Orator O'Rourke

Orator O'Rourke

The Life of a Baseball Radical

MIKE ROER

McFarland & Company, Inc., Publishers

Jefferson, North Carolina, and London

796.357
O74r

Frontispiece: Jim O'Rourke (*Harper's Weekly,* May 16, 1885)

LIBRARY OF CONGRESS CATALOGUING-IN-PUBLICATION DATA

Roer, Mike 1944–
    Orator O'Rourke : the life of a baseball radical / Mike Roer.
       p.   cm.
    Includes bibliographical references and index.

    ISBN 0-7864-2355-2 (softcover : 50# alkaline paper) ∞

    1. O'Rourke, Jim, 1851–1918.   2. Baseball players—
United States—Biography.   3. Baseball team owners—
United States—Biography.   I. Title
GV865.O77R64   2006
796.357092 — dc22   2005031090

British Library cataloguing data are available

©2005 Mike Roer. All rights reserved

*No part of this book may be reproduced or transmitted in any form
or by any means, electronic or mechanical, including photocopying
or recording, or by any information storage and retrieval system,
without permission in writing from the publisher.*

On the cover: Jim O'Rourke, from his 1888-89 Old Judge Cigarettes
baseball card *(Library of Congress)*

Manufactured in the United States of America

McFarland & Company, Inc., Publishers
   Box 611, Jefferson, North Carolina 28640
      www.mcfarlandpub.com

To my Angel Cloud, Sue

University Libraries
Carnegie Mellon University
Pittsburgh, PA 15213-3890

Contents

Preface

Jim O'Rourke earned the nickname "Orator" for a commanding speaking voice that he used to champion the rights of professional athletes. The struggle between ballplayers and owners typified the confrontation between labor and capital in "raging, tearing booming" nineteenth-century America.[1]

The rules governing workers' rights were evolving to assimilate a mass migration of self-directed farmers to northern industrial cities where they would become members of managed teams in the steam-powered factories of New York, Chicago, and Boston.

The rules of baseball were also evolving. As offense or defense invented new strategies, like curving the baseball or stealing bases, new rules had to be written to re-level the playing field, much like the government regulations to maintain a balance between labor and capital.

O'Rourke serves well as a touchstone to this period in the history of the country and its national sport. His career as player, team captain, manager, umpire, owner, and league president encompassed most of the major events along these parallel tracks of history.

His driving motivation was to enjoy the personal dignity he thought everyone deserved — Irish or English, black or white, laborer or capitalist. O'Rourke devoted his career to bringing respectability to the role of professional athlete; indeed to working men and women as a whole. He was polished in his speech and his conduct, even at the plate, where he stood tall and erect. He did not compromise an inch on the ideal that a man who earned his bread by his hands could command dignity.

Over the years, as his renown grew (O'Rourke played on nine pennant-winning teams) his demands upon the ruling classes became bolder. There was even a moment, near the end of his major league career, when he and other baseball "shooting stars" almost turned the power structure of America inside out in a gambit to merge the labor and capital classes into one amalgam of equals.

Macaulay said, "A nation's history is in its newspapers,"[2] and I found that contemporary accounts proved to be the most reliable sources for this biography. Most libraries have local newspapers on microfilm and many have the *New York Times*, which has been thoroughly indexed. SABR (the Society for American Baseball Research) has a number of nineteenth-century volumes of national sporting publications, including *Sporting Life* and the *New York Clipper* on microfilm for loan to its members. SABR members also have Web access to searchable electronic copies of the *New York Times*, *Washington Post*, *Chicago Tribune*, *Los Angeles Times*, and *Boston Globe*.

To be sure, many newspaper accounts contain errors or bias. (Sportswriters seldom blame the umpire for a hometown win.) But human fallibility can be countered by searching out accounts in rival publications. Eventually a pattern of truth emerges.

In contrast to contemporary reporting, I found that recollections published years after an incident are seldom reliable. Dates, places, names and even the outcomes of important contests shift gradually over time.[3]

Published interviews of O'Rourke and his contemporaries were valuable because they shed rare light on the opinions and attitudes of players. The player files at the National Baseball Library were most helpful in this regard. The Orator, thankfully, was easier to flesh out than most players because he was quick to speak his mind and his rhetorical flourishes were very quotable.

Written correspondence, because of its private nature and limited audience, can also tell a lot about a player, and a surprising number of letters survive from the era. A. G. Spalding collected hundreds to and from Harry Wright that are housed along with the personal scrapbooks of Spalding at the New York Public Library. This collection includes letters from O'Rourke in his own hand.

For a good grounding in the history of baseball, I found the following very helpful:

Overview of nineteenth-century baseball: David Voigt, *American Baseball*, Vol. 1.

National Association Era (1871–1875): William Ryczek, *Blackguards and Red Stocking*.

Relationships among players, managers, owners, and media: Howard Rosenberg, *Cap Anson 1*.

For providing access to their collections, I would like to thank the New York Public Library, Bridgeport Public Library, Boston Public Library, Derby (Connecticut) Public Library, Fairfield Historical Society, Enoch Pratt Free Library (Baltimore), Fairfield (Connecticut) Public Library, the Graduate Club of New Haven, Mory's (New Haven), the National Baseball Library, New Haven Public Library, the Norwalk Museum, Pequot Library (Southport, Connecticut), the Society for American Baseball Research (SABR), the University of Connecticut, and Yale University.

In addition, I would also like to acknowledge Frank Williams, Bob Gelzheiser, Howard Rosenberg, and Ed Walton for selflessly volunteering information from their personal files.

Williams and Walton also reviewed the manuscript and offered many helpful suggestions for its improvement.

Mike Roer
Fairfield, Connecticut

Prologue

In 1904, on a cool day in late September, long shadows fell darkly across the grass of the fabled Polo Grounds. The Giants hadn't won a championship since 1889 and it was almost the end of another season. But if manager John McGraw could win this day, the Giants would clinch the pennant.

When the lineup was called, the announcer intoned "James O'Rourke catching for New York." A low murmur rippled through the crowded stands. To most, the name was new, but older fans were carried back a decade to when the Giants were champions and Jim O'Rourke roamed the sun field. Some could even recall two decades earlier when Jim O'Rourke won the National League batting title. A few even remembered three decades back to America's centennial when a young Jimmy O'Rourke rapped out the first hit of the National League.

But the spectators quickly dismissed their reminiscing: the James O'Rourke they knew would be in his mid-'50s.

Then, when the game started, and the Giants catcher strode to the plate with an unmistakable air of dignity, a wave of recognition surged through the stands. It *was* Orator O'Rourke. To inspire his Giants, McGraw had recalled the veteran of New York's last pennant-winning team.

It wasn't long before the entire stadium was standing and applauding; and the game had to be halted so the "the grand old man of baseball" could doff his cap.

Were they not aware of O'Rourke's constant battles with the magnates? Had they forgotten the devastating Baseball War for control of America's national sport?

Or was it they remembered?

1

Beginnings

"Like everything ... American, it came with a rush."[1]
— Hall of Famer John Montgomery Ward

During the first half of the nineteenth century, with the industrialization of the United States and the migration of its population from farms to cities, adults in urban areas adopted "base ball" as a way of obtaining healthy outdoor exercise. Baseball carried both player and observer back to a time and place when *The People* were their own masters.[2]

A third of the population was living in urban areas, whereas before the Civil War, 90 percent lived on farms or in small towns where they enjoyed freedom of space and of their work and routines. Once, an ever-receding frontier had offered a relief valve for crowded cities and tenements. Now baseball fields provided an inner space for the dispossessed to catch a breath of fresh air and gaze upon a reassuring sunlit pasture. Now the trek was made by trolley.

From a handful of clubs in the Northeast during the 1840s, the game spread wherever young enthusiasts were found. Volunteer firehouses, offices, stock brokerages, and telegraph offices were fertile grounds for ball clubs. Bank clerks, typographers, merchants, and jewelers also embraced the sport to relieve stress and strengthen underused muscles. The original Metropolitans of New York were schoolteachers.[3]

Middle-class sportsmen formed organizations much like modern golf and tennis clubs. By 1860, there were 60 ball clubs in the U.S., mainly in the New York area.[4] Then a cataclysmic event brought together young men from all corners of the nation to unify them under one flag, and one national sport.

During the Civil War, soldiers often passed the time playing baseball. Actually, they spent most of the time arguing, until they settled on one set of rules: those of the New York Knickerbockers, the oldest club then in existence. These rules had been written down in 1845 by Alexander Cartwright, an organizer of the Knicks.

Soldiers returning from the war brought back harrowing stories of battlefield bravery, souvenirs, and a universal set of rules for baseball.

The game spread through the country as fast as the new railroads could carry it. Clubs competed for honor, glory, and friendly wagers, as regimental units had done during the war.

Baseball emerged in O'Rourke's hometown of Bridgeport in 1865 when he was 15 years old.

James Henry O'Rourke was born on September 1, 1850. A brother, John, was born a year earlier, on August 23.[5] They were the new beginning in the New World for Hugh and Catherine O'Rourke. Hugh was 33 and Catherine 23 when they arrived in America in 1845[6] with the first wave of Irish exiled by the famine.

By 1851, through long hours and hard work, Jim's parents saved $200 for a down payment on a building lot. They each signed the mortgage with an "X." They constructed a small house, later expanded into a duplex to share with other workers in America's industrial revolution. In time, the O'Rourkes were also able to purchase land to farm with their strapping sons.[7]

The O'Rourke home was on Pembroke Avenue, just around the corner from Waterville Grammar School,[8] attended by Jim and John. The high regard that Hugh and Catherine held for formal education would broaden the range of opportunities for Jim and would become a family tradition.

Hugh and Catherine O'Rourke's American Dream had come true. They had traveled here in the hold of a wooden ship to labor toward the consuming goal of one day owning the land they lived on.

The nineteenth century was an era when industry shared the landscape with parks, homes and schools, and the O'Rourke children grew up in the shadows of factories turning out sewing machines, brass lamps, and rifle cartridges. Dusty streets carried heavy wagons down to barges waiting in Long Island Sound to transport the finished goods to New York warehouses and then the world.

It was in neighborhoods such as these that the new pastime of baseball began to take root. In Bridgeport, the number of organized teams grew rapidly from only three in 1865 to 14 in 1866.

The O'Rourke brothers played in pick-up games at every opportunity. There was no better way for the sons of immigrants to feel a part of the promised land than to immerse themselves in its new national sport. To play baseball was to *be* American.

Jim and John O'Rourke also had plenty of opportunity to witness serious games between organized clubs of adult players whose members gathered on Saturdays to form into teams for socializing and recreation. In Bridgeport, important games were held at Seaside Park, a gift to the city from P. T. Barnum.

The Game in 1866. A Currier and Ives print of a ball game at the Elysian Fields in Hoboken, across the river from Manhattan. Following the Civil War, this scene was commonplace in hundreds of parks around the country, including those in Jim O'Rourke's hometown of Bridgeport, Connecticut.

Note the absence of gloves for the fielders or protection for the catcher and umpire. At least the umpire had the good sense to stand out of the line of fire.

We can see also from this sketch how the shortstop got his name. He played up close to scoop up the short hits and relay them to the basemen, who were already in position to take the throw.

Spectators stood. Modern "stands," although used for sitting, derive their name from the area once designated for baseball's first spectators.

The new horse-drawn trolley made it easy for players and their friends to assemble at ball grounds. For a nickel, a fan could be transported to the expansive green park by the sea while being lulled by the rhythms of a summer day, hooves clopping on paving stones, sailing ships creaking in the harbor, and the aroma of roasts cooking in the restaurants.

When the trolley reached the park, the passengers alighted and walked eagerly along gravel paths toward the ball field, drawn by the sounds of excitement.

As the baseball fanatics—a term later shortened—entered through enveloping shade trees into the bright green clearing, the sensation was not unlike walking into a modern stadium.

Bases of sawdust-filled canvas bags were anchored to the ground by heavy straps. Home base was a round piece of plate iron, painted white.[9]

Well-groomed and gloveless young men warmed up, showing off for the young ladies, as their friends shouted encouragement from carriages ringing the outfield. The trolley passengers bunched under shade trees or stood along the baselines.

Five hundred voices stirred with anticipation as the air advertised roasting peanuts.

An officious man in a stovepipe hat and a long, gray coat walked to the plate, and the captain of each team joined him. A ball was produced by the captain wearing a red bow tie and belt. It was accepted with a nod by the captain wearing a blue tie and belt. The man in the tall hat, the umpire, tossed a coin and looked to the captain of the reds who elected to bat first.

In a booming voice the umpire commanded "play!" and the blues moved sharply to their positions in the field.

A striker strode to the plate with a long thin bat.

A player stood 20 feet behind the plate to catch the pitches on one bounce as they were tossed, underhand, for the batter. The umpire seldom called strikes, and never balls; but he did keep arguments to a minimum by confidently calling close plays on the base paths. After three outs, the entire red team was "out" and the blue team had its "in"-ing.

With each magnificent hit or commendable catch, fans erupted in shouts of triumph, waving canes and parasols for their summer heroes. The O'Rourke brothers must have noted the admiration the young women had for these weekend athletes and resolved to learn the manly arts of throwing and batting. The O'Rourke boys practiced at every opportunity, but their yearning for assimilation and success would be met by a rigorous commitment to exclude the sons of Erin from America's national sport.

2

Jim Joins the Club
(1866–1871)

> "Thin and not so thin, strong and not so strong, Catholic ... and Jew, these were the elements that, fighting, clashing and jarring at first, then slowly mixing, blending, refining, made up a team. Made up America."[1]
>
> — Baseball writer John R. Tunis

In the nineteenth century, ability did not necessarily guarantee admittance to a baseball club. There was animosity between the established nationalities and the newcomers to America. In Bridgeport, Irish youngsters felt they "had to stand up for [their] rights against the Yankees" who appeared to them to be "putting on airs." The Irish thought they were resented because they owned most of the saloons and had "bought up a lot of property."[2]

Jim probably met rejection and ridicule on his initial attempts to join a ball club. This was the era of NINA (No Irish Need Apply). Ironically, he didn't think of himself as Irish. His *parents* were Irish. *He* was American.

Finally, in the spring of 1866, blue-eyed[3] 15-year-old Jimmy O'Rourke — who could heave and wallop the ball far beyond what his years should have allowed — was accepted into the Ironsides, a club for boys 12 to 15 years of age. It was a real team with store-bought balls and bats and they played on a regulation diamond, without the tall weeds and broken bottles common to the sandlots. But most importantly, the Ironsides had uniforms, with breast shields, just like the firemen wore. The manager rooted through an old steamer trunk and drew out a uniform that once was white, and almost fit; two shortcomings his mother would soon correct. When Jim reported home to a beaming father and envious brother, his mother scowled at the uniform and tossed it into a tub. When she was through scrubbing and bleaching the flannel, it was once again white.

In 1867,[4] having proven his worth, Jim advanced to the Unions, an amateur[5] club for young men 16 and up.

The Unions could hold their own in contests with the other amateur clubs in the area. But when the Unions sallied forth to challenge teams from other cities they encountered an increasing number of superteams composed of the best players from all the neighborhood, church and social clubs in one town. These combines were serious endeavors. Because they represented an entire town or county, interest in their contests attracted sizeable crowds. Fans were even willing to pay to see *their* boys whip a rival burg. These serious amateur clubs are the evolutionary link between baseball as leisure sport and as profession. Actually, baseball evolved into a business quite by accident.

The first time admission was charged for a baseball game was in 1858 at a clash between amateur superteams from New York and Brooklyn.[6] Historian Jules Tygiel says the purpose of the gate fee was to recoup the rental cost for the Fashion Course racetrack, the only venue large enough to accommodate the anticipated large turnout.[7] The 50-cent ticket price (the amount reported by most historians) supports an additional purpose: that the gentlemen organizers also wanted to discourage the sporting class from attending what was intended to be a fashionable outing of the carriage set. Especially galling to the gentlemen athletes were the "plug uglies," the lower class onlookers who gathered at games to drink, gamble and spew invectives at the sportsmen for muffing plays that jeopardized their wagers.

Nevertheless, the bettors were not discouraged by the admission price or the

THE NATIONAL GAME.
"Gentlemen,—Owing to Sudden and Severe Illness, I will Be Unable to Attend the Office To-day.
"I am, with respect," etc.

Amatuer Athletes (*Harper's Weekly*, September 12, 1868).

withering stares and raised eyebrows of their betters. As historian Robert Smith points out, the admission fee scheme to discourage the undesirable elements "did not work to utter perfection."[8] However, the later practice of charging a premium for covered seats in a "grand" stand did at least keep them in their place.

If admission fees to baseball competitions failed to maintain the pastime as a preserve of the well-to-do, the enduring benefit, making money, was quickly appreciated by the owners of racetracks and fairgrounds. Charging admission on a regular basis was inaugurated in 1862 by William H. Cannemeyer, proprietor of the Union Grounds in Brooklyn.[9]

By 1863, several clubs were charging between 10 and 25 cents. Initially, players were satisfied by the flattery that people would actually pay to see them play. But that attitude was shortlived. Athletes soon demanded a piece of the action and semiprofessional sport was born. You can see how one thing led to another, although I doubt whether anyone could have predicted that sharing gate receipts with the players would eventually lead to multi-million-dollar contracts, or even that professional baseball would overshadow the sport as gentleman's pastime in less than a decade.

Jim attended high school at Strong's Military Academy in Bridgeport.[10] Every day, after school, he performed his chores on the family farm, and practiced baseball, hoping for a chance to play for one of the superteams.

The ever-increasing importance of winning — rather than merely obtaining outdoor exercise — led to an important evolution in baseball in the late 1860s: "inside baseball," or the fine art of getting men on, then advancing the runners one base at a time by the sneaky and ungentlemanly tactics of stealing and bunting.

The first stolen base was purloined prior to the Civil War. History has not divulged the name of the innovator, but baseball's first commentator, Henry Chadwick, was advising catchers as early as the spring of 1860 on how to guard against the steal:

> When a player has made his first base, the Catcher should take a position nearer the striker, in order to take the ball from the pitcher before it bounds; and the moment the ball is delivered by the pitcher, and the player runs from the first to the second base, the Catcher should take the ball before bounding and send it to the second base as swiftly as possible, in time to cut off the player before he can touch the base.[11]

Chadwick also admonished batters not to let good balls go by in hopes of a passed ball and thereby an opportunity for a teammate to steal. The first stolen base ending in a *slide* was recorded in 1866 by Bob Addy of Rockford.

Tim Murnane, the first player to turn sportswriter, claims for himself the distinction of inventing the bunt; but all other sportswriters credit Dickey Pearce of the Brooklyn Atlantics in 1866 with inventing the "baby hit."[12] Tim may be responsible for naming the tactic. One theory about the origin of the word "bunt" is that it evolved from "butting," the term Tim Murnane used to describe the technique of hitting without swinging.[13]

Inside baseball placed greater demands on the catcher. Until the bunt and steal, the catcher wasn't much more than a manual ball return. He stood far back out of harm's way. However, with the advent of inside baseball, the catcher had to play much closer to the plate to retrieve the short bunts and to hold men on first. This exposed catchers to the risks of busted teeth and noses from foul tips and long bats. It was said you could always spot the catcher: he was the one with the welts and bruises.

The following account of a catcher sheds some light on the lot of back-stops in the late 1860s:

> He went into the game with his right eye almost knocked out of his head and his nose and the whole right side of his face swollen to three times their normal size. Yet, notwithstanding this, nothing seemed too difficult for him to take. Player after player went down before his unfaltering nerve, and although struck four times during the game — once squarely on the mouth by the ball and once on the chest and twice with the bat — he could not be driven away from his position.[14]

Baseball for glory and wagers opened opportunities for rugged young men not afraid of the risks of the faster, physical baseball that was evolving. Still, the conflict between social standing and skill as the accepted rationale for picking players would not gracefully accede to logic. Years later, it was still being debated, as in this example from Yale:

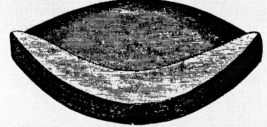

GEORGE WRIGHT'S
Base-Ball Catcher's Mouth Protector.

The above protector for the teeth of Base-Ball Players is the most desirable article for the purpose yet invented; being made of a pure rubber it can be held in the mouth without having any disagreeable taste. Samples by mail, post-paid, each, 50 cents. Address,

PECK & SNYDER, Manufacturers,
124 Nassau Street, N. Y.

Rubber Mouth Protector. This was the only protection available to catchers during the 1860s (*Peck & Snyder Catalog*).

Not only the Yale freshman, but the members of the other classes in the college, openly express dissatisfaction at the way its freshman base ball nine is made up. Recently a game was played by the regular nine and a nine made up of the defeated candidates, and the latter warmed the regulars up to the tune of a score of 7 to 4. This, the students contend, does not augur well for the future success of the regulars. They say that the principle of choosing men on account of their social position is not at all the spirit which should pervade Yale athletics. The feeling is so strong that it may compel changes in the personnel of the nine before the Harvard games.[15]

In 1868, a superteam was organized in Stratford, Connecticut, a town adjacent to Bridgeport and its home park was just over the town line, only two miles from Jim's home. The team, the Osceolas, was organized by a number of prosperous college men and drew players from throughout southeastern Connecticut.[16]

The club's ambition to win matches and the growing importance of skill and athleticism induced the organizers to overlook Jim's Irish heritage and lack of higher education. Jim was called up from the Unions to join the Osceolas.

The club's rival for supremacy in Fairfield County, Connecticut, was the Norwalk Liberty club. In his debut with the Osceolas on August 5, 1868, Jim put out three opponents and scored two runs in a 22–21 victory over the Libertys.[17] The box score listed Jim as "Rourke."

At the end of the 1868 season, the Libertys won a decisive invitational tournament, earning them the distinction of champion ball club in southwestern Connecticut.[18] At the time, weekend elimination tournaments often decided superiority, rather than a season-long schedule of contests.

The Libertys were members of a dying breed, a club composed entirely of gentlemen amateurs. An editorial in the Norwalk *Gazette*, published a week before the game with the Osceolas, provides a parting look at a sport that was about to be dominated by a new breed of player and fan who understood that winning was more important than appearances:

Again, let us give the spectator several hints. Do not crowd the players, give them *plenty* of room, especially near the catcher and 1st and 3rd bases so that they will have a fair chance to run for foul balls; bestow all applause *honestly* upon good playing and not specially to your favorite clubs and frown down all efforts of the *gamin* to lease and annoy players by saucy and annoying remarks and organized yells; if you love the sport, and you like to see a fair and square game do all in you power to discourage *betting* which is especially so shamefully frequent; avoid all loud remarks derogatory to the umpire; finally, remember that all these games are necessarily attached with considerable expense, and that the players cannot afford and ought not be obliged to pay all these expenses, and that a small donation from each spectator would make quite a large amount in the aggregate, and assist the clubs materially in keeping up a good and efficient organization.[19]

I don't know how many games Jim played for the Osceolas in 1868. Box scores were infrequent. Game accounts appearing in the *Bridgeport Standard* on July 27 and August 20 do not list O'Rourke. But the box score of an October 3 game again lists "Rourke" in right field.[20]

It appears from the four box scores that I was able to find that Jim was a substitute in 1868. In fact, most later sources give 1870 or 1871 as the first year Jim played with the regional superteam. A *New York Clipper* feature of October 25, 1879, gives 1871, as does the *Spalding Guide* of 1887. The *Reach Guide* of 1885 and an article in the May 16, 1885, issue of *Harper's Weekly* report that Jim first played with the Osceolas in 1870.

But the promise of glory was to be short lived. Baseball would have to take a back seat to the more basic concerns of the O'Rourke family. On the last day of 1868, Jim's father died at age 56. He simply ran out of life. To make ends meet, the brothers would have to spend more time in the family fields; and less on their field of dreams.

The amateur Osceolas were forced to retreat as well. Prior to the start of the 1869 season, the Bridgeports (a superteam representing the Park City) swooped in to capture the Osceolas' key players. The deserters were probably induced with signing bonuses and a share of the gate.

The new super-combine of the best players from the Osceolas and Bridgeports adopted a new name, the Seasides, after Seaside Park in Bridgeport, where they played home games.

No accounts or notices of Osceola games have been found in any newspaper for 1869. The team ceased to exist. For the 1869 season, Jim returned to the amateur Union Club and continued to improve his skills and knowledge of the fine points of the game. In late summer the O'Rourke brothers found themselves on the opposite sides of the diamond when the Unions took on the powerful T.B.F.U.S.B.B.C. (The Bridgeport Friendly United Social Base Ball Club) or TBs for short. John O'Rourke played for the TBs.

John and his teammates "appeared in their new uniform which consisted of a neat cap, representing our national colors, plain merino shirts, green knee breeches with white stockings and red canvass shoes, the whole making the neatest uniform" the Bridgeport reporter had yet seen. The loud uniforms and the reputation of the TBs may have had the intended intimidating effect on the Unions, for John's team whipped Jim's team 30–15.[21] But the Bridgeport Unions and TBs were both strong amateur teams. In September, the Unions hosted the New Haven Clippers, whom they sent home in defeat.[22]

On the national scene, baseball continued to evolve during the 1869 season in ways that would create new opportunities for aspiring ballplayers like the O'Rourke brothers.

For some time, baseball boosters had been offering signing bonuses to attract players from other towns. This progressed to offering cushy jobs in local industries with liberal paid leave for practices and games. Star players were often exempt from showing up at all. But these dealings had to be arranged under the table as the gentlemanly rules of baseball precluded the paying of players.[23] This convoluted process and secrecy tended to retard the growth of the sport. Yet, defiantly, the number of paid players increased, and they agitated ever more loudly for legitimacy within the National Association of Base Ball Players.

In 1867, to stave off a schism within the national organization, the NAPBBL permitted players to receive pay, but classified those participants as professionals.[24] Although the association thereby acknowledged a practice that was by then commonplace and well known, the sanctioned pros were not allowed to play on amateur teams. From a practical standpoint the ruling had little effect. Professionals could play only on professional teams; but there were few professional teams because clubs did not want to admit they had paid ringers. Teams remained cloaked in the mantle of amateurism.

But then, in 1869, the Cincinnati Red Stockings came out as the first (admittedly) all-professional club.[25] Team manager Harry Wright wrote contracts for the full season at a flat salary, regardless of the gate. This guarantee improved player loyalty and solved the problem of star players "revolving" during the season to greener fields.[26] (Until the advent of undisguised professionalism, managers of supposed amateur clubs could hardly sue a player for breaking a contract.)

Wright attracted the best players, including his younger brother, George, who hit .518 and scored 59 home runs in 1869.[27]

Cincinnati finished the season undefeated.[28] "Their success was so pronounced that other cities who hoped for equal success found it necessary to organize professional clubs."[29]

Chicago boosters—envious of the prestige that a winning baseball team had brought to Cincinnati—subscribed $20,000 to underwrite a professional team[30] "for the express purpose of rivaling, and if possible, defeating the Cincinnati Reds."[31] In Boston, too, investors provided capital to establish a team of paid players.

The Red Stockings had ushered in the era of professional baseball and city boosters everywhere—including the small industrial towns of Connecticut—were scrambling to hire the best amateurs money could buy.

Traveling from Boston to New York, the Cincinnati "Red Stox" passed through Bridgeport at 6:30 P.M. on the 14th of June 1870.[32] Their railroad car was upholstered in rich burgundy velvet and paneled in polished walnut. The air reeked of cigars and adventure. A boy peering into that car would have known right then and there what he wanted to do for the rest of his life.

As he worked the family farm on those hot summer days, Jim must have dreamed of what it would be like to play for one of the full-time professional nines. By the end of 1870, there were five openly professional clubs.[33]

In May[34] of 1870, the Stratford Osceolas reorganized as a semipro club. They had returned to the field with a vengeance, loaded for bear and the

1869 *Cincinnati Red Stockings,* the first openly professional ball team. They were undefeated throughout 1869 and well into 1870, encouraging other cities and teams to discard amateur pretense. George Wright, second from left in the top row, was an expert at place hitting and baseball's first superstar. Older brother and team manager Harry is seated center (Engraving: *Harper's Weekly,* July 3, 1869).

Connecticut Baseball Association championship. Taking a lesson from the Seasides, the Osceolas hijacked pitcher Frank Buttery and catcher Tim Murnane from the Norwalk Libertys. (Ball teams had long since given up the pretense of fielding only homegrown players.)

Buttery had been the Libertys' pitcher since his debut with the team on Saturday, June 27, 1868, in which he "acquitted himself with much credit" in a contest with Yale.[35] Murnane caught his first game for the Libertys in a match against the Seasides on Saturday, September 18, 1869. Although the Libertys lost to the Seasides 27–23, the Norwalk *Gazette* said of its dynamic duo:

> Buttery, faithful fellow, did his work well ... and Murnan[e] proved a capable catch and deserves to remain on the nine.[36]

The Norwalk Libertys ceased to exist after losing their starting pitcher and catcher; and when the Osceolas humiliated the town's second-ranked Star Club in July, the Norwalk *Gazette* lamented:

> As a scientific pursuit, base ball has "gone up" in Norwalk for the present, and we are resting upon our laurels.[37]

The Osceolas also expropriated the Bacon brothers, catcher Walter and left fielder Fred, from the Qui Vives of Derby.[38] The Derby *Transcript*, in an 1870 article referred to its home team as the "once famous" Qui Vives.[39] This no doubt refers to the team prior to the Osceola raid.

In August of 1870, the Osceolas again called up O'Rourke from the Bridgeport Unions, to be the back-up catcher, and parked him in right field. Jim had developed into an "all-around" (utility) player who could hit, cover the outfield or infield and fill in behind the bat.

For the 1870 season, the rules were amended to require the pitcher to swing his arm parallel to his body, keeping the arm stiff and straight, and release the ball underhand, with the hand below the hip.[40] This was an attempt to stop pitchers from putting "stuff" on the ball. Umpires watched carefully for any twist or snap of the wrist upon release, but this was as hard to guard against as kids peering through knotholes. Skirting the rules is as old as baseball itself.

Teams were beginning to realize how grueling were the demands on the pitcher and catcher in light of the ever-increasing speed and deception of pitching. The logical solution was to maintain two sets of pitchers and catchers (batteries) who could rotate each game and provide back-up if a member of the starting pair was injured or wore out during a game. A battery was defined at the time as a pitcher and catcher who are kept together because they have "such familiarity with and knowledge of one another's peculiarities as to cause them to work like a well-trained pair of horses."[41]

To keep down costs, and because no one wanted to warm the bench, the second battery covered other — usually less-demanding — positions until and if they were needed. Teams were called nines not in reference to the number of men on the field, but to the number of players on the team.

O'Rourke's first game with the 1870 Osceolas was during early August,[42] in the first of a three-game series against the Naugatuck, Connecticut, club. O'Rourke was singled out in the game description:

> Rourke, of the Osceola's deserves special notice. His catching and throwing was splendid and elicited encomiums from every side. In his position he is, without doubt, as good as any in the State.[43]

The first game against Naugatuck was won easily by the Osceolas 24–6. The Stratford players expected game two, on their home ground, to be a repeat of the first. Tim Murnane, writing years later, said it was the first game for which Jim received money.[44]

Murnane was catching. O'Rourke was in right field. The game was much like any other. Spectators were perched in carriages fringing the outfield. The catcher clenched a rubber mouth protector between his front teeth and stood only 15 feet behind home plate. The umpire stood 20 feet up the first base line. If the striker seemed too picky, the game officiator would sometimes call "Strike" even if the batter didn't swing.

If the pitcher did not seem to be trying to get the ball over the plate, the umpire might warn him by calling an "Unfair ball!" The rules defining bad pitches were quite complicated and no one really understood them. Few players ever walked, since it required nine balls for a free base.

The game was closely contested, with both teams scoring over 20 runs. Finally, in the bottom of the ninth inning, the Osceolas held a slim lead. If their defense held, they would win the game and the series, advancing their standing in the Connecticut Baseball Association.

With runners on, a Naugatuck batter hit a high fly to Jim. A description of catching a high fly has been left to us by an O'Rourke contemporary:

> There was a high fly hit up to me. I have seen baseballs do strange things, but I don't remember ever to have seen one make so many moves as that one. At one time it seemed to be falling ten feet to my right, and the next instant it had jumped ten feet to my left. I thought it would never come down. I grew lightheaded and faint. It came zigzagging down in such a way that at one moment there seemed to be a half-dozen of them and the next moment I couldn't see any. To make matters pleasanter, a couple of demons stood there, yelling in my ears. 'Run hard! He'll never get it!' I realized my nerve [would] be judged by that catch. I made one last *desperate* effort to collect myself, the ball came within reach, I clutched at it, and it stuck fast in my hands.[45]

And by the same chronicler, a description of the exhilaration and glory of victory:

> The crowd swayed like trees in a tempest and the sound [was] like the roar of a cataract. I stood and listened, lost to the game, forgetful even of the victory just won.[46]

But, alas, there was no joy in Stratford. O'Rourke dropped the ball, "allowing the winning run to score."[47]

Fortunately, Jim had by then proven his worth offensively as well as defensively, and was forgiven the error. The Osceolas came back to win game three and the Naugatuck series.

The schedule of the 1870 Osceolas, Jim's first semiprofessional club, has been pieced together from newspapers accounts. The following publications were checked: the *Bridgeport Standard, New Haven Palladium, Norwalk Gazette,* and *Derby Transcript.* Following are all of the game notices and accounts as yet discovered:

> July 18 (Tuesday) — Bridgeport TBs defeat the Osceolas at Stratford 29–15 in game one of three-game series.[48]
> July 22 (Friday) — Osceolas "easily defeated" the Star Club of Norwalk.[49]

August 6 (Saturday)—Osceolas win game one of three at Naugatuck 24–6.[50]

August 16 (Tuesday)—Osceolas to play Mansfields (postponed).[51]

August 19 (Friday)—Mansfields win game one of three vs. Osceolas, 14–11.[52]

August 29 (Monday)—Osceolas defeat TBs 19–8 at Bridgeport in game two.[53]

September 3 (Saturday)—Osceolas to host Mansfields for game two of three.[54] The Mansfields must have won this game, and therefore the state championship, as no arrangements were made for a third game.

September 6 (Tuesday)—TBs win game three at Seaside Park, 33–26.[55]

September ?—Naugatuck wins game two of their series 32–27.[56]

September 23 (Friday)—Osceolas to play Empires of Thomaston.[57]

October 5 (Wednesday)—Osceolas beat Meriden 32–21 at Meriden.[58]

October 5 (Wednesday)—Yale humbles Osceolas 29–11 at Meriden.[59]

October 7 (Friday)—Osceolas crush Naugatuck in the third and final game of the series by a score of 41–7 on the neutral grounds of the Derby Driving Park Association. O'Rourke caught and was listed in the box score as "J. Rourke." According to the *Derby Transcript*, "Rourke behind the bat caught everything within his reach."[60]

We can imagine from recollections of contemporaries what it was like the first time Jim was sent in to catch. We pick up a hypothetical game in the middle of the seventh inning:

Pitcher Frank Buttery is working from a box six feet square. As he begins his delivery, he moves from left to right across the box while taking two strides to throw his full weight into the ball. By this time, many pitchers were throwing with vim. (A slow toss would make it too easy for a runner to steal.) As the hurler reaches the front of the box, his right arm sweeps forward in a long arc across his body. Just at the end of the pitch, Buttery gives a twist to his wrist. The batter lunges for the ball, but it curves away, out of reach.

On the next pitch, the runner takes off for second. Murnane throws to the second baseman, but not in time, prompting the Osceola captain to yell to his catcher, "Move up or he'll steal third too." Murnane moves closer, to within eight feet of the plate. Before the inning is over, a foul tip smashes into the end of his outstretched hand, splitting the skin.

There was no bench in the early years. A player had to be seriously injured—in the opinion of the *opposing* manager—before he could be replaced. But players already on the field could switch positions. The Osceola captain, after inspecting Tim's hand, waived Jim in from right field. A change of catchers took only a matter of seconds in 1870. There was no cumbersome equipment to don: no mask, no chest protector, no shin guards, not even a mitt.

Jim had many things to be concerned with on that first day, not the least of which was remaining off the injured list himself. His training from the captain was "Don't let the ball get past you."

Jim O'Rourke steps behind the plate. The pitcher uncorks a fastball. Jim sees

the blur of the bat swing through the pitch as he instinctively clamps onto the
ball and lets his arms recoil to absorb the force. It sticks.

The Osceolas became the team to beat in southwestern Connecticut.
The 1870 state championship came down to the Stratford Osceolas and the
Middletown Mansfields. In a three-game series to settle the question, the
Mansfields carried off the palm, winning the first two games.

More was at stake in these games than honor. Rooters bet liberally in support of their favorite sons and emotions ran hot. The opportunity to earn a
quick buck from a rival town led backers to look for ways to improve their
odds. The wagering induced ever more clubs to hire professionals. The amateur spirit of sport played for exercise and honor began to clash increasingly
with the idea of winning at any cost. The games became rougher as winning
became the main objective, convincing the old-line clubs to become owners of
baseball teams and to leave the "playing" to hired mercenaries. The paid ringers
may have been listed as club members, but they were not permitted to vote for
officers, and it was understood they would not participate in social functions.[61]

As the sport grew in popularity, and more people attended games adding
their dimes to club treasuries, teams were able to allocate ever more money
for salaries and signing bonuses.

It was at this time that baseball's underlying economic law emerged: big
cities with big parks took in more money at the gate and could therefore pay
higher salaries, so they wound up with the best players and won the most
pennants. Professionalism had unleveled the playing field, and the amateurs
resented it.

Mounting tensions between the amateurs and professionals finally led
to a rift in the National Association of Base Ball Players. On March 16, 1871,
at the annual convention, the still more numerous amateurs expelled the
professional players. There were over 500 amateur clubs and only a handful of pro teams. It was assumed by those who believed the "all–American
game was being ruined by professionalism" that the cancerous branch, having been cut off, would wither and die. Not so. Representatives from the
professional clubs met in New York City the following day to organize the
National Association of *Professional* Base Ball Players.[62] The original amateur trunk of baseball died out in only three years, but the cutting took root
and eventually grew into organized baseball.

While playing for the Osceolas in 1870 and 1871, Jim acquired an appreciation for the university education of his fellow players and the cultural
advantages of these soon-to-be lawyers, doctors, merchants, ministers, indus-
trialists and politicians. It was from these gentlemen enthusiasts that
O'Rourke honed the vocabulary and elocution that, combined with a strong
and pleasant speaking voice, would make him an effective advocate. In these

formative years, Jim also developed his dignified bearing and an irreproachable conduct on and off the field.

While waiting to be discovered by one of the growing number of professional teams, Jim met 18-year-old Annie Kehoe, recently arrived from the Emerald Isle.[63] The Kehoes lived only a block from the O'Rourkes. Annie had a musical brogue, a permanent smile, light brown hair, and a total disinterest in baseball.

Annie loved ice skating. The popular sport provided recreation and a respectable way for young people to meet members of the opposite sex. Bridgeport's Pembroke Pond, near Annie's home, was a magical place at night, with its impromptu bonfires, the lights and mystery of passing trains, and a brass band setting the tempo. Annie skated at every opportunity, tracing figure eights in her jaunty hat, muff and a daringly short skirt that barely covered the tops of her boots.

Jim, too, was an avid skater. Eventually, the two met on the frozen pond and from that moment, they were inseparable. Annie brought much joy into Jim's life, and perhaps some of the luck that even the best ballplayers need from time to time.

In 1871, the Stratford Osceolas challenged the Middletown Mansfields to a rematch for the state title. The winner would receive a sterling silver ball from the Connecticut Baseball Association.

Jim was now the starting catcher for the Osceolas. Murnane had left the club at the end of the 1870 season to play winter ball in Savannah, where he stayed over for the 1871 season. Coincidentally, during a northern tour Murnane was hired away by the Middletown Mansfields. It would be O'Rourke versus Murnane in the match-up behind the plate.

The Mansfields, heavily favored, won the first game of the series on their home grounds, 40–22. An exclamation point was added to the victory by an outside-the-park home run by a Middletown player.[64]

Since the Osceolas' home park in Stratford was not enclosed and therefore admission could not be charged, the second game was played at a hastily laid-out diamond on the infield of Cameron's Trotting Park, a venue for harness racing in Bridgeport, near the Fairfield town line. The *New Haven Palladium* observed that "The ground was a new one, and never will be very good."[65] But it had that new and all-important feature: a fence that allowed the charging of admission.

Game two at the Bridgeport Trotting Park got off to a late start because of several arguments.

First, there was "considerable wrangling" over who would umpire,[66] "the Mansfields insisting upon their own man"[67] to which the Osceolas eventually relented.

Second, "the Mansfields also insisted upon playing a man who had not been a member of their club the proper time, and this too the Osceolas allowed."[68] The player in question was the Mansfield catcher, Tim Murnane, who had been hired away from the Savannahs only two weeks previously. National Association rules required a player to be a member of a club for 60 days prior to participating in a match.[69] (The intent of the rule was to prevent a club from making a wager on a match, and then bringing in a ringer at the last minute. The provision also discouraged revolving.)

Third, the Mansfields demanded a share of the gate because the contest was in "neutral" territory and not on the Osceolas' home grounds. After more delays, the Osceolas begrudgingly offered the Mansfields $4 . The paltry sum, which did not even cover the train fare from Middletown, intensified the bitterness of the rivalry between the clubs.

After six innings, the youthful and "flashy" Osceolas trailed the more-seasoned Mansfields by one run. But the young men rallied in the seventh and eighth innings, scoring seven runs while whitewashing the Middletown team. The final score was 15–9, in favor of the Osceolas.

A third and deciding game was therefore necessary. It was to be played at Hamilton Park in New Haven on Saturday, September 16, 1871. When the appointed day arrived, "There was a large concourse of people ... to witness the great match between the Osceolas, of Stratford, and Mansfields, of Middletown. The two nines were in the finest condition."[70] According to the newspaper accounts:

> The backers of the Mansfield club tried to "bluff" the friends of the Osceolas, before the game commenced, and during its progress, by offering large odds in favor of the Middletown boys, but did not succeed in frightening them, at all. Considerable money changed hands.[71]
>
> After considerable bickering [again over the selection of an umpire] the game was commenced at about a quarter to three. The contest opened unfavorably for the Osceolas, as their opponents closed the fourth inning with the score standing 8 to 0 in favor of Middletown. After this point, however, the Osceolas rallied, and aided by some wretched plays by the Mansfields caught up and lead them, so that the score stood 12 to 10 in their favor.[72]
>
> The ninth inning would decide the game. The Mansfields went to the bat, were prevented from scoring anything by the indomitable Stratford boys, who were returning from the field in high spirits, when the crowd rushed in on the grounds.[73]
>
> The result was hailed with tumultuous cheers by every one but the clique of Mansfield "backers," as that club has gained no friends by its recent acts. The Osceolas have fairly earned the championship, having now beaten the Mansfields twice, with all their recent illegal importations to boot.[74]

The Osceolas became the state champions and proud owners of a sterling silver ball. The charge of "illegal importations" referred to the recent hiring of Tim Murnane and another player. Of course, as the Mansfields were eager to point out, the Stratford Osceolas had imported players as well,

The Stratford Osceolas, Connecticut State Champions of 1871. Standing, left to right: Fred Bacon (infielder, of Derby), George N. Wells (of Stratford), Wallace Curtis (1b), Charles Smith, Jim O'Rourke (catcher, 21). *Sitting, left to right:* Walter Bacon (infielder, of Derby), N. H. Jones (ss, of East Bridgeport), Frank Buttery (pitcher, of Norwalk), and E. Allen Powers (of Stratford). **Powers would inherit $100,000 within 10 years. The Bacon brothers' father was the proprietor of the** *Derby Transcript.*

including Buttery (Norwalk) and O'Rourke (Bridgeport). Middletown also claimed the Stratford club had members hired from as far away as New Haven and New York, but I have not been able to corroborate these charges.[75]

Lest the young and gentlemanly Osceolas fail to understand that baseball was now about the money, the Mansfields drove home the lesson by absconding with all the gate receipts, no doubt to purchase train tickets home. The Middletown team and its backers boarded the train "one or two thousand dollars"[76] poorer for having bet against the Osceolas.

Mansfield manager Ben Douglas duly noted the names of the players who had cost him the 1871 state championship.

For Middletown's 1872 season, Douglas offered to hire catcher O'Rourke and pitcher Frank Buttery. Jim would play at short for the Mansfields, except when Buttery pitched; then he would catch.

However, before Mrs. O'Rourke would release her son she sought assurances that Jim's share of the gate would be enough to hire a replacement for the family farm.[77] She had negotiating leverage, as it was well known that Jim was "one of the best batters in Connecticut."[78]

For 1872, Middletown joined the National Association of Professional Base Ball Players, still loosely organized, but nevertheless the first major league. It included teams from Baltimore, Boston, Brooklyn, Cleveland, New York, Philadelphia, Troy, and Washington.

There were two types of financial structures for professional ball clubs. The more common variety, the stock club, raised capital through the sale of shares to investors and ardent followers of the game. Shares usually included a season ticket and a pass to the clubhouse. Stock clubs could pay fixed salaries, come rain or come shine, because the amount raised usually was enough to guarantee the payroll for the season. At the end of the year, the club would pay back its shareholders, hopefully with a dividend; then start the process all over the following season.

The Mansfields, however, were a cooperative, in which players were compensated with a share of the gate receipts. Co-ops ranked only slightly above part-time semipro clubs in the baseball hierarchy. Four other National Association teams were co-ops: the Brooklyn Eckfords, Brooklyn Atlantics, Washington Nationals, and Washington Olympics.[79]

Because of their unpredictable and inconsistent wages, it was difficult for co-ops to compete for players against the stock clubs and as a result, the co-ops found themselves in the bottom half of the standings.[80]

Nonetheless, Jim's dream had come true: he was a full-time baseballist.

3

Middletown Mansfields (1872)

> "It is a proud day in the life of any ball player when he signs his first contract. It makes little difference how small the league.... It is at least a part of Organized Baseball and he is a genuine professional." [1]
>
> — Hans Lobert

Hans Lobert, who spent 16 years in the majors in the early 1900s, described the treatment a rookie could expect:

> If he has natural ability enough and faith in himself and has spirit and perseverance enough to stand the sarcasm which is heaped upon him he is bound to make good. But if he becomes disheartened, which is more likely to be the case, he loses his nerve and has no prospect but speedy return to the minors. [2]

O'Rourke would certainly need spirit and perseverance to endure his first professional outing, on April 26, 1872, at Troy. [3] It was the Mansfields' first game of the season, and not at all what he expected.

Gamblers openly exchanged money. Drunks waved bottles and swore at players. The New York combatants were eager to intimidate the rookie in the crisp white uniform with "chin music" and jostling on the base paths. On March 8, only a month before Jim's debut, the New York Times had described the typical professional player as a "worthless, dissipated, gladiator." Jim had not found in the professional baseball ranks the dignity he sought. He wasn't admitted into "the club"; he was merely its hired mercenary.

But there was no turning back. Jim had growing responsibilities at home. In only three weeks, on May 15, 1872, he and Annie were to be married. [4] There was only one thing a proud young man could do: clean up his profession from the inside. He would make baseball respectable. To be sure, Jim did have co-conspirators on the team. Frank Buttery and Tim Murnane were college educated. Buttery would become a minister; Tim Murnane would become a writer after baseball. Both were gentlemen.

First Major League Game of Jim O'Rourke
Middletown at Troy–April 26, 1872

TROY	R	H	O	A		MANSFIELDS	R	H	O	A
Force, ss	2	2	3	1		Clapp, c	0	2	2	1
McAtee, 1b	1	1	0	0		Suttery, 3b	0	0	2	6
Allison, c	1	2	0	0		Bentley, p	0	0	0	4
King, lf	2	1	8	0		Murnane, 1b	0	1	17	0
Bellam, 3b	1	2	1	1		Booth, 2b	0	2	0	4
Martin, rf	0	2	8	0		Tipper, lf	0	1	1	0
Hodes, cf	1	1	3	0		O'Rourke, ss	0	0	0	3
Zettlein, p	1	1	3	7		McCarton, cf	0	0	5	0
Wood, 2b	1	1	1	2		Arnold, rf	0	0	0	0
Totals	10	13	27	11		Totals	0	6	27	18

Troy	000	134	011–10
Mansfields	000	000	000–0

Home run–Wood. Double play–Force, Wood and McAtee. Errors–Troy 2, Mansfield 4. Earned runs–Troy 8. Umpire–James McDonald. Time–2.00.

Source: Ernest J. Lanigan, National Baseball Hall of Fame, Cooperstown.

But they weren't fuddy-duddies. Murnane was always up for a good practical joke. Once, he convinced a young member of the team to disguise himself as a woman and stand in at the plate while a prospective pitcher was given a tryout. The young lady batted his fastest pitches — and his self confidence — all over the field.[5]

It was with the Mansfields that Jim began to travel: west to Chicago, east to Boston, south to Washington, and to points in between. The Pullman sleeper debuted in 1865 and the dining car in 1868, just in time to allow professional baseballists to travel in style.[6]

During their brief brush with glory, the Mansfields played against the strongest clubs in the country, enabling Jim to refine his skills in the fast company.

On June 15, 1872, the Mansfields even crossed bats with the renowned Red Stockings at Boston. (Cincinnati had decided to revert to amateur status after the 1870 season, so Harry Wright accepted an offer from Beantown backers to establish a professional team in the Hub. Harry brought brother George, slugger Ross Barnes, ace pitcher Al Spalding and the team nickname with him.)

In stark contrast to Troy, the Red Stockings relied on skill and were professional in their demeanor. Buttery was tapped to pitch and O'Rourke was stationed behind the plate for the Mansfields. At a crucial point in the contest, with Reds on second and third and only one out, Cal McVey grounded to John Clapp at short, who threw to Jim to catch Ross Barnes coming home. Then, in one of those heads-up plays that can change a player's destiny, Jim fired to second to catch Andy Leonard off the bag and end the inning.[7] Boston manager Harry Wright would not forget the gentlemanly Connecticut catcher with the quick snap to second.

The Bostons met the Mansfields again, in Hartford on July 3, for a contest that the Red Stockings won easily 16–6. The battery was again Buttery and O'Rourke. On Independence Day the teams traveled to the Mansfields' home field for what was to be the first baseball double-header, but an afternoon storm preempted the historic first. In the morning game, with the same battery as the day before, the Mansfields were leading 9–1 after three innings. It looked like they might actually beat the Red Stockings, but 14 Mansfield errors later the Bostons won 25–13.[8]

O'ROURKE

O' Rourke in 1872 at age 21.

More telling of Middletown's prospects than its fielding was the condition of its playing field. "The grass was high and the weeds luxuriant. George Wright amused himself at leisure moments during the game by pulling up the vigorous shoots of plantain and other outlawed plants which flourished at shortstop."[9] The club could not even afford to keep the grass cut.

On August 13, 1872, the Mansfields folded.[10] Cleveland, Troy and the Washington Olympics also went out of business that same summer.

Disillusioned with professional athletics, O'Rourke returned to the family farm to tend the cows and help with the harvest. But he still loved the vigor of the game and the thrill of competition, so he returned to the amateur Unions for the remainder of the season.[11]

Middletown's biggest problem was its small population. Its gate just did not generate enough income. Many clubs refused to visit the Mansfields, leaving the team with unfilled dates. The cost of an away game can be pieced together from the account books of Boston manager Harry Wright. Meals, lodging, and transportation for a team of nine players, plus manager, was over $100, not counting payroll[12]:

Train fare	$82.50[13]
Hotel	12.50
Dinner	10.00
Local transportation to and from ball park	6.00

A *good* turnout in a small town was 1,000 paying fans. At $.25 per ticket, this would produce a gate of $250. The visitor's share would equal only $100; and that was on a good day. Of course, a three-game series in the same town was more profitable due to the savings on transportation, but small towns did not have the fan base to maintain attendance over three days.

The rationale to visit or bypass a city can be seen in a letter from Boston co-owner N. T. Appolonio to Harry Wright, in which he analyzes the financial results of a stopover in Cincinnati:

> I presume the 1500 attendance reported in the press dispatches would boil down to about $150 for our share. I fear that at that rate we will not take enough in Cinti to pay our expenses.[14]

Controversy swirled around the economics of baseball and the arguments were followed closely by Jim, for if the business model could not be perfected, he would have to pursue a more secure and reliable profession.

Besides the conflict between large and small cities, a class struggle raged between clubs that relied on working class patronage and therefore wanted a 25 cent ticket price and clubs that catered to the carriage set and insisted on a 50 cent admission fee.

During the early 1870s, Boston manager Harry Wright argued consistently for a $.50 ticket price. In a March 23, 1871, letter to Nick Young, then manager of the Washington Olympics, Wright agreed that the visiting team in matches between their clubs should receive 40 percent of the gate "with the understanding that the admission fee be at least 50 cents."[15]

Henry Chadwick, the sports editor of the *Brooklyn Eagle,* jumped into the $.25 versus $.50 argument to add his two cents:

> In reference to the discussion concerning the reduction of the charge of admission to champion club matches, we have simply to state that when professional playing was introduced in the West some five or six years ago, all leading contests were marked by fifty cents admission gate money. This charge all the western clubs insisted upon, and the grounds keepers in the East were not slow to follow the example when it was first suggested them. The high rates of admission were first inaugurated in Philadelphia before the [1869–70 Cincinnati] Red Stocking nine became noted, the [Philadelphia] Athletics on one occasion charging one dollar admission to a match between them and the [Brooklyn] Atlantics, and nearly 4,000 people paid this sum on the occasion — it was in 1866, we think. From this originated the high tariff out West, which was introduced here in the exciting times of 1869....
>
> The furor for professional playing being now on the decline, it becomes the pecuniary interest of the ground keepers to reduce the tariff in proportion to the loss of the power to attract large crowds, which the professional clubs possessed two or three years ago. What with "exhibition" games and their sequence of suspected hippodroming [throwing games] the patrons of the game have gradually lost interest in a majority of the club games played, and they will no longer pay the half dollar fee as they did in 1869 and 1871. In those years so

great was the rush that it became advisable to increase the tariff in order to lessen the crowd. Now the reverse action is necessary.[16]

In response, the collectors of those egregious fees wrote to the editor of the *Brooklyn Eagle* with the now-standard defense of blaming someone else for the high price of baseball:

> The directors of the [Brooklyn] Atlantic Club and Messrs. Weed & Decker think that 50 cents admission [at the Capitoline Grounds in Brooklyn] is too much to see any game of ball, but we cannot control the price of admission, as it is at the option of the visiting Clubs. They say, "If 25 cents is the price of admission, we shall expect one-half the gross receipts; if 50 cents is the price of admission, we will take one-third." If the admission is 25 cents the Atlantics receive one-fourth; if 50 cents, one-third.[17]

The math is not consistent, but the point was that clubs like Harry Wright's Boston Red Stockings insisted on a higher percentage of each ticket if the home club chose to charge only 25 cents, versus 50 cents.

The editor of the *Eagle* rejoined the argument two days later, taking exception to the New York Mutuals blaming the out-of-town teams for the high price (50 cents) to see a ballgame in New York:

> The New York dailies are trying to prejudice the patrons of the game against the Boston nine, because the directors of the Club retain the fifty cents fee. So long as they can draw such a crowd at half a dollar admission as they did yesterday, they will of course retain it. It is the public's own fault; they will pay it rather than not see the Reds play. But how about the New York Club? The Reds have nothing to do with the Athletic and [New York] Mutual game charges on Saturday, nor the Athletics either. It remains with the Mutuals whether the charge is to be half a dollar or a quarter admission. When their metropolitan club leads the way, it will be time enough to pitch into outside clubs for not following. The people in Boston Pay the 50 cents fee to see the Reds willingly, but they would not do it if the club charged only a quarter, elsewhere. Hence the directors retain the high tariff. But it is the public and not the club which are at fault. The patrons can stop the high tariff at any time by staying away; but they won't.[18]

The economics of admission fees, and the root of all disagreements is this: in the nineteenth century, most workers earned $2 per day. Fifty cents admission, plus a dime for the trolley, and two more nickels for a hot sausage and a beer, and you've only got a $1.30 left in your pocket after a day's labor.

The smaller towns could not fill a stadium at 50 cents; but they could at 25 cents. Still, small-town teams from Middletown or New Haven loved it when they went to Boston or Chicago and collected even a third of a 50-cent tariff (16.7 cents). The major metropolitan areas had enough wealthy patrons to fill the seats at 50 cents.

But the Boston Red Stockings did not want to schlep to New Haven to collect 40 percent of a 25-cent ticket. It just wasn't worth the train fares, hotel charges, meals, or even the bother. They could stay home and play Harvard, draw a larger crowd *and* charge more per seat.

During America's centennial year the conflict over admission fees would erupt in a revolt by the larger cities to expel the small towns and establish 50 cents as the official admission fee. But still the old argument of 25 cents versus 50 cents would return each season — testing the solidarity of organized ball.

Although the life span of a professional team in the National Association era was somewhat unpredictable, Jim at least did not have to wait long for a new offer after Middletown quit the game.

On Christmas Eve 1872, Boston manager Harry Wright invited O'Rourke to join the Red Stockings. Jim's gentlemanly manner was probably as important a factor in catching the eye of Harry Wright as was his quick snap to second. Managers, including Wright, were experiencing personnel problems with drinking players and with the thin rosters of the early years, Wright had to be able to rely on his players showing up for games sober and on time.

But Jim was not so quick to sign. He had concerns about the solvency of the Boston club. Although the Red Stockings were the reigning champions, they had not yet found baseball's delicate balance of winning games *and* making money. At the close of the 1872 season, the Red Stockings were $5,000 in the red, and the players went home without their last paychecks.[19]

While Jim preferred baseball to farming, he was now a married man and Annie was pregnant with Sarah, their first of eight children. So when O'Rourke received the offer to play for the champion Red Stockings, he wrote back to ask manager Harry Wright what assurances he could give that Boston would not fold midway through the season, owing him money, as Middletown had.[20]

Five days latter, a three-page letter arrived from Boston. Wright said he understood Jim's concerns and promised that the club's backers would make good on his contract. Harry wrote candidly about his personal experiences and the relationship of trust he had with the Boston owners.[21]

In due course, Jim was convinced. In a letter dated March 28, 1873, to Washington manager Nick Young, Wright mentions "We have engaged another player, James O'Rourke."[22] The *Boston Herald* voiced the opinion: "The latest accession of the Boston club, O'Rourke of the Mansfield nine, is a capital one."[23]

Jim reported for duty on Friday, April 11, one day before the first game of the year, a traditional pre-season contest with Harvard.[24]

4

Boston Red Stockings (1873)

"We must make the game worth witnessing,"[1]

— Harry Wright

Challenging the Owners — Episode #1: *Discrimination*

A popular story says that Wright asked O'Rourke if he would change his name to "Rourke," to disguise his Irish heritage.[2] Jim refused, saying: "I would die first before I would give up any part of my father's name. A million would not tempt me."[3] The Boston Brahmins backed off and from day one, Jim was listed in Boston box scores as "O'Rourke"

This anecdote may be apocryphal. We know that Jim was listed as "Rourke" in the Osceola box scores published in 1868 and again in 1870, apparently without objection.

Whether true or not, I suspect that Tim Murnane was the originator of the story. Writing in 1906, Murnane said that he received offers from Boston and Philadelphia in the fall of 1872 to play first base during the 1873 season, and that he recommended O'Rourke when he informed Wright that he was accepting the offer from Philadelphia.[4] According to Murnane, Wright then informed him: "O'Rourke can have the job if he will drop the 'O' from his name, as the public in Boston will not stand for the Irish."[5]

In the new social order of America, with its class system of capitalists and workers, being "manly" (preserving one's dignity) required a worker to stand up for his rights, even if it meant losing his job.[6] Jim would have to put his career on the line many times to defend his concept of justice for workers. For his spunk, he became a hero to the Boston Irish.[7]

Jim boarded with Harry and Carrie Wright at their home in the Highland section of South Boston, not far from the ball grounds.[8] The Highlands are well named. The area is atop a steep hill with a spectacular panoramic view, a fitting perspective for Harry Wright, the visionary "father of professional baseball."

Boarding with the Wrights allowed Jim to save money to send home to Annie and his mother. Jim said the Wrights treated him so well they would have spoiled him had it not been for his mother's counsel.[9]

O'Rourke's salary was $800 for eight months work: more than a factory worker could earn in a year.[10] Some idea of the purchasing power of $800 can be gauged from a personal account book maintained by Harry Wright in 1871[11]:

Income from boarders (Charles Gould and brother George Wright)	$ 42.00 per month.
Suit of clothes (for George)	$ 5.50
Coat and vest for Harry (obviously better dressed than George)	$ 16.24
Icebox	$ 30.00
Bedstead and mattress	$ 9.50
Rocking chair	$ 3.00
Spittoon	$ .35
Teapot	$ .40
Beef	$ .22 per lb.
Fish	$ .09 per lb.
Potatoes	$ 1.25 per bushel
Butter	$ .42 per lb.

An $800 salary would have worked out to about $100 per month (for a baseball season that ran from mid–March, when spring training started, to late October.) Jim was able to send home about $65 a month — about $1,300 in today's dollars — after deducting out-of-pocket expenses for himself and room and board at the Wrights.

Wright took Jim under his wing as well as his eaves and the two became fast friends. Jim gained a rare opportunity to understudy a man who would later be inducted into the Hall of Fame strictly for his skill as a manager. Harry made nightly entries in his expense journals and conducted correspondence with prospective players, other managers, and with railroad offices and hotels to plan road trips.

Since George Wright and Charles Gould also boarded with Harry, the discussions at the dinner table must have been heady. George, Harry and Charles were three of the players on the first professional baseball team, the Cincinnati Red Stockings of 1869. They were also pioneers in the emerging sporting goods industry.

The athletic equipment store of Wright and Gould (later Wright and Ditson) was a year-round gathering place for players and fans alike. The business side of baseball was so important to Gould that he chose to sit out the 1873 season in order to devote full time to the fledging sporting goods business.[12]

Harry Wright invented a score sheet that he sold in bound sets to managers, fans and journalists. He expanded this modest beginning into a full line of baseball supplies and equipment, and for awhile both George and Harry operated competing stores in Boston.

The three veteran ball players were capable, ambitious men who did not "sport away" their earnings in saloons. As in the most respectable households in Boston, the Wrights, Charles Gould and Jim O'Rourke gathered in the parlor after dinner to sing popular songs as Charles fingered the melody on the Wrights' piano. They might have been pharmacists or jewelers or English teachers. Instead, they were founding members of a new profession. They were ballplayers.

O'Rourke's fellow borders reinforced his belief in the importance of projecting a refined image to encourage patronage by well-behaved and affluent spectators (as opposed to brawling, bottle-throwing, gamblers and drunks). The 50-cent admission promoted by Harry also helped to discourage the less savory element.

Harry Wright, like O'Rourke, was clearly concerned about the image of his new profession, as evidenced by a letter he wrote to the manager of the Philadelphia Athletics, winners of the 1871 pennant (baseball's first), discussing the proper respect that should be accorded the "flag":

> I was sorry to see it stated in the papers that the Flags would be on exhibition in a drinking saloon. I think the proper place is or would be the Athletic club room, or some place where *all* who wish could go and see them. To elevate the National game we must earn the respect of all; and now the Athletics are champions—the first legal and recognized Champions of the United States—they will be looked up to as the exponents of what is right and wrong in base ball, and will find it in their power, in a great measure, to make the game a success financially and otherwise.[13]

When Boston won the pennant in 1872, Harry hung the 32-foot streamer in the sanctuary of the Red Stockings' clubroom, where Boston fans were welcome to come in and bask in its majesty.

Harry wanted for baseball the same esteem enjoyed by cricket. Harry's father had been a professional cricket player in England. Because of the decorum surrounding the English national pastime, its adherents were held in higher regard than their poor American relations.

Harry Wright also expected his players to attain a high standard of excellence in the performance of their craft; again, to garner respect for the profession. Harry expected his players to report for training each year on or before March 15.[14] They conditioned in a gymnasium near the ballpark, and on the occasional snowless day the Red Stockings practiced outdoors on their ball grounds. In a letter to a fellow manager, Harry described his spring training regimen:

> Our players will ... receive orders to be at the Gymnasium[15] for exercise from 10 to 12 AM and 2:30 to 4 PM. This will consist in throwing, pitching, and catching, running and jumping, swinging light clubs and dumb bells, rowing, pulling light weights, and in fact doing a little of everything to keep them going and assist in making them supple and active. When the weather is favorable they will meet on the grounds in the afternoon at 2:30 for practice. This will comprise a half-hours indiscriminate throwing, batting and catching; then they will assume their regular positions in the field, with say two taking alternate turns at batting–eight strikes each all hits counting — to be relieved by two others in turn until all have been at the bat. With three men at the bat the bases can be run as in a game giving two or three outs to each batsman.[16]

Either from the hours he spent exercising or from heredity — probably both — O'Rourke developed tree trunk legs that served as a solid platform for batting and catching. The *Boston Herald* reported after one game that "Jimmy O'Rourke's legs were the objects of especial admiration on the part of several ... spectators."[17] Harry Wright once wrote about a futile attempt by O'Rourke to snag a throw over his head: "It is hard work for Jim to leave his feet. I guess his legs are too heavy."[18]

In the gymnasium, Jim ran laps, lifted weights, hit balls into a net, and tossed the ball around with Boston shortstop George Wright and catcher James "Deacon" White.

George could throw behind his back, throw without looking, pretend to muff the ball and then catch it, and roll the ball down his arm and flip it high from the inside of his elbow.[19]

According to writer Robert Smith, before each game Wright and O'Rourke "used to amuse the spectators with exhibitions of juggling. They laughed and joshed as they flipped the ball back and forth, making a striking picture" in their white flannel uniforms, replete with collar, bright red tie and scarlet stockings. O'Rourke was "always merry, full of life and of course full of talk." Smith adds that Jim "had an abundant mustache that seemed to make his loud laugh twice as jolly."[20]

Boston catcher Deacon White was nervously quick and agile as a cat. He had sure hands, and yielded to the ball when catching. In throwing, he was swift and accurate.[21] White earned his nickname for his temperance, polite manner and off-season profession as a preacher.[22]

During the previous season of 1872, White introduced the practice of catching up close behind the batter, even *without* runners on base. That was the year the pitcher restrictions were relaxed enough to allow for curves. Pitchers still had to release the ball below the waist, but were allowed to snap the ball with their wrist or elbow at the end of the delivery. Deacon felt that pitchers would be more effective if they were provided a target.[23]

There was no catcher's mitt at the dawn of the professional era, nor any protection for the backstop. The wear and tear on the hands was the worst. Shaking a catcher's hand was like grabbing a piece of rough-hewn timber. According to White, he also became the first catcher to wear hand protection: "I bought myself a large buckskin glove, put my own padding in it, and stood up behind the batter."[24] (At the time, catchers literally stood behind the plate, legs spread, knees bent, and leaning forward with their hands cupped and held out in front of their chest.)

For 1873, Jim was assigned the roles of right fielder and "change catcher" to back up Deacon White. Substitutions from the bench still were not allowed. If Deacon was injured, he would be moved to right field, and O'Rourke brought in to catch.

Harry Wright, 1878. The first professional manager, and one of the most successful, winning half the pennants during the first decade of major league baseball (National Baseball Hall of Fame Library, Cooperstown, New York).

Since it was difficult to introduce new players during a game, the entire roster of the Red Stockings consisted of only 11 men. Thirty-eight-year-old Manager Harry Wright also covered center field.

Al Spalding was *the* pitcher. In the words of baseball historian Arthur Bartlett, in 1873, "a bullpen was a place you kept bulls."[25]

Before substitutions were allowed, pitchers had to pace themselves. If they threw too much heat, they would not last nine innings, nor would their gloveless backstops. As a result, Spalding used the changeup as much as possible:

His forte in delivery is the success with which he disguises a change of pace from swift to medium, a great essential in successful pitching.[26]

Spalding also relied on control. Catcher Deacon White claimed that Al "would place the pitch where the batter wasn't expecting it."[27]

As Jim waited in right field for starting catcher Deacon White to be

injured, he learned the proper techniques for covering the outfield. Harry
Wright taught Jim to shift left or right, depending on the hitter; and to back
up throws to first base.

During the first half of the 1873 season, Jim was called upon to fill in
behind the plate five times.

Then, in July, Jim was moved from right field to first base to replace
struggling rookie Jack Manning, whom Wright had recruited at the start of
the season to replace Charlie Gould.

First basemen were required to hold runners on first and to defend the
right infield. It is one of baseball's many myths that Charlie Comiskey, in
the 1880s, was the first player to play off the bag at first.[28] As O'Rourke
explains it, players of the day relied on place hitting rather than power, so a
hole next to first base would have resulted in much higher batting averages
than those actually recorded.

O'Rourke excelled at first base. According to one account, he was "very
reliable at holding the difficult high foul flies." Although "one of the youngest
professionals in the business," he was also "one of the best."[29] In one contest O'Rourke put out over 20 play-
ers at first.[30]

The Ball. In the early 1870s balls were
offered in a wide range of elasticity, from
lively to dead. With Spalding pitching,
the Bostons favored a dead ball. Their
strategy was to rely on superior fielding
to hold opponents to low scores. On
offense, the Red Stockings were adept at
place-hitting and could push the ball into
the gaps (ad in *Harper's Weekly*, September 12, 1874).

Jim acquired many of the fine
points of tactics from Harry Wright,
who thought baseball more a game
of wits than brawn. O'Rourke later
remembered that "Harry Wright
spent many an hour teaching me to
hit to right field, for naturally [as a
right-hander] I was a left-field hitter. No team ever has been able to
place the ball more accurately and
safely than that Boston team."[31]

Harry's style of hit-and-run
ball helped the Reds win the pennant in 1873.

In spite of the success of the
Red Stockings and his popularity
with the Boston fans, Jim was
tempted to give up baseball for
a potentially more lucrative career;
and might have done so had it
not been for his "angel cloud."
According to Jim, billowing white
clouds "are the hope of ball players.

Whereas a dead blue sky bewilders a man who tries to catch a batted ball, angel clouds ... guide his judgment."[32] Jim's wife was *his* angel cloud.

Boxer Patsey Sheppard had a popular gym in Boston that Jim frequented to stay fit. Jim became friendly with Sheppard and for a while "James made the English boxer's hotel his home."[33]

Sheppard taught Jim the science of boxing and O'Rourke became handy with the gloves. So much so, that Sheppard prodded him to turn pro. However, Annie reminded Jim of how hard he had fought to overcome the stereotype of the unruly Irishman. O'Rourke did not drink, and his nickname attested to the polish of his speech. At a time when ballplayers were loaded more often than bases,[34] his gentlemanly habits set him apart. The *New York Clipper* described Jim as a "quiet, gentlemanly, Connecticut youth with Irish blood in his veins, and, therefore, full of pluck and courage."[35]

Under the accepted middle-class standard of "manliness," these qualities were not in conflict with one another. While it was necessary for a man to fight back when pushed too far, it was just as important not to lose control. To do so would be undignified. Better to argue calmly, rather than throw a punch or swear at an umpire or teammate.

Jim followed Annie's advice and stuck with baseball, reaffirming his resolve to enhance the image of the sport and its practitioners.

Jim's goal to bring respectability to his profession would not be easy. While there were other notable players with gentlemanly ways, like teammate Deacon White, there were also many attracting unfavorable press, as evidenced by this *New York Times* passage:

> A ball player is a "shiftless member of the laboring class, prone to drink, having a loose moral code, and preferring to avoid an honest days work by playing baseball."[36]

The genteel Connie Mack described the low regard for professionals when he and O'Rourke were players: "The game was thought, by solid respectable people, to be only one degree above grand larceny, arson and mayhem, and those who engaged in it were beneath the notice of decent society."[37]

5

The Red Stockings in Great Britain (1874)

"Their independent bearing and free and easy manner was remarkable."[1]
— The *Dublin Mail*, describing the American "tourists"

In 1874, Jim had a chance to participate in the first goodwill tour to promote America's national sport. The grand adventure was the brainchild of Harry Wright, who thought additional money could be earned by taking baseball to Great Britain. He knew that large crowds turned out for cricket matches; and wasn't American baseball vastly superior?

Prior to the start of the season, Harry sent pitcher Al Spalding to England to line up venues for a series with the Philadelphia Athletic Base Ball Club. Spalding was the perfect choice to parley with the Brits. His imposing 6'1" stature and imperious manner endeared him to the English gentry.

Spalding used the opportunity to hone his skills in duplicity, which he would put to use on more than one occasion over the ensuing years. When in England, it became clear to Spalding that the Brits had no interest in witnessing American baseball; but they were interested in trumping the colonists in a series of cricket matches. So Albert Goodwill Spalding told the Brits that the Americans were accomplished cricketers and would be delighted to meet them on the greensward for some wicket bashing. Then he wired Harry Wright to get the boys packing because John Bull could not wait to see the great American pastime first hand.

On Friday, July 17, the Red Stockings and Athletics steamed out of Philadelphia in the wake of a riotous celebration by fans and families. Former Middletown teammates Tim Murnane and John Clapp were on board as part of the Philadelphia contingent.

A tug followed along, like a whale calf clinging close to its mother, as the *Ohio*, of the one-year-old American Line, headed from the cramped harbor for open water. H. J. Kempton of the *Boston Herald*, one of seven sports-writers sailing with the clubs, provides an excellent description of the passage[2]:

> A few minutes later, and the ship and tug were steaming in opposite directions though "good-byes" were shouted as long as voices could be heard and hand-kerchiefs waved as long as forms could be distinguished. Everybody on board the *Ohio* then realized that we were fairly off, with home and friends behind and 3000 miles of open sea before us.

Ship and Cargo

The curious soon began their investigations to ascertain how we were provided for on the voyage and something definite about our means of conveyance. Upon inquiry it was found that the Ohio, commanded by Captain Morrison, was an iron steamship 350 feet in length and 50 feet deep, with tonnage of about 3200 tons, and an average draft of 22 feet six inches. She had 371 souls on board besides crew, and was far from being full, as the steerage would accommodate about 700. The cabin rooms were all taken, and there was not much spare room in the intermediate quarters.

The passengers were traveling in relative luxury compared to the journey Jim's parents must have experienced traveling from Ireland to America 40 years before. The ship's stores were well stocked with beef, pork, lamb, veal, turkeys, chickens, ducks, geese, flour enough to supply a daily consumption of 700 loaves of bread, besides coffee, tea, vegetables, and spices.

> The storekeeper's compartment showed an ample supply of wines and cordials and to keep the party cool there were thirty tons of ice on hand. The water supply was sufficient and in case accident could have made a lack in this quarter there was a glorious opportunity to draw upon old ocean for an unlimited amount of what the condensers connected with the engines could convert into the best of water.

Down in the hold there was an assorted cargo, consisting of wheat, corn, cheese, tobacco, flour, hides, and a variety of other merchandise.

The Voyage

> As the ship glided over the smooth waters of Delaware bay the weather was delightful and the party lounged about the deck enjoying the cool air and the fine view afforded. The afternoon passed quickly, and at early twilight our pilot left us. Cape Henlopen was passed at about half-past 8 o'clock, and two hours later the ship came abreast of Four Fathoms light house, whose twinkling light was visible when the majority of the party turned in. An unbroken night's rest was followed by a clear bright morning, and it was discovered that as we slept the ship had taken us away from sight of land and we were in the center of a vast expanse of water, bounded by the sky on every hand. Now we began to feel the motion of the waves and it was noticed that breakfast was not heartily enjoyed.

The tourists soon adjusted to the gentle swell and the "whole voyage was a series of pleasant days, with smooth and favorable winds." The delegation was entertained with the wondrous sites of nature. On Friday, the second night out, the sunset was:

remarkable fine, the sun sinking like a great red ball of fire into the waves at the horizon, and leaving the light reds tinged with a beautiful carmine which was gradually transformed into golden and purple shades, finally changing to a leaden gray.

On Saturday morning the Athletics began to grow uneasy of the restraint placed upon them and to look about for means of passing the time, which evidently commenced to hang heavily on the minds of some. There were cards, checkers, chess, and other means for their amusement at hand in abundance, but men used to outdoor exercise demanded something more lively. Shuffle board and ring toss became the preferred diversions.

Arctic Visitors

Sunday and Monday passed without the occurrence of any event of importance, the vessel continuing on her course at an average speed of 11½ knots an hour. Tuesday morning all hands were called out early, the news passing over the ship with great rapidity, that an iceberg was in sight. This was an event indeed, and everybody hurried up so as not to miss the sight. We were in latitude 43.11, and longitude 47.3, and about 1400 miles away from Philadelphia at the time and there about six miles north of us floated the berg. As viewed by us it looked like a shelter tent pitched upon a level plan, being a regular rectangle in form, and lacking those lofty peaks and angular prominences which a novice expects to find in icebergs. The top, to the extent of about an eighth of the distance down, was pure white, as though the mass of crystal were covered with snow. It was estimated that the cold lump was a quarter of a mile in length, and 200 feet high above water. Floating around it, like a brood of chickens around the mother hen, were numerous detached pieces, which were hardly discernible without the aid of the glass, but which were no doubt very respectable sized lumps. During the forenoon a smaller berg floated past us, not more than a mile and a half away. It was irregular in shape, and this, with its pure whiteness, led one of the boys to compare it to a lump of ice cream, which was not a bad simile. This is the "ice month," but it is quite unusual to meet bergs on the southerly course upon which we sailed. In fact, this was the first trip of the season in which it occurred. In going east, however, when the northerly course is adopted on account of the aid received from the strong westerly current, icebergs are seen on every voyage. On the last trip of the *Ohio* from Liverpool she was in sight of fifteen of these stragglers from the North at one time, and they made themselves so familiar that it was necessary to steer the ship in a zigzag course among them to avoid collisions.

Into the Fog

During the night of Tuesday the 21st, we passed out of the Gulf Stream, a fact which was perceptible on the following morning by a fall in the temperature of the air and a drop from 73 degrees to 65 degrees in the water. About noon, Wednesday, a thick fog settled down around the ship, limiting the view to a very few feet around us. The afternoon was misty and damp, and no particular pleasure was to be derived from sitting upon the deck, so that many of the party were driven below. The fog whistle was brought into requisition and was sounded at frequent intervals to warn any ship which might be approaching. In the early part of the evening a ship under good spread of canvas was discernible for a few moments, through the fog, and she passed within a couple of hundred feet of us. This afforded ample opportunity for reflection upon the possibilities of collision, and though no nervousness was expressed, it was doubtless felt by many on board....

In spite of the unavoidable monotony of an ocean voyage, there was something new almost every day. The system and frequency of meals—breakfast at eight, lunch at 12, dinner at four, and supper at eight—did much to make the time pass quickly, and it was a noticeable fact that after the first two days the attendance upon all these meals was wonderfully good. Nobody had reason to complain but the steward, and he probably found the labor of supplying the ravenous crowd no easy one.

The weather grew cooler and the seas rougher as we drew nearer the Irish coast, and overcoats, which had hitherto been unneeded, were brought out and found very comfortable for a stroll on deck. The boys began to get a little tired of so much sea view and to imagine that land would be a pleasant sight....

Land Ho!

Early Sunday afternoon [the 26th of July], the more anxious began to scan the horizon ahead of us for the first glimpse of land, and about 3 o'clock the sharp-eyed could perceive that faint outline of what appeared like a low mound upon the edge of the water, and which was hardly distinguishable in color from the sky. It may be a cloud, but no, the officer on deck says it is land, and that mound is the eastern extremity of the range of mountains extending from Cape Clear to Cork [Ireland].

Upon landing at Liverpool, the players took a few days to regain their land legs (and stomachs). During their spare time, fashion plates O'Rourke and Spalding invested heavily with the London haberdashers. A reporter accompanying the tour panned the dandies with the observation: "The only thing I can say in favor of the various garments is their cheapness."[3]

Then commenced a whirlwind tour of England, staying at Dickensian inns like the Black Swann, and traveling first class in a special car supplied by Mr. Pullman. Fourteen baseball games were scheduled between the two American teams,[4] plus cricket contests with the leading clubs of England.

The Americans also scheduled a side trip to the Emerald Isle. When planning the tour, Wright had suggested in a letter to the Athletics: "We surely must take Dublin in, for with all our Mc's and O'R's, a game there would surely prove attractive and pay handsomely."[5] Boston had Cal McVey and Jim O'Rourke on its roster; Philadelphia had pitcher Dick McBride, infielder Mike McGeary, and center fielder John McMullen. By the early 1870s, baseball was providing an avenue of upward mobility for Irish Americans. On August 24, 1874, a week before his 24th birthday, James Henry O'Rourke stood at home plate in Dublin stadium.[6]

To fulfill Spalding's promise, the tourists also played a series of cricket matches against the blokes from Great Britain, but their playing wasn't exactly—well—cricket.

The Send-Off for the Baseball Tourists. A band played waltzes and gallops, champagne flowed, and according to the *Philadelphia Press*, "hearty good-bys and cheers rent the air." The Ohio sounded a warning and the great ship moved away from the dock. Players hung from rigging and waved to noisy fans. A convoy of small boats and tugs escorted the delegation as far as they dared, blowing off steam to wish the athletes bon voyage.

When the send-off subsided, the players settled into a routine of shipboard life and draw poker (engravings from the *New York Daily Graphic*, August 13, 1874).

The Brits swung at what we would call balls and merely deflected pitches that were right down the middle. This seemed unnatural to the Yanks. Nevertheless, the Americans were under strict orders by Wright to display good form as they were international ambassadors. In the first game, the Americans started rather poorly, but they were "very proper."

Then, out of frustration, Al Spalding wound up the big cricket club and walloped a strike as hard as he could. It sailed clear out of the park. The American players jumped up and shouted themselves hoarse. But Harry, whose father was a famous English cricketer, was mortified at the breach of etiquette.

Spalding started his victory lap when Umpire Williams stopped him short. A hush fell over the crowd. Spalding thought he was to be called out for bad form, but the umpire merely advised, with English understatement: "You needn't leave your place on a hit like that."[7]

The Americans resumed cheering and each in their turn whaled away at the ball. The Yanks won 107 to 105. Of course, their playing wasn't cricket.

Our schoolyard motto: "It's not whether you win or lose; it's how you play the game" must also be of English origin. America is about winning.

A cricket team consists of 11 players, but all 18 of the American ballplayers competed.[8] Since every player on a side has a chance at bat, most American historians state that this gave the Yanks an advantage. Mark Alvarez is most critical of the American venture and says the "tour was considered a joke by the British" who did not take the cricket games seriously.[9] However, the stats from the contests show that a number of the Americans were superior players. At the Sheffield game, for example, the top seven Americans outbowled all 11 players of the English team.

I believe the Yanks would have done well had Wright taken the field with only his 11 best players. The Americans had more experience with cricket than anyone at the time imagined. The Wrights had played cricket professionally, and Harry drilled the Americans prior to and during the voyage over. In addition, the Americans were far better fielders, as this skill had evolved into a fine art in the baseball branch of bat-and-ball games. As one English spectator admitted: "Eleven of those fellers could stand us a tight game."[10] But regardless of whose interpretation of the events you accept, the Yanks get an asterisk next to their cricket wins.

In its post-mortem of the match, a Sheffield, England, paper reported:

> The batting of the Americans generally was of the cross-bat, slogging order, a style learned, no doubt, from their manner of striking at base-ball, but this remark does not apply to the three Wrights and O'Rourke, who showed decidedly superior form.[11]

1874 Boston Red Stockings. **Four are Hall of Famers: O'Rourke (seated far left), Harry Wright (with beard), George Wright (seated on floor holding cap), and Al Spalding (standing with ball), who would soon discover more money could be made making baseballs than by throwing them. Catcher Deacon White is third from left (engraving:** *Harper's Weekly,* **July 25, 1874).**

The American Ballists v. British Cricketers, at Kensington Oval, London (engraving: *New York Daily Graphic,* September 3, 1874).

On August 14, 1874, after the final game in London, a contest was held to see who could throw the ball the farthest. The English gentry were safely enthroned upon their carriages beyond the outfield. Harry Wright stood in center field to mark the distance. When O'Rourke's chance came, he squeezed the ball so tightly the veins bulged from the back of his hand. He filled his broad chest with air and reared back for a full arm swing. His entire body strained to slingshot five ounces of leather and yarn into the clear sky. The ball flew from the son of an Irish émigré, high over Harry's head, past the outfield, and into an astonished crowd of 4,000.[12] "Just before leaving the Oval in London, 'Jimmy' O'Rourke was presented with a handsome cricket ball, as a prize for the longest throw. He threw 123 yards."[13]

Hall of Famer Adrian Anson, who was on the tour with Jim, writing a generation later, had this to say about O'Rourke's throwing:

MENU

Marylebone Cricket Club

Soups.

Thick and Clear Turtle.   Spring.

Fish.

Fillet Soles, Hollandaise.   Red Mullet, Italian.

Grilled Salmon, Caper Sauce.   Boiled Salmon.

Turbot, Lobster Sauce.

Whitebait.

Entrees.

Lobster Cutlets.   Sweetbreads, Supreme Sauce.

Lamb Cutlets.   Fillet Chickens.   Lentiles.

Removes.

Roast and Boiled Chickens.   Ham and Tongue.

Roast Quarter Lamb.   Spinach.

Roasts.

Duckling and Peas.   Goslings.   Haunch of Venison.

Lobster Salad.

Sweets.

Fruit Jellies.   Charlotte Russe.   Ice Puddings.

———

Haddock on Toast.

Dessert.   Ices.

H. Reed, Printer   57 Oxford Street

A typical menu to which the baseball tourists were indulged (Menu: Spalding Scrapbooks, New York Public Library).

At right: Hall of Famer Adrian Anson in 1874. In *A Ball Player's Career,* Anson remembered "Jim" as "a quiet, gentlemanly young fellow, blessed with a goodly share of Irish wit, and a rich vocabulary of jaw-breaking words." As to his playing, Anson said Jim was "a sure catch, an active fielder, a good thrower, and fine batsman. O'Rourke was always to be relied upon" (engraving: *Harper's Weekly,* July 25, 1874).

Bottom: The Lord's Cricket Grounds, where, in August of 1874, Londoners witnessed a baseball game between the Boston Red Stockings and Philadelphia Athletics. All the American players wore white flannel shirts, caps and knickerbockers; the Bostons wore stockings and belts of scarlet, while the Philadelphia Athletics sported blue. At the left is Boston's 36-foot-long National Association 1873 pennant. The English were intrigued by the American pastime, but opted to stick with cricket (engraving: *Harper's Weekly,* September 5, 1874).

Jim O'Rourke threw the heaviest ball I know of. There was a power of muscle behind Jim's throw, and when he threw to the plate and the ball came to the catcher on the fly, a twinge of pain shot through the arm of the backstop in the old days before they wore the heavy gloves.[14]

After weeks of baseball and banquets, the American tourists sailed for home on August 27, 1874, on the steamship *Abbotsford*, arriving in Philadelphia on September 9, after a stormy two-week voyage.[15] Jim traveled in relative luxury compared to what his parents had endured a generation earlier; but still he became violently seasick and vowed never to leave land again.[16]

There would not be smooth sailing, either, in his relations with the Beantown owners.

Challenging the Owners — Episode #2: *Employees Should Not Have to Make Up Operating Losses*

O'Rourke's first showdown over finances concerned a payroll deduction connected to the overseas trip. Miserly Red Stockings owner Arthur Soden (31)[17] deducted $100 from each player's paycheck to cover the cost of their ocean passage, claiming the tour lost money.

Gate receipts from overseas games were only $1,679.70. However, several farewell and welcome-home games netted $6,835.56, which more than made up the deficit.[18] Soden conveniently overlooked this additional tour-related income.

In the early years of professional baseball, when the rules were still being written, the owners continually looked for ways to pass expenses on to the players. And Jim O'Rourke, in turn, challenged every assessment upon the players.

When Jim discovered his final pay of 1874 was light, he stormed out of Boston, threatening: "If the pay is not reinstated I will leave the team."[19] Harry Wright insisted he had told Jim prior to departing for England that the players would be expected to absorb part of the expenses if the tour lost money. Jim denied he agreed to any such thing and countered: "The club has failed to fulfill its contract."[20] Harry offered to put the matter before the board but warned Jim that he would probably lose the fight.[21]

I believe Harry was trying to keep peace in the family. He was divided between his paternal feelings toward his young protégé and his responsibility to the owners of the Red Stockings, at whose pleasure he served. Harry's mixed feelings toward O'Rourke are apparent in a January 2, 1875, letter he sent to Henry Chadwick:

A first baseman should not stand [on] one leg with his arms folded, thinking of "the girl I left behind me" [a popular song of the time], when the ball is being delivered to the bat, as he does frequently, thereby letting many a ball get by him that he should have fielded. Did he not have the best throwing to him of any first baseman in the fraternity, his record would be a poor one indeed. He does not know what it is to get off his base a yard or two for a wild throw and stop it, or handle it and get back as Start or Mills or Dehlman would. He has a stubborn disposition and two or three times last season refused to catch when I sent him behind the bat. Of course he had to go, but I have had to threaten him more than once to send him off the field... His good points are heavy batting and accurate throwing.

The fans and media agreed with Wright's positive assessments of his first baseman and change catcher. According to the *Boston Times* of March 15:

> [O'Rourke] is considered the strongest thrower in the nine, and his batting is very hard.... James O'Rourke is ... a most popular player with the Hubbites.

But this time Jim gave in. Boston was losing money, and Jim did not want to see the team fold, as Middletown had. The sport was growing and evolving at a rapid rate. But it would be the last time Jim would retreat from a confrontation with the owners.

During the following season, Jim would witness two milestones in the evolution of the game: the invention of the fielder's glove and the "bird cage."

6

The Tools of Ignorance (1875)

"We used no mattress on our hands,
No cage upon our face,
We stood right up and caught the ball,
With courage and with grace."[1]
— George Ellard

During the 1870s, the tools of the baseballist were being invented and refined. For example, it was at this time that a few brave and innovative players began wearing hand protection. The commonly accepted originator of the fielding aid was Charlie Waitt, outfielder and first baseman for the St. Louis Brown Stockings.[2] According to popular legend, in 1875, he was spotted sporting a tight-fitting fingerless mitt. Waitt's glove was flesh-colored so as not to draw attention and hooting from the crowd.

Firsts are difficult to authenticate, especially when the originator does not want anyone to catch on that he is doing something that may give him an edge. However, a glove may have been used earlier than 1875, perhaps as early as the 1860s. The *New York Clipper*, in an article appearing *before* the start of the 1875 season suggested pitchers wear

> gloves covering the palms of the hand and the lower part of his fingers. Stout hand gloves will prevent a hot ball from splitting of the hand while admitting of the free grasp of the ball by the uncovered fingers. In fact the gloves we refer to should be used alike by catchers, first-basemen, and pitchers.[3]

The glove described above matches an early style of baseball glove, and the frank discussion suggests that at least some first basemen wore hand protection prior to 1875.

The source of the Waitt legend may have been Al Spalding, who credited Waitt in his 1911 memoir, *America's National Game*, as the first player to wear a glove. The two were teammates on the 1877 Chicago White Stockings.

51

There is even more evidence for earlier users of a glove or gloves behind the plate. For example, DeWitt's *Guide* of 1872, included the following advice:

> The catcher will find it advantageous when facing swift pitching to wear tough leather gloves, with the fingers cut off near the joint, as they will prevent him having his hands split and puffed up. If he has the fingers of the glove on he can not retain his hold of the ball so well.

Other sources credit Doug Allison, Harry Wright's 1869 Cincinnati catcher, as the first to wear hand protection.[4] However, according to the *Toronto Globe*, the first player to wear gloves [plural] behind the plate was Delaverage of the Victory Club of Troy, in 1860.[5]

Whoever was first to deaden the impact of swiftly thrown balls, the glove of the 1870s was hardly the Viking shield of the modern era. The first catcher's glove was little more than a heavy work glove. Typically, catchers wore two gloves: one with the fingers cut off, on their throwing hand (to allow a sure grip on the ball), and a glove with fingers on the other hand.

Another important development during the mid–1870s was the adoption of the catcher's mask. In 1883, *Sporting Life* printed the earliest recollection of the invention of the "muzzle":

> O'Rourke, of the Buffalo club, claims to be the inventor of the base ball mask. In 1877, when with the Bostons, he had two made for his own use, but gave one to [William] Holbert. George Wright obtained his model from O'Rourke.[6]

A second account, and the one most often repeated, says the mask was invented in 1877 by Harvard captain Fred Thayer for his squeamish catcher James Alexander Tyng, who was afraid he'd wind up looking like a prizefighter if he went behind the bat without protection. In a letter to Al Spalding dated May 18, 1911, Thayer recalled adapting the fencing mask to baseball:

> It was up to me to devise some means of having the impact of the blow kept from driving the mask onto the face. The forehead and chin rest accomplished this and also made it possible for me to secure a patent.[7]

The baseball mask was also made of much heavier gauge wire than the lighter fencing mask. According to Thayer, Tyng practiced with the mask during the winter of 1876–77 and debuted it on Fast Day, Thursday, April 12, 1877, in a game with the Live Oaks at Lynn, Massachusetts.[8]

George Wright, who had partnered with Thayer to commercialize the mask, confirmed Thayer's recollection in a letter to Spalding dated May 17, 1911:

> The first time I saw the mask and it being used was by Tyng, when catching in a game on the Harvard nine in 1877. What game it was I cannot remember. But

that fall Mr. Thayer, by appointment, brought the mask to my store on Eliot Street. Harry Schafer, being there, put it on. When we threw several balls at it, which glanced off, he not feeling any jar or effect from them, we pronounced it a success and decided it would come into general use. I made arrangements at the time with Mr. Thayer to patent the mask, control sale of it, and pay him a royalty, and, as you know, after the above date the mask gradually came into general use. Who the first professional player was to use it I cannot say.[9]

Harry Wright also supports the spring of 1877 as marking the first instance of a catcher wearing protection. In an April 5, 1877, letter to *Cincinnati Enquirer* editor O. P. Caylor, Harry heralded armor's debut:

On Saturday 14th, and Tuesday 17th we are engaged to play the Harvard University Nine on our grounds. It will be the first appearance of a catcher in armor, as Tyng will wear Thayer's mask. It is a good thing, as it enables the catcher to *face* the hottest kind of foul tips.[10]

In spite of the fact that the Boston crowd (Thayer, George Wright, and Harry Wright) concur that the mask made its first appearance in Boston in April 1877, protecting the tender countenance of Jim Tyng, there are no game accounts of the first appearance of the strange contraption to corroborate their story. Specifically, the *Boston Globe* makes no mention of a mask in a 68-word description of the April 12 game between Harvard and the Live Oaks of Lynn, in which, according to Thayer and accepted history, the bird cage made its public debut.[11] Nor was there a mention of the "first appearance of a catcher in armor" in the *Globe*'s 178-word coverage of the game of Saturday, April 14, between the Bostons and Harvard, as promoted by Harry Wright.[12]

The mask may have been perfected in 1877, but most likely it had been evolving for two years prior to its highly touted debut. Consider the following evidence.

In 1884, the *Spalding Guide* boasted:

The first Catcher's Mask brought out in 1875, was a very heavy, clumsy affair, and it was not until we invented our open-eyed mask in 1877 that it came into general use.

Even two of Thayer's catchers claim to have worn the mask prior to when captain Thayer claims to have invented it. In an 1896 letter to the editor of the *New York Sun*, teammate Howard K. Thatcher recalled:

When we played our first game in the Spring of 1876, I put on a mask which I had made from heavy wire. The edges were wound with leather, and I had a strap on the chin and another at the forehead. My chum Fred Thayer, helped me to make it, and I confess it was a queer-looking thing. I was ridiculed the first time I wore the mask, partly because it was a new thing, and partly because the people considered that a catcher did not need protection for his face. I threw the mask away but Thayer picked it up and had it patented.[13]

Years later, in an article appearing in a June 1908 issue of the *New York World*,[14] Thatcher admitted that he received a great deal of "guying" from his fellow Harvard players, who said it was "babyish" and cowardly to wear face protection, so he "was not seen very often" wearing the mask, but instead used George Wright's mouth protector.

Harvard catcher Warren Briggs says he wore a mask in the spring of 1876 and "left Boston on the 5th of July" of the same year.[15] Briggs settled in O'Rourke's hometown of Bridgeport, where he became a successful architect.

Spalding added his own recollections in 1911:

> About this time, 1875–6, James Tyng, catcher for the Harvard Base Ball Club, appeared on the Boston grounds one day, and, stepping to his position, donned the first wire mask that I had ever seen. This mask had been invented and patented by Mr. Fred W. Thayer, a Harvard player, now a prominent lawyer of Boston. Like other protective innovations at that stage of the game, it was not at first well received by professionals. Our catcher, James White, was urged to try it, and after some coaxing consented. I pitched him a few balls, some of which he missed, and finally, becoming disgusted at being unable to see the ball readily, he tore off the mask and, hurling it toward the bench, went on without it.[16]

It sounds like the try-out with White took place in 1875, the last year they both played for Boston, but it may have been in 1876, when the battery jumped to Chicago. Here is Deacon White's recollection:

> One day during the season of 1875 at Boston, the papers announced that "The Man with the Iron Mask" would play a game of baseball for Harvard. Harry Wright asked me to go out with him and see the demonstration. A fellow named Fred Thayer, third baseman for Harvard, had made a big cage, much like a bird's cage, out of heavy iron wire. This is the mask Harvard catcher, Jim Tyng, wore during the game.
> "What do you think of it?" Harry asked me.
> Well, I told him such a mask hindered a catcher's work but I believe one could be made which would prove satisfactory.
> "Make one the way you think it should be made," he ordered.
> So I went to an iron worker in Boston and had him make me a mask out of steel wire. It fit over my face only, with padding around it, and was held on with elastic bands. This I used in catching Spalding for two season after that [1876 and 1877].[17]

One final thread of evidence for a genesis of the mask prior to 1877 is a notice discovered by historian Richard E. Noble in the St. Marks (Massachusetts) School *Courier* of May 15, 1875, giving an account of a game versus Harvard in which 16-year-old catcher W. A. Howe wore a catcher's mask developed by him and a member of the school faculty, William E. Peck. According to Noble, the device was a fencing mask, strengthened with copper wire, with eyeholes cut into it. On the Harvard nine that day in the spring of 1875 was none other than freshman F. W. Thayer.[18]

So how do we reconcile all these conflicting recollections? The mask probably made its first appearance in 1875 in a primitive adaptation of a fencing mask that was not very effective or patentable. I believe it evolved through several versions, thereby accounting for the various dates. Fred Thayer and George Wright would naturally want to establish their 1877 patented iteration as the first mask; therefore Harry's letters to the press announcing the first appearance of a mask, and the synchronized stories decades later by Thayer, George Wright, and Harry Wright. Thayer and George Wright successfully sued Spalding in August 1883 for patent infringement.[19]

O'Rourke's mask may have been a missing link between the modified fencing mask and the final patented product, but I have not been able to find

Catching in 1875. In this painting one can see just how vulnerable the catcher was. Note also his half-crouch stance. Wes Fisler is at the bat. John Clapp, who alternated behind the plate with O'Rourke on the Mansfields, is probably the catcher (1875 watercolor by Thomas Eakins: "Practice Session of the Philadelphia Athletics").

a second source to corroborate Jim's account. Of course, at the time, Jim was not interested in establishing precedence for a patent claim. He was just a catcher who didn't want to be or look like a prizefighter.

In one of history's intriguing coincidences, most of the characters in the mask story appeared on the same ballfield on April 8, 1875 (Fast Day). The Bostons were playing their first game of the season against a picked nine made up primarily of Harvard players. Briggs was at short for the collegians, Thatcher right field, Tyng was at third, and Jim O'Rourke caught for the college nine. Deacon White was behind the plate for the Bostons, who won 8 to 0.[20]

Although the mask gradually began to win acceptance in 1877, it would be years before it was universally adopted. The face-saving device was not mandated, so it was a matter of individual choice. As a case in point, the *Boston Globe* reported in the spring of 1878:

> During the few days' practice of the past week, Charley Snyder, the new catcher, has succeeded admirably in adapting himself to Tommy Bond's pitching. He has also been experimenting with Thayer's patent mask for catchers, and it is not unlikely that he may adopt it.[21]

In 1879, a gruesome incident may suggest why some catchers were reluctant to trust the mask. As reported in the *New York Clipper* of June 7, 1879:

> In a recent game, [John] Clapp, of the Buffalos, met with an accident through wearing a catcher's mask, a wire being driven in his head above the left eye. After having the wound dressed, he pluckily finished the game.

And three months later,

> During the Boston-Cincinnati game at Boston, Mass., on Sept. 12, Kelly, the Cincinnati catcher, while wearing a wire mask, was hit by a foul ball with such force that one of the wires cut a gash over his left eye, causing temporary suspension of the game.[22]

Even as late as 1880, many catchers still refused to wear a "bird cage." In that year, 20-year-old Fred Pfeffer demonstrated "the folly of facing swift pitching behind the bat without the protection of a mask."[23] As reported by the *Clipper*:

> He was struck between the eyes by a foul tip and fell senseless to the ground. He remained in an unconscious condition for some time, and an examination disclosed that his nose had been broken, and that he had sustained an ugly contused wound on his forehead.[24]

That same year, Holbert, Troy's catcher, was "hit in the eye by a foul ball."[25] (Obviously he wasn't wearing the mask given to him by O'Rourke. Or perhaps Jim had not yet parted with his extra mask and it was this incident that prompted him to do so.) In either event, having gained a healthy appreciation for the tools of baseball, Holbert opened a baseball emporium in Troy the following season.[26]

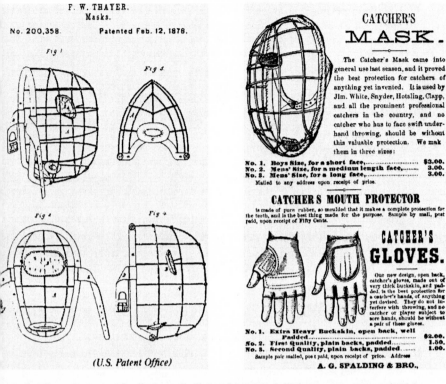

F. W. THAYER.
Masks.

No. 200,358.   Patented Feb. 12, 1878.

Fig 1

Fig 3

Fig 4

Fig 4

(U.S. Patent Office)

CATCHER'S
MASK.

The Catcher's Mask came into general use last season, and it proved the best protection for catchers of anything yet invented. It is used by Jim. White, Snyder, Hotaling, Clapp, and all the prominent professional catchers in the country, and no catcher who has to face swift underhand throwing, should be without this valuable protection. We mak them in three sizes:

No. 1. Boys Size, for a short face, ... $3.00.
No. 2. Mens' Size, for a medium length face, ... 3.00.
No. 3. Mens' Size, for a long face, ... 3.00.
Mailed to any address upon receipt of price.

CATCHER'S MOUTH PROTECTOR

Is made of pure rubber, so moulded that it makes a complete protection for the teeth, and is the best thing made for the purpose. Sample by mail, post paid, upon receipt of Fifty Cents.

CATCHER'S
GLOVES.

Our new design, open back, catcher's gloves, made out of very thick buckskin, and padded, is the best protection for a catcher's hands, of anything yet devised. They do not interfere with throwing, and no catcher or player subject to sore hands, should be without a pair of these gloves.

No. 1. Extra Heavy Buckskin, open back, well Padded .... $2.00.
No. 2. First Quality, plain backs, padded .... 1.50.
No. 3. Second Quality, plain backs, padded .... 1.00.
Sample pair mailed, post paid, upon receipt of price. Address

A. G. SPALDING & BRO.,

Left: Thayer's Patent for "A Base-Ball Catching Mask." The patent was applied for on January 15, 1878. *Right: 1878 Tools of Ignorance.* The Spalding mask is clearly a knock-off of the Thayer patent. Note also the primitive catcher's gloves, that were worn as a pair (*Spalding Guide,* 1878).

Catching without a mask—as Jim did from 1873 through 1875—may seem incredible, in light of the full suits of armor worn by modern backstops. But there was another baseball tradition, *off* the field, that would be even more improbable today.

An anachronistic carryover from the time when baseball teams really were clubs, professional organizations maintained clubhouses for their "members": the players, stockholders, and season ticket holders.

In 1875, the Boston clubhouse was moved to 39 Eliot Street, behind George Wright's store. The *Boston Herald* described the quarters:

At the rear of this is an apartment to be used as a chess room measuring 17 × 20 feet, and this opens upon a parlor 30 × 20 feet in dimensions. The parlor will be handsomely fitted up, and will contain a piano, etc. Adjoining the parlor will be the private office of the directors. The rooms are admirably lighted and ventilated. The entrance to the club is independent of the store, but the store and rear rooms are connected. Keys will be furnished to members of the club.[27]

The championship flag and pennant of 1875 [are] on exhibition at the new rooms of the Boston club, on Eliot Street. The flag measures 30 feet by 10; the groundwork is white with red trimmings; and the inscription in red and blue letter is as follows: "Boston 1873–1874–1875 Champions." The pennant is 40 feet in length, and resembles that of last year.[28]

The *Boston Times* described what one might encounter on a typical spring evening of 1875 in the Red Stockings clubhouse:

A visit to the rooms of the B.B.B.C. ... at about 8 P.M., exhibits them filled with young men, for the most part discussing the features of the last game, and deciding among themselves who among the boys did the most. As a rule each disputant has a favorite, and whilst some are loud in the praise of O'Rourke, others again think "George" the best.[29]

And of course they would discuss the likelihood that their team would win the pennant, enumerating the reasons Boston should go all the way. At the start of the 1875 season, the Red Stockings were the unrivaled champions of the diamond, having won the pennant during the previous three years "due to teamwork and harmony, a marked advantage over clubs in which changes in personnel were frequent."[30]

So, when Hartford won its first 12 games of the 1875 season, it looked like it might be a horse race. The Red Stockings were also undefeated, with a 16–0 record. On May 18, for the first match-up of the two front-runners, a crowd of 9,000 fans from all over Connecticut packed the Hartford stands, a record for New England baseball. "Talk about baseball excitement.... The whole state went wild."[31]

When the game finally commenced, the Hartfords fought valiantly, but in the end, only Boston remained undefeated. The game was decided by crucial errors by the Hartford Dark Blues, who were unaccustomed to the rarified air at the top of the standings. The final score was 10 to 5.

Mark Twain witnessed the great game, and afterward placed the following notice in the *Hartford Courant*:

TWO HUNDRED AND FIVE DOLLARS REWARD — At the great base ball match on Tuesday, while I was engaged in hurrahing, a small boy walked off with an English-made brown silk umbrella belonging to me, and forgot to bring it back. I will pay $5 for the ... umbrella. I do not want the boy (in an active state) but will pay two hundred dollars for his remains — Samuel L. Clemens.[32]

Although Hartford won an impressive 66 percent of its games in 1875, Boston posted a 90-percent win rate, taking the pennant again.[33] But the Red Stockings' permanent possession of the championship was about to be threatened.

The seeming invincibility of the Boston dynasty led one of its rivals to a desperate plot to even the odds. In the midst of the 1875 season, the Chicago club raided the heart of the Boston order. In the furor that followed, the baseball establishment would be turned upside down, and the players would find themselves on the bottom.

7

Boston Red Caps (1876–1878)

White Stockings owner William A. Hulbert was tired of losing the pennant year after year to the Red Stockings. So he bribed Al Spalding to defect to Chicago for the 1876 season, and to recruit other key players from the unbeatable Bostons. Spalding signed up teammates Ross Barnes, Deacon White, and Cal McVey.[1] They were a formidable combination. In 1875, Spalding racked up 54 wins with only five losses. Catcher McVey hit .355, Barnes .364 and White led the league with a .367 average.

On July 20, 1875, the *Chicago Times* broke the story of "A New Chicago Club," and included O'Rourke in the list of defectors. The *Chicago Tribune* of July 20 also listed O'Rourke in the 1876 Chicago line-up, as a "substitute." O'Rourke did not jump to Chicago. If he was considering joining the White Stockings, he soon changed his mind.

The Chicago raid was a clear violation of the National Association agreement. As the *Clipper* had reminded everyone only months earlier, "No player can sign a contract ... until the close of the regular championship season."[2] A player doing so could be expelled from the league.[3] The intent of the rule was to avoid players having divided loyalties. Players who signed with another club prior to the end of a season were suspect of giving less than 100 percent when they competed against the club that had already hired them for the following season.

To preempt disciplinary action, Hulbert and Spalding conspired to break away from the National Association and establish a rival league of their own. Hulbert found that other owners were also willing to desert the player-run National Association. On February 2, 1876, William Hulbert formally organized a new league made up of teams from New York, Boston, Philadelphia, Hartford, Chicago, St. Louis, Cincinnati, and Louisville.[4] The new association would be known as the National League of Professional Base Ball Clubs.

The National League constitution excluded clubs from cities with populations under 75,000 or that were within five miles of any club already in the league. Only a unanimous vote of all the clubs could exempt an applicant from these restrictions. The effect was to purge major league baseball of its small-town teams. The five-mile limit was to guarantee an exclusive franchise to the first club admitted from each metropolitan area. The five-mile rule would affect bordering cities like New York and Brooklyn. New York was a charter member of the National League, so Brooklyn would have to watch from outside organized baseball. Eventually, new competing leagues would provide an opening for Brooklyn. The smaller cities, like New Haven, that were excluded from the National League, would be accommodated by professional minor leagues, which would begin to sprout within a year to fill the void.

To improve the image of baseball and curb rowdiness in the stands, open gambling would be banned from ballparks.

But the overriding goal of the new National League would be to maximize profits for owners at the expense of the players. The *Boston Herald* of February 6, 1876, was the first to notice the shift in focus:

> The new organization "was to be called the "National League of Professional Base Ball *Clubs*," instead of an "Association of *Players*" as before.

The men who played the game had lost control of their profession. Between 1871 and 1874, the president of the National Association was an active player, the first — and last — to serve as the head of a major league. During this period, "the professional players held firm control, ... but it was to be a short-lived worker's paradise."[5]

An important separation had taken place in the 1860s when players ceased to be the club members. The worker-players could not provide the capital necessary to build and maintain ballparks, much less provide salaries for themselves during deficit seasons. The role of financial backing fell to the wealthier members of the club, a group distinct from the players. Al Spalding described the paradigm shift: "The function of baseball *clubs* in the future would be to manage baseball *teams*."[6]

Originally, during this new epoch, "Individuals of means and leisure organized clubs for pleasure, and were perfectly satisfied if at the close of the season ... receipts balanced expenditures."[7] However, as baseball became more popular and clubs began to make money, a new class of owners was attracted. These investors, interested more in profits than in sport, became impatient with the gentlemen patrons of the game, and took control.[8]

For his part in sabotaging the "worker's paradise" Spalding was promised a $500 raise and offered the roles of manager and field captain of the Chicago White Stockings, in addition to the job of starting pitcher.[9] Spalding was also supported in his intention to enter the sporting goods business.

Hulbert, who owned the White Stockings, steered its business to Al and put in a good word with the other owners.

On November 17, 1875, Spalding entered into a contract to distribute the Mahn ball.[10] With an $800 loan from his mother, Al and his 19-year-old brother, Walter, opened their first store at 118 Randolph Street in Chicago in March of 1876, just in time for the inaugural season of the National League.[11]

Challenging the Owners— Episode #3:
Eight Hours Pay for Eight Hours Play

O'Rourke was the National League's first holdout. With four of its veterans off to Chicago, Jim was one of the most experienced players left on the Red Caps (the name Boston took when they signed on with the new National League[12]). In three years with Boston, Jim had not been given a raise and he refused to sign for 1876 unless he received a substantial increase.

The *Boston Herald* came to his defense, saying Jim was "one of the strongest players in the country."[13] However, the Boston paper did not hold out much hope for one lone player against the baseball establishment. Just two days before the season opener, the *Herald* reported the club's reaction to Jim's demands:

> The managers are not disposed ... to modify the ... contract ... and therefore O'Rourke will find himself out in the cold so far as his playing with any other club.[14]

Translation: if he did not play ball, he would be blacklisted by the Boston owners and would never play baseball again.

To its credit, the *Herald* also published Jim's reaction:

> If O'Rourke's demands are not met, then he "will return to Bridgeport ... to engage in business other than base ball."[15]

On April 21, 1876, the eve of opening day, Boston was scheduled to play an exhibition game against Yale. Jim umpired. After the game, the Red Caps and citizen O'Rourke boarded the five o'clock from New Haven. Jim would either get off at Bridgeport or continue on to Philadelphia to play in the first game of the National League. The following day, the *Bridgeport Herald* announced happily that "O'Rourke has come to harmonious agreement with the Bostons, and will rejoin the nine."[16]

Jim's salary doubled to approximately $1,600.[17]

Annie exhaled.

For the 1876 season, Jim was reunited with his old teammate Tim Murnane when the latter was hired by the Red Caps to cover first base. This was the third team Murnane and O'Rourke played on at the same time, the prior occasions being the 1870 Osceolas and the 1872 Mansfields.

Jim thought of Tim as a great athlete. He said he once saw Murnane jump over a second baseman to avoid being tagged.[18]

The paths of Murnane and O'Rourke would cross again off the diamond as well, once as allies, and once as bitter foes.

Murnane Teamography

Year	League	City	Team	Position
1869	Semipro	Norwalk (CT)	Libertys	c
1870	Semipro	Stratford (CT)	Osceolas	
	Semipro (winter ball)	Savannah (GA)	Savannahs	c
1871	Semipro	Savannah	Savannahs	
	Semipro	Middletown	Mansfields (Sept.–Oct.)	c
1872	National Association	Middletown	Mansfields	1b
1873	National Association	Philadelphia	Athletic(s)	cf, 1b, 2b
1874	National Association	Philadelphia	Athletic(s)	of, 2b, 1b
1875	National Association	Philadelphia	Phillies	1b, of, 2b
1876	National League	Boston	Red Caps	1b, of, 2b
1877	National League	Boston	Red Caps	of, 1b
1878	National League	Providence	Grays	1b, of
1879	National Association	Rochester	Flour Citys	cf
	National Association	Albany	Capitol Citys	cf
1880	National Association	Albany	Capitol Citys	lf
1884	Union League	Boston	Unions	mgr, 1b, of
1885	Eastern League	Jersey City	Jersey Citys	1b, of

The opening game of the National League pitted the Bostons against the Athletics in Philadelphia, two blocks from the Centennial Exposition[19] where young Alex Bell was demonstrating his talking novelty.

Boston was up first. The great George Wright grounded out to

Tim Murnane. Tim became a well-known sportswriter, first with the *Boston Globe*, in 1887, and then *The Sporting News*. Born Timothy Hayes Murnan, he altered his last name when he made the transition from scooping up grounders to scooping rival publications. Evidently, "Murnane" was more acceptable to the Brahmins in Boston (engraving: New York *Clipper*, c. 1879).

BASE BALL
The First Championship Game of the Season
Boston and Athletic

The championship season of 1876 was opened on Saturday afternoon by the Boston and Athletic, on the ground of the latter at Twenty-fifth and Jefferson streets. As was anticipated, there was a large turn-out to witness the game, which was well worth seeing, both nines being in full force. The first inning was a blank for both clubs, although O'Rourke, for the Boston, and Fisler and Meyerle, for the Athletic, made clean hits, the latter's being a two-baser. In the second inning, owing to Sutton's wild throwing, McGinley scored for the Boston, and on the other side Coons got home on a good hit by Hall. In the third inning, owing to the failure of Fisler to catch a difficult fly in short right field and hard hits by Murnan and O'Rourke, the latter sending the ball far over Eggler's head, the Boston scored two runs, giving them the lead. Good batting and base-running by George Wright and Leonard gave the Boston another run in the fifth inning, but in the next inning the Athletic, thanks to good hits by Fisler, Coons and Hall, and a base on called balls given to Meyerle, tied their opponents. Both clubs were blanked in the next two innings, McGinley and O'Rourke for the Boston being "doubled up" by Eggler's fine catch and rapid handling of the ball to the home plate. In the ninth inning, Murnan and Schafer made safe hits. The former stole a base and both came in on Manning's hot grounder to Fowser at second. A double play by Force, Fowser and Fisler retired Manning and Parks, and then, amid intense excitement, the home club went to the bat. Knight led off with a hit to the left-field fence, stole third and came home on a fly by Force to Parks. Eggler got his second on a difficult fly missed by Parks, and Meyerle was muffed by Schafer. Neither reached home, however, as Sutton went out on a weak hit to Borden. The Athletic excelled at the bat, and Fisler's playing at first base, and that of Knight and Coons in their positions, was very fine. For the Boston, McGinley and Murnan carried off the palm, though Leonard and Manning did well. At the bat, Leonard, O'Rourke and Murnan did the best work. Another game will be played to-day on the same grounds, and from the excellence of Saturday's game and the closeness of the result, the game this afternoon will be still more interesting and be even better attended. The following is the score:

BOSTON.	R.	1B.	P.O.	ATHLETIC.	R.	1B.	P.O.
Wright, s.s.	2	1	3	Force, s.s.	0	1	0
Leonard, 2b.	0	2	0	Eggler, c.f.	0	0	4
O'Rourke, c.f.	1	2	0	Fisler, 1st b.	1	3	13
Murnan, 1b.	1	2	8	Meyerle, 2d.	1	1	4
Schafer, 3b.	1	1	1	Sutton, 3b.	0	0	1
McGinley, c.	1	0	8	Coons, c.	2	2	1
Manning, r.f.	0	0	3	Mali, l. f.	0	2	1
Parks, l.f.	0	0	3	Fowser,	0	0	2
Borden, p.	0	0	1	Knight, p.	1	1	1
Totals	6	8	27	Totals	5	10	7

Box score of the first National League game.

short. The second batter was also out. Then Jim O'Rourke singled to left, and "The League" was officially open.

In the same game, Boston teammate Tim Murnane chalked up the circuit's first stolen base.[20]

The first game of the National League may have been historic, but for Jim, an even more important contest was the first time Chicago visited Boston. The Hub fans had taken the defection of Spalding, McVey, Ross and White as a personal affront.[21]

The first meeting of the 1876 season between the two superpowers was eagerly anticipated. This would be the game that for years to come Bostonians would claim to rapt grandchildren to have witnessed. The responsibility for avenging Boston's honor rested on the broad shoulders of its remaining veterans, George Wright and Jim O'Rourke.

As Al Spalding's White Stockings left their hotel for the ballpark, their carriages had to thread through countless streetcars creeping toward Boston's South End Grounds. The way became increasingly jammed with Bostonians eager to witness the comeuppance of the Chicagos. Three blocks from the park the White Stockings abandoned their conveyances and waded into the mob. Cal McVey marched ahead of the team with the bat bag to spearhead the push through the throng.

Although the game was not to start for two hours, the stadium was already filled to capacity, and then some. When they arrived at the ball grounds, the Pale Hose found the stadium sealed at every entrance against the hoard of fanatics poised to storm the smallest breach. The Chicago nine had no choice but to scale the fences to gain admittance. This bold act gave heart to the rejected patrons milling outside the gates. Besieging fans poured in behind the Chicagos and swarmed over the field. Before the game could begin, the teams had to link arms with the police to recapture the field.[22]

Jim O'Rourke in 1876 (photoengraving: Tuohey, *History of the Boston Base Ball Club,* 1897).

The fans were then rewarded with a pregame show performed by the Boston and Chicago catchers:

> O'Rourke, who was to catch for the Bostons, was, of course, very anxious to outdo Cal McVey, who caught for the Chicagos.... O'Rourke and McVey turned back somersaults at the plate ... to show their athletic superiority one over the other. The performance was hugely enjoyed by the immense crowd of partisan spectators, who ... praised [O'Rourke] for his gameness in not taking a back seat to the great Cal McVey.[23]

In spite of Boston's pluck, Chicago carried off the palm. In fact, Boston lost the first 9 of 10 games against the White Stockings.[24] In the 10th meeting of the rivals, O'Rourke scored the winning run for Boston. The way the crowd erupted you would have thought Boston had just won the pennant.

Jim earned his hard-fought raise for 1876, leading the team in hitting with a .312 average, a full 20 points ahead of George Wright, who ranked second among the Red Stockings.[25]

But the four-year veteran's offensive leadership did not guarantee harmonious relations with the front office. The following year, Jim would face another critical confrontation with the Boston owners.

Challenging the Owners — Episode #4: *Employees Should Not Have to Pay for Required Uniforms*

For the 1877 season, Al Spalding organized a scheme to deduct $30 from each player to cover the rising price he was charging for uniforms.[26] The uniform fee was adopted by the National League at its annual meeting on December 7, 1876. The league also voted to charge players 50 cents per day for meals while on the road.[27]

Spalding had been shifting his attention from playing to managing his growing sporting goods business. Spalding knew his days as a player were numbered, so he used the little time he had remaining on the field to promote his baseball products. Because his 1860s style of pitching was no longer effective, he played most of 1877 covering first base for the White Stockings. To demonstrate the value of a fielding glove, he wore one in his new position; but not the common tan variety. The Chicago star flaunted a very visible black glove.[28] While there is some debate as to who first wore hand protection, there is no doubt that the player most responsible for popularizing the glove was Al Spalding. By wearing one openly, the sporting goods merchant helped to popularize hand protection. Spalding eagerly made gloves for the sore hands of pitchers, catchers, and first basemen (the positions that handle the most throws). Spalding offered the glove for sale in his 1877 *Guide* at prices ranging from $1 to $2.50. The fingers were cut off and an inconspicuous amount of padding was stuffed under the palm.

In 1877, Spalding also received an assist from the president of the National League. In 1876, when the league was founded, Morgan G. Bulkeley of Hartford was installed as its first president. But in its second year, White Stockings owner William Hulbert took command. Hulbert procured for Al Spalding two plums that would assure the success of the young entrepreneur. The first was to adopt the Mahn brand as the official National League Ball for 1877 (Spalding held the Chicago distributorship for the Mahn ball.) Wait, it gets better. To assure uniformity, the league required all clubs to purchase their balls through the League office.[29] Where was the league office? Chicago.

Of course the idea of standardizing the ball was good for the game. The old choice of dead or lively balls was out. Every team would use identical balls in every game. But this was a rule easier to write than to enforce.

The first balls shipped by Mahn in 1877 were too dead. In a May 11 game between Harvard and the Manchesters of New Hampshire, a full 24 innings were played without either club scoring a run. This was hailed as "The longest and finest game on record,"[30] (a game of extraordinary defense), but I suspect a mushy ball had a lot to do with it. Then, after a 1–0 loss by Chicago to Boston on May 16, National League secretary Nick Young "notified all clubs that the latest ball furnished by Mahn was illegal, one of the old or soft kind was used."[31] The *Boston Globe* observed:

> The fielding was very sharp and the hitting rather weak throughout, as might have been expected from the character of the ball.[32]

Mahn altered the composition, and the balls shipped during the second half of May were "very lively," resulting in "a large increase in errors."[33] Eventually, through this trial-and-error process, the ball evolved into what Spalding described as "not too lively, not too dead."[34]

During 1878, Spalding began to have balls made to his standards with his now familiar logo. So at the 1878 meeting of the National League, chaired by Hulbert, the Spalding ball was specified for all official games, effective with the 1879 season.

In the first major league baseball licensing agreement, Spalding paid the National League $1 on every dozen balls used. Although Spalding did not receive payment for the balls he supplied — perhaps as many as 1,000 per year — he was, by his contract authorized to advertise that his was the "Official League Ball." The promotional value of the contract was inestimable. By 1880 Spalding was selling so many baseballs that he had to contract with Al Reach, his biggest competitor, to manufacture Spalding baseballs.[35] After the 1882 season, the *Clipper* estimated that "about five mil-lion balls are made each year."[36]

The second plum Hulbert dropped in Al's glove was the right to publish the annual *Official League Book*, which outlined National League rules and reg-ulations. The Spalding Company announced that it had paid "liberally" for the privilege of publishing the League book, beginning in 1877.[37] Al Reach held this contract during the National League's inaugural year of 1876.

Spalding also began to publish his own *Official Baseball Guide*, which, in spite of its title, was not an official league publication. The *Spalding Guide* was more comprehensive and included standings, stats and rosters from the prior season. It soon supplanted the league guide in popularity. Since Spald-ing controlled the content, he was able to use his *Guide* to shape public opin-ion on the rights and roles of owners over their overpaid and underworked players. The *"Official" Spalding Baseball Guide* was also liberally decorated with ads for Spalding sporting goods.[38]

I'm sure Jim was proud and happy about the business success of his for-mer teammate; but, as the self-appointed defender of the rights of baseball workers, O'Rourke balked at the $30 uniform fee. He thought the cost could easily have been reduced simply by eliminating unnecessary items such as the silk necktie. To Jim, it was just one more instance of the owners chip-ping away at the players' rightful share of the baseball gate.

This battle Jim won. Either because of his hitting or popularity with the fans, he was exempted from the uniform fee.[39]

Jim knew he was in a strong bargaining position as he was earning kudos from the sportswriters. In one game with the Brooklyn Hartfords, he was twice credited with earning the lead for Boston:

> O'Rourke opened the play for the Bostons by earning his first base on a good hit, and by swift base running reached his third. Sutton, after two hands were put out, followed with a base hit, on which O'Rourke scored. This gave them the lead, which they held up to the fifth inning, when the Hartford tied the score.... O'Rourke again won the lead for his side in the next inning by his dar-ing base running, assisted by a splendid drive for three bases by White.[40]

But Jim's proudest accomplishment that season was also one of the high points of his career. Late in the season, Boston and Louisville were battling it out for first place. As Jim recalled:

> It was early in October when the Louisvilles came to take back the champi-onship with them.... I remember that it was my good fortune to be of material aid at critical points in the two decisive games of the series. I look back upon the winning of those games as the proudest events of my career.[41]

The games may have been a high point in O'Rourke's career, but they marked a low point in major league baseball. For it was in this series that

Louisville pitcher Jim Devlin was accused of throwing games for gamblers. Although the National League had banned pool sellers from the ballparks, outside "halls" that sold chances on gambling "pools" continued to satisfy this demand. Along with the daily box scores, the *Boston Globe* published the "Pool Quotations" for the following day's games.[42] With gambling so common and accessible, it is not surprising that a number of players were tempted to supplement their income.

As this incident occurred during the National League's second year, and because Spalding and Hulbert had partly justified their takeover of baseball in order to rid it of the gambling influence, they came down hard on Devlin, who was blackballed for life, as Charlie Comiskey's Black Sox would be 50 years later, and Peter Rose more than a century after Devlin.

Jim O'Rourke in 1877. In his fifth season in Boston, Jim batted .362 and led the National League in runs scored (68), and walks (20) (*National Baseball Hall of Fame Library*, Cooperstown, New York).

Boston won the 1877 pennant by seven games over second-place Louisville.

The source of Arthur Soden's financial desperation — therefore the incessant clashes between him and O'Rourke over money matters—can be seen in the following chart.

Profit (Loss) of the Boston Base Ball Club

National Association Era		National League Era	
1872	($ 3,000)	1876	($ 777)
1873	$ 4,020	1877	($ 2,223)
1874	$ 833	1878	($ 1,433)
1875	$ 3,261	1879	($ 3,347)

Source for 1877: Boston Globe, January 6, 1878; other years: David Voigt, American Baseball, Vol. 1, 1983, p. 57, 77.

The Boston Red Caps were losing money. Ironically, the Boston owners faired better during the National Association years when the players were in control than they did under the owner-dominated National League. Obviously, the players did not make such a mess of things as Major League Baseball asserts. Historian David Voigt observes that "Ranged along-side the modestly profitable Association era, it goes far to debunk the myth of League superiority."[43]

Major League Baseball has justified the coup that eviscerated the National Association of Players and created in its place the National League of Clubs, by arguing that the original circuit had an erratic, unenforced schedule, and therefore had to be rescued from the incompetent management of the players. This is rationalizing by the owners after the fact. The players, too, would have eventually settled upon the National League improvements of arranging the season schedule at an annual meeting and relegating smaller cities to minor leagues.

Evolution of the Game: Diamond Layout, 1877. The batter's box was added in 1874 to combat intentional fair-foul hitting, the then-legal tactic of running up to chop the ball at a sharp angle so that it hit fair but then careened off the playing field (at the time a ball was fair even if it rolled foul before reaching first or third base). Although the sneaky tactic of the fair-foul hit was outlawed in 1877, the batter's box has remained (engraving: *Spalding Guide,* 1877).

The National Association has since been further discredited by the Official Records Committee of 1969 by its claim that the NA was not a major league. Baseball historian David Voigt explains why:

> It was a player-run league, with a player president, and its stockholder "owners" functioned mainly as patrons. That major league baseball was born of such parentage must have been anathema to modern owners and the sort of heritage one seeks to conceal.[44]

Ironically, organized baseball confers upon Jim O'Rourke bragging rights for the first major league hit, in 1876. It was the first hit of the National

League, but not the first major league hit. Deacon White made the first major league hit, with Cleveland, on May 4, 1871.[45]

Challenging the Owners — Episode #5:
Employees Should Not Have to Pay for Cleaning Required Uniforms

By 1878, as noted in the previous chart, the Red Caps were still awash in red ink. Boston owner Arthur Soden[46] was desperate to balance his books. For away games, he housed the Red Caps in fleabag hotels and cut their meal allowance. Soden even charged players' wives to attend games.[47]

Then he went too far. He demanded each player pay $20 per year to cover the cost of uniform cleaning while on the road. The players were already paying $30 per year for their uniforms; and were required to keep them clean when the team was at home.

O'Rourke balked. It wasn't just the principal of drawing a line against an unending stream of pay envelope deductions; for O'Rourke it was a personal insult. He always kept his uniform immaculate, even on the road. He knew he'd catch heck from his mother if he didn't.

In an effort to resolve the impasse, the fans took up a collection to pay the fee. But it wasn't about the $20. Jim was fighting for a principle, for the precedent of how a baseball player — indeed any worker — should be treated. The same struggle was being played out in coal mines in Appalachia, in factories in New England, and on farms in Georgia. If the workers did not resist, they would all end up owing their souls to the company store. Once more Jim felt he had to take a stand. After six years with Boston, Jim O'Rourke let it be known that he was amenable to offers from other clubs.

For its 1879 season, the Providence Grays were scouting for socially mature and thoughtful players who might attract the affluent fans who could afford to take an afternoon off and pay 50 cents for a ticket. O'Rourke, with his gentlemanly ways, was just the man for the job.

Boston teammate George Wright was also disgruntled because Soden had demanded he accept a $500 pay cut in 1878. At first George had held out, refusing to sign. But then, on Saturday, February 9, as other players were already working out in the gym, George signed, acknowledging the financial reality that "Times have changed from what they were a year or two ago."[48]

As a sporting goods proprietor, George, too, fit the Providence mold.

Backers from the Providence Grays came to Boston to interview Wright and O'Rourke, agreed to their terms, and signed both for the 1879 season.

Jim, however, did not leave the Red Stockings in the lurch. He found for them a replacement outfielder: his brother, John.

This set up the unique situation whereby two sets of brothers would play on rival teams: Jim O'Rourke and George Wright on the Grays; John O'Rourke and Harry Wright on the Reds. In 1879, the Providence and Boston teams would battle each other in a close race for the National League pennant.

During the 1878 season, John had played center field for the Manchesters of the International Association.[49] Previously, he played centerfield for the TBs (The Bridgeport Friendly United Social Base Ball Club). "Social" indicated amateur status. This may have been true in 1869 when the club was first organized, but by 1875 the players were paid by the team's owner, P. T. Barnum.[50] The TBs included three future major leaguers, James Roseman, Fred Goldsmith, and John O'Rourke. They were so good that it became difficult for the TBs to arrange matches. No one wanted to suffer the almost-certain humiliation. So the "Friendly Social" club challenged major league teams to duels on the ballfield. Five teams accepted the challenge.[51]

When not playing baseball, John ran the family farm and worked as a spring bender in a shop that served a large carriage-building industry in the Park City. Carrying on a family tradition of public service, John also ran successfully for a seat on the Bridgeport City Council. John's one-year term began in April 1875. The mayor at the time was P. T. Barnum.

In 1879, John was the lead-off batter for the Bostons.[52] On April 12, 1879, the *New York Clipper* led off its baseball news with praise for John's major league debut:

> John O'Rourke, brother of James O'Rourke of the Providence team, had a creditable record in the new nine on Fast-day, viz., one base-hit out of four made in the game by the Bostons, two put out, three assists—marked by a double play—and no error, every chance offered him from the bat being accepted. If the other new men turn up like this, the nine will do.[53]

On defense, as of July 1, John was the leading center fielder in the National League.[54] On offense, the left-handed batter had a knack for lofting balls over right-field fences.[55]

Praise by the *New York Clipper* continued throughout the season:

> July 26—O'Rourke's batting and Burdock's second-base play contributed largely to the Boston's success.
> August 9—The chief features were a splendid one-handed catch by O'Rourke and his excellent batting.
> August 30—O'Rourke and Morrill's batting and Snyder's catching were noteworthy on behalf of the Bostons.
> September 13—O'Rourke led at the bat.

At season's end, John led the majors in slugging (total bases divided by times at bat)[56] with a .521 average. He also ranked second in home runs, with six; and tied for the lead in RBIs with 62 (a new single-season record). Ironically, some historians credit these last two distinctions to John's better-known brother.

John might have done even better had he not been injured near the end of the season:

> John O'Rourke, the Boston's best batsman, had his left hand so badly injured in the Boston-Cleveland game of Sept. 19 that he has gone to his home in Bridgeport, Ct., to place himself under the care of his family physician."[57]

He did not return to the lineup until October 9, when the regular season had ended.[58]

In spite of John's contribution to the Red Caps, owner Soden still bristled at the fact that brother Jim had defied him by walking out the door and into another clubhouse. He would see that this did not happen again.

John O'Rourke, Forgotten Star. (BL, TL, 6' 180 lbs.)The *Bridgeport Post* on June 24, 1911, reported: "John was always a splendid specimen of muscular strength. Tall and well proportioned, and remarkably agile for a man who carried close to 200 pounds when in fine athletic trim" (detail, 1879 team photo, Tuohey, *History of the Boston Base Ball Club*, 1897).

8

Providence Grays (1879)

George Wright was assigned to play shortstop and manage the Providence Grays. Jim played right field and filled in at first, third, and behind the plate when the starting catcher needed a day to heal.

Jim shared the outfield grass with Paul Hines, a hearing-impaired player. Hines and O'Rourke worked out a system to avoid collisions in the outfield. As *Sporting Life* noted:

> Hines ... is so deaf that he cannot hear the umpire call the balls; he depends on the captain of the nine to inform him.[1]

It would be for the benefit of players like Hines that hand signals became an integral part of baseball.

An urbane player already on the Grays' roster was 18-year-old John Montgomery Ward. Young, debonair, and a "college man," Johnny was also a star pitcher.

In 1878, his rookie year, he led the National League with a 1.51 ERA.[2] Ward was of the new generation of pitchers who came of age in the emerging curve ball era. For the young pitchers, the movement felt natural, not artificial, as it must have seemed to veterans like Spalding. The following contemporary account of Ward is a rare description of a pitcher in action:

> Ward, the Providence pitcher, is as full of tricks as a circus mule. He will bear watching by the umpire to see that he does not violate the rule which requires the pitcher to face the batsman. When he pitches he first wipes his right hand on his pantaloons until he gets tired, then crooks his arms funnily and crowds the ball into the right side of the back, then gives his body a quick twist, unwinds his arms and shoots the ball at the batsman.[3]

O'Rourke, the outspoken advocate for worker rights, must have discussed his ideas with Ward as they whiled away hours on late-night trains,

1879 National League Providence Grays. This photograph shows the once-common racetrack style grandstand. During the next decade, stands would begin to wrap around the playing field.

The screen was invented in Providence in 1879 when fans began referring to the area behind home plate as the "slaughter pens."

Pitcher Johnny Ward is standing second from left; manager George Wright is at center on one knee; Jim O'Rourke is standing third from right. At the far right is center fielder Paul Hines (Providence Public Library).

for one day the two would rally the major league players for a daring bid to retake control of the national sport.

The natural rivalry between Jim and John seemed to propel both brothers to the heights of their abilities, especially when Boston and Providence faced each other. In a June double-header between the rivals, Jim was eight for nine at the bat and brother John belted out two home runs. The Grays and Red Stockings split the double bill.[4]

In 1879, Johnny Ward led the National League pitchers with 47 wins. Paul Hines led in hitting with a .357 average, and Jim O'Rourke was second at .348. Brother John O'Rourke of Boston was fourth at .341. Jim also led the National League with a .371 on-base percentage.

With the top two hitters and the league-leading pitcher, Providence took the pennant, igniting fireworks on the field, and off.

The *New York Clipper* gave Jim the following rave review at the end of the 1879 season:

He has filled the position of right-field for the present League champions with a most creditable amount of skill. O'Rourke has made a brilliant record for himself as an outfielder, being an excellent judge of a ball, a swift runner, and making

Top left: Jim O'Rourke at the end of the 1879 season (engraving: *New York Clipper*, October 25, 1879). *Top right: Johnny Ward* in 1879. The cosmopolitan Ward was a student of the innovative language teacher Maximilian Berlitz (engraving: *New York Clipper*, September 6, 1879). *Bottom: Paul Hines* in 1879. Hines was the first outfielder to wear sunglasses (engraving: *New York Clipper*).

the most difficult running-catches with the utmost ease and certainty. As a thrower, too, he stands pre-eminent, being credited with a throw of 365 feet, the next to the longest yet accomplished by any player. His average each season has proved him to be in the front rank in handling the bat, and shows that his usefulness is not merely confined to his fielding abilities. He has always enjoyed the reputation of being a thoroughly reliable and honest player, and one who works hard for the best interests of his club. His gentlemanly conduct, both on and off the ball-field, has won for him a host of friends. In conclusion, we would call attention to the fact that he has formed one of the champion nine each season, with the solitary exception of 1876, since he has been playing professionally.[5]

The Grays were feted at a "grand reception" on the evening of Tuesday, September 30, 1879. The Boston Red Stockings, who were scheduled to play their final game of the season in Providence on the same afternoon, were also invited to attend the evening festivities.[6] The *New York Clipper* previewed the gala celebration:

> The nine, with the Bostons as invited guests, will be banqueted at the Park Garden, after which badges will be presented to each member of the nine by mayor Doyle. As each member appears on the platform his name will be displayed in bright fire, and then in the glare of an electric light, the presentation will take place. Such, at least, is the announced programme. This is the merited reward of honest and manly play.[7]

Of the invited rivals, only three put in an appearance: catcher Charles Snyder, substitute Bill Hawes, and pitcher Charles "Curry" Foley. I do not know why more of the Boston players did not attend. The Providence papers accused Boston manager Harry Wright of poor sportsmanship, charging that he had prevented his team from attending the celebration. In his defense, Harry insisted that "he could not attend himself but that all his men were at perfect liberty to go."[8] Perhaps the second-place Reds just weren't in the mood for rejoicing with the first-place Grays, who made sure to humiliate their invited guests with a 14–3 defeat in the afternoon ball game.

The Providence owners were also conspicuously absent. They were meeting in Buffalo behind closed doors with their fellow National League club owners.

Notwithstanding the absence of the Beantown rivals and club management, the event was even grander than the Providence fans and players had been promised. The *Clipper* described the scene:

> A calcium light was burning brightly just back of the platform, and the players were seated in a half circle in front, facing an audience of over four thousand persons. Mayor Doyle of Providence, R. I., on being introduced to the audience, made a speech praising the nine and congratulating them on their success.[9]

The band played victory airs and toasts were given for the players, the directors, the press, even the umpires. Then the Grays were honored individually. As James O'Rourke was called forward, and the mayor pinned the golden badge on his breast, a fuse was touched, and the name O'Rourke appeared in "living fire." The evening concluded with a display of more fireworks.[10]

As Jim was being honored in Providence, Boston owner Arthur Soden, still seething that Jim was able to evade his authority,[11] was at the Annual Meeting of the National League in Buffalo, introducing the now-infamous reserve clause. Under its terms, the owners agreed that each club would reserve five players that the other owners would not attempt to hire.[12]

The players reserved for the 1880 season were[13]:

Boston — Snyder, Bond, Burdock, [John] O'Rourke, Sutton.
Buffalo — Galvin, Clapp, Richardson, Crowley, Walker.
Chicago — Williamson, Quest, Anson, Flint, Hankinson.
Cleveland — McCormick, Kennedy, Glassock, Richmond, Shaffer.
Providence — Wright, Start, Hines, Ward, McGeary.
Troy — Evans, Caskins, Cassidy, Ferguson, Goldsmith.

Why Soden suggested five as the number to reserve may be deduced from a letter by Boston co-owner N. T. Appolonio to Harry Wright, dated July 17, 1878, in which he updates Wright on Soden's latest thinking regarding contract negotiation strategy:

Mr. Soden's plan is now that if we can hold on to *Snyder, Burdick,* they with *Bond, Sutton and Morrill,* would form a pretty good nucleus with which we could afford to be in no great hurry to negotiate with the others.[14]

Substitute "reserve" for "hold on to" and you have the reserve clause.

The owners had previously adopted a rule that no club could negotiate with a player on another team during the season. This at least restricted competition to the winter months and set a definite starting time for the annual scramble for star players. It was this compact that Chicago owner William Hulbert violated when he secretly signed the "Big Four" of the Bostons in July of 1875 for the 1876 season.

Soden, who was the victim of the Chicago raid, was aware of the inherent weakness in the former agreement not to engage players during the season. He realized that, "If any club respects [the agreement] literally, the others will gain an unfair advantage."[15]

A final inspiration for the 1879 Reserve Rule was a letter from Buffalo owner Jonathan B. Sage to Soden, dated

1879 Championship Badge. Before there were championship rings there were gold medals that hung from pin badges. The 1879 pennant badge displayed the player name and position in blue enamel[18] (National Baseball Hall of Fame).

August 21, 1879, in which Sage casually suggests "changing the agreement made at Buffalo, so that we can contract or engage our present men for another season."[16]

Ironically, the reserve system — before it was extended to the full roster — gave an ego boost to the five players who were picked. A reserved player could relax during the winter, confident he had a job the following year. Indeed, not being reserved said you were not a star; you were one of the expendable players; you might be replaced by a rookie next season. Better worry this winter.

Considering the economics of spectator sports, the reserve clause was probably inevitable. Until this agreement among the owners, any player could sell his services at the end of a season to the highest bidder, "revolving" from club to club. One star of the 1870s, George Zeitlein made eight jumps in six years.[17] Prices were spiraling out of reach of smaller cities and even the large metropolitan areas were feeling the financial pinch.

Boston experienced a $5,753 decline in revenue during 1879 to $19,603.[18] A 20-percent decline in income would cause any businessperson to search for ways to control expenses. Besides his scheme for reserving players, Soden also gave up the space the club was renting above George Wright's store[19] as a gathering place for its members, thus ending the last vestige of club tradition.[20]

The day after the National League adopted the reserve clause, President William Hulbert issued a press release, which read in part:

> The financial results of the past season prove that salaries must come down. We believe that players in insisting upon exorbitant prices are injuring their own interests by forcing out of existence clubs which cannot be run and pay large salaries except at a large personal loss. The season financially has been a little better than that of 1878; but the expenses of many of the clubs have far exceeded their receipts, attributable wholly to the high salaries. In view of these facts, measures have been taken by the League to remedy the evil to some extent for 1880. It has also been decided that a uniform contract with players shall be used by each club and that no money shall be paid players until it has been earned — in other words, that no advance shall be given. The contracts will hereafter extend from April 1 to October 31.[21]

No mention of the reserve clause; only the cryptic "measures have been taken to remedy the evil [of high salaries]." The intent of the vagueness was to keep the pact a secret, but word soon leaked.[22]

The owners were hoping that the reserve clause would finally end revolving and its attendant annual escalation of wages. To the owners, players were a tangible asset. Why, they argued, would anyone invest money to start a club if his assets could walk away at any time? They asserted that this was unfair. Their contention had already been tested in the courts, and the judge had favored the owner over the worker. The precedent involved an opera star who refused to appear for an engagement. The star argued that no damage was done because the theater owner could hire another singer. However, the courts agreed that certain performers are exceptional and not easily replaced. Star performers, by definition, are not interchangeable. Replacing a pitcher isn't as easy as replacing a ticket taker.

Moreover, it was argued, a popular baseball player leaving a club could affect attendance and therefore a club's profit. The reserve clause reduced the investors' risk by insuring that at least the critical players of each team stayed put.

While it may not be due solely to the reserve clause, baseball profits increased dramatically in the 1880s. In 1880, Soden lost $3,316,[23] but in 1881 the Boston club earned $2,850.[24] Three years later, Soden and his Boston co-owners were earning over 10 times this amount.[25]

The dilemma of how to protect the investors—without trampling on the individual rights of players—confounds professional sports to this day.

George Wright was an early victim of the reserve rule. George was reserved by Providence and in spite of winning the pennant his salary was "slashed." The owners were affirming the new relationship with the players. They were now in charge and the players could take what was offered or leave the game.[26]

George refused to play in Providence in 1880; and the Grays refused to allow him to play anywhere else. This impasse pointed up an inequity in the reserve clause soon after its adoption. As the *Boston Herald* explained:

> The object of the famous Buffalo agreement was ... to prevent players from "auctioning" their services ... but its use and abuse were not intended in the way to which the Providence management has put it in the case of George Wright. Wright will not, under any circumstances, play in Providence the coming season, and thus he has been driven from the league by the selfish and arbitrary action of one of its members.[27]

In early October 1879, while other men decided their fates, George and Jim donned their old cricket togs and joined a team of ball players barnstorming with a pro team from Britain.[28]

During the tour, George Wright suffered a career-threatening injury. "Several bones in his hand were broken by a fast-bowled ball."[29] This was as serious for a shortstop as it would be for a piano player.

In late October 1879, George went home to Boston to attend to his sporting goods business. In mid–November, the following note appeared in the sports press:

> George Wright has not signed as yet with any club for next season, and it is on the cards that he may abandon the ball-field and devote his entire attention hereafter to his business. In partnership with Mr. Ditson, he opened last week a new and centrally located baseball headquarters at No. 580 Washington street, Boston, Mass.[30]

George Wright, manager and shortstop with the champion 1879 Providence Grays (engraving: *New York Clipper,* 1879).

It was a good bluff. A number of former ballplayers were earning all or part of their income from businesses, many related to the sport they knew and loved so well, the most notable and most successful being Al Spalding. So it was not far-fetched that a player might eschew the uncertain future and unending travel of a baseball player for the settled life of a business proprietor. The following year, an article in the *New York Clipper* pointed out that no fewer than six current or former Boston players had "engaged in business in that city," not far from the ball grounds[31]:

George Wright	Sporting Goods Store	580 Washington St.
Harry Wright	Porting Goods Store	765 Washington St.
Tim Murnane	Billiard Hall	Springfield and Washington
Andy Leonard	Wineroom	Springfield and Washington
Harry Schafer	Clubroom	15 Essex Street
John Manning	Grocery Store	Tremont Street

In the *New York Clipper* of December 20, 1879, as part of a continuing game of blinkmanship with the Providence owners, George reaffirmed his position:

George Wright, whose playing, management, and captaincy contributed to secure the League championship for the Providence nine, peremptorily refuses to sign with that organization for 1880 at a reduced salary.

This was a way, indirectly, of notifying the Grays' front office that he would sign for the *same* salary as last year. He may have begun to appreciate the security of a regular paycheck. The day before, his wife gave birth to a son.[32]

The Providence owners responded with their own press release:

Peters, who was dropped by the Chicagos this year, has made an application for George Wright's position as shortstop with the Providence Club; but the managers of that organization prefer to wait for Wright, who writes that he has not yet made up his mind to play anywhere; but if he plays at all, it will be in Providence.[33]

Finally, on February 21, the *Clipper* reported an ultimatum from the Providence owners:

> The directors ... now wish to force Wright into signing with them for another season at a reduced salary, and threaten that they will engage Peters or Macullar to fill that position in case he does not sign at once.

This helped George make up his mind, but it had quite the opposite effect from the one intended by the Providence magnates. George decided not to play baseball at all in 1880. When the owners received George's answer, they backed off from their firm stand[34] and offered to at least maintain his salary level, but it was too late. George Wright, on April 15, informed the management of the Providence club that he would not make any engagement to play ball for the 1880 season.[35] As the *Clipper* reported, when all was said and done:

> The directors of this club did wisely in retaining the services of a majority of their players.... They made a decided mistake, however, when they failed to reward George Wright for his valuable services in 1879 by retaining him in the manager's position on his own terms, when it was possible for them to secure him last Fall. What the cost of this error will be next October will show; but that it was a mistake there is no doubt. George Wright has closed his career as a baseball professional with éclat. He is now the superintendent of an amateur organization in Boston, designed to present a model recreation ground in that city for all amateur field sports.[36]

The impasse continued through the 1881 season: George refusing to abandon his business and family in Boston, and the Providence owners keeping him on reserve, so that he could not play in Boston, where his own brother was willing and eager to have him back.

Finally, in 1882, brother Harry was hired to manage the Providence Grays.[37] (Soden had fired Harry after back-to-back losing seasons, even though his overall record as a Boston manager was six pennants in 11 years.[38]) George returned to the Providence lineup. But the exile had been too long. He had lost his edge, or perhaps his will. The season of 1882 was his last.

George Wright is the only manager to win a pennant in his first year as a manager and never manage again. However, baseball's first superstar was not forgotten. In 1937, at age 90, he was among the first inductees into the Baseball Hall of Fame.

9

Return to the Boston Red Caps (1880)

On September 27, the day before the start of the National League conclave in Buffalo, the *Clipper* reported that Providence wanted both O'Rourke brothers. However, Boston also wanted the O'Rourke brothers, and Soden wound up with both of the sluggers.

A side deal may have been made at the September National League meeting between Providence and Boston for Jim O'Rourke. The following note appeared in the *New York Clipper* of October 11, 1879:

> It is said that all the Providence nine will be retained for next year, with the exception probably of O'Rourke, who is wanted by Boston.

And in the same publication on November 11:

> Only one change occurs in the Providence team, and that is the substitution of Dorgan as change-catcher and right fielder for O'Rourke, the latter being likely to return to Boston.

I do not know whether the return of O'Rourke to Boston was discussed as part of baseball's new Fugitive Slave Act — considering that it was his mocking of club authority that led to the reserve clause in the first place — or if the Bostons simply wanted the return of their star player.

Whatever the motivation of the Red Stocking owners, Jim was eager to join his brother in Boston. There was no love lost between Jim and Arthur Soden, but he was still on friendly terms with manager Harry Wright.

Once Soden finalized the deal with Providence for Jim, he probably assumed the matter was settled. He would send contracts to Jim and John, demand they sign on his terms and that would be it. However, dealing with one O'Rourke brother was difficult enough — as Soden surely remembered — but the two, bargaining collectively, would be much more than Soden had bargained for. The Boston owners were accustomed to negotiating with one player at a time, but they could not divide and conquer the O'Rourke brothers. There would be a lot of hard negotiating, brinksmanship, and press spinning by both sides before contracts would be inked.

Challenging the Owners — Episode #6:
Defying Reservation

The primary sticking point was that Jim wanted it stipulated as a condition of his return to Boston that neither he nor John would be reserved at the end of the season. Of course, it was this free agency that Arthur Soden, the father of the reserve clause, was trying to end.

Notes buried in the sports pages telegraphed the maneuverings, offers and counteroffers between the O'Rourkes and the Boston owners.

Herewith the salvos as picked up by the *New York Clipper* (with translations):

November 1, 1879: "The announcement that the O'Rourke Brothers had signed in Boston for next year is premature."
This was probably planted by the O'Rourkes. Translation: we're available and open to offers. It was a common practice for clubs to mislead the press (and thereby rival clubs) into thinking a star player was already signed when he actually was not. This was a clever way to eliminate competition for a player. The O'Rourke press release reversed the impression.

November 29: "Cincinnati is negotiating with the O'Rourke brothers."
This may or may not have been true. It doesn't matter. Jim and John wanted to play in Boston, near their home. Besides, John had no choice; he was under reserve by Boston, so it is unlikely anyone was negotiating for the pair. I'm sure this was a plant by the brothers in an effort to keep their name in the press, worry the Boston owners, and improve their negotiating position.

December 6: "The Boston team for next season will be as follows: Bond, pitcher; Brown or Sullivan, catcher; Foley, Burdock and Morrill on the bases; Sutton, Shortstop; with Jones, John O'Rourke and James O'Rourke in the outfield."
John and Jim had not signed. This was another attempt to discourage other clubs from talking to Jim O'Rourke.

December 6: "The Clevelands ... are making efforts to secure Jas. O'Rourke to play first base and captain their nine in case he has not been engaged by the Bostons."
Plant by Jim.

December 27: "Harry Wright has secured his team for 1880, and it consists of the following players: Battery, Brown and Bond; basemen's team, Foley, Burdock and Morrell [sic]; shortstop, Sutton; outfield team, Jones, John O'Rourke and Jas. O'Rourke."
Nope, not true. Neither John nor Jim had signed. They were still holding out for their terms. Plant by Boston.

January 10, 1880: "The O'Rourke Brothers— John and James— declined to sign contracts with the Boston club so long as the directors of the latter refused to cancel the clause taxing them thirty dollars each for uniforms, and 50 cents each daily while traveling. The lovers of the game in Boston, Mass., then subscribed the required amount, and the O'Rourkes will probably sign."

This was a truthful press release from the Boston organization, even if it omitted the more important concession regarding the reserve clause. The Boston owners, the inventors of the reserve, understandably were not eager to notify organized baseball that they caved on this issue. The O'Rourke brothers had won their main concession and then had browbeaten (the no-doubt prematurely aging) Soden to roll back the payroll deductions for Spalding's uniforms and board while on the road.

January 24, 1880: "The contracts of John and James O'Rourke with the Boston Club, duly signed, have arrived at [National League] headquarters."

The Boston Herald *revealed that the contracts contained an amendment that the brothers were to be "released from reservation."[1] Translation: Life is good.*

In case you think it a bit far-fetched that Victorian-era ballplayers carried out media campaigns—as would present-day press agents—consider this 1879 *Clipper* editorial remark about a story then circulating that a group of Buffalo players were moving to other clubs:

This rumor is probably a bid that they may be re-engaged by the Buffalo club.[2]

In 1880, the *Clipper* commented on the prevalence of press manipulation:

Nines are being made upon paper in quite a lively manner for the coming season. Players have a trick of getting themselves advertised by sending communications to the papers that they are about to sign with the so and so club, or that they have been sent for by such and such a manager, or are in demand by one city team or the other.[3]

The O'Rourke brothers began the 1880 season for Boston with the same exceptional performances they had demonstrated the prior season. Herewith some sample reports from April contests that appeared in the New York *Clipper*:

The Bostons won a pre-season exhibition game on April 30, "John O'Rourke doing some terrific batting."[4]
James O'Rourke had the best batting average ... in the 13 games played by the Bostons in April.[5]

For John, it almost ended in May 1880, when he was again seriously injured. The following notice appeared in the *New York Times*:

TROY, N. Y., May 24,—John O'Rourke, of the Boston Base-ball Club, while attempting to make a difficult play this afternoon in the Troy City-Boston game, ran against a fence. A gash was cut in his throat five inches long, and it is supposed he received internal injuries.[6]

The *Washington Post* added that he was knocked unconscious by the impact with the wooden fence and had to be carried from the field.[7] However, he was back in his old form in June, staying even with brother Jim in drawing comment from the sportswriters. In a June 19 game, Cincinnati pitcher Will White (Deacon White's brother) was "hit hard, John O'Rourke making a home-run and James O'Rourke a three-baser."[8]

Then in July, John had a serious relapse:

> J. O'Rourke the ball player is in a hospital at Boston under treatment for the injuries received some time ago while playing at Troy. He has grown much worse and his condition is considered dangerous.[9]

But by season's end, both brothers were again in top form. In a 4–1 victory over Worcester on September 11, John O'Rourke made a "home-run hit over the right-field fence" and "made a difficult running catch."[10]

In a 5–4 win on September 15 over Providence, "Jim O'Rourke made a good catch off Hines' bat in the seventh, near the left-fence braces, that looked good for two or three bases." John had four hits in five chances off Providence pitcher Johnny Ward in the same game.[11]

At season's end, Jim led the National League with six home runs; John had three. However, they had identical batting averages of .275. Jim hitting from the right, John from the left. The 1880 Boston batting order was Charley Jones (lf) batting first, Jim second, John third, and Curry Foley (1b) fourth.[12]

But it would be the first and last season the brothers played for the same team. In an economy move following a financially dismal 1880 season, "The Boston team of 1880 was disbanded by Manager Harry Wright after their game with the Troys on Sept. 30," the final championship game of the regular season. However, the player contracts called for a fixed salary through October 31. The Boston owners planned to keep the players on for post-season exhibition games "as long as the weather will permit," but to pay them on the old "cooperative plan," that is, a share of the gate receipts, as semi-pro players are compensated.[13]

Soden was again testing the limits of unfair play. In an earlier incident, Charley Jones was suspended for refusing to play when he did not receive his August pay when he asked for it on September 2. According to Jones, the club also owed him $128 of his July salary. Soden promptly suspended Jones and fined him $100 for insubordination and refusing to play. The team was in Cleveland at the time, so Jones went home to Cincinnati. Whereupon Soden expelled him from the league for leaving the services of the club without permission. All for asking to be paid what was due him.[14]

John was fit to be tied. He sent the *Cincinnati Enquirer* a long list of player grievances against Boston management. On October 5, the paper reported that John had "begun suit against the club for breach of contract" for unilaterally canceling his contract as of October 1, causing him to lose a month's pay.[15]

John and Jim did make an appearance, reluctantly, for a post-season series between Boston and Worcester on October 12 and 13, but it was soon apparent that the barnstorming games would be a financial failure. Only 100 fans paid 50 cents each to witness the first game. John did not show for the second game, forcing the Bostons to recruit an amateur on the spot to take his place. For game two, the admission fee was reduced to 25 cents, but fewer than 100 showed, producing only "$17 and some cents" for the players to divide, or about 85 cents each.[16]

Since the brothers could not be reserved, they were free agents, and they were fed up with Arthur Soden and the Red Stockings organization. The feeling may have been mutual. The *Bridgeport Standard* thought Boston had "a lot of old players there they cannot manage."[17]

Rival clubs wasted no time in courting the O'Rourke brothers. Buffalo began negotiating with both Jim and John on October 16, 1880.[18]

John was ambivalent about playing baseball anywhere. Life following the 1880 season was not going well for the 31-year-old brother. John had suffered two serious injuries in two years and the Boston owners stiffed him for his final month's wages.

For the off-season, John accepted a lucrative position with the New Haven Railroad from a hometown political crony, Col. William H. Stevenson. The *Bridgeport Post* explains the connection between John, Stevenson, the railroad and politics:

Mr. O'Rourke was active in old Sixth ward Democratic circles and was as skillful in directing party affairs as in work on the diamond.... He it was who secured for Colonel Stevenson the delegation of the Sixth ward, which made it possible for the colonel to receive the Democratic nomination for mayor in 1879. But party factions were displeased, and Colonel Stevenson was defeated. It was shortly after that Colonel Stevenson, then connected with the old Housatonic road, took Mr. O'Rourke and other Bridgeporters into the service of that company and when the road was absorbed by the New Haven, Colonel Stevenson found nice places with that great corporation for his friends.

On First Fast Train [Between Boston and New York]

When the New Haven road instituted its five hour service the famous Bay State Flyer was its first train. It leaves Boston around ten o'clock and the return train starts from New York at the same hour. The west bound train passes through here [Bridgeport] about 1:50. The East bound about 11:00. Mr. O'Rourke was made baggagemaster on this train from the start, one of the best positions in the fast train service."[19]

In late August 1881 John was still in a stew over his treatment by the Red Stockings, or else his new career was on the fast track. He received an offer of "an engagement for the remainder of the season by the Cleveland Club," but, the *Clipper* reported, "it is doubtful whether he will accept."[20]

Two months later he received an offer from the National League Worcestors for the 1882 season. In January 1882 it was announced he had been "secured by the Worcestor Club and will re-enter the professional arena." In mid–February, John signed a contract for the 1882 season, Secretary Young of the National League being duly notified.[21]

During March, brother Jim was "practicing daily" with two other professional ballplayers living in Bridgeport: Fred "Tricky" Nichols and catcher Ed Rowan.[22] But John was not. He was riding the rails between Beantown and Manhattan. At least he was getting some exercise handling baggage.

Then, on April 8, 1882, came the Worcestors' first contest, a tune-up game against Brown University.[23] John was not on hand for the game. On April 18, the Worcestors were in New York for a series of exhibition games with the Mets. But still no John.[24]

A week later, a hint from the *Clipper*:

John O'Rourke was in Boston last week. He is not very desirous of playing this season, and unless his arm is in good enough condition to enable him to get the requisite practice, he will not join the Worcestors on [opening day] May 1.[25]

On opening day the Worcestors were at Boston (where John had an apartment), but John was not in the lineup.[26] John O'Rourke would sit out the 1882 season, as he had 1881. I don't know what, if anything, was wrong with his arm. This may have been a cover story for the benefit of the Worcester organization.

John was understandably reluctant to once again trust his fate to organized baseball. His suit against the Bostons to collect his October 1880, back pay was still tied up in the courts. Nor did he need a job. He had a lucrative position with the railroad. Although he had a standing offer to take a leave of absence to play baseball should the right opportunity come along, he may have felt that a noncommittal attitude toward his year-round job might affect his chances for advancement. He hoped to be promoted to conductor.

Oh, but how this 33-year-old must have been torn between the safe, secure railroad job versus the possibility of even one more year as a major league star.

In December 1882, John finally received a settlement of his lawsuit from the Boston owners:

Case No. 334 on the Superior Court list at Boston, Friday, Nov. 24, was the long-pending case of John O'Rourke vs. the Boston Baseball Association. O'Rourke sued for $185, the amount of salary claimed to be due for services rendered during November, 1880, and the jury found for him in the sum of $205.[27]

(The reference to November is incorrect. The suit was for the month of October.) Based on the amount of the claim, John's salary must have been around $1,300 per year. John was once again at peace with organized baseball, having challenged the trust, and won.

Jim's Odyssey after Boston was not fraught with the same distress and dilemma. Upon his release from Boston at the end of the 1880 season, the National League Buffalo Bisons offered him the chance to manage and he jumped at the opportunity. While Jim had not had experience leading a team, he was a major league veteran of nine years, and he knew the fine points of almost every position. During the 1880 season alone, Jim caught, covered first base, shortstop, and third base, and played all three outfield positions.[28]

10

Buffalo Bisons (1881–1883)

Upon learning that Jim O'Rourke would manage the National League Buffalo franchise in 1881, the *Clipper* compared the Bisons' management structure to that of the League champion White Stockings:

> The Chicago ... appointed club-captain runs the team with undivided control. Buffalo, too, profiting by the costly lessons of the past, has now placed its club-team in the hands of a competent manager.[1]

Both O'Rourke and Chicago manager Cap Anson were appointed by the owners, as opposed to being elected by the players, a common practice of amateur and college clubs, but disastrous within professional organizations. The *Clipper* editors also thought it was significant that the Chicago and Buffalo clubs had undivided leadership: that is, Anson and O'Rourke were both club manager *and* field captain. As captains, they made the strategic pregame decisions of establishing the lineup, battery, and batting order; then they directed tactics during the game, from shouting out who should catch a fly ball to questioning unfavorable calls by the umpire.

As managers, they made travel and hotel arrangements, and monitored expenses on the road. It was also a manager's job to make sure his club received its proper share of the gate at away games.

O'Rourke and Anson had complete control of the players on and off the field, giving them a firm authority that neither was hesitant to exercise.

Jim was well prepared for his opportunity to manage. He had understudied the winning style and strategy of Harry Wright for eight years. Even the *Post and Mail* in rival Chicago had praise for the veteran Boston manager:

> The reason that the Bostons hold the pennant is that the nine are composed of men who keep themselves in condition to play ball, and are never to be found hanging around beer saloons and low variety dives. They indulge in no dissipation,

go to bed at a reasonable hour, and the next day they are fresh and active. Harry Wright has taught his men that sobriety and temperate living are the chief requisites in a first-class ball player, and to this added a course of strict discipline.[2]

When Jim signed with Buffalo during the last week in December 1880,[3] he again ducked the reserve clause. He did, however, give verbal reassurances that he would not desert the Buffalo club after the 1881 season. As a result, the club did not have to waste one of its five reservations on O'Rourke: he had given his word he would re-up for the next season, and that was good enough.

The Buffalo owners were not enthusiastic supporters of the reserve rule anyway. At a meeting of the National League in Rochester on October 4, 1880, the Buffalo representative, E. B. Smith, spoke out against the "five-man rule." He came close to overturning it. The Worcester board was divided, and even the original author, Soden, was having misgivings. (He wanted to retain more players than the five covered by the original agreement.)

Cincinnati was also against the reserve rule, but National League president William Hulbert of Chicago challenged the right of the Cincinnati delegate to participate unless he first ratified the league ban on liquor sales at ball grounds. Hulbert insisted that "The meeting could not go on with their further business [renewing the reserve rule for another year] until this matter was definitely settled." The Cincinnati representative, after consulting with his board via telegraph, offered "to have the sale of liquor restricted to a bar under the grand-stand," and said he would give his word that the directors would exert themselves to do away with the custom as fast as the prejudice in its favor could be overcome." But this was not good enough for Hulbert and the offending club was expelled from the National League.[4]

The proponents of the reserve clause then safely outnumbered its opponents four to three. The *Clipper* reported what transpired next:

> With the distasteful element from Cincinnati out, the gathering proceeded to hold a more than ordinarily secretive conclave. Each delegate solemnly swore, as we are informed, not to disclose the results of their deliberations. After a two hours' session their business was concluded, and representatives came downstairs. Our representative was enabled to gather an outline of the result of the afternoon's proceedings. The five-men matter was discussed. The Buffalo representative opposed it vigorously, and made a desperate fight, but he was outnumbered. The other delegates had made up their respective minds, and decided to send their pet policy through flying. All law, courtesy, and everything else was thrown aside to let Worcester, Troy and Cleveland have their best men. Buffalo was most emphatically sat upon, and the six [other] delegates voted to renew the reservation agreement signed at Buffalo in 1879. Among

other things learned was the fact that the Boston delegate, who had not been in favor of the plan, was pacified by the agreement of all not to approach Snyder and permit Boston alone to sign him. All but Buffalo signed this bond and the baseball Slavery-act once more became a reality. Such cramping of the interests of the players, and designating where and how they shall play, is preposterous. The delegates all left home without doing anything further with the Cincinnati matter.[5]

Michael Scanlon, representing Washington, reported that the owners "also signed an agreement that no player should receive over $1,200, so that each club could live within its receipts."[6]

Secret agreements to fix a ceiling for player salaries, along with the reserve clause, would exacerbate the relations between players and magnates to the breaking point before the end of the decade.

In their next issue, the *Clipper* editors said that the action against the Cincinnati club was "untenable" and that the reserve clause was a "disgrace." The publication then took the courageous action of offering a strategy to overthrow the National League monopoly and thereby the stranglehold of the reserve rule:

In regard to any action looking to an effective opposition to this five-men rule by players themselves, we see nothing better that can be done than the adoption of propositions to form a new League outside of the six clubs comprising the five-men rule League. Thus far but two clubs have "kicked" against the personal rule. But these two, by the aid of newly-formed clubs in cites like Detroit, Cincinnati, Buffalo and St. Louis, in the West and New York, Philadelphia, Baltimore and Washington, in the East can by judicious and combined action utterly destroy the five-men rule. The question is, will they do it?[7]

The position held by the Bisons' directors in regard to the reserve clause may well have influenced Jim's decision to accept their offer to come to Buffalo.

On the field, Jim's strategy was to overwhelm opponents with heavy hitting. The average weight of the Buffalo players was 168 pounds.[8] For 1881, the Buffalo owners also hired heavy-hitting Curry Foley from Boston. At the time, it was common for club owners to do all the hiring and firing, negotiate salaries, and prepare the reserve list at the end of each season. Managers had little authority in this area. Although they were free to offer recommendations on who to sign and who to release, and O'Rourke probably recommended fellow Irishman and former teammate Foley to the Buffalo front office, the final decision rested with the man who signed the paychecks.

In 1878 Henry Chadwick wrote that Cap Anson was the only manager with the "whole power of selecting and managing his team"; and in 1891, Chadwick again named Anson as the sole manager with the "power to engage and release players." Since these dates bracket the years Jim managed in Buffalo (from 1881 to 1884), we might assume that O'Rourke numbered among the other managers who Chadwick described as "handicapped to a more or less extent by official interference at the hands of club presidents and directors."[9]

O'Rourke also encouraged former teammate Deacon White to join the Bisons in 1881 as a utility player. White lead the league only four years earlier with a .387 batting average, and like Jim, he could play most other positions, including catcher.

The Bisons had finished seventh in 1880. On June 6, 1881, under O'Rourke's management, the team was only one game behind the first-place Chicago White Stockings.

The rivalry between Buffalo and Chicago, between O'Rourke and Anson, grew so intense that by midseason the two captain-managers were not on speaking terms.[10]

On June 9, the Bisons won a classic 13-inning 1–0 game at Boston against Jim's former teammates.[11]

On August 1 and August 20, Buffalo was still in second place.[12] However, at the end of the season, the Bisons were in third place, seven games ahead of Boston.

It is remarkable that Buffalo performed as well as it did against much larger cities. The notoriously frigid Buffalo climate and relatively small population conspired to keep attendance low, resulting in limited funds for salaries. Jim had to stretch every dollar far beyond what was required of Cap Anson and his other big-city competitors. So, when shortstop Johnny Peters asked Jim for a $10 advance, O'Rourke replied in his patented vague rhetoric:

> The exigencies of the occasion and the condition of our exchequer will not permit anything of that sort at this period of our existence. Subsequent development in the field of finance may remove the present gloom and we may emerge into a condition where we may see our way clear to reply in the affirmative to your exceedingly modest request.[13]

But Peters was not to be so easily befuddled:

> Dear Manager O'Rourke: I don't want any of this funny business or horse talk. I want ten bucks ... and I want it right now or the blanket comes right off the horse and I quit.[14]

The blanket stayed on the horse.

The following financial report of the Buffalo Baseball Association at the close of its inaugural season shows how challenging it was to keep enough cash in the bank just to meet the monthly payroll:

Buffalo Baseball Club — 1878

Receipts

Gate Receipts, at home	$11,236.51
Gate Receipts, out of town	4,669.75
Season Tickets	160.00
Contributions	95.00
Receipts from Advertisers and Concessionaires	325.00
Player Fines	81.77
Interest on Bank Balance	46.95
Rental of Grounds for Lacrosse	75.00
Total Income	$ 16,689.98

Expenses

Railroad Fares	$1,782.66
Hotels	1,131.89
Transportation to Hotels and Ball Parks	196.42
Salaries	11,068.33
Maintenance of Grounds	331.15
Balls and Bats	140.10
Uniforms and Equipment	320.48
Rental of Grounds	700.00
Printing, Bill Posting, Advertising	631.40
Telegrams	257.03
Incidentals	336.01
Total Expenses	$ 16,895.47
Net Profit (Loss)	($ 205.49)

In 1878, the Buffalo organization also sold $4,920 in shares of stock to secure cash to fit out the grounds and provide working capital. Of this amount $1,138 was spent leveling and preparing the playing field and $3,328 to construct fences and accommodations for the spectators.

By the time Jim came aboard, the club apparently was doing no better financially. Prior to the start of the 1881 season, the stock authorization was increased from $5,000 to $7,000.[15] This would indicate the organization needed to raise cash.

However, at the end of 1881, Jim's first season as manager, game receipts were $23,666 and salary expenses $13,851.[16] Note that revenues were up almost $8,000 over 1878, while salaries increased less than $3,000. Jim's first year as manager was a very good year for the Buffalo stockholders.

Succeeding in baseball's delicate balance of winning games and making money requires a manager to attend to countless details on and off the playing field. We can glean an idea of what a manager's routine was like on the road from a piece written by Abe Yager of the *Brooklyn Eagle* as he tagged along with Brooklyn manager Billy Barnie:

Managing a base ball team on the road is full of little incidents entirely outside of actual play on the ball field. A manager is his own advance agent, advertiser, property man and everything else. He has to arrange every detail, look out for trains, telegraph ahead for busses and baggage wagons to meet the team at the depot, detail men to work the gate, announce when the game is to start and what time the men must leave the hotel for the grounds, telegraph or telephone the line up [sic] of the team for the score cards and perform a dozen other duties that keep a manager busy all the time.[17]

On overnight trains, Jim purchased sleeping berths. He tossed the tickets into a hat and the men drew for the coveted lower berths. The players entertained themselves by telling stories and singing songs in the smoking lounge while drawing on strong cigars.[18] While the other players were relaxing, Manager O'Rourke, had his head buried in his account book, posting amounts paid to porters to load baggage and the cost of the dinners in the dining car. Jim would finger his pocket watch as he recalculated the time it would take to get from the hotel to the ballpark the following afternoon, decide where meals would be eaten (they were cheaper in the hotels than on the trains), recount his cash to make sure he had enough for the next two days, and compute the profit or loss so far on the current road trip.

With the finances and logistics under control, Jim would switch gears and contemplate the game just played and the one on the morrow. Newspaper box scores would be scoured for what they revealed about opponents, and whether rival Chicago won its last game. Win-loss records would be updated to figure the number of games Buffalo was out of first place.

Finally, time and fatigue permitting, Jim would write home to Annie and the kids.

A manager is also responsible for grooming new talent. O'Rourke kept Buffalo in the first division by being able to spot and develop players, like slugger Dan Brouthers and pitcher "One-Arm" Daily.

The hulking Brouthers had played for Troy of the National League in 1879 where he hit .274. He began the 1880 season with Baltimore of the National Association, batting .297 in 20 games[19] before the Baltimores disbanded in the latter part of June. Brouthers then joined the newly organized Rochester team, also of the National Association, where his hitting declined to .250 in the 12 games he played for the club[20] before Rochester, too, folded. The Bisons tried to hire Brouthers in mid–August, but the owners refused to meet his salary request or even to pay his travel expenses to Buffalo.[21] The big first baseman returned to Troy, where he finished out the 1880 season hitting a disappointing .167 in three games.

Brouthers began the 1881 season with the Brooklyn Atlantics,[22] but by the end of May he was finally corralled as a Buffalo Bison. He was described by one reporter as "knock-kneed, a giant in stature and a man who seldom uttered a word."[23]

With Jim's coaching, Brouthers become the first player to win back-to-back batting titles, hitting .368 in 1882, and .374 in 1883.[24] Brouthers was a power hitter, one of the first to use the full length of the bat and to bring the combined power of his shoulders, legs, arms, and wrists into the swing.[25]

Jim saw to it that Dan was amply rewarded for his contributions. Although Brouthers earned only $800 his first year with the Bisons, the slugger received a $400 raise in each of the following three seasons.[26]

With Brouthers, Jim O'Rourke, Deacon White, Jack Rowe, Hardy Richardson and Curry Foley in the line-up, the *Clipper* referred to the Bisons as the "big batting team."[27] Singles hitters need not apply.

To fortify his defense, Jim scouted for a second starting pitcher. Managers were beginning to rotate their pitchers to rest their arms (instead of waiting for a pitcher to request relief). During the 1880 season, the *Clipper* noted:

> With the hard work our pitchers have to attend to, playing in every game is too much of a strain.... Three pitchers are not too many to have in a first-class team, each with his own catcher.[28]

Jim scouted Hugh "One-Arm" Daily, "a mean, tall, mutton-chopped string-bean"[29] of a pitcher with piercing eyes and an "abominable temper."[30] As a result of a childhood accident, at the end of his left arm, instead of a hand, was a leather pad. But Daily could be given no quarter for his disability; he had to hit and field as well as pitch.

Jim had a chance to see Daily in action during 1881 in two closely contested exhibition games between the Bisons and the then-independent New York Mets.[31] He liked what he saw, so in spite of Daily's handicap, O'Rourke gave him a shot at the majors and the chance to find out what it was like to pitch to men who were paid more than college professors for their ability to hit baseballs.[32]

Jim put Daily in the box on May 17, 1882, against the world champion White Stockings, whose player-manager, Cap Anson, was leading the National League in hitting with a .399 average.

Daily pitched the complete game against Chicago, holding the White Stockings to six hits for a 6–2 Buffalo victory.[33] Daily won 14 more games for the Bisons in 1882 and even filled in at second and short "for a couple of games."[34]

The following year, Daily pitched a no-hitter against Philadelphia.

In one game, Daily threw 20 strikeouts. For 100 years, this feat stood as the all-time major league record.[35] Some statisticians differ over the number of single-game strikeouts. Some credit Daily with only 19 because the catcher dropped one of the third strikes, then threw wildly to first, allowing the batter to reach base safely. But even at 19 strikeouts, it was still the all-time record until Kerry Woods and Roger Clemens each threw 20 K's that made it into the record books.[36]

A manager must also motivate his club to excel. To accomplish this, each member must feel he is treated fairly and equally. In addition to managing, O'Rourke played left field and some of the Bisons thought he was harder on them than on himself. So, one day when he muffed a low liner, Jim called time to announce:

> Mr. O'Rourke, I am pained and astonished at the hopeless incompetence displayed by you in your futile effort to trap that daisy cutter. If you do not quickly improve the quality of your play, it will be necessary for you to retire from your present position, and join a less pretentious organization. I trust I shall not again be compelled to bring this matter to your attention.[37]

As a manager, O'Rourke was also an innovator. On May 22, 1881, he laid off left-handed hitter Deacon White when an opponent put in a southpaw pitcher, thereby beginning the practice of platooning: starting a left-or right-handed player in a position depending on who was pitching for the other team.[38]

The rule makers, too, were experimenting, in an effort to liven up the game. The National League adopted a series of restrictions on the pitcher intended to produce more hitting. In 1879, the pitcher's box was narrowed to four feet so he couldn't move around as much before delivering the ball. To further restrict distracting moves, the pitcher also had to face the batter as he began his delivery.[39]

The pitcher was still required to deliver the ball underhand, but that was difficult to police. Early in the 1880 season, a Mr. Stevens, writing in the *Boston Herald* observed:

> Several pitchers have an illegal delivery a large part of the time, and, though the rule might bear hard on them, it ought to be either enforced or rescinded.[40]

ADRIAN C. ANSON.
ALLEN & GINTER'S
Cigarettes.
RICHMOND. VIRGINIA

Cap Anson, the swaggering manager and first baseman for the Chicago White Stockings (Allen & Ginter card, 1887).

By season's end, the issue still had not been resolved. George Wright complained that several pitchers, including Will White (Deacon's brother) and Johnny Ward, "throw the ball almost direct from the shoulder, and should be ruled out."[41] And even two years after that, the *Clipper* noted:

> There is scarcely a League pitcher that does not infringe the rule requiring the hand holding the ball in delivery to pass forward below the line of the [waist]. Either umpires should enforce the rule or it should be repealed.[42]

The problem with enforcing the underhand rule, was that the penalty was so severe that umpires looked the other way. When a pitcher's hand was above his waist when he released the ball, the umpire was to call a "foul balk." Three foul balks and the game was to be called in favor of the other team. The umpires knew this would cause a near riot for such a minor infraction. A less drastic penalty was needed for illegal pitches. The *Clipper* suggested the following punishment to fit the crime:

> In the case of three foul balks being called each base runner occupying a base at the time should be allowed to score a run. This would amply suffice to stop any violation of the existing rule, while the forfeiture of the game is altogether too severe a penalty.[43]

But the advice was not heeded. As a result, pitchers inched their arms higher each season, realizing they could get away with it.

In another effort to level the playing field, the pitcher was moved back five feet to 50 feet from home plate.[44] According to the *Clipper*:

> The design of the amendment was to give the batsman a better chance to judge the ball as it comes from the pitcher's hands; the increase of distance, too, must necessarily affect the speed of the ball.[45]

However, the longer pitching distance gave pitchers an unintended benefit in that it gave balls more time to curve. Jim thought the advantage still rested with the defense. Writing years later, Jim noted:

> The pitcher was only 50 feet away from the batsman ... and there was no penalizing him if he hit you with the ball, as there is now. The result was that the pitcher had the batsman at his mercy more than he has today, and in those old days many a pitcher tried to intimidate the batsman by striking him with the ball.[46]

To achieve another advantage over hitters, batteries also began to develop signals, so the catcher could call for a specific pitch: a curve in, a curve out, a change-up, fast ball, or even a pitch-out to pick a player off base.[47]

With innovation rampant in baseball, Jim even began to experiment with colorful uniform themes. In 1881 the home uniform was a conservative gray with red trimmings[48]; but for the road he chose an adventurous lavender and blue combination. Unfortunately, the free rein he allowed his choice of colors may have given encouragement to Al Spalding in a disastrous scheme the following year.

Spalding supplied the uniforms under contract to the National League.[49] Prior to the start of the 1882 season, Spalding pushed through a rule to attire players in color-coded uniforms, corresponding to their *positions*, instead of their teams. This was an early attempt to help the fans identify players. The uniform scheme was adopted at the National League annual meeting in Chicago on December 9, 1881.[50]

Ever the shrewd businessman, Al also knew his scheme would require teams to purchase all new uniforms and make it more difficult to mix and match team inventory for new players. Also, it made life much simpler for the Spalding company. He had to stock only nine uniform combinations. Perhaps it was O'Rourke's order for lavender and blue that drove Al over the edge.

But the Orator could not keep silent about what he saw as an affront to the dignity of professional athletes:

> It is an insult to all of us to make a professional baseball player dress like a clown. If we are unfortunate enough to play near a lunatic asylum, we are likely to wind up inside looking out.[51]

Even Oscar Wilde was roused to comment that the Spalding costumes were not quite to his aesthetic tastes.[52] Another contemporary pointed out:

> The umpire seems to have been entirely overlooked. Serpentine pantaloons, in imitation of a barber's pole, harlequin jacket and a circus clown's wool hat would give them a neat and not particularly gaudy suit, and afford a kaleido-scopic effect as they skipped up towards first-base along with a batsman. A log-cabin quilt, worn as a toga, would heighten the effect and add dignity to the office.[53]

However, the full extent of the fiasco of the "monkey suits" was not apparent until the season began. On several occasions when a first baseman walked or singled, the pitcher threw over to first to hold the runner on, only to find that he had thrown to the wrong first baseman. The startled base runner would duck and scamper to second as the exasperated real first baseman chased after the ball.[54]

After two months, the new uniform code was abandoned.[55] Spalding, of course, was only too happy to sell every team all new outfits. (The following year the *Cleveland Herald* would report that Spalding had earned $200,000 since the founding of his company, an average of $25,000 per year.)[56]

The Bisons returned to their natty gray and red uniforms for the balance of their 1882 home games,[57] but promotion-minded O'Rourke selected a "flaring green" outfit for the Bisons' road trips.[58]

For the following season, a league color scheme was applied to the stockings only: red for Boston, gray for Buffalo, white for Chicago, navy for Cleveland, light blue for Providence, brown for Detroit, blue and white check for Philadelphia, and crimson and black for New York. In addition, the home team was required to wear white; the visitors could wear any color except white.[59]

As bad as the monkey suits were to the reputation of the game, Spalding's folly paled in significance to the pervasive and sinister influence of gambling. Jim would have endorsed, and probably helped to promote, the outlawing of pool selling in Buffalo. As the *Clipper* reported on May 6, 1882:

> The Board of Police in Buffalo, N. Y., has prohibited the baseball pool-combination betting, in violation of the State law. The punishment is a $2,000 fine. The *Buffalo Express* says: "The suppression of combinations will redound to the general benefit of the game."

The 1882 Chicago White Stockings modeling their boss's "circus outfits." Manager Cap Anson, holding cap, is in the center. Second from left in the back row is Mike "King" Kelly, and far right in the same row is pitcher Fred Goldsmith, a claimant to the invention of the curve (engraving: *Harper's Weekly*, October 14, 1882).

As the 1882 season progressed, the Bisons maintained a third-place ranking on the field, but the blustery fall weather in Buffalo made financial success increasingly difficult. When September rolled around, it was mathematically impossible for Buffalo to move up in the standings, but it was not too late to improve its performance as a business. When the Bisons were scheduled to play a three-game series at home against the White Stockings, O'Rourke obtained clearance from the National League office to play the games in Chicago to take advantage of its warmer climate and larger market.

During September of the prior season, only 75 fans showed up for a game against Chicago. Jim understandably wanted to avoid the possibility of another such "vast assemblage" in Buffalo.[60] As the *Clipper* understood the arrangement:

> The ostensible object in making the change is that both clubs' finances may be increased by playing in Chicago. The Buffalos will have the same financial arrangement that they would have if the games were played on their own grounds, Chicago getting only 15 cents per head.[61]

The Providence Grays, under the management of Harry Wright, were neck-and-neck with Al Spalding's Chicago White Stockings in the race for the pennant. Harry Wright, who naturally was rooting for Buffalo to sweep the series, wrote to Jim, objecting that the change of venue would give a home field advantage to Chicago. Jim replied on September 25[62]:

> Friend Harry:
>
> Bancroft delivered your well composed request which was indeed exceedingly clever. I thought it too good to keep so gave it for publication.
>
> And let me here say, Harry, although going to Chicago— without Prov[idence's] consent, I shall have each and every man play as he never played before. If they [Chicago] win games, much better ball playing will they have to do than I think they're capable of. Prov[idence] people I hope will not say we are going to let them win. As we are prejudiced against them. Such is unworthy of notice. We are going with an object in view namely to defeat them if not the majority, sufficient to enable your club to win the championship.
>
> I feel our club is equal to the emergency. And regret in as much as our rules and constitution make no provision for a case of this kind we did not obtain your affirmative vote. Assuring you of our utmost confidence and determination to win, I Remain Yours &c,
>
> James

The *Clipper* sided with Wright, arguing:

> By entering into this agreement the Buffalo management do the Providence team an injustice. Every club has an advantage in playing on its own ground, and this year the Chicagos especially have done miserable work when away from home.[63]

1882 Buffalo Bisons manager Jim O'Rourke, with handlebar mustache, is in the center. Below O'Rourke, right of center, is Dan Brouthers. Below O'Rourke, left of center, is Hugh Daily (with mutton chops and bow tie). Other players, clockwise from the very top are: Hardy Richardson, Davy Force, Jim Galvin (the first pitcher to win 300 games), Deacon White, Blondie Purcell, Tom Dolan, Jack Rowe, and Charles Foley. In addition to O'Rourke, Brouthers and Galvin are Hall of Famers (National Baseball Hall of Fame Library).

When Chicago swept the series from a "strangely passive"[64] Buffalo team, Wright "screamed vain protests."[65] In a follow-up letter to Wright on October 12, 1882, O'Rourke offered the following explanation for the rout in Chicago:

> Were it not for a Bogus Umpire we should have assisted you by winning at least two games from Chicago out of three. But in every manner he favored them and this advantage defeated us.[66]

It is possible that the umpiring was partial to the White Stockings, but I suspect Chicago bested the Buffalos because they were fighting for the pennant against a team to whom it no longer mattered.

In an effort to smooth the Grays' ruffled feathers, the National League arranged a post-season series between Chicago and Providence, which the White Stockings won handily.

At the close of the 1882 season, Jim's contract was renewed.

He and the Buffalo owners were still opposed to reservation on moral grounds; and one last noble attempt to permanently rescind the reserve clause was planned for a special meeting of the National League called for September 22 in Philadelphia.

Autocratic National League president William Hulbert had passed away "after a lingering illness" on April 10, 1882.[67] Spalding was elected to succeed Hulbert as president of the White Stockings organization, on April 26, 1882.[68]

Vice President Arthur Soden automatically became president of the league until the annual winter meeting in November 1882, when a successor would be elected.

At a special National League meeting to discuss the reservation system, in September 1882, Soden held the gavel, and Spalding, as a new owner, wielded a vote. Also present was W. O. Thompson of Detroit, who eloquently led the fight among the magnates to defend the rights of their workers:

> Mr. Thompson ... spoke at considerable length upon the abuses contained in what is known as the "five-men rule," under which a manager could have any five players as long as he chose, and could then summarily discharge them without notice. The speaker held that this rule was unjust to the players, inasmuch as it prevented a player from improving his prospects, and frequently kept him from getting an engagement, as managers often took advantage of the rule to extend their season until after all the other clubs had been filled for the ensuing year."[69]

But it was a lost cause. There was a great deal of peer pressure to support and indeed strengthen the reserve clause. Not only was the policy continued for 1883, the number of players a team could reserve was increased from 5 to 11, which, at the time, represented an entire roster. The reserve clause was also adopted by the American Association and the Northwestern League. These organizations, along with the National League, drew up the

Tripartite Agreement to honor each other's reserve lists, further limiting a player's options. This was the first National Agreement or formal baseball trust.[70]

At the annual meeting of the National League, in November 1882, although some of the Western papers suggested Spalding, A. G. Mills was elected to head the league, replacing interim President Arthur Soden.

During 1883 it became common knowledge that Jim was evading reservation. His defiance of the policy was a galling embarrassment to the National League office and a dangerous inspiration to other players, who were beginning to follow O'Rourke's lead.

The new National League president, A. G. Mills, counterattacked. In October 1883, the *Boston Globe* obtained a copy of a letter to the club owners in which Mills wrote that he had learned that "certain reserved players are signing for 1884 with the proviso that if they attach their names to a contract they will not be reserved for 1885." Mills urged clubs not to sign any more such contracts until after the annual meeting in October, "when the matter will be discussed." Mills warned the magnates that that "if players are accorded this privilege" the reservation scheme will ultimately fail.[71]

Nevertheless, Jim and the Buffalo directors continued in their gentlemen's agreement whereby he agreed verbally that he would renew his contract at the end of the season, and in return they gave him an exclusion from the perpetual clutches of the reserve system.

O'Rourke enjoyed the complete trust and backing of the Buffalo board. Earning the confidence of the media and the cranks was not as easy.

Unlike modern managers, and even most of his contemporaries, player-manager O'Rourke was daily judged by fans and the press for his performance as a left fielder *as well as* team captain and manager. Fortunately, Jim was up to the challenge, though the dual role must have been a strain.

As of July 3, 1883, Jim had appeared in 319 *consecutive* National League games, a new major league record. By the end of the 1883 season, Jim had played in a total of 510 National League games, also more than any other player.[72] The previous year, Jim had also taken the lead for most lifetime runs scored, a record he held through 1893, his final major league year. Anson took the lead in 1894. He had it taken away in 1928 by Ty Cobb, who lost the title to Pete Rose in 1985.[73]

However, the sportswriters did not always focus on the good news out of Buffalo. In some rival Western cities, the press seemed to enjoy needling the Orator. Perhaps they were trying to outpsych the competition, or it may have been intended to discredit Jim and the success the Bisons were enjoying against much larger cities and better-financed teams. In any event, as a major league manager, he was fair game. Here's an example of a potshot from the *Cleveland Leader*:

It is most amusing to note the turkey-cock strut and loud and affected voice with which Jim O'Rourke seeks to let the public know that he is the captain of the Buffalos. Nine tenths of his directions are unnecessary, and when guidance and coaching is necessary, none comes from him.[74]

The previous season, Buffalo had nosed out Cleveland for third place with a 45–39 record, versus Cleveland's 42 wins and 40 losses.

Fortunately, the more common slings and arrows Jim had to endure were lighthearted spoofs he inspired. The *Boston Courier* published an essay entitled "The Great O'Rourke":

The great O'Rourke then, is a warrior not yet of middle age, and remarkable for his noble moustache (tawny of color like a bundle of fragrant straw), and for his yet nobler legs, which may be termed the columnar perfection of flesh and blood. As a terrific batter, base fielder and outrunner he is equaled by some and surpassed by but few! Kindly to his foes and fierce to his friends, fleet of foot and nimble of eye, with accurate pose of head upon his shoulders and correct adjustment of his breeches, according to the severest principles of decorum, O'Rourke is the master spirit of the field, the glory of the game. Whole pages could be more than filled with the story of his daring feats and wondrous achievements. Space forbids the enlargement of this holy theme, but even the austere editors who object to Latin may permit him to say that he has been known to make a base hit in the course of a game, and even to run to first base in the agony of his excitement. Such facts, it is true, border on the superhuman, but who can doubt them when even reporters believe? Fearsome will be the contest when Sir James enters the arena on those splendid legs, and lightly will wave the kerchief of the gentle welcome from jeweled hand and blushing cheek.[75]

Even in the local press, a losing manager, then as now, will incur uncomplimentary scrutiny. As one sportswriter admitted:

A couple of weeks ago, O'Rourke's management was universally condemned in Buffalo—because the club was losing. Now he is the biggest man in Buffalo—because the club is winning. Such is popular judgment.[76]

Things were better in Jim's personal life. In 1883, he built a new home for his growing family. In May, a fifth child, Ida, was born to Annie and Jim. Fortune was also smiling on older brother John.

11

John O'Rourke Joins the Mets (1883)

For the 1883 season, John received offers from Cincinnati,[1] Cleveland,[2] and the Mets. The Mets joined the major league ranks on October 24, 1882, when they signed on with the American Association.[3] John signed with the Mets for their inaugural season. And showed up. *Sporting Life* welcomed John back to The Show with the announcement:

> Manager James Mutrie, of the Metropolitan Club, last Monday signed a contract with John O'Rourke to play with the club during the present season. O'Rourke is a brother of the well-known player of the Buffalo club, and has been for a long time identified with base ball interests. He used to be a heavy batter and a good general player."[4]

And in the *New York Times* on opening day, John read the following encouraging words:

> John O'Rourke, who will take his position on the Metropolitan team today, is well known in the professional ranks and is everywhere regarded as a good player. He played centre field for the Boston club for a term of three years [actually two], and during that period gained a reputation as a heavy batter and a daring base runner. O'Rourke will cover first base and it is thought he will strengthen the in-field.[5]

The Mets' season opener was a blaze of color. Besides the usual banners, bunting, and band uniforms, the New York opponents, the Baltimore Canaries, were dressed in bright yellow uniforms, hence the team nickname. Not to be outshone, the Mets were resplendent in dark-blue stockings, bluish-gray pants, white and blue polka-dot shirts fashioned from fabric "imported from England," capped off with a different brightly colored hat for each player, depending on position (much more sensible than the Spalding uniform scheme — and a lot less expensive). Even the gatekeepers and groundskeepers were "appropriately uniformed."[6]

In the opener, John led the Mets offensively with 4 hits, but alas, he also led in errors, with three in his only game at first base. He played the rest of the season in center field.[7]

For awhile, the brothers were neck-and-neck offensively, both ranking 16th in batting as of July 1 in their respective leagues. Jim was hitting .305 with Buffalo in the National League, and John .294 with the Mets in the American Association.[8]

At season's end, Jim ranked fifth in the National League, with a .328 batting average, and third in hits and runs scored. Brother John finished with a less impressive .270 average, yet still distinguished himself with his hitting. In late August, *Sporting Life* reported:

> John O'Rourke, of the Mets, who made the longest hit on the [Philadelphia] Athletic grounds, is credited with the same feat on the [New York Mets] Polo Grounds.[9]

On Monday, September 10, 1883, John was injured in one of his "famous" headfirst slides. *Sporting Life* informed the fans:

> John O'Rourke of the Mets, will play no more ball this season, ill health having compelled him to leave the nine and go to his home in Boston.[10]

Such is the uncertainty of a baseball career. Henceforth, John "decided to give up the game for railroading."[11] He is listed in the *Bridgeport City Directory* under the title "Ball Player" from 1881 through 1883, and in every successive year as "baggagemaster." He is listed in the *Boston City Directory* as a ball player in 1880, no listing in 1881, and as baggagemaster in 1882 and subsequent years.

John O'Rourke Teamography

Year	League	City	Team	Position
1866	Amateur Boys' Club	Bridgeport	Pembrokes	cf
1867	Amateur Boys' Club	Bridgeport	Pembrokes	
1868	Amateur Boys' Club	Bridgeport	Pembrokes	
1869	Amateur Boys' Club	Bridgeport	Pembrokes	
1870	*Unknown*	Bridgeport	*Unknown*	
1871	*Unknown*	Bridgeport	*Unknown*	
1872	*Unknown*	Bridgeport	*Unknown*	
1873	*Unknown*	Bridgeport	T.B.F.U.S.B.B.C. (TBs) ?	
1874	Semipro	Bridgeport	T.B.F.U.S.B.B.C. (TBs)	cf
1875	Semipro	Bridgeport	T.B.F.U.S.B.B.C. (TBs)	cf
1876	Semipro	Bridgeport	Bridgeports	cf
1877	International Assn.	Manchester, NH	Manchesters	
1878	International Assn.	Manchester, NH	Manchesters	cf
1879	National League	Boston	Red Caps	cf
1880	National League	Boston	Red Caps	cf
1881	*none*	*none*	*none*	
1882	*none*	*none*	*none*	
1883	American Association	New York	Metropolitans	cf, 1b

12

National League Batting Champion (1884)

Meanwhile, Jim was experiencing a setback of his own. The Buffalo lease expired in late 1883 and Jim had to find a new field for his Bisons to roam.[1] The club had played all its home games on rented grounds at Fargo Avenue and Rhode Island Street. The property owner, Alexander Culbert, notified the Bison organization that he intended dividing the ball grounds into building lots. (Baseball fields, with their broad expanse of clear level land on transportation routes, have always been coveted by developers.)

Jim used the need to relocate as an opportunity to construct a new and improved stadium.[2] To increase attendance, a crescent-shaped grandstand was constructed that was enclosed on three sides to keep out the chill Buffalo winds. The ladies' grandstand was replete with "gaily painted caned arm-chairs."[3] For the carriage trade, Jim built a covered parking area.[4] The parking fee was 15 cents per game, or $5 for a season pass.[5] General admission, according to National League bylaws, was 50 cents. O'Rourke also fashioned a new scoreboard that was the first to show results of other games.

The new home for the Bisons, with the grand name of Olympic Park, was built at a cost of $6,000. The Bisons also paid $1,500 per year to rent the land.[6]

Besides contending with the need to find new space, Jim also faced a particularly vexing personnel problem during the 1883 and 1884 seasons. His centerfielder, Charles "Curry" Foley, was a friend and former teammate with the Bostons. Foley had joined the Bisons in 1881, the same year as Jim.

Foley was reserved at the end of 1883, but the Bisons did not sign him for 1884, nor did the club release him so that he could join another team. The club was later criticized for its actions. These are the facts of the Curry case:

In 1881 and 1882, Foley was a producer for Buffalo. On May 25, 1882, he became the first major leaguer to hit for the cycle (homer, triple, double,

Olympic Park. Built by Jim O'Rourke in 1884, the venue accommodated 1,764 spectators under the grandstand and another 1,984 on the lower-priced bleaching boards.

Note the single players' bench. At the left end of the bench is a new requirement for all ballparks, mandated in 1883: the bat rack. Prior to then, bats were strewn about the grass like pick-up sticks (National Baseball Hall of Fame Library, Cooperstown, New York).

and single in the same game.) O'Rourke accomplished the same feat two years later.[7]

Foley returned to the club for a July 5 game at Detroit. He had one hit and one error, playing center field.[8] On Thursday, July 19, 1883, Foley had three hits including a triple and no errors playing center field, but then he was out for another six weeks.

On September 4, 1883, Foley again returned to the lineup in right field. He rapped out one single and made no errors. The following day he played center, hitless and errorless.[9] It was his last game for Buffalo.

On September 8, the club celebrated the last home game of 1883 with a balloon ascension, and, in keeping with the festive spirit, announced, "the present nine will be retained to a man."[10] At the same time it was reported that "Foley, of the Buffaloes, has been in poor health and unable to play with the team, but has improved, and left Buffalo on Monday to join the team. He meets it in Boston,"[11] his hometown.[12]

On Saturday, September 15, 1883, Jim's second child, Anna, aged nine years, "died suddenly, ... necessitating O'Rourke's return home at once."[13]

But Foley did not catch up with the team, so Jim had to rush back to keep the outfield up to strength. O'Rourke was again in the line-up on Wednesday, September 19th.

By late October, Buffalo had "signed all its present team but three."[14] By year's end, all reserved Buffalo players had been signed except Foley.[15] Indeed all reserved players of both the National and American leagues had been signed by this time except 10, and some of these were holding out for better offers, including Hugh "One-Arm" Daily and Johnny Ward. By the start of the 1884 season, all except Foley found teams. Hugh Daily and two others jumped to the new Union Association, which did not recognize the reserve clause. As a result, Daily was blacklisted by the National League for violating the reserve. This did not seem to disturb Daily, for as *Sporting Life* reported:

> The one-armed pitcher of the Chicago Unions, has, in the 11 games in which he has twirled the sphere on the home grounds, made the remarkable record of 107 strike-outs.[16]

One reason Foley may not have been given his release was that O'Rourke thought he was malingering (pretending to be ill) to win his release in order to accept a higher offer from another club. A note in the *Sporting Life* of September 24, 1883, suggests this possibility:

> It is said that some of the Buffalos are playing poorly with the hope that they will not be put on the reserve list. This will give them a chance to accept outside offers at higher salaries.

Charles "Curry" Foley (engraving: *New York Clipper*, October 1, 1881).

The *New York Clipper* had let slip prior to the 1882 season that the Worcester club was negotiating with Foley.[17]

In hindsight, it does not appear Foley was faking. In a letter written several years later to the sports editor of an unidentified newspaper, he describes himself as "a man who can hardly walk from the effects of rheumatism."[18]

Interestingly, another Buffalo player, Kennedy, was also ill at the same time as Foley and, apparently, with the same debilitating rheumatoid arthritis. In late May, *Sporting Life* reported:

> Foley and Kennedy of the Buffalos have been given 20 days' leave of absence. Owing to the bad weather they have not improved as fast as expected. It is said Foley will visit Mount Clemens, Michigan.[19]

And two months later:

> Kennedy of the Buffalos was released on Wednesday at his own request."[20]
> Kennedy suffered from a "rheumatic shoulder."[21]

Another plausible reason Foley was reserved at the end of 1883, but not signed to a contract in 1884, is that *he* was holding out; stalling for a better offer. As late as February 1884, the club reported to the *Buffalo Courier*:

> It was expected that ... Foley would sign with the home club, which would then have a full complement of 13 men.[22]

This report begs the question: was Foley holding out, or was management waiting for Foley to demonstrate that he was in top form? The language seems to suggest the club and player could not agree on salary. The next mention of Foley seems to support the latter scenario:

> Foley is ... reserved by the Buffalo Club, but has not yet signed. He is sulky. It is said, because he was refused $300 advance money. The Cincinnati Unions have been after him and offered him big money and $500 in advance, but [Foley] hates the black list and refused."[23]

It seems Foley was angling for a release, not for poor health, but to obtain a better deal elsewhere. There is no question that a star performer could find deeper pockets than those in Buffalo. Cincinnati, with an 1880 population of 255,000, had a bigger gate than Buffalo, with its 155,000 population and damp and chilly climate. Four National League cities had populations greater than 500,000.

The profit of the Buffalo club in 1883 was $5,000. By contrast, Chicago earned $20,000 for the season, and Boston a whopping $48,000.[24] Buffalo, not surprisingly, ranked seventh in payroll among the eight National League teams.[25]

Years later, it would also be claimed that Foley was again reserved at the end of 1884 for the 1885 season, but this was not the case. *Sporting Life*, on October 29, 1884, p. 3, printed the list of all players officially reserved, and Foley was not among them.

Another episode, in 1884, demonstrated concern by O'Rourke for his players: the invention of the chest protector.

Pitchers' arms were still creeping higher. As a result, in 1883, the National League decided to legalize what the authorities had been unable to prevent, sidearm pitching. Legally, the ball could then be released above the waist, but no higher than the shoulder. Pitchers observed this new restriction almost through the first inning of opening day. Then the arm began to inch higher still.

Finally, in 1884, the league office gave up trying to police pitching. As Jim explained it, for 1884:

> There was no restriction placed upon [pitchers] as to delivery, and they could double up like a jack-knife and deliver the ball [overhand].[26]

When overhand pitching was legalized, it took a heavy toll on the catchers. This inspired manager O'Rourke and catcher Deacon White to develop the chest protector.[27] It was made of rubber-coated cloth, inflated with air, and weighed only one and one-half pounds.

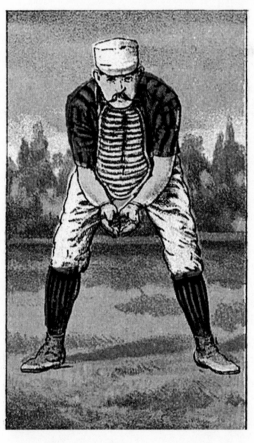

Jim O'Rourke models the pneumatic chest protector that he developed in 1884 with catcher Deacon White to reduce the bruising and broken ribs caused by overhand pitching. Note also the barely discernible flesh-colored glove on each hand (1887 Buchner Gold card).

There is some confusion over the exact date the chest protector was introduced, and its source. The root of this confusion is that there were really three types of breast protectors developed during the 1880s and 1890s.

First, there was a flexible sheepskin pad worn under the uniform. Since it was virtually invisible, we will never know for certain who first wore one, or how popular they were. I suspect they were widely used. They were inexpensive and undetectable, thus avoiding ridicule for the wearer.

The second iteration, still used by some umpires, was a thick but awkward cushion that hung in front of the chest like a shield.

The third iteration of the chest protector was the lightweight, air-filled, cloth and rubber invention of Wright and O'Rourke that was worn externally. It caught on quickly and is the direct ancestor of the modern chest protector.

The first mention of a protective device (probably the sheepskin) was by *Sporting Life*, in its April 2, 1884, issue:

The latest base ball tool is an abdomen protector for catchers, and the Cleveland Club is likely to adopt it.

Hall of Fame historian Lee Allen says the chest protector was first worn in a major league game on June 5, 1884, by Jack Clements of the Philadelphia Keystones of the Union Association, a league in existence for this one year only.[28] Allen adds, "It was first called a 'sheepskin' and was generally ridiculed." The inflatable protector was not a sheepskin nor did it remotely resemble one.

The *New Haven News,* in May 1884, reported on the debut of the next stage along the evolutionary path of body protection for backstops:

> [Baseball's] latest fashion is a huge pad which the catcher of the Detroit Club hangs in front of his manly person as he faces the projectiles from the pitcher behind the home plate. We saw him in his place last Saturday, with his frontal livey-pad, his hands cased in thick gloves, the familiar wire helmet on his head, and looking for all the world like an animated combination of a modern bed bolster and a medieval knight.[29]

Then, on June 4, 1884, *Sporting Life* reported on the emerging use of the ultimate protective device, the O'Rourke-White model:

> The catchers outside of the [National] League have not yet taken to the body protection. McKenna of the Washington Nationals wore one in Cincinnati last week, which was the first time it had been seen in use in that city. The protector is an excellent invention, and will ultimately be used by all catchers.[30]

Apparently, *Sporting Life* was not above plugging its advertisers' products in the editorial sections, for coincidentally, an ad appeared in *Sporting Life,* June 4, 1884, for Grays' Patent Body Protector for Catchers:

> Made of Rubber Cloth and inflated with air, weighing 1½ lb. Impossible to be injured in any part that is covered by the Protector. Does not interfere with throwing or running, but gives the catcher entire confidence.

The protectors retailed for $10 and were sold by Reach, Spalding, Wright & Ditson, and Peck & Snyder. The device was patented by Bill Gray, a Hartford player.

I know of no connection between Gray and O'Rourke or White; except that Gray and O'Rourke both lived in Connecticut at the time. The various histories are in conflict with one another; unless O'Rourke, White and Gray collaborated on the research and development and Gray patented and sold the protector. Their respective motivations were different. Gray was interested in the device as a potential source of income. O'Rourke and White were just trying to survive 90-mile-per-hour fastballs.

On June 10, 1884, p. 7, *Sporting Life* again championed the chest protector:

The rubber breast protector now used by all catchers when facing swift pitching is as valuable an adjunct of a catcher's article as the wire mask; and the catcher who refuses to wear such a protector from severe injuries simply because "It looks so queer," or because a lot of fools in the crowd laugh at him, is no better than the idiots who quiz him.

The *Sporting Life* campaign was working. On July 23, 1884, the publication reported:

The chest protector is coming into general use. It is as necessary as the mask.

Once manager O'Rourke was satisfied that his catcher, Deacon White, was adequately protected from the faster overhand pitching, player and batsman O'Rourke had to learn how to adjust to the new pitching style himself. This he did well. In fact, Jim led the National League in hitting in 1884, with a .347 average.

Jim presented the bat he used to win the batting title to the baseball team at Yale. Two years later it was reported that the bat was still effective at getting hits:

The majority of base hits made this season thus far by the Yale nine have been made with the bat which Jim O'Rourke led the League in 1884.[31]

The *Spalding Guide* praised Jim for more than his batting during the 1884 season:

He has made a brilliant record for himself as an outfielder, being an excellent judge of a ball, a swift runner, and making the most difficult running catches with the utmost ease and certainty.... His gentlemanly conduct, both on and off the field, has won for him a host of friends.[32]

For 1885, Spalding introduced an "O'Rourke" signature bat.

In a bit of revisionist history, the 1884 averages were altered 85 years later. Jim's figure was lowered to .347 in some compendiums when the Baseball Records Committee of 1969 recomputed the averages based on newspaper box scores. At the same time, Mike Kelly was belatedly awarded four additional at bats and seven more hits, elevating his 1884 average to .354.[33] The Macmillan *Baseball Encyclopedia* of 1969 contained the revised stats and listed Kelly as the 1884 batting champ.

However, some sources, including *The Sporting News*, continued to recognize O'Rourke as the 1884 batting champ.

Then, in 1999, statistician Frank Williams presented the following arguments, which convinced Major League Baseball and *Total Baseball*, the official encyclopedia of Major League Baseball, to reverse the actions of the 1969 committee[34]:

1. Box scores are prepared by local — and not necessarily objective — sportswriters. They are often at variance with the official scores as submitted to the league secretaries. It is these official records — that show O'Rourke as the 1884 batting leader — that served as the basis for the annual guides of the era. The original records, however, were destroyed in a fire in 1903. For this reason, the Committee of 1969 relied on box scores to recompute averages prior to 1903.

2. The 1969 Committee added in stats from tie games in 1884, but this did not become official practice until 1885.

3. O'Rourke was recognized as the batting champion in the 1885 Spalding and Reach *Guides*, with his picture. He was listed in all subsequent guides, baseball encyclopedias, and compendiums through 1968 as the 1884 batting champion.

For John O'Rourke, the 1884 season was far less auspicious. A notice in *Sporting Life* on December 19, 1883, remarked cryptically:

John O'Rourke will not play with the Metropolitans next season. If he plays at all, it will be with the New York [National] League Club.

This sounds like John was the source of the information. If so, it may indicate a falling out or inability to come to contract terms with the Mets. Like his "stubborn" brother, John had refused to sign a contract that included a reserve clause. As *Sporting Life* later revealed:

Jim O'Rourke, champion batsman of 1884. In Giants of the Polo Grounds, *writer Noel Hynd says O'Rourke had a dignified stance while at bat, and a powerful swing (engraving: Spalding Guide, 1885).*

John O'Rourke has not yet signed with any club and is not reserved. He did not sign a contract with the "Mets" last year, but played on a verbal contract and for big money. John is a baggagemaster on the Eastern Shore line and gets a leave of absence when he plays. He expects to be made a conductor before long, but will play ball this season — for the earth.[35]

Sporting Life, April 9, 1884, reported:

Tim Murnan[e], George Wright and John O'Rourke are mentioned as likely to play on the Boston Unions. This would be the nucleus for a formidable team.

The Boston Unions did get off the ground for 1884, but John was not on the roster.

John was in the baseball columns even after the 1884 season opened. On May 7, *Sporting Life* noted that: "The Washington Club has not yet given up hope of securing John O'Rourke."[36] However, on June 4, 1884, the national sporting publication let it be known that:

> The negotiations between John O'Rourke and the Washington Club have fallen through as O'Rourke *only* wanted $2,800 for his services.

The *Washington Post* added, "It's a wonder John did not ask for the Capitol."[37]

Sporting Life felt high salaries would kill baseball. To put John's $2,800 asking pricing in perspective, the St. Louis team, "generally regarded as the highest-salaried club in the American Association" paid $2,500 to its manager, Jimmy Williams. Third-year veteran Charles Comiskey was earning only $2,100.[38]

John had a good job with the railroad and while he did not outright quit the diamond, he priced himself out of the market. Like his brother, he had savings and income property. The following year, John would build a boarding house on land he owned in Bridgeport.[39]

John O'Rourke was never again seen in a major league uniform.

13

New York Giants
(1885–1887)

"Athletes don't hate other athletes. The fact of the matter is that they all hate management."[1]
— Screenwriter Ron Shelton [*Bull Durham*]

Because of his high batting average, the New York Giants offered O'Rourke $4,500 for the 1885 season, the largest sum yet paid a ball player.[2] The record salary was the result of a bidding war among five clubs; just the sort of thing the 1879 reserve clause was intended to prevent. But O'Rourke was not under reserve. Each year with the Bisons, as he had with the Bostons, O'Rourke steadfastly refused to sign a contract unless the club promised *not* to reserve him at the end of the season. As *Sporting Life* confirmed at the end of 1884, "O'Rourke leads the batting average of the League; [yet] could not be reserved by Buffalo. He is in the market."[3] Amazingly, O'Rourke also negotiated the reserve clause out of his 1885 contract with the Giants.[4]

James Mutrie, general manager and part-owner of the Giants, had apparently had his eye on O'Rourke for some time. *Sporting Life* reported in November 1883:

The manager of the New York team is on the lookout for several players of note. One is James O'Rourke, the captain of the Buffalo Club.[5]

In a follow-up article later that month, *Sporting Life* added:

James O'Rourke received liberal offers to play with the Athletics and New Yorks next season, but, with a sense of honor as fine as it is rare in base ball players, refused them, because, although not reserved, he had pledged his word to play in Buffalo [in 1884].[6]

When he signed for 1884, he gave no verbal pledge to return to the Bisons in 1885. (After the death of his daughter in 1883, he gave the Buffalo owners notice that he wanted to look for work closer to home after the 1884 season.[7]) Playing in New York, Jim could spend Sundays with his family in Bridgeport when the Giants were at home.[8]

During the second week of November 1884, Jim O'Rourke officially signed with the New York Giants.[9]

This was only the Giants' third season. They were organized in 1883 when the National League dropped the small towns of Troy and Worcester and transferred those players to New York and Philadelphia, respectively.[10] John Day and Jim Mutrie, owner and manager of the New York Mets of the American Association, were only too willing to accept the National League franchise for Manhattan as well.

Day and Mutrie brought in Jim Price to manage the Giants in 1884, but he was let go when the Giants placed fifth in the National League. Rumors were rife in the winter of 1884–85 that Jim would manage the Giants in 1885. After all, he had just managed the club that placed third in the standings, two rungs ahead of New York.

O'Rourke had a reputation of being a tough taskmaster. An example of his no-nonsense approach to discipline had appeared in *Sporting Life* during July of the 1884 season:

> Galvin was ... fined $20 by O'Rourke for remarking that he ought to have shown better judgment than to send [second baseman] Collins for fly balls which he could not reach.[11]

Two weeks later, the paper added:

> Every member of the Buffalo team, it is said, has soured on Jim O'Rourke, the captain, for the arrogant way in which he treats them. The same is said to be the case with Anson, of Chicago.[12]

From the tone and subject of this quote, the source may be Galvin himself. Even after Jim had left the Bisons, Galvin was still tormenting him from Buffalo:

> Galvin is quoted as saying, that If Jim O'Rourke had remained with the Buffalo's he Galvin would not have played this season.[13]

It is not known whether Jim's reputation among his players worked for or against him while he was being considered for the manager's job by New York. A certain amount of player resentment of authority is

Jim Mutrie, manager of the New York Mets and Giants (engraving: *New York Clipper*, November 12, 1881).

expected, and anything Galvin said was probably taken with a grain of salt. In the year prior to Jim taking over the leadership of the Bisons, the *Clipper* accused Galvin of being responsible for "a division in the team."[14]

According to press reports of the firing of the previous manager, firm leadership may have been just what the Giants were seeking:

> Manager Price, of the New York League Club, has been discharged. President Day says that the club had done well during the first few weeks of Price's management, but that after that he had been unable to control them and they had done as they pleased. President Day lays to Price the failure of the club to obtain a better place in the championship race. He has faith in the nine and believes that with proper management they will make a good record next season.[15]

In the end, internal politics ruled. Mutrie, a part-owner, wanted to take the helm, and he had enough votes and experience to assume the position. In late December 1884, Giants president John Day, in an effort to stem the rumors, affirmed that "O'Rourke will not [manage] the club. The team will be under the management of Mr. Mutrie."[16]

Then speculation percolated that Jim would be the field captain. As late as March 18, 1885, *Sporting Life* rendered the opinion that "O'Rourke will probably be the New York's field captain." However, when the season began the press announced, "Johnny Ward captains the New Yorks."[17] Mutrie probably felt he could control Ward more easily than O'Rourke. He would be proven correct.

Ward, you will recall, was Jim's teammate on the 1879 pennant-winning Providence Grays. Ward transferred to the Giants when that team was organized in 1883.

Ward was an ideal captain, not easily discouraged by adversity. Although Johnny pitched the second perfect game in major league history in 1880, by 1883 his arm was worn out from too many double-headers. That would have convinced most players to change careers. Not Johnny. He taught himself to play shortstop, and then proceeded to lead the league in double plays.

In 1884, the first year of overhand pitching, Ward was hit hard several times. As a result, he began to shy away from the ball. To overcome his habit of stepping back from pitches, Ward switched to batting from the left side.[18]

O'Rourke got along well with field captain Johnny Ward. However, as a former general manager, Jim was not reticent about offering unsolicited advice to the front office.

The New York fans immediately took to Jim. He "received quite an ovation" the first time he came to the bat as a New York Giant. That was in an exhibition game on April 1, 1885, against Manhattan College.[19] A week later, during a series against the New York Mets, the press gave him an ovation in print:

O'Rourke distinguished himself by making two pretty catches and taking part in a double play, cutting off a base runner at the home plate. His efforts were warmly applauded, and it is evident that he will prove a favorite here this season.[20]

At the end of May, Jim received a new suit of clothes from "an up-town tailor" for scoring the most runs during the Giants' first month of league play.[21] He also had the fewest errors: one.[22] (In 1888, Jim made it through the first two months without an error being charged to him.)[23] Of his early achievements in 1885, a sportswriter also noted:

> O'Rourke, the champion batter of 1884, has done good work, but his record has been impaired somewhat [he was hitting .340 at the end of May] by making "sacrifice" hits, and taking his base on called balls a number of times. This, however, is a very good fault, and confirms the belief that he plays for his club and not for a record."[24]

In July, more kudos from the sporting hacks:

On the Diamond Field
The New Yorks Best the Detroits Easily
O'Rourke Shows Up Well Behind the Bat

O'Rourke led in the heavy batting. He made a home run, three-base hit, and a single.... In order to give [catcher Buck] Ewing a rest [centerfielder] O'Rourke exchanged places with him in the seventh inning. The genial James put on the mask, gloves, and chest protector, and to the intense delight of the spectators, he caught a good game.[25]

JOHN M. WARD.
ALLEN & GINTER'S
RICHMOND. Cigarettes. VIRGINIA.

Although O'Rourke was no longer the manager, his reduced authority did not prevent him from innovating new plays. In 1885, Jim introduced the "Rabbit Ball Trick" of slipping into play at a critical moment a well-tenderized ball that "the heaviest sluggers couldn't drive past the pitcher's box."[26] In an exhibition game, centerfielder O'Rourke decided to have some fun with the Washington Nationals. *Sporting Life* recounted the play-by-play:

> A dispute arose in the first inning which delayed the game a long time and nearly broke it up. The first striker, Baker, after seven balls had been

Right-handed Ward batting left. Johnny had a shortstop's build, neatly trimmed mustache, and melancholy eyes. Like O'Rourke, he was a gentleman's gentleman; but would occasionally explode from pent-up frustration (Allen and Ginter card, 1887).

called, took first base. The ball used was an Eastern League ball and bore two distinct stamps. After Baker had gone to his base the ball was passed around to O'Rourke, of the New Yorks, who it is alleged, put it in his bosom and threw out a dead ball. The next striker detected the changing of balls and called upon O'Rourke to show the ball said to be in his bosom, but he defied them to search him. On examination no stamp was found on the ball in use, the ball being not even soiled. After half an hour's wrangling another new ball was thrown out and the play resumed. The next day's game with the New Yorks was canceled by the Nationals. O'Rourke's action was severely denounced on all sides. In defense, O'Rourke wrote a letter to the New York World excusing his conduct on the ground that the ball was soft and impossible to bat, and that he changed it in order that the spectators might see a good game, which was impossible with the ball furnished. O'Rourke should keep quiet. A bad excuse is worse than none, and only makes matters worse. The regular ball used by the Nationals was the Shibe ball, as good a one as is made.[27]

The *Washington Post* added that during the rhubarb both nines were huddled about O'Rourke, yet he steadfastly refused to admit to having a ball concealed inside his shirt, even though "it was bulging out in plain view of all the spectators and players."[28] We now know that at least the following, and perhaps the entire New York bench was in on the dodge: Manager "Truthful Jim" Mutrie, pitcher "Sir Timothy" Keefe, and Roger Connor, who passed the good ball to Jim.[29]

The Washington club was founded by the Internal Revenue Service, never known for an easy sense of humor. However, Jim would not tolerate cheating in a league game — where it mattered. When he was managing the Bisons, one of his pitchers, "Blondie" Purcell "was fined $100 for cutting the ball." The fine was levied not by the umpire in the game, but by the Buffalo ball club.[30]

Innovations instituted by the league were somewhat less controversial than O'Rourke's Rabbit Ball. For the 1885 season, the National League voted in a new rule, and ended a 40-year tradition. As reported in *Sporting Life*, "The home base may be made of solid white rubber instead of marble, as formerly used. This change will prevent many accidents to players through sliding at home."[31] However, the players did not appreciate the new rubber plate. "No use tapping that with the bat; it gives forth no sound."[32]

It was also in 1885 that the modern (heavily padded) fielder's glove first met the light of day. In order to protect two broken fingers, while playing for the National League's Providence Grays in 1885, shortstop Arthur Irwin taped padding to the outside of one of the common buckskin gloves that had been in use for years. He soon realized that the larger size of the glove improved his fielding average. When New York shortstop Johnny Ward saw Irwin's glove, he immediately adopted the new invention.[33] By the late 1880s, the padded glove was in general use. Within a decade, a small web, the size of a half dollar, began to appear between the thumb and forefinger.

These were halcyon days for the players, but the champion of player rights did not dare become complacent. The owners were scheming anew for Jim had once again inspired them to action, this time because he pushed the top salary well beyond what the owners wanted to pay. He had set a dangerous precedent.

The baseball magnates were frustrated that they could not control wage rates, as owners in most other industries were doing. A typical factory worker earned less than $500 per year, or about one-tenth what Jim earned for six months in 1885. Even as late as 1891, a factory worker earned on average only $1.57 per day, still less than $500 per year.[34]

The problem for the owners was that baseball workers, even after the reserve clause, still had a great deal of bargaining clout. Unlike factory jobs, their work could not be automated. A steel mill could replace the independent village smithy and reduce his job to many components that required little skill. Steel workers lined up to compete for scarce jobs, thus keeping wages low. But in baseball, owners bid for players.

There was only one thing left for the owners to do: rig prices. On October 17, 1885, they set a salary ceiling of $2,000.[35]

Five days later, O'Rourke, Johnny Ward, pitcher Tim Keefe and most of the other Giants responded by organizing the Brotherhood of Professional Base Ball Players.[36]

Ward — who had earned a law degree from Columbia the previous May — was elected president. O'Rourke and Keefe became "prime movers" in the brotherhood.[37]

One of the first things the brotherhood did was to collect dues from its members to underwrite a benefit fund for injured players. Accidents were commonplace. In fact, two years prior to the formation of the union, the *Clipper* had suggested a similar program:

> The numerous accidents during the past season have given rise to a suggestion that the professional players form a benefit association, to which each should contribute a small amount monthly. When a player becomes disabled, ordinarily his pay is stopped, and if he is obliged to remain idle for any length of time he is apt to become embarrassed.[38]

But make no mistake, the new brotherhood was a union, intent on protecting its members from the concerted efforts of the owners.

Jim, who was well over the salary limit, wasted no time in responding to the salary cap. For the benefit of the Giants organization, he planted a story in his hometown newspaper that suggested he was ambivalent about playing with the Giants:

> What the Bridgeport supporters of base ball are mainly looking after is a capable manager. There is a fair prospect but by no means a certainty that Jimmy O'Rourke, of last season's New Yorks, may be induced to accept this position....

The New Yorks want him but he will not play with the New Yorks, or any other club under the $2000 limit. As probably the best all around player in the country he knows he is worth more and can get more. But as a Bridgeporter, Mr. O'Rourke feels considerable pride and interest in Bridgeport's base ball prospects, and seems inclined to give his services to Bridgeport the coming summer for less than he would accept an engagement for in a professional club.[39]

This was the same tactic employed by Jim a decade earlier when he negotiated a raise out of the miserly Arthur Soden. On that occasion he notified the *Boston Herald* that unless his demands were met he would return to Bridgeport "to engage in business other than base ball."[40]

The stratagem worked again. Bridgeport did field a minor league ball club during the 1886 season, but there was no discussion of O'Rourke managing. That was pure bluff.

By Christmas Jim had worked out the terms of his 1886 contract with John Day, owner of the Giants. In a December 26, 1885, interview, Jim reported:

I have perfected such arrangements with the president of the club as are mutually satisfactory for '86. These arrangements will be carried out at a future time ... I am the only one of the team who has thus far made arrangements for next year. Undoubtedly the personnel of the nine will be the same as it was last year.[41]

The reporter added that "O'Rourke doesn't believe a single league club will live up to the new salary [limit]."

However, since Jim — at his request — was not reserved, his salary level was not protected and was reduced to $3,000 for 1886, which was comparable to what most other star players were earning. (Or, the $4,500 may have included a $1,500 signing bonus.) Jim also negotiated an extended winter vacation so he could pursue a lifelong ambition.

14

O'Rourke at Yale Law School (1885–1887)

Serious about the players' union and preparing for a career after baseball, Jim used his record baseball earnings to enroll at Yale following the 1885 season. He played baseball for the Giants in the summer and studied law during the winter in New Haven, a half hour from his home by train.

Although there were only about 30 students in Jim's class, the presence of the major league batting champion caused barely a stir among the ancient elms of the Yale campus. But another new law student "created a furor of excitement": the first woman to be admitted to Yale outside the art department. On October 1, 1885, the opening day of the new term, Ms. Alice Jordan was front-page news:

YALE COLLEGE INTERESTS
A Young Lady Law Student

A young lady of prepossessing appearance and intellectual mien, climbed the stairs of the county building this afternoon, to the library of the Yale law school, where she registered herself as a member of the senior class of the institution. Her name is miss Alice B. Jordan.[1]

At the time, Jim was in Chicago for a series against the White Stockings and so was spared the humiliation of discovering that he would not have been the star attraction at registration. Jim caught up with his Yale classmates after the term had already commenced, amid relative anonymity in a student body that had already been "tremendously stirred"[2] by an even more improbable law student.

In 1885 the Yale Law School offered "A two years' course, mainly devoted to the practical side of legal education; but also giving some introduction to the general ideas and sources of jurisprudence."[3] It was this standard two-year program into which Jim enrolled. Yale also offered a supplemental two-year graduate program, leading to a degree of doctor of laws. Alice Jordan already held a law degree from the University of Michigan, and it was the opportunity to enroll in the advanced course that brought her to New Haven. At the time, Yale was the only school offering graduate coursework in the field of law.

Jim also served as the Yale baseball coach while a student at the university. Colleges were beginning to take their sporting teams seriously as expeditionary forces to impress their superiority upon rival schools. For the 1885–'86 season, Yale went so far as to erect a new building for baseball training. The student newspaper described the training facility as a

> plainly built shed-like building, about 60 feet in length and not more than one-quarter as wide. It looks as much like a hot house as it does like a photograph gallery. It is lighted only by a big skylight in the roof, which on the inside is protected by a strong wire netting. The structure will be kept comfortably heated and pitching and catching can be practiced in it to great advantage.[4]

The building had a dirt floor, rolled to replicate an infield.[5] It was completed in mid–December 1885, in time to begin practicing for the spring college baseball season. The *New Haven Union* reported in December 1885 that O'Rourke "intends to begin training the Yale nine after the holidays."[6] During the 1886 season, Jim led the Yale nine to a 8–1 record, beating out rivals Harvard and Princeton for the college championship.[7]

In spite of the team's success, Jim enjoyed no more celebrity as the coach of the Yale nine than as a student. The first professional coaches were just that: coaches. It would be a slow evolutionary process and a gradual erosion of student authority before overbearing adults would rule college sports. The Yale student newspaper does not even mention that O'Rourke was the baseball coach. The first appearance I have found of his name in a Yale publication was in the April 9, 1886, issue of the *Yale Daily News* that read:

> O'Rourke, of the New Yorks, will leave his club for a short time in June to take his regular examinations at the Law School here.

It wasn't that the Yale newspaper did not cover athletics thoroughly. It did, but the students received the credit and blame for the outcome of competitions, not their coaches, who remained on the sidelines of the field and of the glory. O'Rourke suggested; students decided. Coincidentally, Yale's rivals were coached by friends and teammates of O'Rourke. At various times, Keefe coached at Princeton, Harvard and Tufts. (Tim's family home was in Cambridge, Massachusetts.[8]) Ward, who coached the Harvard and Princeton nines at different times, was one of the first professional college coaches. Princeton had hired him as early as 1882 to beat rival Yale.[9] A *Clipper* account suggests an almost innocent relationship:

> John M. Ward, the pitcher of the New York League team, is a member of the freshmen class at Princeton College, and in his spare moments is coaching the 35 collegians who are trying for positions on the baseball nine.[10]

Coaches Ward and Keefe would have employed the same nourishing attitude as O'Rourke. None of these gentlemen would have considered using physical or psychological intimidation; nor would they have upstaged the student team captains. They were teachers.

In the 1880s, college athletics were still student clubs intended to provide healthy recreation. But all the requirements for the impending commercialization were already in place by 1885:

1. An intense desire by students and alumni to best rival schools and thereby demonstrate the superiority of their institution.

2. Graduates with excess time and money on their hands and nostalgic ties to their alma mater. Alumni were already offering money, pressure, and advice on how to beat you know who.

3. School administrators anxious to earn income from student athletic competitions. During the 1885–86 season, the Yale ball club charged 50 cents per game,[11] as much as the National League.

In an odd juxtaposition of roles, the New York Giants played two preseason exhibition games against the Yale nine during April 1886. Jim played centerfield for the Giants and Amos Alonzo Stagg the same position for Yale.[12] There was no mention in the Yale newspaper that the O'Rourke listed in the Giants line-up was a Yale student or coach. But the students were not oblivious to their campus celebrity. The Yale student body did take quiet satisfaction in the exploits of its summer hero. The *Yale Daily News* of May 27, 1886, reported in passing that "O'Rourke, of the New Yorks, at present leads the League with a batting average of .400." While the student newspaper did not point out O'Rourke's connection to the university, it was common knowledge on campus. The *New Haven Union* does provide us a vivid description of *student* O'Rourke:

> Mr. O'Rourke, to gaze down at him from the lecture desk in the Law School recitation room, strikes one as being an earnest student. He pays the closest attention to the words of wisdom that come from his instructors' lips. Mr. O'Rourke is of medium size, with a light moustache, blue eyes that keep up a constant twinkle of merriment when he is talking with anybody, rather fair hair, and features that indicate firmness and determination. The first look at him would convince the observer that he is a man of great physical strength. He is a very pleasant talker, uses excellent English, and can chat for hours entertainingly on base ball topics.[13]

O'Rourke was typical of most New York ballplayers. The sport became fashionable with the carriage set in Manhattan because few of the Giants succumbed to the temptations of excess, to which an inflated income can sometimes lead young men.

The brotherhood founders set the same high standard of personal conduct for all members of the union. The strategy was designed to garner a sympathetic press and to establish a responsible image for the union opposite that of a band of bomb-throwing anarchists. Every club had men who were rejected. As a family man, civic leader, supporter of youth clubs,[14] and a true gentleman, O'Rourke was a model representative for the brotherhood.[15]

15

The Brotherhood
(1886–1887)

During the 1886 season, the brotherhood secretly organized chapters in each National League city. In August, the *Sporting News* broke the story with the headline: "Big Surprise. A Ball Players' Union Fully Organized."[1] It was quite an accomplishment to keep the organizing efforts under wraps. If the owners had caught wind of what the ringleaders were up to, they might have blacklisted the early recruits and thereby discouraged others from joining.

The blacklist was a particularly effective form of intimidation.[2] To give it even greater clout, the major leagues adopted the National Agreement to honor each other's blacklists as well as reserve lists. Even semipro teams avoided a blacklisted player because no professional club would play a team that employed a blacklisted player. The players had nowhere to run.

However, by the time the magnates found out about the union, most players had already joined. They couldn't blacklist everyone.

During the season of 1886 season, in its first official act, the Brotherhood prevailed upon the National League to drop the salary cap. It had become a dead issue anyway, ignored by the owners who were anxious to offer whatever was necessary to obtain the star players. It seemed as if the players and magnates had struck a fair and equitable balance. But would it last?

In 1886, O'Rourke and 25-year-old Buck Ewing alternated between the outfield and catching.[3] This arrangement would seem unnatural to modern catchers whose position, when not back-stopping, is next to the water cooler. But in the nineteenth century, the last place any player wanted to be was on the bench. In the words of teammate Johnny Ward, "In those days, the greatest punishment you could inflict on a ballplayer was to keep him from playing. We all wanted to be in every game that was played."[4]

During the 1886 season, Jim caught 47 games and played in an additional 63 contests in the outfield and two at first.

In November 1886, Spalding attempted to trade 29-year-old centerfielder George Gore to the Giants for Jim O'Rourke. Although the Giants did get Gore, the deal for O'Rourke fell through.[5] For the 1886 season Jim had signed a contract with a reserve clause[6] and was therefore at the mercy of the New York club.[7] Owner John Day could have sold his contract to Spalding, but it wouldn't have done any good. Jim would never have moved to the Windy City, reserve or no

Catcher "Buck" Ewing (Allen & Ginter card 1888).

reserve. O'Rourke was in the middle of a two-year course of study at Yale and he liked it just where he was. The Giants' Manhattan field was only one hour by commuter train from his home in Bridgeport. He probably apprised John Day or Spalding of his intransigence, and as a result, the discussions did not proceed.

When an article appeared in *Sporting Life* suggesting that Jim was disgruntled over the hiring of another outfielder, Jim sent a letter to the editor to welcome his new teammate:

> The unjust and very unkind imputation of being disgruntled over the engagement of Mr. George Gore by the New York Club, I repel as preposterous; in fact, it is simply too ridiculous to entertain for an instant. On the contrary I mingle my rejoicings with those of all other enthusiastic admirers of the Giants upon this grand acquisition to their representative club, wishing only for Mr. Gore the grandest success of his life, and may the distinguishing achievements of this, our celebrated, happy and genial brother professional on the ball field in the past, winning for him the renowned distinction he is now enjoying, pale into insignificance when contrasted with his giant record of 1887.
>
> Your truly, James H. O'Rourke, New York B. B. C.[8]

As an outfielder, Gore was definitely a match for O'Rourke. Both were 34 years old. Gore led the league in batting in 1880; Jim in 1884. In 1886 Gore hit .304; Jim .309. They were interchangeable. But only one was trying to negotiate time off for school. This may have been a worryin' situation for O'Rourke.

By the time Gore was officially signed, on Wednesday, November 25,

1886,[9] Jim was already back at Yale, continuing his studies and coaching the college ball club. According to the *New York Tribune,* there were great expectations of the Yale nine for the upcoming 1886–1887 season:

> There is great interest at New Haven ... and the baseball enthusiasts are confidently predicting success.... The nine has been coached all winter by James O'Rourke, of the New York nine, who is a student at the law school and will graduate this year. He is revered by the New Haven people about as much as Kelly is by Bostonians.[10]

Jim would have received only a modest amount of income — if he was paid at all — for coaching the collegians. His bread-and-butter job was still as a major league ballplayer. Baseball contracts ran from April 1 to October 31. So when Jim had not heard from the Giants by late March, he planted the following article that appeared in the *New Haven Register* on March 28, 1887:

> James O'Rourke has not been signed by any club as yet. He has been expecting to receive an offer from the New Yorks, but they seem rather dilatory in making up their nine. O'Rourke says he is not particular about playing at all this season, as he will graduate from the Yale Law school in June, and really needs the time to prepare himself for the event.[11]

O'Rourke in 1886 (engraving: *Leslie's Illustrated,* July 10, 1886).

Four days later, on April 1, Giants owner John Day sent Jim a telegram "ordering him to report for an exhibition game" on Saturday, April 2, 1887.[12]

Jim was under reserve for the first time, so he was at a disadvantage in negotiating with the Giants. Since he could not use offers from other clubs as bargaining chips, his ploy was to make it appear that he was once more quite prepared to return to Bridgeport "to engage in business other than base ball." The following letter was reprinted in the *New Haven Register* on April 2, 1887:

Bridgeport, Conn., April 1, 1887.

John B. Day, Esq.:

Dear Sir — In answer to your telegram, I may briefly say that in consequence of not hearing from you earlier I have neglected to ask or to solicit any special arrangements with the Yale faculty in reference to my examination.

Unless I can make special arrangements satisfactory to them I shall be obliged to forego the pleasure of playing with the "Giants" earlier than June 26.

If the weather is suitable for playing tomorrow, however, I will come down; otherwise not for the present.

Yours, truly,
James H. O'Rourke[13]

It snowed on Saturday, so Jim spent the day with his family in Bridgeport. Despite the weather, I'm sure Giants' president John Day was pretty hot under the collar. Just to make sure all of his fans saw his response, Jim also sent it to the *New York Times:*

> James O'Rourke notified the Giants' president that, unless satisfactory arrangements were made by which his law studies should not be interrupted, he would be unable to report until June 26.[14]

On Monday, April 4, Jim watched a game between the Yale nine and the Bridgeport minor league club at Yale Field. The following day he visited the Giants' front office where, fortunately, "satisfactory arrangements" were made for Jim to take time off for examinations. As he wrote to a friend,

> NEW YORK, April 5, 1887. I was received right royally by President Day and the boys. My arrangements are far in excess of anything anticipated. So signed this afternoon. James H. O'Rourke.[15]

Three days later, on Friday, April 9, the Giants played the Yale club in New York, beating the O'Rourke-trained collegians, 15–4.[16]

And as to the Gore matter, Danny Richardson (no relation to Hardy Richardson of the Buffalo Bisons) was shifted from the outfield to second base to make room for the new player and Gore was assigned to center field.

For the 1887 season, Manager Mutrie again alternated Ewing and O'Rourke as catchers.[17] The rotation of the two catchers continued through the next season as well. The one not scheduled to catch played left field. This was the intention all along.[18] It was Jim's ability to catch that made him indispensable to the Giants, as it had to the Bridgeport Osceolas in 1870. Jim made good in his new dual role as outfielder and change catcher. After the Giants' first road tour, *The Sporting News* commented:

> The catching of O'Rourke in the West has been creditable, but when he is put behind the bat the out-field is weakened considerably.[19]

Both Gore and O'Rourke played a full season in 1887. Jim's baseball career and his studies toward a future law career would both progress unabated.

Following the 1887 season, the *New York Times* reported:

O'Rourke Becomes a Lawyer

NEW HAVEN, Conn., Nov. 5.— James O'Rourke, the ball player, was made an attorney at law and a member of the Connecticut Bar to-day. He graduated at the Yale Law School last June, but his engagements with the New York nine kept him away from New-Haven at the time the other members of this class were sworn in by the Supreme Court.[20]

As confirmation that he successfully completed his law studies and passed the examination, Jim is also listed in *The Catalog of the Officers and Graduates of Yale University* as having earned a bachelor of law degree.[21]

After his formal admittance to the bar, attorney O'Rourke opened a law office in Bridgeport, in the Post Office Arcade on Main Street, which still stands.[22]

Lest John Day, George Gore, Buck Ewing, *et al.* assume that attorney O'Rourke was ready to hang up his cleats, he set the record straight in an interview with *Sporting Life*:

"I find that it is the opinion among a great many friends of mine," said attorney James O'Rourke, the well-known ball player to-day, "that now I have fledged out as a lawyer, secured a place to sit down and displayed my shingle that my days of tossing the ball in a professional way were at an end. Perhaps it might interest you to rectify this mistake if you think it worth while. For some years to come the law business will be a side issue with me. I am young yet, in good health and I see no reason why I should give up a several thousand dollars' bird in the hand for the sake of a few hundreds in the bush. Fully six months in the year I shall have time for briefs, musty law books and all that. This will sort of counter-balance my athletic life for the remainder of the 12 months and give me a chance to do a little head work, such as studying and perfecting myself as much as possible. A ball player wears out eventually and at that time I shall drop out of the National game, and as some of my enthusiastic friends declare, blossom out at a level-headed age into a luminous legal light of the Park City. You needn't say this, however, for perhaps I may be a dismal failure. I'll tell you later what I am going to do with this bat and ball in '88."[23]

Meanwhile, teammate and fellow rabble-rouser Johnny Ward — who had already graduated from Columbia Law — was pursuing less serious interests. Although a dedicated athlete, Ward was drawn at night to the gaslights of Broadway. He was the toast of New York society and "could handle all the knives and forks at a fancy dinner party."[24] One night, stage-door Johnny met his soul mate, Broadway producer and actress Helen Dauvray.

Born Ida Gibson, Helen had worked her whole life as an actress, beginning with childhood roles in *Richard III* and *Uncle Tom's Cabin*. She spoke French convincingly on Parisian stages, entertained cattlemen in Australia and 49ers in America's gold fields, where she was billed as Little Nell the California Diamond. In 1885, Helen settled in New York and within a year earned the starring role in a new Broadway drama, *One of Our Girls*. Helen went on to manage the Lyceum Theatre at Fourth Avenue and 23rd Street, where she starred in several plays that she also produced. She has been described as an animated brunette with an "expressive face, striking gestures, and often fascinating movement"[25]

How did the stars of Helen and Johnny happen to cross? Ball players and Broadway performers felt an affinity for one another. As paid entertainers, they both realized they were regarded with some condescension by society and were assumed to possess less than a saintly moral code.

The New York Giants took to spending their evening leisure time at the theater; and dramatic players found themselves wiling away daytime downtime at the ballpark. Helen was a regular attendee at Giants home games and usually sat on the first base side in the upper grandstand next to the press box. She was a conscientious scorekeeper and would often compare notes with the reporters.[26] "Her tiny hands beat each other rapturously at every victory of the Giants and her dark eyes were bedewed at every defeat."[27]

Baseball star Ward and Broadway star Dauvray met sometime in 1886.[28] Both had escaped from small Midwestern towns and spoke French to dye their roots. By 1887, Johnny (27) and Helen (28)[29] were an item. They were married in October 1887 while attention was focused on the World's Series. A quiet ceremony, witnessed by a few friends and family members, was held at an undisclosed location to evade a media feeding-frenzy.

Johnny referred to Mrs. John Ward as "The Goddess," and on a pedestal is where he wanted to keep her. But the headstrong Helen Dauvray Ward insisted on maintaining her career. Although Johnny wanted a stay-at-home wife, *he* was constantly traveling with the Giants or on union business. Their conflicting careers and jealousy over the other's fame led to a stormy relationship, not unlike that of DiMaggio and Monroe.

Ward introduced Giants' pitcher Tim Keefe to Helen's sister, Clara, a statuesque sculptress

The Dauvray Cup. When Helen Dauvray discovered there was no World's Series trophy, she commissioned an eight-pound sterling silver loving cup. Awarding the cup was inaugurated with the 1887 World Series (engraving: 1888 *Season Guide* published by the Detroit Free Press).

and suffragette. The two hit it off immediately and were soon married.[30] Unlike Ward, Keefe was tolerant, even supportive, of Clara's desire for a career and her own identity. They would remain married for life.[31]

To prepare for a post-baseball career, Tim practiced shorthand at night in his hotel rather than carouse with his teammates. For his note-taking skill, Keefe was elected secretary of the union. Like George Wright and Al Spalding, Keefe was also a player-entrepreneur who owned a sporting goods store in Manhattan.

Keefe and O'Rourke had a lot in common, besides being teammates and co-founders of the Brotherhood. Both were sons of Irish immigrants and eschewed tobacco and alcohol.

In 1886, Keefe suffered a nervous breakdown after he hit Boston second baseman Jack Burdock in the temple with a "swift-pitched ball" on August 12.[32] Burdock dropped like a stone right in front of Jim, who was catching Keefe that day.

Burdock, like Jim, was one of the original members of the National League. They had been teammates on the Boston Red Caps of 1877 and 1878. Prior to the Keefe incident, Burdock had already received at least three serious head injuries. In 1881, according to the *New York Clipper*:

TIMOTHY KEEFE.
ALLEN & GINTER'S
RICHMOND. Cigarettes. VIRGINIA.

"Sir Timothy" Keefe (Allen & Ginter card, 1887).

John J. Burdock, the second-baseman of the Boston Club, met with a severe accident on the afternoon of April 8. It appears that he was on the rear platform of a horse-car, on his way to the ball-ground for practice. As the car passed a place where the track was being repaired it struck a stone, and the shock threw Burdock from the platform head foremost, striking the pavement with the back of his head. He was picked up in an insensible condition, and an examination of his injuries developed the fact that he had received a concussion of the brain, but just how severe the injury is cannot be fully determined at present. The physicians expressed an opinion that there was no immediate danger of his life, but it will probably be a long time before he will be again able to play ball. At the latest advices he was still in a critical condition at his home, and is in a comatose state most of the time.[33]

Fortunately, Burdock recovered rapidly from this head injury.[34] But then on April

24 of the following year, he collided with another player while chasing a fly ball:

Burdock was severely injured, lying in an unconscious state on the field for some time. A similar accident occurred to Burdock and Rowen in the morning-game in Detroit, Mich., July 4, both sustaining severe injuries.[35]

It is the remembrance of such accidents that can lead a player to distraction. Although Burdock also recovered from this latest accident, the haunting vision was not easy for Keefe to shake off. Clara patiently helped Tim rid his mind of the nightmare of the ball curving into Burdock's head, and he, too, after several weeks, returned to the game.

Players could eventually forgive each other for unintended injuries, for they needed to stand united against the common foe: the magnates. And the fragile peace of 1886 between players and owners was soon broken. In 1887, 24 years after the Emancipation Proclamation, Al Spalding sold superstar Mike Kelly to Boston for $10,000.[36] Everyone in baseball was stunned by the size of the deal and to the brotherhood, selling a player—at any price—was a violation of the original intent of the reserve clause. Moreover, the players were dismayed that Kelly received not a penny from the transaction, nor did he have any say in where he was sent.

The sale did have one benefit for the players. It gave the union a membership boost, for it showed the disregard the owners had for their employees, and gave evidence of just how much profit they were earning off the labor of the ballplayers.

Jim O'Rourke playing center field for the Giants in 1887. The striped shirt and socks were maroon and black (detail of an 1887 chromolithographic Album).

The union took the players' case directly to the fans through articles in popular magazines. In a *Lippincott's* piece, Johnny Ward asserted the reserve clause "invested the club with a questionable right ... to *retain* the services of the player; not ... to *sell* him."[37]

But the National Agreement, the formal collusion between all clubs to recognize each other's reserve list, in effect gave the right to sell a contract (with its renewal right of reserve) to another team. It was the magnates' version of the Fugitive Slave Law and the player had no way out. Consider, for example, the desperate case of Paul Hines:

> Hines, of Providence, declared that rather than submit to that club's reservation he would stay idle for a year. The construction was then evolved that even this would not free the player from the reservation, — that, though the term of his contract had expired, and though the reservation was so distasteful that he would prefer the loss of a year's salary, yet he would still be held by it.[38]

A player could not shake off the shackles of the reserve clause even by staying out a season. In a case similar to that of Paul Hines, Jim McCormick pitched for Pittsburgh in 1887 but refused to sign for 1888. The club reserved him anyway at the end of 1888 for 1889, and every year thereafter, preventing him from ever signing with another club.[39]

A year later during the World's Series, while the spotlight of public attention was on baseball, a second article by Ward, this one in *Cosmopolitan* magazine, raised the level of rhetoric by arguing that the reserve clause was "a dishonor to our national sport."[40]

The object of all this attention, Mike "King" Kelly was a "tall, muscular Irishman with a fierce mustache and a fiery eye. He was reckless, frolicsome, open-handed, sentimental, self-indulgent, and without fear. He enjoyed being a hero"[41] and dressed to match his personality, a Beau Brummel in patent leather shoes, spats, checked pants, cane, red carnation, and cocked bowler.

On the field, Kelly was an aggressive base stealer, especially when the fans intoned: "Slide, Kelly, Slide." Neither base paths nor rules could hem him in. In the 1880s, when there was only one very harried umpire to watch the ball and the base runners, Mike would often skip third base when racing home from second. One time Mike reached home well ahead of the ball, but was still called out. "Out?!" he protested, prompting the umpire to explain, "Aw, Michael, you got here too quick."[42]

Another case held up by the union as an example of the "cruel repression" of the Reserve Clause was the Foley Incident. Although O'Rourke knew the real story, he may have kept mum so the players

Mike "King" Kelly (engraving: *Sphere & Ash*, 1888).

could gain some sympathy. Nevertheless, the case of Foley as victim may have been weakened by a spoof of the Orator that appeared about the same time. (Note who wrote it.)

Jim O'Rourke's Return from Yale College

SCENE—John B. Day's office (New York City) April 1.
Enter Jim O'Rourke.

John B. Day–"Why, Jim O'Rourke! How are you, my dear boy?"

Jim O'Rourke–(Smilingly)–"I am right well, thank you."

John B. Day–"How is everything down in Barnumville?"

Jim O'Rourke–"You mean Bridgeport, do you not?"

John B. Day–"Certainly; you don't suppose I mean any other place?"

Jim O'Rourke–(Beginning to warm up)–"I will tell you Mr. Day, Barnum's 'Equescuriculum of Megathetherian Monstrosities' have evacuated the town, and the grief of the demoralized and isolated population is inexorable."

John B. Day–(thinks he has struck a hornet's nest)–"Great Gawd, Jim! Where have you been all winter with you summer clothes on?"

Jim O'Rourke–(Solemnly)–"I have been an indefatigable and studious 'Impresario' at Yale College."

John B. Day–(Wants to change the subject)–"What do you think of the umpiring for next season, Mr. O'Rourke?"

Jim O'Rourke–(Thoroughly at home on the subject)–"I will tell you, Mr. Day, we want unostentatiousness and the effervescence of imputrescibility conglomerated and all umpires who are unsophisticated, incapacitated, or whose pedigree is not well authenticated, or even men who get intoxicated should be emasculated. My mottos are: *Sesquipedalian* Verba; Sic Semper Tyrannis Paregoric; Vive La Republique.

John B. Day–(Extensively satisfied)–"I am quite busy now, Jim; but will see you later."

Jim O'Rourke–(Smiling as a conqueror)–"Not if I see you previously, Mr. Day."

The Demosthenenes of the ball field will then wend his way to the Polo Grounds, where he will be heartily greeted by Count Munchausen (Mutrie) and the rest of "the Giants." Then look out "Gore."[43]

Yours, rheumatically, Chas. J. Foley

16

The Color Line
(1887)

The owners were not deterred by union rhetoric or articles in popular magazines sympathetic to the players. They were flexing capital's muscle, and they liked the feeling. Spalding had one more demonstration to give, lest there be any doubt as to who was in charge of America's national sport. O'Rourke would witness prejudice once again, directed not toward the Irish for their nationality, or workingmen for their class, but against certain players for their race.

In the spring of 1887, Giants' captain Johnny Ward was in the process of recruiting black minor league pitcher George Stovey. A family friend from his hometown of Williamsport, Pennsylvania, provides us this description:

> From his earliest youth he was recognized as a pitcher with marvelous speed, great cunning and boundless energy.... He was also a champion marble shooter, an incomparable sprinter, and a harmonica player the like of which you have never seen.[1]

The Giants wanted Stovey to pitch in an important series against the Chicago White Stockings. According to *Sporting Life*:

> New York has been seriously considering the engagement of Stovey, Jersey City's fine colored pitcher. The question is would the League permit his appearance in League championship games?[2]

Stovey was more than qualified for the promotion. In 1886, he led the International League with 33 wins.[3] This feat is all the more remarkable when one considers that Stovey was in the league for only a portion of the season, having played earlier in the year with the independent black Cuban Giants and an unidentified Canadian club.[4] Stovey also struck out 22 men in a game against Bridgeport, and ended the 1886 season with a 1.13 ERA.[5] The game in which he wafted 22 opponents must have been a heartbreaker,

Right: Adrian C. "Cap" Anson. Was he the one person responsible for the segregation of baseball, or has he earned that title because history demands simple answers? More likely, it was a general, unwritten consensus by many players, owners and fans to ban blacks. But Anson was their willing spokesman (engraving from *Sphere & Ash*, 1888).

as Stovey was the losing pitcher.[6] The fielders on the otherwise all-white Jersey Citys did not support their black pitcher to their fullest ability.

Giants' president John Day was in full agreement to hire Stovey, but powerful Chicago owner Al Spalding and his team manager, Cap Anson, would have nothing of it. As the publisher of the *Official National League Guide*, Spalding was a powerful force in the shaping of the national sport and public opinion. And Spalding and Anson

The Cubes of 1887. They were the undisputed champions among all black teams. During the summer of 1887, the Cuban Giants became the first black club in organized baseball. They played in O'Rourke's hometown of Bridgeport, Connecticut, for two weeks in the Eastern League, but then pulled up stakes, saying they could make more money barnstorming (National Baseball Hall of Fame Library).

wanted the nation's pastime to mirror their waspish image. No blacks need apply.

The Giants received pressure from Chicago not to hire Stovey. Cap Anson, who was also a part owner of the White Stockings, insisted "There's a law against that."[7] In the past, Anson had refused to allow the White Stockings to play exhibition games against minor league teams with black players.

Probably because of his visibility on the field in these incidents, history has labeled Anson as the man most responsible for the color line. However, Anson's boss, Al Spalding, did not overrule or reprimand his manager. The precedents were allowed to stand.

If this happened today, Spalding's company would be singled out by the media and pressured to change its policy. However, in the 1880s, the baron of baseball was no more autocratic than other captains of industry. The magnates were in charge of the national sport and they decided who worked.

The color line was etched even deeper when the World Champion St. Louis Browns— with the exception of Comiskey and Knouff— refused to play an exhibition game on September 11, 1887, against the all-black Cuban Giants. To his credit, Browns owner Chris Von der Ahe upbraided his mutinous players. Contrast this with Spalding's conspicuous silence in the wake of Anson's repeated outrages to black players.

The New York Giants traveled to Jersey City on October 10, 1887, to play the Cuban Giants.[8] Clearly, the Giants counted their black brethren among the collective definition of "The People."

But it was too late to turn the tide.

17

Orations (1888)

The Cuban Giants exhibited a flair in their patter and physical humor similar to the comic pregame antics of Jim and George Wright during baseball's innocent youth.

O'Rourke maintained his sense of humor throughout his career and his memorable sayings were intended primarily for amusement.

However, he was not hesitant to unsheathe his prodigious vocabulary if he thought it might discombobulate an umpire or an opponent. His arsenal of $10 words and thunderous orations sometimes so befuddled the men in blue that they changed their calls. Then one day Jim met his match in tough-as-nails arbiter Tim Hurst. On a pitch that appeared to Jim to be a ball, umpire Hurst expressed an opposing view:

Strike!

The Orator objected vociferously, postulating on the umpire's ocular deficiencies, to which Hurst calmly replied:

Mr. O'Rourke, I have the most profound respect for you both as a ball player and as a parliamentarian, but I have come to the conclusion that you are altogether too loquaciously disputatious this afternoon, and I shall therefore proceed to say play ball. You lose.[1]

The silenced Orator knocked the next pitch out of the park, then couldn't resist asking:

I suppose that was a strike, too?

To which Hurst responded:

No, James, that was a home run; but the question will cost you five bucks.[2]

The umpire always has the last word.

I think Jim played at words. When asked why the Giants had dropped to fourth place in 1887 from second in 1885, the Orator responded with a politician's vagueness: "We lack the necessary requisite."[3] Herewith, a dictionary of O'Rourke orations, uttered a half century before another Hall of Fame catcher, Yogi Berra, earned renown for one-liners:

- Self-importance: "*Elephantiasis of the skyline.*"[4]
- On the Orioles' having two doctors: "*An allopathic superfluity of medicos.*"[5]
- On manager Gus Schmelz's whiskers: "*A phosphorescent trellis work of agitated hair.*"[6]
- On an umpire's ability to catch a pitcher off the rubber (hunching ground): "*An optical impossibility.*"[7]
- Opposite of heads-up ball playing: "*Ossification of the brainery.*"[8]
- To admit being wrong: "*To bow the pregnant knee of respectful obeisance.*"[9]
- A man of few words: "*An epigrammarian.*"[10]
- Predict a small gate: "*Register a pessimistic forecast.*"[11]

An example of a classic O'Rourkism is the reply given a Chicago reporter when asked why the Giants lost a game to the White Sox:

Unfortunate combination of heterogeneous circumstances compelled us to succumb to the simultaneous and united endeavors of our opponents.[12]

The *New York Telegram* observed: "Catcher O'Rourke relishes a dish of Webster salad with a little dictionary sauce."[13] The most famous example of O'Rourke's dictionary relish is the Gilligan letter that has been oft reprinted. But was he the real author? Here's the story. You decide.

When P. T. Barnum's Bridgeport winter quarters caught fire on November 20, 1887, escaping animals roamed through the surrounding neighborhood and into Mrs. Gilligan's back yard. Hearing a commotion in her barn, she went to investigate and found a lion attacking a calf. She beat it off with a broom, thus inspiring a letter later published in the New York *Sporting Times.* The following excerpt conveys the style and essence of the epistle:

Mrs. Gilligan:

We should extol your bravery to the coming generations in words more lofty than my unprepared efforts can faithfully depict, for your name hereafter will be synonymous with fearlessness in all that the word can unconsciously imply.

Standing before a wild, unrestrained pitcher with a mellifluous and unconquerable courageousness is as of nothing compared with the indomitable fortitude exhibited by you when destruction seemed inevitable — when pandemonium rent the oxygenic atmosphere asunder with the tragic vociferation of Barnum's untamed and inhospitable intruder.

A thousand blessings to you!

Yours admiringly,
James H. O'Rourke[14]

Although Jim's name was appended to the letter, it strikes me as too flowery even for Orator O'Rourke. One might also wonder how the *Sporting*

Times came by a private letter from O'Rourke to a fellow Bridgeport resident.

O'Rourke did not use five-syllable adjectives without a purpose (like confusing umpires). Yes, Jim would occasionally throw out some arcane and Brobdingnagian words, but no more than I have in this sentence. The Gilligan letter is saturated with multi-syllable words.

On another page of the Gilligan letter, Jim defends his own verbosity. Is this something one would do with a perfect stranger? It is written as if directed to a larger audience. The passage in which Jim defends his manner of speech reads:

> The exuberance of my verbosity is as natural as the chrysanthemums exhibited at the late horticultural exhibition, so in reality it cannot be called ostentation, even though the *sesquipedalian* passages may seem unintelligible to the untutored personality.

The passage may contain a clue to the identity of the real author: the obscure word "sesquipedalian" (meaning: characterized by the use of long words), that also appears in the March 1887 spoof "Jim O'Rourke's Return from Yale College" reprinted in a previous chapter. That parody, we know, was written by Charles "Curry" Foley.

Foley, who could wield a pen like a bat, also wrote an early *Ball Four* article for *Sporting Times* in April 1890 that elicited outraged reactions from players:

> "What do you think of that fellow?" asked Dick [Johnson]. "There is a fellow I have often put my hand in my pocket for, and yet I no sooner get in the town before he writes a lot of lies about me."
> "Why that's nothing," said Dan Brouthers, ... "that fellow has roasted every friend he had in the world long ago. All I have to say is that anyone who reads his fakes is worse than he is."[15]

I believe the Gilligan letter was written by Foley. If you're a conspiracy theorist, you may find it interesting that *The Sporting Times* was owned by Albert Goodwill Spalding. It is generally acknowledged that the purpose of the publication was to discredit the Brotherhood and promote the National League party line.

But rather than a clever conspiracy to embarrass a veteran organizer of the rebellion, the Gilligan letter was probably just a prank, a bit more cerebral than shaving cream in the catcher's mitt, but a practical joke nonetheless.

O'Rourkisms were delivered orally. He was, after all, "Orator" O'Rourke. Half the effect was in the delivery and the twinkle in his eye; and according to John Kiernan of the *New York Times*, Jim had "a most pleasant full voice."[16]

Orator O'Rourke might have been successful as an actor. Cap Anson and Mike Kelly found the stage lucrative in the off-season, but probably more for their baseball fame than for their thespian skills.

"TEN THOUSAND EYES WERE ON HIM
AS HE RUBBED HIS HANDS WITH DIRT"

"BUT THERE IS NO JOY IN MUDVILLE—
MIGHTY CASEY HAS STRUCK OUT"

"WHENEVER HOPPER APPEARS
BEFORE THE FOOTLIGHTS"

Davenport sketch. A. G. Spalding, *America's National Game*, 1911.

The New York Giants occasionally invited their adversaries to a Broadway show, a quaint throwback to the time when gentlemen's clubs entertained opponents at sumptuous banquets.

It was at one such theater outing with the White Stockings, on August 14, 1888, that actor DeWolf Hopper first read "Casey at the Bat."[17] Wallack's Theatre on the northeast corner of Broadway and Thirteenth[18] was packed with 3,000 patrons. The urbane ballplayers were ensconced in boxes flanking the gas-lit stage. They were quite the dandies in their tuxedos, top hats, black canes, and white spats.[19] When they heard the surprise ending, they jumped on their seats and cheered,[20] for Hopper had captured baseball's "Glorious Uncertainty."[21]

Hopper made a career of "Casey," performing it over 10,000 times.[22]

On another visit to New York, the White Stockings poked some fun at the Giants' garb. In a lapse of common fashion sense, the Giants adopted daring all-black, tight-fitting outfits for the 1888 season. The Chicagos wore their traditional white flannel uniform, accessorized with black silk ties, silk caps, and formal swallow-tailed coats with white boutonnières. "The spectators looked upon the innovation as a joke and laughed heartily."[23] The next day, the Giants showed they could take a ribbing by adding white linen dusters and white top hats to their uniforms for their grand entrance.[24]

Maybe the new look was "the necessary requisite" to which Jim had alluded. In 1888, the Giants found themselves serious contenders for the pennant.

18

*The Giants Win
the Pennant (1888)*

The 1888 pennant race whipped baseball enthusiasm to a fever pitch, described here by *Leslie's Illustrated:*

> *That furor of enthusiasm which used to draw the old Romans to the Coliseum, eighty thousand at a time, to witness combats of man and beast, the modern Man-hattanese expends upon the baseball game. His arena is the diamond; his coliseum, the Polo Grounds enclosure; his favorite gladiators are the uniformed Giants, who strive in Titanic combats to clutch for New York the silken pennant of the champi-onship in the season's record of games.*
>
> *The democracy of sport could not be better illustrated than in this Polo Grounds multitude, or its counterpart in any of the other cities where the League contests are waged. All creeds, castes and professions are telescoped together on the grand-stand, and representatives of the exclusive four hundred are separated from those of the unselect millions only by a fragile rail. Nobody is too dignified to roar and howl at the unsatisfactory decision of an umpire, or too partial to withhold frantic applause for a home run, no matter to whose score it is added.*
>
> *There is a fascination about the pitching of a "Mickey" Welch, the batting of a "Buck" Ewing, or a Connor, the short-stopping of a Ward, which no man, woman or child, once inoculated with the fever of the game, can possibly resist; and the glory of a winning record hedges round each member of the successful club.*
>
> *Only last week, the President of the United States shook the New York Giants individually by the hand, and wished them the championship; whereupon they went out and "whitewashed" the Washington "Senators" on their own ground.*
>
> *We may be without a national poem or novel, or a distinctively American school of art, but clearly we have a national game.[1]*

The Giants won the pennant in 1888 and went on to capture the Dau-vray Cup. Veteran Jim O'Rourke supported his club defensively as well as offensively, setting a new major league record for outfielders with a .960 fielding average.[2] Jim was aided by fielders' gloves, which were gaining in popularity. According to a claim in the Arthur Irwin catalog, O'Rourke was using their gloves in the outfield at least as early as 1888.[3] These were really

Left: Tim Keefe modeling the Giants tight-fitting all-black uniform for 1888, which were made by his sporting goods firm. I suspect his wife, Clara, and sister-in-law, Helen Dauvray Ward, had a hand in the *avant garde* styling. (Helen designed the costumes for her plays.) The following year the Giants returned to traditional uniforms (engraving: *Harper's Weekly*, October 20, 1888).

Right: The Baseball Furor: A Scene at the New York Grounds. Note the calm of the players in the eye of the storm of fans swirling about them, gripped by the pennant fever epidemic of 1888.

just leather work gloves with the fingers of the right glove cut off to allow for a better grip for throwing.

Jim wore gloves behind the plate even earlier. A note in the *New York Times* of May 15, 1887, offered a reward for the return of his "favorite pair of catcher's gloves" that were stolen from under the players' bench during a game.[4]

But there was only so much a pair of gloves could do to protect the catcher. The gloves were small so the catcher had to cup both hands together to trap the ball. The greater danger was to the throwing hand, that was only partially gloved.

As a catcher Jim received his share of injuries, breaking both hands multiple times. Near the end of his playing days a reporter noted the "bent and twisted fingers" of his right hand and secretly admired these mementoes of the baseball fray.[5]

The catcher's mitt (fingerless glove) first appeared during the 1888 season and quickly replaced the glove behind the plate. The "mattress" was here to stay, and would continue to grow in popularity and size as it took most of the sting out of catching and allowed the ball to be caught with one hand. The throwing hand still needed to be at the ready to make sure the ball did not bounce or fall out of the mitt. Today, with a modern fly-trap glove, a catcher can capture the ball securely with one hand while completely shielding the throwing hand behind his leg.

For every advantage the players received on the field, the owners seemed to devise some new scheme to weaken the players' position at the bargaining table.

The rallying cry of the Giants' fans was, "We are The People." The motto of the owners must have been, "We are the rulers." By 1888, the magnates had established three precedents to affirm their control: the adoption of the reserve clause, the blacklist, and the National Agreement among the leagues to recognize each other's reserve lists and blacklists. Still, the failed attempt to cap salaries was an embarrassment to the magnates' goal of absolute control. But they had a plan to fix that.

After the 1888 season, Albert Goodwill Spalding announced an around-the-world tour of the Chicago White Stockings and an "All-American" nine made up of players from other teams. The mission of the tour was to promote America's national sport. It went without saying that the Spalding company would be only too happy to supply baseball equipment to any country that wanted to adopt the sport.

Spalding recruited Johnny Ward to captain the All-Americans. Ward was a natural choice. He had management experience and spoke five languages. However, Spalding may have had other motives for inviting the union president on an extended tour.

On November 22, 1888, while Brotherhood president Johnny Ward was conveniently out of the country, the league owners announced a ploy to roll back salaries: the classification scheme.[6]

A report of the November interleague Committee on Playing Rules read:

The Committee whose actions were so closely watched was composed of Messrs. Rogers, Day and Spalding for the League, and Byrne, Barnie and

Schmelz for the Association. The committee went into secret session at 11 o'clock A.M., and were in continuous session until far into the night.[7]

It is hard for me to believe these high-powered men spent a whole day debating rule changes. Although Spalding is mentioned as being present in New York, he was at this time on the *Alameda*, two days out of San Francisco.[8] Of course, as a member of the joint rules committee, he may have been aware of proposals that were to be presented by fellow National League magnates John Rogers and John Day at the "secret session."

Ward did not learn about the scheme until he read about it in an American newspaper in Egypt. When Ward confronted Spalding with the report, the later claimed ignorance of the new plan to cap salaries; and, according to Ward, said it was as a "dangerous experiment."[9]

However, Chicago second baseman Fred Pfeffer — who was also on the tour — said, "Spalding knew all about the classification while on the trip around the world." Pfeffer was a minority owner of the White Stockings and had inside knowledge. As Pfeffer explained, "As a stockholder in the Chicago Club, Spalding often talked schemes with me."[10]

Ward arrived home on March 23, 1889,[11] He had left the tour early, giving the excuse of an emergency back home.[12] This would prove to be an understatement.

A "system of graded salaries" was being urged upon the magnates by *Sporting Life* as early as 1883 and 1884 — as a *substitute* for the reserve clause — that included "an extra sum to be given to each player on the score of good conduct off the field."[13] The influential Cincinnati sportswriter O. P. Caylor suggested a low of $1,000 and a high of $,2500; not far from the $1,500–$2,500 range adopted four years later.[14]

President Howe of the Cleveland club first proposed a plan to limit salaries at the National League meeting at the end of the 1882 season.[15] Two years later, an article in *Sporting Life* presented a comprehensive argument by F. N. Brunell, the Cleveland scorer, for salary limits, including the often-overlooked problem for the smaller cities, that even with the reserve clause, they had to bid for rookies, and the prices they were forced to pay were "ruinous." Brunell predicted in 1884 that a classing of players in some manner "will be adopted by the League within two years."[16]

In 1888, the owners chorused the now-familiar refrain that the exorbitant salaries paid to athletes were ruining the sport.

The Brotherhood fired back that if a club could not pay big-league salaries, it should transfer to a minor league rather than reduce the income of all major league players.[17] The union also countered that if the big cities really were concerned about their smaller brethren, they could split the gate receipts 50–50.[18] By giving the home team the lion's share of the gate, the clubs in the larger cities became richer, adding to their economic advantage over teams in smaller cities. The union had resurrected an issue that had bothered baseball since the dawn of the professional era.

During the early 1870s, the formative years of professional baseball, the admission rate and the split of the gate was negotiated between the individual teams. Harry Wright usually offered 40 percent of the gate to the visitor, and expected the same share when his team was on the road. In a letter to Nick Young, manager of the Washington Senators, at the start of the 1872 season, Wright suggested the visitor's share be reduced to 33 percent of the gate.[19]

In 1877, the National League, at its first annual meeting, on December 7, 1876, "The visiting clubs in games were voted fifteen cents for each admission to a game."[20] This is equal to 30 percent of a 50-cent tariff.

In 1878, the visiting team's share of the gate receipts was reduced to 25 percent.[21]

For most of the early 1880s, the visitor share was 30 percent.[22] A surviving 1883 receipt shows how the visitor's share was computed[23]:

1,517	Through turnstile at $.15	$ 227.55
622	Through other gates $.05	$ 31.10
2,139	Total	$ 258.65

"Other gates" indicates the large number of freebies wheedled from the Detroit owners by the press, politicians, and parasites. The nickel payment to the Giants may have been a negotiated amount, as it was penciled in on the form.

In 1886, the visitors' share in the National League was changed to a flat rate of $125. For 1887, the rate was increased to $150, or 25 percent, whichever was greater.[24]

The specifics of the classification scheme read as follows:

The compensation for all league players ... shall be regulated and determined by the classification of grade to which such players may be assigned by the secretary of the league after the termination of the championship season as follows:

class	A,	compensation	$2,500
class	B,	compensation	$2,250
class	C,	compensation	$2,000
class	D,	compensation	$1,750
class	E,	compensation	$1,500

Class A being the maximum, and E minimum. In determining such assignments the batting, fielding, base running, battery work, earnest team work, and exemplary conduct on and off the field will be the basis for classification.[25]

It was clear that this time the owners were serious about enforcing the salary ceiling. An additional provision stipulated that:

Each player upon executing a League contract shall make affidavit in form prescribed by the secretary of the League to the effect that the consideration prescribed in said contract includes all salaries, bonuses, rewards, gifts and
emoluments and every other form of compensation expressly or impliedly
promised him for his services as player during the term of such contract, and ...
any false statement ... shall blacklist him.[26]

Translation: no side deals to skirt the salary limit. The old league rule
to cap salaries at $2,000 was ineffectual because owners were willing to make
supplemental deals outside the playing contract to obtain a star performer.
For example, in 1887, Mike Kelly received $5,000 from Boston. To circum-
vent the salary cap, Mike's contract called for a $2,000 salary plus a $3,000
license fee for the use of his picture.[27]

For the 1887 season, the Brotherhood had agreed to the spelling out of
the reserve clause in the player contract.[28] As you will recall, the clause was
originally part of the National Agreement, a contract among teams and
leagues. In return for acknowledging the reserve system by the union, the
owners agreed to consider lifting the salary cap and promised not to arbi-
trarily cut the salary of any reserved player when signing him for another
season. (If a player *was* offered a lower salary, he had the option of accepting the offer or becoming a free agent.)[29]

The classification scheme violated the agreement not to reduce the salary
of any reserved player when renewing contracts.[30]

Although the agreement referred to "reserved players," these provisions
applied to virtually all major leaguers, since the reserve clause had been
extended to additional players. From the original five at the end of the 1879
season to:

- 11 players per team in 1883,
- 12 in 1886, and
- 14 in 1887 (a typical roster at the time).

To the credit of the owners, when the reserve was extended in 1883 to
what was then the usual number of players on a team, a $1,000 minimum
salary was also established as a "safeguard" to the players.[31] Nevertheless, the
classification scheme pushed the players too far. Each year the magnates had
been tightening the yoke about the players, squeezing every dime in revenue
from their brief careers as athletes, and then discarding them when they
became sick or injured or old.

Even more degrading to the players was the taking of their freedom by
the blacklist and reserve, and being bought and sold "like so many sheep."[32]

Moreover, the classification scheme, with its rating of off-field conduct,
treated the players like children. They were told when to go to bed, and how
to eat and dress. They were tailed by Pinkertons and fined for missing a bed

The Giants New Home for 1889. A New York politician did not feel he received enough free passes to ball games, so he decided to build a new road through the middle of the Polo Grounds. Since you can't fight Tammany Hall, the Giants began building a new park farther north at 155th Street and 8th Avenue, but it was not ready for the start of the 1889 season. So for over two months, the Giants played their home games at an outdoor theater at St. George, Staten Island, with spectacular views of New York Harbor and the construction of the Statue of Liberty. The park featured baseball and lacrosse in the afternoon, and concerts and illuminated geysers in the evening (engraving: *Harper's Weekly,* May 15, 1886).

check, drinking when off duty, or, as in one case, eating pie with a spoon. It was too much to swallow for grown workingmen whose fathers had enjoyed a large degree of autonomy as farmers and craftsmen in pre-industrial America.

The storm was about to break. It may have been triggered by the classification scheme, but it had been brewing for years.

O'Rourke was a veteran of many a baseball skirmish. At the end of the 1888 season, he was one of only seven original members of the National League still active since its founding 13 years earlier. The other six were Cap Anson, Paul Hines, Deacon White, John Burdock, John Morrill and Ezra Sutton.

Jim was invigorated by the impending battle. On May 8, 1889, *Sporting Life* said he was "bathed in the waters of youth." President Day of the Giants was buoyed by O'Rourkes "hard hitting."

19

The Baseball War (1889)

"It was the irrepressible conflict between labor and capital."[1]
— Albert Goodwill Spalding

On May 19, 1889, union reps from all eight National League teams met in New York to decide how to respond to the classification scheme. For the first time, the players were organized. Nearly every eligible member of the National League had joined the Brotherhood.[2] The players debated striking, but "cooler heads" prevailed. They would first attempt a peaceful settlement through negotiations with the owners.

Twice in June of 1889, they tried to meet with National League representatives,[3] but Spalding obstinately refused to negotiate or even meet with the union during the spring and summer of 1889.[4] Years later, Giants' pitcher Tim Keefe recalled Spalding's intransigence as "The crowning point to the arrogant despotism of these dictators" and added that in response, "the players revolted at this contemptuous disregard of their rights as men and laborers."[5]

Spalding was stalling. He wanted to wait until the regular annual meeting of the league in November to meet with the union reps.[6] But the Brotherhood leadership knew the union would be at a disadvantage in the postseason against the owners, huddled in one hotel room, while they were scattered about the country engaged in their winter pursuits.

After being repeatedly snubbed by Spalding, Brotherhood representatives from each of the teams met again on the centennial of the French Revolution, July 14, 1889, at the Fifth Avenue Hotel in New York, and voted to form the Players' League.[7]

Spalding probably got wind of the meeting, for he chose July 14 to finally offer a compromise. He was clearly worried. Spalding suggested that players who led exemplary lives and had played for at least three years in the majors would *not* be classified. Spalding also offered to share a fourth of sales proceeds with the transferred players.[8]

At its annual meeting in November, the National League went even further by amending its rules to allow a player to negotiate his own sale, with a club of his choosing, provided the releasing club accepts the negotiated compensation for its loss. According to Spalding, "This action does away with the system of sales, over which there has been such an outcry by the seceding players and their organs." In an even more desperate attempt to regain players and favorable public opinion, the new sections relating to classification were stricken from the National League constitution.[9]

Although Spalding's efforts toward compromise offered more than token concessions, the players were wary of promises. Previous regulations protecting players had been ignored by the owners. Besides, the iron was hot.

During the next two weeks, Brotherhood leaders met secretly with players and investors. The plan was to organize teams in each National League city. That way, players and fans could defect *en masse*. Needless to say, there would be no reserve clause or salary cap in the Players' League. However, to provide stable team rosters "absolute one-year contracts with privilege of renewal for two years were substituted" for the reserve.[10]

To maintain secrecy, the players developed a code for their war traffic over the public telegraph system. The magnates were animals. (Spalding was "Fox"). Individual players were inanimate objects (chair, table, etc.). Historian Bryan Di Salvatore mused "It must have been thrilling, this subterfuge."[11]

First, the secessionists needed to raise money for grounds and salaries. The rebels realized they needed the support of capitalists, but the players and investors would manage the league together and share the profits. "Each [Brotherhood] representative was asked to check the feasibility of securing capital in his own city.... The results were all encouraging."[12] Actually, baseball had never been more profitable: the New York Giants and Mets had earned $750,000 in 10 years for their owners.[13] As Ward later revealed:

> Men were found willing to advance the money to start a new league.... Many [investors] were even willing to put in the capital without any return whatever, out of love for the sport and a desire to see it placed on a plane above that upon which it was being operated. The feature of the old system specially repugnant to all was that which permitted one set of men to trade on the future services of another, and denied to the latter any right to make a free contract. A fundamental principle of the new League is therefore that no player shall be transferred from one club to any other without his consent and never for any monetary consideration. Neither shall he be held in any perpetual bondage, but at the end of this term of contract, whether that be for one year, two or 10, he shall be at liberty to dispose of his own services as he chooses.[14]

The players were also asked to participate in the capitalization of the new clubs. *Sporting Life* described the game plan:

> The brotherhood has appointed a committee of four players for each city. These players have the right to dispose of the stock of their respective clubs to the amount of $20,000, 200 shares at $100 each. They can subscribe the entire amount themselves if they so desire, but in any event they are to hold a controlling interest.[15]

Each player was expected to invest at least $500, a significant sum in 1889. Ward alone invested $3,800 in the Brooklyn club. In New York, Ward, Keefe, and catcher Buck Ewing owned $9,500 of the $20,000 stock of the Players' League Giants.[16] At a meeting of the directors of the Brotherhood Giants Jim O'Rourke and Roger Connor "promptly made good for their shares of capital stock in hard cash."[17]

In Chicago, Fred Pfeffer, White Stockings second baseman and Players' League organizer, also invested heavily.[18] Pfeffer ran a popular and profitable restaurant in the Windy City.

Former Buffalo players under O'Rourke, Jack Rowe and Deacon White, had purchased the Bisons in 1889. For the 1890 season, they moved the organization, lock, stock and bat rack into the Players' League. They quickly raised their $20,000 capital quota, each personally contributing $1,000. Connie Mack threw his lot in with White and Rowe, purchasing $500 of the Bison stock,[19] which represented his life savings.[20] In 1889 he earned $2,750.[21] The lease on Jim's Olympic grounds in Buffalo had expired, so Jack and Deacon had to dismantle and haul Jim's old grandstand and fences to a new location at Michigan, near Ferry Street.[22]

Albert Goodwill Spalding in 1889. Spalding was never president of the National League, but he was in control of the national sport, as powerful a force in 19th-century baseball as Kenesaw Mountain Landis would be in the twentieth century.

William Hulbert, the first National League president (1877–1882) was succeeded by A. G. Mills (1883–1884) and Nick Young (1885–1901), but it was with Spalding that the union leaders conferred. And it was Spalding who commanded the strategy and resources of the National League magnates during the Baseball War (engraving: *Athletic Sports*, 1889).

In Pittsburgh, John Tenor and Ned Hanlon stepped up to the plate to purchase stock in the Players' League club slated for Steeltown.[23]

In Boston, Big Dan Brouthers was a major investor[24] and manager Mike Kelly "plunked down $500 in payment for his stock."[25] Kelly, who never had two dimes to rub together, borrowed his $500 ante from his old boss, Al Spalding. I wonder if Spalding knew what the money was for.

After raising financial backing, the players next needed to line up ball-parks. In New York, the Brotherhood leased land for $4,000 from James Coogan, who also leased the land occupied by the National League park. The Brotherhood grounds, located just north of the National League's park, still needed grading, stands, and fencing.[26] The *Clipper* provides additional details:

On Jan. 13 [1890] workmen began work on the grounds of the New York Club, of the Players' League, in this city. They are situated at Eighth Avenue, between One Hundred and Fifty-seventh and One Hundred and Fifty-ninth Streets, extending from the avenue line back to the bluff, a distance of 800 feet. The grand stand will be situated under the high bluff west of the grounds and the men will bat toward Eighth Avenue. The grounds will be very large, and there will be plenty of room inside the inclosure [*sic*] for all necessary purposes. When finished, there is no doubt whatever, they will be among the finest grounds in the country.[27]

Sporting Life added more details:

Plans were filed Feb. 4 [1890] in the Building Department in New York City for the proposed improvements of the new Players' League grounds on Eighth avenue, between 157th and 159th streets. The contract for the grand stand and other buildings has been awarded to Geo. W. Cram for $15,000. He is also the contractor for the big fence which is to enclose the grounds. Work will begin immediately on the grand stand, which is to be built first, and it is expected that it will be finished by April 1. It is planned to make that the best structure of the kind in the country. Special pains have been taken by Architect D. W. King to make it a model as regards comfort and security and for the purpose of observation. It will be two stories high, substantially built and easy of access."[28]

In similar fashion, ballparks began to take shape in each of the Players' League cities. Organizers in Chicago obtained an option on a lot on the cable car and steam train lines. The *Clipper* reported in January 1890:

The grounds secured by the Chicago Club, of the players' League, are said to be located at Thirty-third Street and Wentworth Avenue, Chicago, and are not far from the old grounds of the Chicago Club of the National League. There will be plenty of room for the players and work will at once be begun upon the grounds. The grand stand and free stands, fences, etc., will be built and other improvements made. The new grounds are accessible, being on the line of the cable cars and the steam roads, and have been leased for a long term.[29]

In February, *Sporting Life* added:

The Game in 1889. In this rare action photograph taken in Philadelphia, we can see the ball and runner racing each other to second as the sole umpire darts up the first base line for an unobstructed vantage (engraving: *Athletic Sports*, 1889, p. 147).

Work has already been commenced on the new base ball park of the Chicago Players' Club. The diamond will be so arranged that the clubs will bat toward the north. An elegant club house will be erected for the players. It will be fitted up in the latest improved style and will be supplied with hot and cold shower baths. Quarters will be reserved for the visiting clubs and all arrangements made to properly entertain them. There will be no open stands. All will be properly covered to protect the audience from the sun and inclement weather. This means the abolition of the "bleachers." It is expected that the grounds will be completed April 1 and that the improvements will cost $20,000.[30]

A week later, the *Chicago Daily Tribune* provided some insights into the fine points of building a first-class ballpark:

The contract for the laying out of the Players' League grounds, at Thirty-fifth street and Wentworth avenue, was let Monday to Contractor Reynolds. A grand stand seating 4,000 will be put up on the Thirty-third street side and will be filled with opera chairs. The bleaching boards are to be roofed in a substantial way, and will bring the total seating capacity up to 7,000. In the field, which will be made under the supervision of Billy Huston, a thorough system of drainage, coupled with firmness of ground, will be sought for. The diamond will be sodded, and also the outfield points, the rest of the ground being sown with lawn grass. Everything is to be in readiness April 1, and the contract price is $25,000.[31]

To accommodate Boston's entry in the Players' League, an existing park on Congress Street was rented. The grounds had been used by the Boston club of the ill-fated Union Association of 1884.[32] In February of 1890, *Sporting Life* reported:

Work on the grounds of the Boston Players' League Club is progressing rapidly and satisfactorily, and contractor Manning says that if it is necessary he can have them in playing condition by March 10. Architects are busily engaged on plans for the grand stand, which will be submitted during the week. The club gave out a contract on Tuesday last for several thousand opera chairs for their pavilion to the Harwood Manufacturing Company. The New England Railroad decided at a meeting Feb. 6 to build a station close to the new grounds and run trains every five minutes through South Boston and the suburbs as far as Hyde Park for one fare of five cents."[33]

The grandstand was to be an elaborate double-deck affair with pavilions atop two seventy-five foot towers that would allow fans a panoramic view of Boston Harbor. With bleachers, the park could accommodate 16,000 fans.[34] The field was conveniently located on the New York, New Haven, and Hartford rail line that ran along the northeast border of the park.

In Brooklyn, Brotherhood backers put money down on property near the Grand Concourse.

Philadelphia-based *Sporting Life* reported on activity in the City of Brotherly Love:

The contract for the improvement of the Philadelphia Players' Club grounds has been given out, and on Monday next 140 carpenters will start on the erection of the new grand stand, open field seats, fences, etc. The contractor agrees to have the job completed by April 1st. He is under bonds to carry out his part of the agreement, and will forfeit $100 for each day work has to be carried on beyond that time to complete the job. The entire lot, which is 568 by 520 feet, is a level plot of ground, and will make one of the finest grounds in the country. The distance from the home plate to the center field fence will be 612 feet.... The grand stand will be erected at the corner of Broad and York streets, and will gave a seating capacity for 600 people, about 500 on the lower tier, 750 on the upper tier, and 250 in the private boxes. The open seats will accommodate, so the building committee claims, nearly 10,000 more people. There will be 24 private boxes, including the press box, which will be located in the center directly back of the home plate. Improved opera chairs have been contracted for, and no others will used in the pavilion."[35]

In St. Louis,

A. L. Spink, editor of the *Sporting News*, to-day closed a contract for the lease of the Amateur Baseball park for a period of two years, and improvements to the amount of $10,000 are to be made on it at once. The name of the park is to be changed. It is to be known as Brotherhood Park.[36]

As Ward, O'Rourke, and other leaders traveled with the Giants during the 1889 season, they secretly conferred with players in other towns. Combatants by day, they were allies by night as they planned their *coup* by lamplight in hotels guarded by sympathetic policemen.

"The secret was so well guarded that ... there was no word of suspicion uttered to warn the club-owners."[37] Word did not leak to the press until September 1889.[38] Even then, the National League owners thought it all just a charade to coerce higher salaries for the following season.[39] Giants owner John Day was so confident in the loyalty of his players and the prospects for the National League that he turned down a $200,000 offer for his club.[40]

Even some of the players thought the proposed Players' League was just a ruse. Supporting the bluff theory was an article in the *Chicago Tribune* of September 10, 1889:

> Two years ago a similar project was talked of in Brotherhood quarters. John Ward was behind it.... It was a "bluff" at the League magnates and brought to the players some concessions in the way of modification of a cast-iron and unfair contract. Since then, a new necessity for a new "bluff" has arisen. The classification law, which aims at ultimate reduction of all salaries to $2,500 per season and less, has been at work for a season.[41]

Indeed, the idea for the Players' League may have begun as bravado and a ploy to roll back the salary cap, but the new league had begun to take on a life of its own.

To affirm that the Players' League was a serious endeavor, the Brotherhood called a press conference on September 22, 1889.[42] Seven writers were present, including Tim Murnane, now writing for the *Boston Globe*; Al Spink, editor of *The Sporting News*; and Frank Richter, editor of *Sporting Life*.

Although Murnane, Spink, and Richter were sympathetic to the Brotherhood's cause,[43] the players did not entirely trust the press to deliver its story to the public. Team owners signed advertising contracts[44] and the big-city dailies were known for their anti-labor position.[45] So the players took their story directly to the fans. The Elks Clubs—of which O'Rourke was a member—was one venue used to reach fans directly. Jim declaimed in his grandiloquent style: "Our ascension from thralldom is positive, uncoupled from all doubts, notwithstanding the warning of the master magnates and the snapping of their whip."[46]

Jim also took on the National League through the media. After Spalding fined player Charlie Bastion $125, because Anson reported he was intoxicated on a Chicago streetcar, Jim fired off a blistering letter to the sporting press:

With all the peculiar hoggishness and avarice which characterizes the very existence of the organization, it proceeded in its might to rob this innocent player of the balance of his year's salary upon the bold and false accusation of a creature [Cap Anson] whose intolerable brutality to players makes him shunned by the reputable element in professionalism, and upon the assumption that he was a poor defenseless ball player without courage to enforce his legal rights against this would-be king of the base ball trust.[47]

While an attempt to beat the owners at their own game may appear to have been a brash undertaking, the players did have capable generals. As already noted, Chicago's Fred Pfeffer was a successful restaurateur. Tim Keefe hired away long-time Spalding employee W. H. Becannon to join him in a new sporting goods emporium in New York City.[48] *Sporting Life* likened Tim to another player turned sports entrepreneur:

As Spalding ... grew up with the National League, so the enterprising young firm of Keefe & Becannon, scarcely a year old, is growing up with the Players' League. The Keefe ball, which is to be the official ball ... is also sure to make a hit and add to the already excellent reputation of this great young firm."[49]

Moreover, Ward and O'Rourke had law degrees and the bold move of forming their own league required confidence by the players that they could defend themselves in the courts. Indeed, Spalding leaked a story to the *New York Times* in which he named O'Rourke as one of the "ringleaders" of the players' movement.[50] These old friends and former teammates when both were young now found themselves on opposite sides of the war.

The magnates had met their match. Most importantly, the fans were with the players. No longer was the struggle just about baseball. This workers' revolt had implications far beyond the boundaries of the ballpark. In the Brotherhood model, owners and workers shared the power and the wealth. In 1889, this was a radical idea, and it was being promoted by men familiar to every worker in America.

Industrialist Albert Goodwill Spalding could not allow such dangerous ideas to survive.

First, he attacked the players where they were most vulnerable: in their wallets:

Word comes by way of St. Louis that Spalding will discharge his entire team October 15, so as to save two week's salary, for he is convinced that the players intend to put a rival league into the field.[51]

In an effort to intimidate the Players' League financiers, the National League announced it would cut attendance prices to bankrupt the new league.[52] Spalding and the other owners were prepared to lose millions to crush the workers' revolt.

Next, the National League ordered every player to report on October 21, 1889, to sign a contract for the following season, or be barred from baseball

Left: Charlie Comiskey, manager of the St. Louis Browns from 1883 through 1889 (engraving: *Harper's Weekly,* October 27, 1888). *Right: Cornelius McGillicuddy.* Connie used to slip a frozen ball into play that victims said was like hitting a croquet ball. By all appearances, the ball was normal. By the time anyone grew suspicious and asked to inspect the ball the surface temperature was normal. It was the opposite of O'Rourke's rabbit ball. The two catchers were lifelong friends (1887 Goodwin card).

for life. Only one player showed up to sign: Cap Anson. (Spalding promised minority shareholder Anson that he could one day buy controlling interest in the White Stockings — a promise Spalding would never honor.) Also, Cap had signed a five-year contract in 1888, so he was legally bound to the White Stockings anyway.[53]

Anson revealed Spalding's next legal maneuver by taunting the strikers:

Brotherhood clubs would be in a pretty bad box, if, with grounds all ready for the playing of their first scheduled games, the courts would issue an injunction in favor of the League clubs.[54]

The Brotherhood, too, went on the offensive, grabbing up many of the National League's star attractions, like young Connie Mack.

Mack and O'Rourke had a lot in common. Both were catchers, both were involved in the player revolt, and both would own and manage teams after their playing days. Connie enjoyed a record 64 years in major league baseball as a player and manager.

Another coup for the Players' League was the signing of Charlie Comiskey,[55] the player-manager of the St. Louis Browns. Commy was anxious to get out from under the reserve clause: "America is a free country," he said, "and after a man has lived up to his contract for a season ... he ought to be allowed to go where he can do the best."[56]

Commy wanted to return to his hometown, so he was appointed to manage the Chicago Players' League team.

20

The World's Series (1889)

In the midst of all their organizing, the New York Giants found time to win the National League championship.[1]

It was Jim's eighth pennant. Since the inauguration of the major leagues in 1871, O'Rourke had played for more championship teams than any other player. Second was George Wright, with seven. Deacon White, Andy Leonard, and Cap Anson each had six pennants to their credit.[2]

For the National League pennant presentation, the Giants' vaudeville friends held a gala benefit on the evening of October 20, 1889. The Broadway Theatre was packed with 3,000 cheering fans. According to the *New York Times*: "Hundreds of people were turned away, and outside the building, both on Broadway and forty-first Street, there was such a jam that the police had to interfere to make a passage way [on] the sidewalks." [3]

Approximately $6,000 was raised that evening from admission fees and souvenir sales. The proceeds were divided among the players for bringing the pennant and pride to New York City.

Over 22 acts appeared, including DeWolf Hopper reading "Casey at the Bat." For the finale, the team members were called up to the stage as a sign was lowered that read "We are The People."[4] Like one great wave, the entire audience rose and gave the Giants a cheer that rocked them back. The Giants' slogan had struck a responsive chord with the fans. The people found vicarious glory in their summer heroes from factory neighborhoods, lifted now from gray streets to fields of green.[5]

Then the signed slipped, almost hitting some of the players.

Two days after the benefit, the National League New York Giants entered the World's Series against the American Association Trolley Dodgers. (The team earned its nickname from all the trolley lines that crisscrossed the city, especially in the area of the Brooklyn ballpark, where several systems converged.)[6]

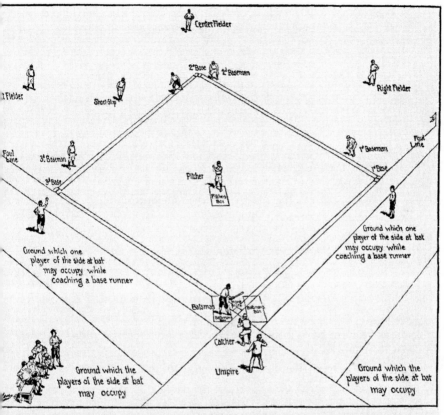

THE FIELD.

The Diamond in 1889. Two years previously, the pitchers' box was cut down to 4 feet wide by 5.5 feet deep. The pitcher had to keep one foot in contact with the rear line of the box, and could take only one step in delivering the ball.

The coaches' boxes were also added in 1887. Although intended to restrict coaches to a prescribed area, their large size created problems, both accidental and intentional (engraving: *Century Magazine,* October, 1889, p. 833).

This would be the first series between New York and Brooklyn. Since the subway hadn't been built yet, fans shuttled back and forth across the six-year-old Brooklyn Bridge.

GAME ONE: The first game of the 1889 World Series was played on Friday, October 18, at Manhattan Field. The stands were crowded with 8,455 fans who

shouted, cheered, hissed, yelled, stamped their feet, clapped their hands, and acted as only baseball "cranks" can. Every minute point of the game was watched with eager eyes, and no play worthy of applause went by unnoticed. In fact, every play, commonplace or otherwise, was cheered to the echo, and the contestants could not complain of lack of enthusiasm. If anything, there was too much, and at times the coachers made themselves heard only with difficulty.[7]

After seven innings, the scoreboard showed New York ahead of Brooklyn, 10–8. The few remaining fans were shivering and the October sky was darkening. No matter, seven innings were enough for the game to count. The Giants began to put on their jackets and shove bats into bags. However, the umpire was not disposed to call the game just yet, and the players were told to go back onto the field. The Giants objected vigorously. Buck Ewing pointed out that the electric lights were already on in the elevated trains. But to no avail.

By the time the Dodgers came to bat in the bottom of the eighth, it was so dark you couldn't read the Spalding ad on the outfield fence. In the waning light, easy outs rolled past infielders or dropped next to startled outfielders for hits, and the Dodgers pulled ahead.

Then the Dodgers began to curse the darkness. In the strangest World's Series game ever played, Brooklyn became desperate to make a third out quickly, and New York was determined to stretch the inning out as long as possible. If the umpire called the game because of darkness before the end of the inning, the score would revert to the end of the last complete inning — when the *Giants* were ahead.

All of a sudden, Tim Keefe had trouble finding the strike zone. But the

The Giants' Second Ballpark, Manhattan Field, on the east side of the island, between 155th and 157th Streets at Eighth Avenue. This view is looking toward the northeast. The park was opened on July 8, 1889 (engraving: *Leslie's Illustrated*, July 27, 1889).

Dodgers soon had the book on Keefe and started swinging at his wild pitches. When "Strike three!" was called on the final batter, the umpire ended the game on account of darkness, with Brooklyn the winner.[8]

GAME TWO (Saturday, October 19): The Giants won to tie the series.

GAME THREE (Tuesday, October 22): The Dodgers jumped out to an early lead, but O'Rourke brought the Giants to within one on a three-run homer. But, again, the Dodgers stalled until it was too dark to continue. This was the second game the Dodgers won by questionable methods. However, the Giants would get even.

GAME FOUR (Wednesday, October 23): In near-freezing weather, the umpire again kept the game going after dark. "Then Burns hit a fly that O'Rourke was unable to see on account of the darkness. Before the ball could be found Smith, Collins, and Burns had scored and the Giants were beaten again."[9] Although the Giants were charged with 10 errors during the game, none were credited to Jim. The official scorer knew it was too dark to see the last hits of the game.[10]

The umpire had a more difficult

CLARK, C., Washington
COPYRIGHT BY GOODWIN & CO., 1889.

Fielder's Glove, 1889. In the late 1880s, gloves became larger to allow for padding around the fingers and thicker cushioning for the palm (1889 Goodwin card).

judgment call. O'Rourke was coaching at third when Ward had a chance to score from second on a deep hit to left. Jim ran alongside Johnny after he rounded third, shouting encouragement. The throw in from left hit Jim in the back. After a half hour of deliberations, the umpire eventually ruled that Ward would have been safe had the ball not been blocked, and therefore the run counted.[11]

A less innocent form of interference was invented by St. Louis Browns manager Charlie Comiskey, who noticed that the lines allowed coaches access to the home plate area. Commy stood right next to the visiting catcher to supply him with an analysis of his ancestry. Because of Commy, coaches' boxes are now much smaller and well away from the plate.[12]

Following a Game. On newspaper row in Manhattan, newsies and fans watch the play-by-play as updates arrive from the ballpark by telegraph (engraving: *Leslie's Illustrated*, July 27, 1889).

The Giants were now down 3 games to 1. For the remaining games of the World Series, the umpires agreed to an earlier start time so that darkness would no longer be a factor.

GAMES FIVE AND SIX (October 24–25): Both games were won by the Giants to tie the series at three games apiece. When Johnny Ward scored the winning run in the 11th inning of game six, the fans' "corked-up enthusiasm knew no bounds, and they shouted as only metropolitan 'cranks' can. Hats, canes, and umbrellas were thrown in the air; old men, young men, middle-aged men, and small boys slapped each other on the back, and a feeling of joy pervaded the atmosphere."[13]

GAME SEVEN (Saturday, October 26): This one made history.[14] O'Rourke led off the record-breaking second inning with a double. This started a rally, allowing Jim to come up a second time in the inning. O'Rourke then broke two records by lining a drive over the center field fence. The *New York Times* said it was probably the longest home run at the Giants' stadium "as it cleared the fence by at least thirty feet."[15] The home run also capped the highest-scoring inning of a World's Series: eight runs, two of which were tallied by Jim. "The spectators cheered vociferously."[16]

But the Dodgers rallied, narrowing the Giants' lead to four runs. Worse, they filled the bases with Trolley Dodgers.

Then it happened. Germany Smith lined a shot over Jim's head and over the fence. It was freezing cold and the outfield stands were empty of fair-weather fans. Jim watched the ball bang around the wooden bleachers with a hollow sound that matched the feeling in his stomach. Every ballplayer knows the frustration he felt as he watched the runners round the bases. His chance to drink of the Dauvray Cup was slipping away.

He couldn't just stand there, watching the Dodgers' victory parade. He ran to the fence, clamored over it, retrieved the ball, and hurled it back onto the field. Johnny Ward at short saw what Jim was up to and moved into position to take the throw. Ward relayed the ball to Giants catcher Buck Ewing who held it up to the startled Smith as he loped into home.

"Out!" said the umpire.

"Out?" said a thousand Brooklynites. The entire Dodger bench protested the call. Although there were two umpires, Lynch and Gaffney, neither saw the ball go over the fence. They said they were busy watching the runners, who were known to cut corners. But O'Rourke knew the real reason: the umps couldn't see the fence in the dark! The call stood. The Giants won the game and went on to capture the Dauvray Cup.

Although O'Rourke hit .389 in the 1889 World Series, the 37-year- old may have already been contemplating plans for a career after baseball. During the series, *Sporting Life* noted that: "Counselor O'Rourke has legislative aspirations which may some day be gratified, as Sir James has something of a political pull in the Connecticut district in which he resides."[17]

1889 World Series — Game 7

Brooklyn	A.B.	Runs	1b.	S.H.	S.B.	P.O.	A.	E.
O'Brien, lf	4	1	0	0	1	3	0	0
Collins, 2b	4	1	1	0	0	3	1	0
Burns, rf	2	2	0	1	0	0	0	0
Foutz, 1b	4	2	2	0	0	8	0	0
Pinkney, 3b	4	0	1	0	0	3	1	1
Corkhill, cf	3	1	0	0	0	4	0	0
Smith, ss	4	0	1	1	0	1	3	1
Bushong, c	4	0	0	0	0	2	2	0
Lovett, p	1	0	0	0	0	0	1	0
Caruthers, p	2	0	0	0	0	0	1	0
Total	32	7	5	2	1	24	9	2

New York	A.B.	Runs	1b.	S.H.	S.B.	P.O.	A.	E.
Slattery, cf	4	2	0	1	0	3	0	0
Tiernan, rf	4	2	2	1	1	1	0	0
Ewing, c	5	1	3	0	0	4	2	0
Ward, ss	5	0	1	1	0	4	3	1
Conner, 1b	4	1	2	0	1	14	0	1
Richardson, 2b	5	1	2	0	0	1	4	0
O'Rourke, lf	5	2	2	0	0	0	1	0
Whitney, 3b	4	1	2	0	0	0	2	0
Crane, p	2	1	0	0	0	0	1	1
Keefe, p	1	0	1	0	0	0	2	0
Total	39	11	15	3	2	27	15	3

Runs Scored Each Inning

Brooklyn	0	0	4	0	3	0	0	0	0	–	7
New York	1	8	0	0	0	1	1	0	X	–	11

Earned runs—Brooklyn, 1; New York, 7; First base on errors—Brooklyn, 1; New York, 3. Left on bases—Brooklyn, 9, New York, 8; Base on balls—off Lovett, 1; off Caruthers, 1; off Crane, 9; off Keefe, 2. Struck out—by Lovett, 1, by Caruthers, 1; by Crane, 0; by Keefe, 2. Home runs—Richardson, O'Rourke. Three-base hit—Smith. Two-base hits—Conner, O'Rourke, Whitney, Keefe. Sacrifice hits—Burns, Smith, Slattery, Ward, Tiernan. Hit by pitcher—Connor. Passed ball—Ewing. Umpires—Messrs. Lynch and Gaffney.[18]

The morning after they won the 1889 World Series, the Giants went to see owner John Day, who, over the years had shown them fairness and kindness, and who they were soon to abandon for a league of their own. They told Day they had no grievance against him personally, but that they were all planning to support the Players' League.

Day still could not believe the league would split in two. He took the players out to Barier's Casino for a sumptuous lunch, music, and an abundance of wine; and informed the players that their share of the World Series came to $380 each.[19] This would be the last cordial meeting between players and owners.

21

Players' League Giants (1890)

"I am for War without quarter."[1]
— Albert Goodwill Spalding

Following the World Series and the expiration of the 1889 player contracts on October 31, the Brotherhood players formally broke from the
National League and issued a statement to their fans. The *New York Times*
carried the story of a meeting held on November 4, 1889, to establish the
new league:

BASEBALL WAR DECLARED
The Players Have Deserted the League
THEY PAY NO ATTENTION TO THE LEGAL OPINION
SECURED BY THE LEAGUE MAGNATES

As was predicted in these columns, the members of the Brotherhood deserted
the League clubs at the meeting held yesterday in the Fifth-Avenue Hotel. This
in defiance of the threat of the officials, means another baseball war. The players
are determined and feel assured of success. The magnates are bitter and declare
that they will spare neither pains nor expense to kill the movement and punish
the ringleaders....

When the meeting was called to order the following delegates answered to
their names: New-York, James O'Rourke; Boston, Daniel Brouthers; Philadelphia, James Fogarty; Washington, Arthur Irwin; Chicago, Frederick Pfeffer;
Pittsburg, Edward Hanlon and John Rowe; Indianapolis, Edward Andrews; and
Cleveland, L. G. Twitchell....

Ward, O'Rourke, Pfeffer, Hanlon, and Brouthers were selected a committee
to draw up a statement for presentation to the public.[2] The following was
adopted:

"*To the public*: at last the Brotherhood of Baseball Players feels at liberty to
make known its intentions and defend itself against the aspersions and mis-
representations which for weeks it has been forced to suffer in silence. It is
no longer a secret that the players of the League have determined to play next
season under different management, but for reasons which will, we think, be

understood, it was deemed advisable to make no announcement of this intention until the close of the present season; but now that the struggles for the various pennants are over, and the terms of our contracts expired, there is no longer reason for withholding it.

In taking this step we feel that we owe it to the public and to ourselves to explain briefly some of the reasons by which we have been moved. There was a time when the League stood for integrity and fair dealing; to-day it stands for dollars and cents. Once it looked to the elevation of the game and an honest exhibition of the sport; to-day its eyes are upon the turnstile. Men have come into the business for no other motive than to exploit it for every dollar in sight. Measures originally intended for the good of the game have been perverted into instruments for wrong. The reserve rule and the provisions of the national agreement gave the managers unlimited power, and they have not hesitated to use this in the most arbitrary and mercenary way.

Players have been bought, sold, and exchanged as though they were sheep, instead of American citizens. 'Reservation' became with them another name for property right in the player. By a combination among themselves, stronger than the strongest trust, they were able to enforce the most arbitrary measures, and the player had either to submit or get out of the profession in which he had spent years in attaining proficiency. Even the disbandment and retirement of a club did not free the players from the octopus clutch, for they were then peddled around to the highest bidder.

That the player sometimes profited by the sale has nothing to do with the case, but only proved the injustice of his previous restraint. Two years ago we met the League and attempted to remedy some of these evils, but through what has been politely called 'League diplomacy' we completely failed. Unwilling longer to submit to such treatment, we made a strong effort last Spring to reach an understanding with the League. To our application for a hearing they replied 'that the matter was not of sufficient importance to warrant a meeting,' and suggested that it be put off till Fall. Our committee replied that the players felt that the League had broken faith with them; that while the results might be of little importance to the managers, they were of great importance to the players; that if postponed until Fall we would be separated and at the mercy of the League, and that, as the only course left us required time and labor to develop, we must therefore insist upon an immediate conference.

Then upon their final refusal to meet us we began organizing for ourselves, and are in shape to go ahead next year under new management and new auspices. We believe that it is possible to conduct our national game upon lines which will not infringe upon individual and natural rights. We asked to be judged solely by our work, and believing that the game can be played more fairly and its business conducted more intelligently under a plan which excludes everything arbitrary and un–American, we look forward with confidence to the support of the public and the future of the national game.

THE NATIONAL BROTHERHOOD OF BALL PLAYERS."[3]

With the Baseball War inevitable, Ward notified Spalding of the Players' League 1890 schedule so the National League could avoid overlapping dates. No point in being suicidal. However, instead of using the Brotherhood information to *avoid* conflicts, Spalding "boldly scheduled" the National League games to *coincide* with Players' League games "to make the battle short, sharp and decisive."[4] The leagues would compete head-to-head in the same cities, on the same days, and at the same times. With characteristic hubris, Spalding trumpeted to the press: "I want to fight until one of us drops dead."[5]

O'Rourke responded by saying that the Players' League would be the one left standing at the end of the year.[6]

But Spalding still had a few trick pitches left in his arsenal. Displaying a willingness to win at any cost, he strengthened the National League by casting off weak tail-enders Washington and Indianapolis,[7] and used their players to fill in the ranks of the New York Giants and other teams whose rosters were thinned by defections to the Players' League. To bring the National League back up to eight teams, clubs in Cincinnati and Brooklyn were admitted. The Brooklyn team had recently resigned from the American Association, allowing Spalding to pick up an intact roster of major league players.

In an effort to embarrass the union, Spalding offered Mike Kelly, the Players' League Boston manager, $10,000 to break his contract.[8] In essence, Spalding was asking Kelly to do what he himself had done in 1875: sell out his fellow players. (Kelly's drinking was now apparently less of a liability to Spalding than the specter of power in the hands of workers.) Spalding was offering Kelly as much as he had sold the ball player for three years earlier — an act, ironically, that had helped to foment the player unrest that led to the Baseball War.

Spalding knew the spendthrift Kelly was in debt and near the end of his playing days. With $10,000, Kelly could have paid off his debts, bought a house, and retired in style. But Kelly told Spalding he "would sooner cut off his right arm than go back on the Brotherhood."[9]

Giants owner John Day tempted Danny Richardson with $15,000, but this bribe, too, was "scornfully rejected."[10]

Cap Anson attempted to bribe Buck Ewing. Several meetings were arranged in carriage rides under cover of darkness, on platforms of small town train stations, and in the smoke-filled back room of a cigar store. In February 1890, Giants' owner John Day was also trying to entice Buck to remain with the National League — and Buck was listening. After a late-night negotiating session between the two in Cincinnati, the Chicago Tribune carried the following story:

"Buck" Ewing Weakening
The Catcher Believed to Think Pretty Well of Day's Offers.

Cincinnati, O., Feb. 17.–[Special.]— The baseball sensation that is being hourly expected to culminate has not yet reached that point. "Buck" Ewing denies that he has forsaken the brotherhood, but his talk shows that he is weakening. The matters that transpired during the midnight conference have been kept secret, both parties refusing to talk. Today was spent by Ewing and Day in promenading about the city taking in the sights. Last night they were corralled in a restaurant and interviewed upon the subject of contract-signing. Mr. Day was asked if he had secured Ewing's name to a contract. Said he in reply: "I will not say anything one way or the other. I am more than satisfied with the result of my visit to the city. Now, draw your own conclusions."

"Buck Ewing" was then attacked and his discourse ran as follows: "No, I have not signed a League contract, nor will I sign one. If four certain men — Crane, O'Rourke, Connor, and Richardson — should happen to sign league contracts with the New York club then perhaps it would make a change that would affect me."

There is a peculiar significance attached to these remarks, as it was a subject of common talk yesterday that these very men were awaiting the example of Ewing to desert the brotherhood and jump to the League.[11]

I am not aware of any evidence that O'Rourke or any other Giant was contemplating returning to the National League. To squelch the rumor, Jim sent a dispatch to the Players' League office saying that "all such reports could be put down as fabrications."[12]

This was probably a rumor spread by the National League agents to soften up Ewing. Spalding was planting false stories about star players deserting the Players' League, then advising others not to wait too long to return to the National League — as all positions would soon be full.[13] The *New York Clipper* of January 18, 1890, was filled with reports and rumors of contract jumpers.

The offer (bribe) to Ewing eventually reached $8,500 per year for three years.[14] Buck wavered, but in the end he refused to break with the Brotherhood. However, few of the rebels trusted him after his waffling over the Players' League.[15]

Eventually, the coercion began to chisel away at Brotherhood solidarity. Ace pitcher John Clarkson accepted a $10,000 bribe to disavow his Players' League contract.[16] All in all, Spalding was able to successfully coerce or intimidate 30 Brotherhood members into walking out on their contracts. He assailed the players with the carrot of a huge signing bonus in one hand, and in the other the stick of a lawsuit and blacklisting for life. O'Rourke derided the turncoats:

> The poor, miserable wretches who have permitted bribers to label upon their flesh the price of their dishonor excited my pity rather than my anger, and I shall allow them to rest in peace if it is possible for them to find it on this green earth.[17]

Some Brotherhood supporters wanted the union to entice players who had signed National League contracts to break them and join the Players' League. But the Brotherhood took the high ground and refused to sign players already under contract in another league.[18]

Jim was even against taking back players who had deserted the Brotherhood. O'Rourke, along with King Kelly, Dan Brouthers, Arthur Irwin, and 10 other players signed a "vehemently worded" protest against reinstituting players that had broken Players' League contracts.[19]

Spalding then carried out his threat to sue individual players. On December 11, 1889, Ward was sued for violating the reserve rule.[20] An aggressive litigation strategy extended to most of the New York members of the Brotherhood. The Giants were harassed for months by League lawyers. As late as March 1908 the *Chicago Tribune* reported:

> Tim Keefe, the famous pitcher, when about to leave New York for Princeton this morning, was served by a Deputy United States Marshal with a writ in the injunction suit brought against him by the New York [League] club. The writ is returnable March 25. Papers were served on Gore yesterday and a writ was sent to Elmira for service on Danny Richardson. These suits will be followed with similar ones against Brown, Slattery, O'Rourke, Connor, O'Day, and Crane as soon as service can be made on them.[21]

Based on the decisions in these test cases, either all players would be free, or all the runaway slaves would have to return to their former owners. *Sporting Life* added additional insight into the magnates' unrelenting legal strategy:

> The policy of the National League toward its new rival, the Players' League, is now well defined. Failing in the Herculean efforts to win any more of the old players back by means of money, the law will be appealed to in the case of every man who left the old League. It is not denied that this is to be tried. The hour is all that is in doubt. It is said that the home address, or the exact place where they can be served most readily with papers, of every Brotherhood player is known and marked. At the hour appointed over fifty injunction suits will be begun against the picked men, and these suits will be pushed to the end.... The League magnates intend to go further and sue the backers of every Players' League club under the conspiracy law and for exemplary damages.[22]

Spalding's war committee spent a fortune on lawyers and the weight of intimidation from the suits cannot be overstated.

To soothe the understandable anxiety of the union members and to discourage further desertions from the ranks, O'Rourke argued publicly that the reserve clause could bind players to clubs only within existing leagues and then only if the contract is specific on terms. He insisted it was "ridiculous and absurd" to assume that the reserve clause made it illegal for a new league to sign players.[23]

The key to the Brotherhood's argument was that the reserve rule only prevented a player from signing with another team that was a party to the National Agreement (the National League, American Association, and the Northwestern League). But the Players League was not a party to the National

Agreement, so therefore, the Brotherhood argued, it was not bound by the reserve clause and could hire any player from any other league.

On January 16, 1890, the day of Ward's trial, AFL president Samuel Gompers and three other labor leaders pledged their support for the Players' League.[24] It was becoming clear even to the general public that the Baseball War was about much more than baseball — it was about the social structure of America. The Giants' refrain: "We are The People" was now a battle cry in the contest for worker rights, for the rights of the citizen against the ruling magnates, who now had more control and effect over their lives than did government or religion. In their stadia they were united, strong in number, a force to be reckoned with. They were *The People.*

In January 1890, the courts ruled that the reserve agreement did *not* apply to the Players' League. O'Rourke dashed off a letter to Frank Richter of *Sporting Life* proclaiming the players had defeated the "crafty ... and unscrupulous owners."[25]

Even though the players eventually won all the suits brought against them, the legal actions disrupted recruiting by the Brotherhood. For years, it had been customary to give players an advance upon signing, to carry them through the winter.

Spalding, ever alert for new ways to earn money from the national pastime, actually made advances a profit center by charging the players 8 percent interest. By 1890, players owed Spalding $36,000.[26]

The Players' League, however, was short on cash for advances because its backers were withholding funds, awaiting the outcome of the test cases.[27] *Sporting Life* tried to put a brave face on the Brotherhood situation:

> The triumph of the Players' League in the Ward injunction suit has had the expected effect. Desertion has been entirely stopped and the work of preparation for the now fast approaching season has been expedited to a remarkable degree and to all intents and purposes the new major league is ready to take the field to-day.[28]

The players may have won the court battles, but Spalding and his cohorts continued to pursue them with ever more tantalizing bribes to desert the Brotherhood ranks. To remove their players from temptation, the Boston and New York teams escaped south for spring training.

On March 15, 1890, King Kelly and his Boston Players' League team took the train to Grand Central Station, where they were met by nine New York players, including Jim O'Rourke, Roger Connor, Buck Ewing, George Gore, Danny Richardson, and Ed Crane. In the afternoon, the two teams sailed for Savannah "to play a series of games for practice."[29]

In spite of vows made after he returned from the Great Britain tour of 1874, Jim spent St. Patrick's Day in mid-ocean. But it was worth it. By conducting spring training in the South, New York and Boston kept their players out of Spalding's reach. According to Tim Murnane, "National League agents were everywhere trying to tempt the players to jump, and by keeping together the players were not easy to get to."[30]

By the start of the 1890 season, the Players' League had recruited over 100 major leaguers.[31] The National League, on the other hand, managed to sign only 60 veterans. (They retained 38 of their own players–25 percent of their 1889 National League roster — and raided 22 veterans from the American Association.)[32] The older league was forced to dip into the minor and amateur ranks for 53 of its players for 1890.[33]

Although the Players' League successfully recruited twice as many major leaguers as the National League, it was not enough of a margin for the hoped-for lay-down. The rebels' original strategy was to hire away at least 90 percent of the National League players, leaving Spalding's league an empty shell.[34] But Spalding had turned enough Brotherhood members to maintain credibility as a major league.

As a result, the war would drag on, its outcome determined by fortune's wheel: the turnstile.

To strengthen the weaker franchises of the National League against the Players' League onslaught, Spalding increased the gate share for visiting clubs from 25 percent of the 50-cent admission fee (12.5 cents) to 40 percent (20 cents).[35]

To make it difficult for the Players' League to arrange preseason exhibition games, Spalding put all college and minor league teams on notice that if they engaged the upstarts, they could just forget about ever playing any club in organized baseball.[36] This did hurt the Players' League. The preseason exhibition contests it had planned for the first half of April were critical for raising cash and tuning up.

Sportswriter O. P. Caylor summed up the impending battle when he predicted:

> There is no possible, probable shadow of doubt but that one of the two organizations will in time have to surrender. Some of the cities occupied by both [leagues] cannot possibly support two clubs.... It therefore follows that the season just opening will be the most exciting and the most important in the history of the national game.[37]

Prior to the initial skirmishes, Spalding escalated the rhetoric with the declaration:

> We will spend all the money that is necessary to win this fight. From this point out it will simply be a case of dog eat dog.[38]

There were two teams claiming to be the true New York Giants, but only one could survive. Which team and league would the fans recognize as the real New York Giants? Opening day would tell.

Before the crucial first game, O'Rourke's daughters ceremoniously scrubbed and bleached his white wool uniform. They were carrying on a family tradition. Years later, baseball writer Noel Hynd wondered how Jim always looked like he just stepped out of a sporting goods catalog: "For some reason, his uniform was always crisp and clean."[39] If O'Rourke's uniform wore out before the end of a season, it wasn't from sliding into second.

Opening day for the Giants was Saturday, April 19, 1890. The New York National League and Players' League parks were side by side below Coogan's Bluff on the Upper East Side of Manhattan.[40]

Outside the parks, rival hawkers steered fans to "the real New York Giants."[41] But patrons divided along class lines: fashionable ladies and men with top hats directed their chauffeured carriages south into the National League park; workers alighting from crowded streetcars melded into the throngs funneling north to their new whitewashed cathedral. Grizzled men whose youth lay buried on Civil War battlefields surged forward in colorless jackets. Factory workers still stained from the grease of their machines emerged from the long dark tunnel under the stands onto their bright green communal lawn and squinted at an unfamiliar sun. The smells of fresh pine and sod melded with the aroma of roasting sausages. The vast greensward was surrounded by a high white fence. A gleaming white grandstand decked out in red, white, and blue bunting curved around the infield.

The *New York World* described the crowd:

> The uncompleted grandstand was thronged, the bleaching boards were crowded, and in the outfield was a fringe of humanity, backed up by a glittering array of coaches and four-in-hands, all crowded with the exultant adherents of the Players' League. The actors of the city who compose the Five A's [the name of a popular Broadway play at the time] were on a stage drawn by eight grays, and a couple of stages, each pulled by six horses, were drawn up close by the left field limits. It was a noisy crowd. They cheered at every possible opportunity, and when not cheering, were blowing horns.
>
> It was just 3 o'clock when the Phillies appeared at the lower end of the grounds. The Sixty-Ninth Regiment Band led the march and the blue-clad visitors received an ovation.... The mass of people rising and sitting seemed like a huge, dark wave.
>
> The band plays "Let Her Go Reilly, Galaugher Is Dead," and Buck Ewing ... gives the word to march. Stalwart and even handsome they appear in their neat-fitting white uniforms with black-lettered "New York" on the breast. Every man seems a king and surely feels prouder than any monarch as he walks up the cinder path. It is a scene of wild enthusiasm. The people are simply frantic. For hoarse throats they care not. They are there to greet the Giants and they cheer wildly. They cheer again and again when the photographer takes a snapshot, and yell loudly as the favorites take their places on the field."[42]

Across the street, the National League Giants hoisted their 1889 Pennant. Not to be outdone, the Players' League Giants raised *their* 1889 pennant on a

New York Players' League Giants on Opening Day. The Giants, in white, are in the field. Note center fielder Slattery is making a Willy Mays catch in this rare action photo. Jim is out of view, standing in left field, or what would soon become known as the sun field, as home plate was directly in line with the sun. Coogan's Bluff is in the background (engraving: *Illustrated American*, May 10, 1890, p. 293).

one-hundred-foot pole, high enough to be seen across the street. The huge white pennant with blue border proclaimed the Brotherhood Giants to be: "The Only World Champions."[43]

Two umpires dressed in white surveyed the battlefield as if to satisfy themselves that it was ready for the contest. This was the first time two umpires officiated at a regular season game.[44]

Then umpire Robert Ferguson, who 15 years earlier presided over the last league to be run by players, announced in his stentorian voice: "Play!"

The next day, the *New York World* devoted its entire front page to the opening salvos of the Baseball War. Across the country, the Players' League drew twice the fans as the National League. Whereas 12,113 fans had crowded into New York's Brotherhood Park, the National League Giants drew only 4,644.[45]

Each day witnessed a battle whose victor was determined by attendance figures, reported in the morning papers, as if casualty figures from the front.

But ticket sales don't tell the whole story. The Brotherhood players were winning the hearts and minds of the fans. When the Giants visited Boston for their first game with the Reds, Johnny Ward gave the following impression of the reception "accorded the two clubs" as the players rode to the ballpark:

THE NEW BATTLEFIELDS OF THE BASEBALL WAR.

Instantaneous Photographs of the Grounds of the New York Players' and National Leag
Taken Yesterday for the "Sunday World" by the Largest Camera in Town.

THE PARK OF THE BROTHERHOOD.

The Above Photograph Shows the Players' League Grounds as the Game Was About to Begin in the Presence of 12,013 Enthusiastic People.

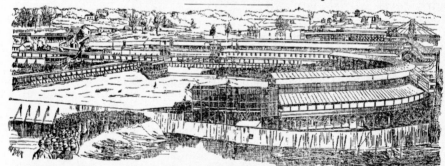

THE FIELD OF THE OLD NATIONAL LEAGUE.

Our Photographer Gives the Magnates the Benefit of a Snap Shot While the Game Is in Full
Progress. Attendance, 4,644.

Front Page News: April 20, 1890. Although O'Rourke had two triples in the opening day game of 1890, the Players' League Giants lost to the Philadelphia Quakers, 12–11.

The streets lined with people, the windows of the large structures, to their very tops, crowded with lookers-on, all anxious to have a peep at the boys, and all waiving their hands, caps and handkerchiefs.[46]

Although the Brotherhood was winning the battle of the turnstiles, Spalding began releasing false attendance figures to obscure the poor showing of the National League. O'Rourke called Spalding on the fabrications, inform-ing the media:

> The attendance at the [National] League grounds is not one-fifth as large as that on our grounds. In one Philadelphia game it was but 250, and it was given out as over 700.[47]

Spalding later admitted,

> If either party ... ever furnished to the press one truthful statement [about attendance], a monument should be erected to his memory.... We [played] two games—baseball and bluff."[48]

In his memoir, Spalding told the story of a reporter asking the National League secretary how many fans were at a Chicago game. Without a moment's hesitation, the official replied: "Twenty-four eighteen." Spalding knew there were nowhere near 2,418 people in the park; so after the reporter had moved on he asked the official how he could say their were twenty-four eighteen. "Why," the official replied, "Don't you see? There were twenty-four on one side of the grounds and eighteen on the other. If he reports twenty-four *hundred* and eighteen, that's a matter for *his* conscience, not mine."[49]

In an effort to control the press and public opinion, Spalding bought the New York *Sporting Times* from Erastus Wiman and installed O. P. Cay-lor as editor. He tried to brush back *The Sporting News* with threats to pull advertising, but Al Spink had too much courage and integrity to cave into the bullying. Spalding even organized hate-mail campaigns directed at pub-lications that did not parrot his party line.[50]

Nevertheless, the baseball journals were, in my opinion, balanced in their reporting. But while the press did not favor either of the combatants, the sportswriters did, unwittingly, help to create a no-win situation. By dili-gently and fairly reporting every accusation and counterclaim in the ongo-ing squabble, the fans were soured on the game and attendance declined in all leagues.

To make the game "worth witnessing" Jim played his heart out. In July, he was injured and went home to recuperate.[51] But in August he came back revitalized, hitting safely in 21 consecutive games.[52] For the season, O'Rourke's batting average was .360, third highest in the Players' League.

In spite of Spalding's duplicity, by the end of the season it was clear to all that the Players' League had won the attendance battle and the Baseball War.[53] However, it was a pyrrhic victory. Although the National League lost between $231,000 and $500,000, the Players' League also lost money, $125,000 by one account.[54] According to Spalding, throughout the industry, "Scarcely a club ... paid its expenses."[55] There were just too many teams. At the con-clusion of the 1890 season, the sporting press counseled consolidation of the

National and Players' Leagues.[56] The leaders of leagues agreed, the poor attendance having bankrupted both their war chests.

Still, reconciliation would not be easy. There had been recriminations
back and forth during the war. O'Rourke had called Spalding an unscrupulous tyrant. The tyrant responded by pointing out that O'Rourke's income
had doubled during the decade of the reserve clause, as had the income of
other shooting stars like Ward and Ewing.[57]

There was even bad blood between players. The Brotherhood Giants
were again suspicious of Ewing's fealty. In August of 1890, Al Spalding, Cap
Anson, and National League Giants owner John B. Day were again trolling
for strong players with weak character to jump the Brotherhood ship. They
set their sights on the managers of the Boston and New York Players' League
clubs, Mike Kelly and Buck Ewing. After interviewing the two targeted players, the *Chicago Daily Tribune* reported: "Kelly has declared himself against
the old league, but Ewing says he is out for the stuff."[58] A *Tribune* reporter
sent a dispatch from Boston on August 8 that read in part:

> John B. Day came on here Thursday night and held a long conference with the
> New York Captain. They sent out a messenger to find Mike Kelly, but the King
> sent back word that he had no use for the League Magnates. A. G. Spalding was
> said to be close at hand with a big pot of money. The magnates have worked
> hard to make the Players believe they can break their three years' contract at the
> end of the season. Ewing was said to have a contract on hand to get Connor,
> Keefe and Dan Richardson to go back, but these men would not even listen.[59]

In spite of the mistrust between the players and magnates and even
among some of the players, O'Rourke sent a fence-mending letter to the
press in which he said it would be best for the two sides to reconcile. Harry
Wright was in the National League camp, and he, too, favored compromise
over war.[60]

The Brotherhood took the lead and called for a peace conference.[61] And
why not? At the end of the 1890 season, the union was in the catbird's seat.
The Cincinnati Reds had cried uncle on October 5 and sold out to a syndicate of Players' League investors.[62] The National League Pittsburgh franchise
was bankrupt,[63] and New York was tottering. John Day, the owner of the
Giants, had lost everything in the Baseball War and was ready to sell out to
the Players' League. At this point, the Players' League controlled more teams:
nine versus seven National League clubs. The stars and the fans were also with
the players. Spalding later admitted the National League owners were "dazed."

But Spalding rallied his troops. To keep the National League New York
team afloat and out of the hands of the Brotherhood, he raised over $80,000.
Spalding and Boston owner Arthur Soden each put up $25,000.[64] (The for-
tunes of Boston magnate Arthur Soden had improved substantially from
soaring baseball profits during the 1880s.)[65]

Spalding then audaciously went on the offensive, taking aim at the crown jewel of the Players' League: its New York franchise. He accepted the Brotherhood's invitation to a parley, but before the official summit, he met secretly with backers of the Players' League Giants. Spalding told the Wall Street crowd that the National League was profitable and that they should trade their Players' League stock to him for shares in National League clubs.[66] "Fifty percent of something, or a hundred percent of nothing" is the way Spalding put it. Of course, Spalding was lying about the National League's financial health, but the Players' League Giants were also in dire financial condition. The club owed money to five of its players, including O'Rourke, who had not been paid for September and October, the final two months of the 1890 season.[67]

Spalding had the advantage in knowing that baseball was a good long-term investment. But the Wall Street financiers had not experienced the good years in the industry. They had been told by the players that they would make money in baseball but instead lost their jerseys. As a result, the Players' League Giants owners took the bait and sold out to Al Spalding.

Spalding then set his sights on the Players' League franchise in Brooklyn. "'Won't you walk into my parlor,' said the National League spider to the Players' League fly. The invitation was accepted." Spalding outfoxed the Brooklyn backers as deftly as he had the New York investors.[68]

While Spalding was wooing the Brooklynites, other National League generals attacked the Players' League Pittsburgh franchise. There, too, the Brotherhood backers capitulated and merged their team with its National League counterpart.

The bold and coordinated attacks took the Brotherhood by surprise. Notwithstanding the loss of so much valuable ground, some of the rebels believed that all was not lost. Deacon White, for one, thought the tide could yet be turned:

> There's a powerful nucleus left to battle against the National League if only the players will hold together.... Determined action at the present moment can defeat the treachery.[69]

In a late-inning attempt to get something going, the Brotherhood appealed to its members to buy out the interests of their wavering capitalist backers. But the players hadn't the means or inclination.[70] Taking risks and investing is the job of capitalists.

When the official summit between the two leagues eventually took place, the score was reversed. It now stood 10 clubs to six in favor of the National League. The players' skill in the field had ill prepared them for negotiating in smoke-filled rooms. When the smoke cleared, the Players' League had been absorbed by the National League. In the words of historian Thomas Gilbert, "The winning side surrendered."[71]

Deacon White offered the following post-mortem, even before the Players' League had been completely consumed:

It looks dark for the Players' League now, but do you know what is killing it? It was the purchase of the Cincinnati Club. They gave $40,000 for nothing. Up to the time the Cincinnati deal was mentioned the Players' League was running along as smoothly as oiled machinery. The capitalists had hard work to scrape together the money. They were in it pretty deep, and this new deal pinched them all the harder. This young Talcott, of the New York Club, had a heap of money in it and got scared. He secured himself at the expense of the other Players' League clubs by consolidating with the National League. Talcott saw a chance to get even and grabbed it. Pittsburgh made the same break, and a more foolish thing I never heard of. Why, the Players' League had the National League whipped, and in a few weeks more the National League men would have been on their knees asking for quarter.[72]

Sporting Life's explanation for the demise of the Brotherhood's Utopia was more succinct:

The Players' League people compared with the League men, are but as clay in the potter's hands.[73]

The *Sporting News* obit was bitter:

The workers ... were crowded to the rear and choked off, while the dress parade element posed and plumed itself in the sunlight of public observation and admiration until its conceit, incompetence and disloyalty ran the concern into the ditch it now lies in helplessly wrecked.

Under the settlement between the Players' and National leagues, there were to be no reprisals against the strikers. The renegade players returned to their former teams for the 1891 season, save one, Philadelphia's Louis Bierbauer, who was grabbed illegally by the Pittsburgh Innocents, who, ever since, have been called the "Pirates."[74]

On the morning of January 16, 1891, the Players' League ceased to exist with the ratification of a new National Agreement, organized baseball's self-granted charter, to which the only signers were the National League and the American Association. (If they knew what Spalding had in store for them, the American Association owners would have attempted to merge with the Players' League. But that was another missed opportunity.)

That evening, Brotherhood supporters held a wake for the Players' League at Nick Engel's Home Plate Saloon. The restaurant, at 16 West 27th Street, had served as an unofficial headquarters of the Brotherhood.

The rebels raised their glasses to their league and to each other for the good fight well fought.

Al Spink of *The Sporting News* observed that although the Brotherhood revolt failed, "the fight had some good results for it led to a much better understanding between owners of clubs and players and a respect for the latter's rights."[75]

Connie Mack, who lost all his savings in the Players' League[76], noted that the National League owners paid dearly to learn a valuable lesson: "Ballplayers must be given a fair deal or [they will] rebel."[77]

The consolidated New York ball club was incorporated on February 6, 1891. The name of the new organization was the National Exhibition Company, with capital stock of $250,000. The old New York National and Players' League clubs were disbanded.[78]

Frank Richter, **Editor of** *Sporting Life* **and a supporter of the Players' League to the very end (engraving:** *Athletic Sports,* **1889).**

As part of the settlement, Jim was sent a check in December 1890 for the two months salary due him.[79] O'Rourke also wound up a stockholder in the new Giants organization. He was a stockholder in the Players' League Giants[80] and may have opted to be bought out with stock in the new club. He had ample financial resources and could afford to take the risk of accepting replacement shares in lieu of cash. The *Boston Globe* (Tim Murnane) estimated Jim's wealth at $50,000 in 1891.[81] O'Rourke received 13[82] shares in the new National League Giants organization.

The Orator was not content to be a silent partner. He attended stockholder meetings and forcefully voiced his opinions, prompting the *New York Times* to observe: "His likes and dislikes are too strong to suit the New York stockholders."[83] The other magnates tried to buy his shares, but O'Rourke "refused to part with them."[84]

The new New York Giants club would have a 17-man roster, composed of the best players from the two New York clubs of 1890.[85] As his first official act as president of the new club, John B. Day "sent word to Richardson, Roger Connor, Ed Crane and O'Rourke to report at New York the coming week and sign."[86] At the signing ceremony, a sportswriter commented that "The utmost good feeling was shown by all."[87] In an interview, O'Rourke said:

> As the Players' League is a thing of the past, it is the duty of every player to put his shoulder to the wheel and work in harmony so as to place baseball on its former basis.[88]

The new National League Giants took over the New York park built by the rebels, and renamed it the Polo Grounds.

The most serious threat to the social order in America was dead. Now began the burying process. To the victors go the rights of writing history, and although O'Rourke and Ward were inducted into the Hall of Fame, their bronze plaques make no mention of the great revolt.

Spalding's vision prevailed: owners shall rule; workers shall obey. Spalding called this the "only possible system which will yield financial success." In referring to baseball workers, he added: they "may be able to throw curves but know nothing of business."[89]

Spalding then proceeded with his next mission: to eliminate the American Association, the only remaining threat to the absolute supremacy of the league he created. As reported by the *Chicago Tribune*, at the annual spring meeting of the National League in 1891,

> A. G. Spalding spoke in a most emphatic manner for some time. He believed in doing anything to crush out the American Association.[90]

Coincidentally, while Jim was fighting the good fight on behalf of the Brotherhood of Baseball Players, John O'Rourke was actively engaged in the struggle for workers' rights as a union organizer. In 1890, the year of the Baseball War, John was one of four Grand Trustees (national board members) of the Brotherhood of Railway Trainmen that represented 20,000 brakemen, switchmen, yardmasters, conductors and baggagemen.[91]

On July 21, John attended a meeting of 500 Brotherhood members in Hartford where they endorsed a bill pending in Congress that would require the use of automatic brakes and couplers on freight trains. The union explained the need for the new regulation:

> There are 150,000 miles of railroad in the country, and on nearly all of this the old-fashioned hand coupling and brake is still used. Two thousand men lose their lives every year on account of this wretched economy. Three quarters of this slaughter might be stopped by the use of automatic brakes and couplers. They are not adopted because blood is cheaper than iron.[92]

At the annual convention in Los Angeles on October 20, 1890, it was reported that the union paid out over $300,000 in benefits to disabled members or as death benefits to heirs during the past year.[93]

The lobbying for safer working conditions and the custodianship of the benefit fund was important work by John and his fellow trustees on behalf of the rank and file. While scanning issues of the *Railroad Trainman's Journal* from the 1880s and 1890s, I couldn't help but notice that most of the advertising was for prosthetic limbs and life insurance.

During the October convention, in celebration of their solidarity, 800 members of the Brotherhood paraded through the streets of Los Angeles behind a platoon of mounted police and a full band. John marched proudly in the van with the other national leaders of the Brotherhood. A reporter described the passing train:

A number of them wore silk hats and all were well dressed and looked more like presidents of roads than plain brakemen, switchmen, engineers and firemen. The boys were frequently cheered by the audience on the sidewalks and they gracefully acknowledged the honors paid them by raising their hats. After marching to the Pavilion the procession broke up and the boys made their way down town and spent the rest of the afternoon meeting friends and talking over old times.[94]

But the solidarity was not to last.

After the next semiannual convention in April 1891, union grand master (president) S. E. Wilkinson summarily dismissed John and the other grand trustees. The trustees had distributed a circular critical of the grand master, who had held the union's highest office for five years.[95]

The dispute was over the control of the sizable member benefit account. The union was taking in $30,000 per month for its life and accident fund. John and the other trustees felt it was incumbent upon them to insure the integrity of the fund in order to maintain the trust of the members. The union had almost been bankrupted seven years earlier by an embezzling treasurer.

John and the three other trustees, responded to their dismissal by filing an injunction restraining Grand Master Wilkinson from "appointing a new board and from interfering with the old board in the performance of its duties."[96] As reported in the *New York Times*:

> The bill charges the Grand Master with improper motives in discharging the Trustees.... It holds that the Grand Trustees were elected to guard this money and as a check on the one-man power of the Grand Master or the Grand Secretary. It charges that the Grand Master wants a board that will be subservient to his wishes: that will change the depository of money; allow the making of assessments for improper and extravagant purposes; permit funds to be handled by the Grand Master and Secretary, and one that will help these two officers in illegal designs to secure the entire management of the money.[97]

Two months later, in June 1891, Wilkinson answered the court, denying the charges, and suggesting that the union be allowed to resolve the dispute internally at its semiannual convention in October. John was no rookie when it came to politics, but he was no match for the gruff and determined Wilkinson.[98]

In September, the "old board" demanded to inspect the books of the union, but Wilkinson refused them access.[99]

At the climactic convention on October 5, 1891, "Grand Master Wilkinson was in the chair. The contending Boards of Trustees occupied chairs facing one another."[100] In the ensuing vote to settle on which was the rightful board, John and his faction lost. Wilkinson was able to win (buy?) enough votes to stay in power and keep John out.[101]

Two years later, Wilkinson lost favor with the rank and file when he sided with management against Eugene Debs in the great Pullman strike. (John had suspected Wilkinson of selling out to management on previous occasions.) Wilkinson finally resigned in disgrace in May of 1895, after admitting to lapses in his duty to the union and the "indiscretion" of a three-month vacation in California.[102]

While no longer in the forefront of the national labor movement, John remained active in his union local. "In the counsels of this organization, his advice was always sought and his views always commanded the greatest respect."[103]

In 1891, the year John faced the failure of his attempt to wrest control of the railroad union from corrupt elements, brother Jim was coming to grips with the aftermath of his failed attempt to regain control of the baseball industry for the benefit of *its* workers.

To return once more into the breach of the good fight requires strength of character, a quality the O'Rourke brothers enjoyed and may have encouraged in each other by their conduct.

22

Return to National League Giants (1891–1892)

Learning to persevere after failure is one of the more practical benefits of the baseball experience. No major league team has ever had an undefeated season.

Of course, dealing with extreme success is just as difficult. Players like O'Rourke, who learn how to live with success, save their surplus earnings from their salad days; those who do not dissipate their fortunes and their health, surrounded by fans eager to buy them a drink to own a piece of their soul.

But failure, baseball teaches well. "Batters fail more than half the time" is a cliché. Fielders must regain their composure after muffing a hot grounder or bobbling a pop-up. And what pitcher has not suffered the humiliation of having his best pitch knocked out of the ballpark.

Jim and his fellow revolutionaries were equipped psychologically to deal with the end of the Players' League. What they were not prepared for was having to team up with strikebreakers and contract jumpers who had helped the magnates rob them of their dream. But that was the deal: forgive and forget all around. Still, it was a bitter pill, and one Jim never quite swallowed.

O'Rourke feuded with Giants catcher Buck Ewing, who he suspected of attempting to coerce Brotherhood players to defect during the Baseball War. Jim told a reporter that he had no faith in Buck Ewing.[1] In return, Ewing quipped that outfielder O'Rourke "couldn't cover enough ground to bury himself in."[2]

Fortunately, life was happier on the home front. Jim was building a new home at 274 Pembroke in Bridgeport for his growing family.[3] By 1891 he had seven children: Sarah Jane "Sadie" (17), Agnes (11), Jim Jr. (10), Ida (7), Lillian (5), Irene (4), and Edith (1). His mother was also living under the same roof.

On the ball diamond in 1891, Jim's 20th year in the majors, the 41-year-old outfielder hit .295.[4] The 1892 season began auspiciously as well. Jim's

O'Rourke in 1891, sporting his signature handlebar mustache. Long flowing mustaches were common on ballplayers during most of the 19th century (National Baseball Hall of Fame Library; Cooperstown, New York).

performance in the Giants' opening-day victory over Philadelphia was duly noted in the press:

> The batting of O'Rourke, who made a hit each of the four times he was at bat, and the fielding of Allen were the features of the game.[5]

But the National League was not doing well financially. The clubs were still paying off debt incurred during the Baseball War. At a special meeting of the league, held in June 1892, "each club was given permission to cut salaries from 30 to 40 per cent." All teams except Brooklyn and Philadelphia cut salaries; and only one player, Tony Mullane

The home of Jim O'Rourke in Bridgeport.

of St. Louis, refused to accept the arbitrary salary reduction. He was forced to remain idle for the balance of the season.[6]

In 1892, O'Rourke exceeded the .300 mark offensively and ranked in the top third in fielding among the National League left fielders.[7]

However, Pat Powers had replaced Mutrie as manager, and in spite of Jim's best efforts, the former world champions dropped from third to eighth place in only one year. The club was losing games, fans, and money.

O'Rourke openly blamed management for the lackluster season. The former Buffalo manager had always been outspoken in his opinion of how the Giants should be run. He was known around the Giants' clubhouse as "The Counselor" not only for his law degree and law book language, but for "his ability to best [General Manager James] Mutrie in post-game arguments."[8] One quarrel escalated to his winging a shoe at Mutrie.[9] Jim was no less attentive to Powers when it came to helping him appreciate the full range of his shortcomings as a leader.

But manager Powers decided that the problem was with the players, and began cutting loose the veterans. (Rookies earned less than members of the old guard, and were less likely to talk back to management.) Six players were let go, including "the veteran with the exemplary habits." Jim O'Rourke was released on September 10, 1892.[10] Powers explained it this way:

> The demand for young and speedy players has caused the New York management to release out-fielder James O'Rourke, and engage James Knowles, the well-known third baseman. O'Rourke has been of little or no use to the club. In the outfield his work has been of a very poor character, his base-running was slow, and his batting was always done when the bases were empty. The club officials say that he did not play for the team, but was always looking for a personal record. They do not want record players in the nine, so O'Rourke had to go.[11]

But the stats say otherwise:

- With a .304 batting average, O'Rourke ranked second among the Giants.
- He had the fewest errors of any player on the team.
- He was third in RBI (so his batting was not "always done when the bases were empty.")
- As to playing for the team or his personal record, it should be pointed out that he had 10 sacrifice hits in 1892, which was typical of other players.
- As to speed, Jim was slowing down, but he stole 16 bases in 115 games in 1892 (an average of .139 bases per game); James Knowles, his "young and speedy" replacement stole only two bases in 16 games (.125 bases per game). And Knowles' batting average was only .153, less than half of Jim's. (Regardless of how fast a runner, he has to get on before he can steal a base.)

Others apparently saw that Jim's record did not match Powers' rheto-

The 1892 New York Giants. Jim O'Rourke, age 41, is on the extreme right. Manager Pat Powers is under the derby. O'Rourke's body language is indicative of the still-lingering ill will in the post–Baseball War era. In contrast to the mood of the players, the Polo Grounds are bedecked in festive opening-day bunting (Supplement to *New York Recorder*).

ric. O'Rourke was immediately picked up by Washington as manager and player for the 1893 season.[12]

The Giants owners eventually realized, too, that the losing season was the fault of the manager, and not the players he had used as scapegoats. Powers was replaced by Johnny Ward. This made Jim and Johnny friendly adversaries, each managing teams in the National League in 1893. Another former Brotherhood ringleader, Charlie Comiskey, was leading the National League Cincinnati team. Other Brotherhood figures would later manage in the majors, including Clark Griffith and Connie Mack.

23

Washington Senators (1893)

In 1889, four years before O'Rourke assumed command, Washington finished in last place in the National League with a 41–83 record. The franchise was dumped from the circuit prior to the 1890 season in an effort to strengthen the league for its impending war with the players.[1] In 1891, Washington joined the American Association, where they also finished last with an even worse 44–91 record.[2]

The American Association had fared the worst during the Baseball War and in its weakened financial state Spalding was able to push the league into its grave prior to the start of the 1892 season, thus consolidating once again the monopoly over major league baseball he had enjoyed between 1876 and 1881. Spalding made room for a number of the American Association franchises, including Washington, in an expanded 12-team National League.[3] According to Frank Richter:

> Secret negotiations running over six weeks, and so quietly conducted that not an inkling escaped, resulted in an agreement whereby four Association clubs were to be purchased outright and the other four admitted to the National League for a term of 10 years. This deal was consummated at a special meeting held in December [1891], in Indianapolis. The Chicago, Boston, Milwaukee, Columbus and Washington Clubs were purchased outright at a total cost of $135,000. The Washington franchise was vested in George Wagner, of Philadelphia, and that club, together with Baltimore, St. Louis and Louisville, were admitted to the National League. So the ill-fated American Association passed into history.

His work accomplished, Spalding began to cut back on his leadership roles in organized baseball. In 1891, he resigned as president of the White Stockings, an organization he had headed since 1882.[4]

The Washington National League club in 1892 finished 10th among the 12 teams, running through three managers in the process. The Washington managers had no say in hiring or firing players. This was handled by the owner, George Wagner, with the singular goal of immediate cash profit. Nevertheless, each manager, in turn, was blamed for the team's poor showing in the standings, and fired.

Into this challenging situation, James Henry O'Rourke arrived in 1893.

When asked about the team's chances, Jim responded diplomatically:

> The Senators will start the season comparatively new to each other, and until the men get accustomed to one another's play, the best results cannot be expected. We have excellent material and I am more than satisfied with the men as individual players. After they have acquired teamwork then look out for some mighty interesting exhibitions of ball.[5]

This statement provides some insight into Jim's management style. Whereas some managers churn through prospects looking for exceptional individual performers; the more deliberate managers realize that the pennant is won by the best *team*, which, when well directed, is greater than the sum of its parts. Jim gave his players time to gel as a unit, to work out signals, to learn one another's strengths and weaknesses, to attempt enough double plays to shave a 10th of a second off their turn time, and to settle on who will take balls hit between fielders and who will back up.

As with all changes in management, the new administration began with the usual optimism. At the Washington club's board meeting on March 7, 1893, President George Wagner assured the directors:

> In securing O'Rourke as manager, I am sure of having made a ten-strike, as he is a veteran in the business, having successfully managed and captained the old Buffalo club. He called on me in Philadelphia Saturday last and within one hour had signed to captain and manage our team.[6]

Henry Chadwick agreed. In a letter to the sports editor of the *Washington Post*, the "Father of Baseball" said:

> Through you I beg to congratulate the club on the excellent selection they have made in the choice of so capable and experienced a manager, so able a captain of a team, and so fine a team worker at the bat, and excellent a catcher and out-fielder as I know O'Rourke to be. I have known him for many years and have watched his most creditable career with great and increasing pleasure, for educated, gentlemanly, exemplary, and professional ball players like James are as yet in the minority in the fraternity, and exceptional characters of his class are not to be seen every day. O'Rourke as a player is one of the best "coaching" catchers in the League and a fine out-fielder, but it is in his team work at the bat — batting so as to forward runners— that he specially excels. Then, too, as a manager he is especially considerate of his players, while being a strict disciplinarian in keeping his men up to the right mark in regard to their physical condition, and, too, as a captain he is well up in every strategic point of the game.[7]

Commenting himself on his management style, Jim said:

The men know me to be easy to get along with as long as they keep in line; and there will be no internal dissensions or cliques permitted to interfere with the success of the team.[8]

From the owners, Jim received assurances that he had "full charge and his word will be law."[9] However, by the time Jim assumed control on March 28, the roster had been signed.

In keeping with his policy of cashing in talent for immediate profit, George Wagner had traded ace pitcher Frank Killen to the Pittsburgh Pirates for switch-hitting catcher Duke Farrell. Under Jim's tutelage, the 26-year-old Farrell improved his batting average from .215 when he was with the Pirates to .280 in 1893. But it would not make up for the loss of Killen.

During a preseason interview, Jim tried to reassure the fans that the Senators could survive the loss of their star pitcher:

The pitching department has been weakened by Killen's loss, but we will have Duryea, Meakin, and Maul to rely on, as well as one or two others who are being negotiated for.[10]

From the lack of conviction in his pronouncement, I doubt that Jim — or any fan — believed the Washington pitching staff was up to the task; and beginning in 1893, the task would be more difficult.

It was in 1893 that the pitcher was moved back to the current 60'6" (from 55'6"); and the pitcher's box eliminated entirely, replaced by a one-foot strip of rubber, from which the pitcher had to begin his delivery.

Jim thought that moving the pitcher back would make it too easy for batters to pick up cheap hits by dumping the ball into the deeper gap between the pitcher and catcher. He was right. Even though the league abolished the use of a flat bat, bunting became a decisive tool in the hands of players and managers that understood when and how to use it.

At the end of the 1893 season, confirmed slugger O'Rourke called upon the National League rule makers to abolish the bunt. He was joined in this appeal by Cap Anson.[11] They lost. Inside baseball would remain king until two other sluggers, named Ruth and Gehrig, reasserted power hitting as a winning tactic.

As to the effect the new 60'6" distance would have on the pitcher, Jim predicted:

Pitchers with speed and change of pace will be the cracks under the new rule, and all three men under contract with Washington possess the requisite qualifications. Maul is positive he has regained the full use of his arm, and if such is the case he will prove a winner. My knowledge of Duryea and Meakin is limited, but I have understood they are both speedy twirlers and will be able to hold their own.[12]

And as it turned out, in 1893, Washington pitchers Al Maul, Jouett Meekin, and Jesse Duryea won a combined total of only 26 games; whereas

Killen — the lefty pitcher the Senators sold to the Pirates — won a league-leading 36 games,[13] including a humiliating 19–0 shutout of the Senators.[14]

In spite of the hand Jim was dealt, the Senators started the 1893 season strongly, reaching first place in the 12-team National League on May 6.[15] But O'Rourke held onto first place for only a day. Injuries began to thin his front ranks, and without depth, particularly in his bullpen, his team began to slide slowly backward. By August, Washington was in last place, where it stayed. It would be 12 years before Washington again held first place for even a day.[16]

This would be Jim's final year as a major league player. At the end of 1893, Jim's lifetime batting average stood at .313. Only one player racked up more hits or more runs during the nineteenth century: Cap Anson.[17]

The year 1893 would also be Jim's last as a manager. In keeping with Washington tradition, O'Rourke, too, was given his walking papers at the close of the season.[18]

Jim could have just walked away, forsaking baseball to concentrate on his law practice and real estate investments in Bridgeport. He was considered to be the second wealthiest ballplayer, behind Cap Anson, who, like Jim, had enjoyed many years of star income and had invested his surplus earnings in real estate.[19]

24

National League Umpire (1894)

"The necessity of discovering among the lost arts an automatic, never-failing, level-headed umpiring machine grows more apparent every day."[1]

—*Sporting Life*

After playing all nine positions plus captain and manager, there was still one role Jim O'Rourke had not tried: umpire. At the spring meeting of the National League, the question of umpires came up. The *Chicago Tribune* reported the outcome of these discussions:

> As a result of that talk five umpires have thus far been chosen, at the head of the list being the veteran manager Harry Wright. After this honor was conferred upon the baseball hero of a quarter of a century it was suggested that a good companion for him would be Orator James O'Rourke of last year's Washington team, and his selection was unanimously endorsed.[2]

Jim assumed that his 25 years of experience arguing with umpires had more than prepared him for the challenge. He therefore accepted the stress-free position of a National League arbiter. Lawyer O'Rourke would now be Judge O'Rourke.

Once again, he would be working for the courteous and competent Harry Wright. What could possibly go wrong? No more worrying over his batting average. (He would no longer carry a pencil and paper with him to recompute his average after every at-bat.) No more chasing long fly balls or legging out bunts on 43-year-old legs. His new position would be no more difficult than that of scorekeeper or spectator. He would be paid to watch major league games from "the best seat in the stadium."

However, when the season commenced, reality hit home. Jim discovered that he had to put up with abuse from other orators of the diamond eager to take exception to his every decision, and without his wit or gentlemanly demeanor. His first assignment was the season opener between Brooklyn and Boston on the old South End grounds in Beantown, where he had covered first base for Harry Wright. The dispatches from Boston chronicled his initiation:

> Jim O'Rourke officiated as umpire in his initial game and the best that can be said of his work was that it was impartial. Several of his decisions on the bases were decidedly off, and kicking was common on both sides.[3]

It gets worse. Much worse. The sportswriters were relatively easy on the Orator after his first foray into the fine art of making losing teams and fanning batters believe they were fairly treated. For the return match between Boston and Brooklyn, the gloves came off:

> "Please Don't Shoot the Umpire!" was one of the familiar signs on baseball ground in the far West some years ago, and, perhaps, the placard touched a sympathetic chord in the hearts of the exasperated spectators when the poor official was doing his best, thus preventing bloodshed. It is a rare thing to see a spectator on a ground in the East prepared to order the umpire to throw up his hands, but unless Mr. James H. O'Rourke improves in his work or is removed by President Young from the staff of League umpires one may expect to hear of a homicide on some of the diamonds in this vicinity.
>
> As a matter of fact President Byrne of the Brooklyn club is seriously thinking of having the sign painted: "Please Kill the Umpire," to be used in the future whenever occasion demands it.
>
> To say that the work of the umpire yesterday was poor would be using a very mild term. From start to finish he gave the Brooklyns the worst of all decision, and, in short, prevented them from winning the game. At one stage, in the third inning, he refused to allow Daub to go to his base on four balls, claiming that he struck at a ball, and then declared him out on strikes, enabling the Bostons to make a double play, leaving only one man on base with two out, whereas, the correct decision would have placed three men on bases with nobody out.
>
> It was, however, in the ninth inning that the umpire made his best effort. Treadway, who had made a three-base hit, was on third with two out, and Daub was at the bat. The score was 7 to 4 in favor of Boston. Daub hit far over Bannon's head for three bases, sending in Treadway and changing the score to 7 to 5. Daly walked to the plate prepared to bat, but, to his astonishment, the umpire had declared Daub out for failing, as he claimed, to touch first base on his long hit. Before the onlookers were informed of what had happened the umpire disappeared in the dressing room. In this he showed good judgment, as the spectators, who had seen Daub touch every base, were wrought up to a high pitch of excitement and were liable to forget themselves.
>
> It was an exciting game from start to finish, but Mr. O'Rourke made all the excitement. His rulings on balls and strikes and his base decisions merited the condemnation that they received. Unlike the Saturday game, in which Mr. O'Rourke was impartial in his mistakes, he gave everything to Boston. In short, the champions can alone thank the umpire for the victory credited to them.[4]

This searing review was from the *New York Times*. Writers further removed from the battlefield gave a more balanced report of O'Rourke's second attempt at umpiring. The *Washington Post* said:

> The Brooklyns attribute their defeat to a wet ball and to a strict interpretation of the rules by Umpire O'Rourke.[5]

The Washington writer's analysis was insightful. Some umpires are intimidated into calling close plays and ties in favor of the home team[6]; others, like O'Rourke, get run out of town on a rail. If you call 'em as you see 'em, you better have thick skin and fast legs, or, like Hurst, able to defend yourself. Counselor O'Rourke, who had played left field because of his strong arm, and who received professional training as a boxer, could have stood up to the unruliest player, but Sir James did not feel an authority figure should have to. Rules and umpires, like contracts and league constitutions, were to be respected and obeyed. Sir James was, after all, a lawyer. Umpire O'Rourke was as surprised and offended by the belligerent reaction his wise decisions aroused on the ball field as Counselor O'Rourke would have been if an attorney was abusive to a judge in a court of law.

On April 25, when O'Rourke officiated at a game in Philadelphia, the *New York Times* returned to the subject of O'Rourke's fitness as a baseball judge:

> As soon as the reports of O'Rourke's poor umpiring reached Harry Wright, the chief of the umpires, he packed his grip and left for his Philadelphia home to make a personal observation. Yesterday O'Rourke umpired a fairly good game, and there was no cause for complaint, but the youths in the bleachers had not forgotten the exhibition of the day before, and Chief Wright was surprised to her these shouts:
> "Who's a robber? Why O'Rourke's a robber."
> "O'Rourke, we're making up a collection to send you home."
> "Scorers, how many assists did you give Mr. O'Rourke yesterday?"
> Finally the crowd grew tired of guying the unfortunate official.
> Chief Wright says that O'Rourke's fault is nervousness. He promises to keep him away from the vicinity in the future.[7]

O'Rourke was not the only umpire targeted for venting by players and fans. After the *Times* piece hit the stands, the *New York Sun* came to the defense of O'Rourke and umpires in general, saying there was entirely too much kicking and umpires should not put up with it:

> Players continue to gather around the umpire after a decision has been rendered, and also show a tendency to give him no end of back talk. In the case of Lynch, Hurst, Swartwood and O'Rourke, these umpires allow players more freedom of speech than should be tolerated....
> Section 1, rule 56, which provides that no person except the captains shall be allowed to address the umpire or question his decisions, has been repeatedly violated. In Saturday's New York-Baltimore game Lynch allowed McMahon to

dress him down for calling certain balls and strikes. He also permitted [feisty Baltimore manager John] McGraw to "chew" at him without inflicting the required fines. Kelley also abused Lynch roundly; and was only threatened with a $25 fine and expulsion from the game. When he declared Brouthers out on Brodie's interference with Murphy, Lynch was surrounded by the entire Baltimore team and allowed them to unnecessarily delay the game.[8]

When, on May 4, Jim officiated at a game in Washington that was won by the visitors, the local press made an attempt to give a balanced assessment of the performance of the umpire, who, during the prior season, had been the manager of the home team:

> Mr. James O'Rourke had his Washington debut as an umpire yesterday. He has not yet reached the Hurst standard of excellence, but he was a big improvement over the work done here by Lynch last week, and as he is still a little new to the business his few slip-ups of yesterday should be overlooked, even if they were costly to the Senators. There were only three decisions in the game which could have been called close, and in two of these instances the locals were in such position that they should have received the benefit of the doubt. But Mr. O'Rourke thought it best to give the Bostons each one of these decisions, and it would be idle to say that they did not have some bearing on the result. Outside of this O'Rourke's work was good. He has an exceptionally good voice for umpiring, and was prompt in making his decisions and in enforcing order on the field.[9]

Two weeks later, Jim accepted a request to umpire a ball game at his alma mater against rival Princeton.

> The grandstand was full of spectators, the bleachers were crowded, hundreds lined the diamond at every vantage point, and the place assigned to the carriages was completely filled. The blue of Yale waved jauntily in every quarter, and the delegations that had been selected to do the cheering for the home team were as vigorous in lung power as ever, sending wave after wave of cheering encouragement to their representatives on the field.[10]

This sunny outing at Yale among the genteel students must have been a welcome respite from confrontational professionals whose incomes depended on batting averages. Yale won 1–0. There was no mention of the umpiring. Decisions, rightly, were accepted as unassailable fact.

In time, Jim gained confidence and experience overseeing contests and the press paid less critical attention to him. Then, one day in Cincinnati, where the belligerent Charlie Comiskey managed the home club, it all came crashing down. The hometown press dispatch read:

> CINCINNATI, June 21.— Incompetent and wretched umpiring by James O'Rourke is claimed by Cincinnatians to be responsible for the loss of to-day's game. In the first inning, after two men were out and [Louisville's] Brown had scored, Grim was retired at the plate, but the umpire sent him back to third, claiming he was not ready to watch the play. Richardson's hit scored him.

Comiskey was hit three times in the last inning but was not allowed his base. A small riot was narrowly avoided, as the crowd was in a fighting character and mad.[11]

A new rule in 1894 prevented a batter from taking his base if, in the opinion of the umpire, he intentionally allowed himself to be hit by a pitch. Chief of umpires Harry Wright knew this would be a cause of grief for umpires because it required them to rule not on what the fans saw, but on the intent of the batter. Intent, Harry knew, was a difficult thing to judge. Jim thought Commie was purposely stepping into pitches to draw a walk in the close game. A week later, he was interviewed while passing through Cincinnati and called Comiskey a "contemptible, dirty ball player."[12] Jim was not alone in this opinion. Years earlier, *Sporting Life* had said of Comiskey his "sole claim to distinction rests upon his glib use of profane language."[13]

Of course the Cincinnati crowd hadn't seen it that way and nearly attacked the enforcer of the rules. Jim said, "It was an impossible job to make a decision that would please a fan who was previously resolved to stand by his team, right or wrong."[14] Of course, a less rigid wielder of authority would not provoke the reaction Jim received in Cincinnati. Two days later, Jim wired National League president Nick Young to tender his resignation, saying the duties of the position were too "trying."[15]

To this day, the 1890s are considered the worst decade ever for umpires.[16] Ironically, Jim was always respectful of the difficult role of the umpire when he was a player and never gave cause to be ejected from a game.

Jim's replacement, former teammate Tim Keefe, fared no better. Here are a few headlines of accounts of games in which Keefe umpired:

"Tim Called the Game. Plenty of Daylight Left but the Umpire Was Tired."[17]
"Vigorous Kicking at Keefe."[18]
"Umpire Keefe is Blamed" for Cincinnati Loss.[19]

Finally, Tim could take no more. While umpiring a game in St. Louis "marked by constant wrangling over decisions,"[20] Keefe walked off the field in the middle of the fifth inning. When interviewed the next day, Keefe gave the following explanation:

My sole reason for leaving the field yesterday, and for then and there determining to sever my connection with the National game forever, is that baseball has reached a stage where it is absolutely disgraceful. It is the fashion now for every player engaged in a game to froth at the mouth, and emit shrieks of anguish whenever a decision is given which is adverse to the interests of the club to which he belongs. This may not be wearying to the general public, but it is certainly disgusting to the umpire, who gives decisions disinterestedly and as he sees the plays. The continual senseless [and] puerile kicking at every decision has been infinitely trying to me.[21]

Note the use of the term "trying" that Jim used in recounting his reason for resigning.

Not long after he surrendered his indicator, Jim was introduced by Tim Hurst to a group of people at a baseball meeting at the Fifth Avenue Hotel as: "Formerly one of my companions in misery," to which Jim implored: "I beg of you, Timothy, do not allude to that unfortunate period."[22]

After O'Rourke retired from baseball, he was able to devote full time to his legal practice and real estate investments in Bridgeport.[23] His law clients were mainly other ballplayers and members of his church, neighborhood, and social clubs who, from time to time, required the services of a lawyer. Most cases were routine and low profile, and so they seldom made the news. However, if a reporter spied some humor in a case, especially if it was at the expense of the high-profile lawyer, as in the following account, the story might make the rounds of the national press:

> One day, he happened to be examining a young widow in the circuit court recently, and the following conversation occurred:
> "Can you give an idea of your late husband's stature?" asked the attorney.
> "Yes; he was about six feet tall."
> "What about his physique?"
> "He was big in proportion, hearty and healthy, and was what would be called a handsome man."
> "Then he was all that makes a perfect, manly man, was he?"
> "Yes," answered the witness.
> Jim arose, buttoned up his Prince Albert coat and, posing as a manly man, asked: "How was he as compared to me?"
> "Well," returned the witness, "my husband was a very handsome man."[24]

Occasionally, O'Rourke stopped by the Yale gymnasium to check up on his championship bat and talk law and baseball with the students. It may only be coincidence, but it was in 1894 that Yale invented the squeeze play[25] (a run-and-bunt stratagem with a man on third). Before steroids and short fences, runs were ground out 90 feet at a time.

Jim had not given up umpiring entirely. Over the years, he continued to umpire Ivy League college games. Instances I am aware of include:

June 1, 1895:	University of Pennsylvania at Brown[26]
June 8, 1895:	Yale at Princeton[27]
June 25, 1895:	Yale at Harvard.[28]
April 20,1896:	Brown at Holy Cross[29]
May 30, 1896:	Princeton at Harvard[30]
June 6, 1896:	Pennsylvania at Harvard[31]
June 5, 1897:	Princeton at Yale[32]

Nor had he really quit playing. On the few days in 1894 that he had not been umpiring or traveling, Jim caught for a prominent semipro team, the St. Josephs, "one of the top semipro teams in the state."[33] With the additional free time on his hands, Jim took over the duties as coach and trainer of the club. O'Rourke's 13-year-old son, Jimmy, was the team's batboy.

The St. Joes also had a future major leaguer, Billy Lush, who, as Jim had done, would also coach the Yale nine.

The St. Joes played against small-town clubs along the east-west and north-south rail lines out of Bridgeport. Opponents included Milford, Derby, Torrington, and Winsted, Connecticut.

Jim also organized an exhibition game against the Boston National League champions. Jim pulled together a picked nine from the St. Joes and other local teams plus Dan Shannon, a teammate from the Players' League Giants and fellow Bridgeport resident.[34]

Beginning a new relationship with organized baseball as a developer of talent, Jim secured for Billy Lush a place on the Rochester club for 1895. As the season and his protégé matured, Jim recommended Lush to the Washington Senators, who snapped up the outfielder in August of the same year.

This new life had to be the very definition of happiness for O'Rourke. No more travel. He was home with his family, a respected lawyer in his community, and he got to play baseball with a crack team on Saturdays.

But for a man who had played on eight championship major league clubs, it wasn't enough.

In 1895, Jim took advantage of his new freedom to pursue a life ambition: to run for public office. Jim's name had been floated in mid–September as a possible candidate for the state legislature.[35] His affable nature, name recognition, and legal training made him an ideal candidate. As a member of the Royal Arcanum, Knights of Columbus, Elks, and Bridgeport Social Club, he was accessible to Bridgeport voters.[36] In October, Jim O'Rourke was formally nominated at the Bridgeport Democratic Party convention.

Years later, Jim described himself as a Theodore Roosevelt Democrat. Teddy was a baseball fanatic and was living in New York in his early '20s, when Jim played for the Giants. The two may have met, as Teddy's home was not far from the Old Home Plate Restaurant, the hangout for Giants fans and players. A Roosevelt Democrat would have supported an interventionist foreign policy and a strong defense. We also know Jim supported racial equality and we can assume he favored women's suffrage (something he would have had to accede to in order to insure domestic tranquility in a household of nine women).

In his acceptance speech at the 1894 Bridgeport Democratic Convention, Jim promised to look out for the best interests of the city and said that he hoped to merit the approval of the people by the faithful discharge of his duties. According to the *Bridgeport Post*, "his remarks were enthusiastically greeted."[37]

On election night, Tuesday, November 6, 1894, Jim and Annie stood in the crowd on newspaper row to watch the election returns projected by a "mammoth" stereopticon. During lulls in the news, pictures of the candidates were projected onto a large canvas sail.[38]

As the night wore on, the crowd began to drift away, as from a ball game in the ninth inning. Jim stayed to the end. At the final tally, he had 4,874 votes; his Republican opponent over 5,200.[39]

The headline the next day was "Snowed Under! The State and Local Democratic Tickets Buried Beneath Republican Ballots."[40]

The post mortem attributed the Democrats' losses to the poor economy: "hard times" and "empty dinner pails."[41] A depressing economic report published the week before the election wailed:

Situation at Present Not So Hopeful — Delay in Demand for Holiday Goods — Depressing Tendencies Rule the New York Stock Market.[42]

Not even a candidate with a "name and face familiar to nearly every resident of Bridgeport"[43] could withstand a landslide caused by a nervous economy.

25

Bridgeport Victors (1895–1897)

When spring came in 1895, the 44-year-old lawyer began to pine for the crack of the bat, the scent of a well-oiled glove, and the feel of a shiny white ball fresh out of the box.

Jim gathered the best players from the local amateur and semipro teams as he had done for the challenge match against the Boston club the prior season. He coached them into an unbeatable nine and called them, appropriately, the Bridgeport Victors.[1] His timing could not have been better, as new advances in transportation technology allowed for large numbers of people to be gathered in one place at one time. The season of 1895 was the first that Bridgeport had an electrified trolley. Instead of the small, slow horse-drawn coaches, modern 60-passenger cars scooped up fans and sped them to the ballpark.[2]

An attempt had been made as early as March of the previous year to organize a first-class professional league, to be made up of eight clubs from New Haven, Bridgeport, Meriden, New Britain, Waterbury, Winsted, Hartford, and New London.[3] These efforts did not bear fruit.

Then, anonymous backers attempted to gain entry for a Bridgeport club into the fast Eastern League that had two openings in its eight-club circuit. Newark also applied for one of the openings. But the Eastern League opted for Rochester and Toronto. This was probably a better fit, since the Eastern circuit already had clubs in Buffalo and Syracuse.[4]

The decision was probably best for Bridgeport, too. The Eastern League was far flung, and Bridgeport would have been on the fringe. As a local sportswriter pointed out:

Bridgeport is hardly prepared for a team in a league as large as the Eastern and whose expense account must necessarily be very large. It would be far better to start in a state league or one embracing towns in nearby states close to the border line. A good, lively team in a league of this kind, managed by the right people in a way to command the confidence of the base ball loving public would pay without a doubt.[5]

A week later, there was encouraging news along these lines:

> There is considerable talk of forming another league in this part of the country and Bridgeport is mentioned as a likely member of it now that we cannot have a team in the Eastern league. The name for this proposed organization is the Atlantic league, and besides this city it will include, if plans mature, New Haven, Danbury, and Waterbury in this state, Newark and Jersey City in New Jersey and two cities in Pennsylvania.[6]

Perfect. Unfortunately, plans did not "mature."

Bridgeport was a baseball town without a league. Frustrated and impatient, O'Rourke went to bat organizing a league of his own. Having traveled throughout Connecticut with the St. Joes during the 1894 season, Jim was familiar with the teams, towns, and potential backers around the state.

By mid–January of 1895, O'Rourke was working the Connecticut media. When asked by the *Waterbury Republican* as to the prospects for a state league in 1895, Jim responded confidently:

> I take pleasure in saying though the movement is still in embryo it is not so embryonic as it was. I have been interested in the formation of either a state or interstate league for a period of some weeks, and have received encouraging assurances of cooperation from the following named cities in our state: Hartford, Meriden, New Haven, Waterbury, Norwich, and Bridgeport.
>
> My preferences lean toward the organizing of an interstate league composed of eight clubs. This includes Patterson and Newark, cities which would be a [valuable] acquisition to any league. My judgment, however, will conform to the one agreed upon by the promoters as the most feasible. In the course of a few days I am in hopes to be able to arrange matters so as to issue an invitation to the parties in interest to come together for the purpose of developing definite plans of organization. The time is flying and we ought to make progress.[7]

There was no lack of encouragement from the sportswriters or promoters. Former major leaguer Jerry Denny wrote to Jim that Norwich, where he resided, was eager to join a league. In Hartford, a traction company offered to build a ballpark for a league club.[8] Ex-governor Morgan G. Bulkley, the first president of the National League, stepped up to help finance a Hartford club.[9] The trolley line to the New Haven ballpark was electrified and the local traction company offered "to take considerable stock" in an Elm City ball club.[10] In New Britain, the electric trolley company provided ball grounds and promised free transportation to the ballpark for the players.[11] The baseball editor for the *Bridgeport Post* summed up the situation by saying "All that seems to be needed is to get the right kind of start."[12]

With baseball fever in the state running high, Jim called a meeting for February 4 at the Tontine Hotel in New Haven "for the purpose of forming a state league."[13] Representatives attended from Hartford, Meriden, Bridgeport and New Haven. An account of their discussions appeared the following morning in the *New York Times*:

> NEW HAVEN, Conn., Feb. 4 — A meeting of prominent baseball men of the State was held in this city to-day and it voted to form a State league. Among those present were J. H. O'Rourke, Bridgeport; John Henry, Arthur McManus, Hartford; Thomas Reilly, Meriden; W. T. Kearney, Waterbury; J. A. McKee, New Haven. It was decided to have a league of six teams, including New Haven, Hartford, Bridgeport, Meriden, Waterbury, and one other city not yet decided upon. A telegram was received from "Ted" Sullivan, formerly with the Washington (D.C.) Club, saying that he would put in a club at New Haven, and his offer was accepted. The next meeting will be held in this city Monday, Feb. 18, when officers will be elected.[14]

The meeting was followed by a frenzy of activity in each of the targeted cities. Former major league manager Ted Sullivan wired O'Rourke to tell him he had a club ready to go in New Haven.[15] Sullivan had managed the 1883 St. Louis Browns to a second-place finish. In 1888, Sullivan — like O'Rourke — had ended his managing career at the helm of the hopeless Washington Senators. (The two must have had a great deal to commiserate over.)

The following evening, a ball club was organized in Hartford with $2,500 in capital. In Meriden, a meeting was held for "those interested in the formation of a baseball club." Over $300 was raised on the spot through the sale of stock at $5 per share, against an eventual goal of $1,000.[16]

Prospects for a Connecticut baseball league had never been brighter. The *Bridgeport Herald* reported optimistically:

> The organization of a state league is in better hands than ever before and the movement is being inaugurated at the right time. With Henry, of Hartford, and O'Rourke, of Bridgeport, in the lead the national game will be a success in Connecticut.[17]

The *Bridgeport Post* carried a front-page cartoon of O'Rourke accompanied by a ditty:

> Base ball, it is hoped, we will have in the Spring.
> If O'Rourke can make the state league just the thing.
> The cranks on "the corner" are anxiously calling
> For the umpire's squeak and the coacher's bawling.[18]

At a meeting on February 18, 1895, to formally establish the Connecticut League, six cities were represented: New Haven, Hartford, Bridgeport, Waterbury, Meriden, and New Britain. There was probably an intention to align the new league with organized baseball, as Robert H. Young, the son of National League president Nick Young, was also present at the meeting and had stayed at Jim O'Rourke's home the previous evening.[19]

Jim was unanimously elected president, secretary and treasurer of the league. The members voted that each club must post a bond of $250 to guarantee playing out the season. An $800 monthly salary limit was established to maintain a level playing field. The delegates also decided that each club would play four games per week, two at home and two on the road. The visiting clubs guarantee would be $40 against 35 percent of the gate. The playing season was established as May 4 through September 14.[20]

With such enthusiasm, harmony, and detailed planning, what could possibly go wrong?

Everything.

Two weeks later, the *Bridgeport Post* sports editor, who, up to this point, had been cheering on the organizers, suddenly realized, "Things are looking a little shaky just now and there are suspicions in some quarters that the league will fizzle out after all."[21] In spite of the grand pronouncements, clubs were not being organized; funds were not being raised; players were not being hired. It was well known by this time that the optimum number of clubs in a league is eight, and the minimum workable number is six. In fact, a league could not join organized baseball in 1895 with less than six teams; and without permission to sign the National Agreement, the players and territory of the Connecticut League could be pirated by other leagues.

On March 6, the New Haven organizers went on record as refusing to continue unless the league had at least six cities, and they voiced pessimism at this likelihood.[22] The following day, more disappointing news:

> Discouraging news also comes from Hartford about the State league. It was supposed that the Capital City was in excellent shape, but according to the Hartford *Times* those who first started in have lost heart and it is almost decided to abandon all idea of organizing a team this year. Several persons who had announced their willingness to take stock backed out and others who it was thought would do so refused.[23]

Jim said he was "greatly surprised that Hartford was financially unable to back a club" but was not ready to concede the game. He did admit the league was "decidedly shaky" and sized up the situation in a March 13 interview:

> There are just three cities left that are solid. Bridgeport, Meriden and New Britain are all right but New Haven will not come in unless five other cities can be secured. Waterbury dropped out and it's difficult to get anyone to take its place. Winsted will [not] come in and neither will Danbury [because they do not have an enclosed field and therefore cannot charge admission].
> I have written to Norwalk but have not heard from anyone there yet and am in hope that they will think favorably of the league.
> I have spent time and money to make the league a go and I am almost discouraged now over the failure of the cities to come in. But if there is no league formed we will have a good club in this city and I think that we'll be able to get as many as two games a week without much difficulty.[24]

Then two days later, in the bottom of the ninth, headlines blasted:

League Not Dead.
President O'Rourke Says Prospects Are Now Bright.
Hartford Will Stay In.

President O'Rourke of the league said to-day: "The prospects are now brighter than they have been at any time since the organization of the league. Hartford has come to the fore after it was feared that the effort to locate a club there was about to fail. Last evening I received word from the Hartford people that the city would not drop out. Tommy York, the veteran baseball man [who began his 10-year National League career in Hartford in 1876], will place a club there, and every thing is now rosy for the success of the scheme. I have not been able to secure a sixth club, but it is still possible that another city will want to enter the association. If it does not the league will go on with five clubs or if New Haven decides not to come in a good schedule for four teams can be made out."[25]

But the prospects of the new league were as uncertain as a baseball game. Hartford did not organize. The league did not form. In its lead sports story on March 30, 1895, the *Bridgeport Post* finally pronounced the game over:

The last sad rites might as well be said over the State league. It has not had strength enough to make a move in over a week. It looks as though Bridgeport would have to be contented with a game now and then during the season which is now almost upon us.

Creating a new ball club is hard enough; but to assemble a league requires the organizer to cajole seven other groups of investors in seven cities to invest simultaneously in a project of uncertain future. This requires a great deal of diplomacy and salesmanship on the part of the league organizer and absolute faith by the magnates in each other.

Remember how skeptical Jim was in 1873 about the prospects of joining the Boston Red Stockings, an existing club with famous stars, the "father of professional baseball" Harry Wright as manager, a ballpark and grandstand already built, and a board of directors of committed investors? Remember the long letters back and forth between Jim and Harry, just to allay the worries of one rookie to quit his job and join the most famous team of its age?

Now, two decades later, Jim had to convince hundreds of investors and players to commit to a league that did not exist. It's a wonder leagues ever get formed.

The *Washington Post* said Jim was "disconsolate" because the Connecticut League failed to materialize. But the veteran baseballist dusted himself off and began arranging exhibition games for his professional Bridgeport Victors. All the players were from the Park City, making the club one of the few that still represented a city in fact as well as in name.

To open the season of his one-team minor league, Jim invited the Cuban Giants to Bridgeport on April 12, 1895. Fast Day.

In June, for their third home game, the Victors played another all-black team, the New York Gorhams.[26] That same month, Jim hired a black outfielder, Harry Herbert.[27] A Bridgeport native,[28] Harry had played for Pawtucket in the New England League in 1894, where he hit a respectable .262.

I don't think Jim was out to change the world. He was just colorblind. He wanted to win ballgames and deliver the best sort of baseball to the fans. Of course, it is by millions of just such small actions that the world finally does change.

Herbert was apparently the right man for left field. He had a strong arm to throw runners out at the plate — a quality that had earned O'Rourke the job of left fielder for the New York Giants. In a throwing contest at Pleasure Beach, Herbert bested all his Bridgeport teammates, including catcher James O'Rourke.[29]

On August 13, the *Bridgeport Post* also lauded Herbert's offensive contribution:

> Herbert of the Victors has been doing some terrific batting in games of late. In the last seven games he made 12 hits with a total of 27 [bases], including three home runs.

That same day Harry demonstrated the praise was not unwarranted. In the final game of a series against South Norwalk, in the bottom of the ninth, with two out and Jim O'Rourke on first, Herbert "lined a great drive to center field, on which O'Rourke just got home by a splendid slide" winning the game 7–6.[30]

With Jim firmly committed to field a professional nine in Bridgeport, with or without a league to play in, other Connecticut cities were encouraged to field independent professional teams. As a result, Jim wound up with more than an ample number of competitors. In 1895, Jim's professional club played 58 games, winning 37, losing 20, and tying 1.

Connecticut opponents during the 1895 season included teams from Ansonia, Darien, Derby, Hartford, Meriden, Milford, New Haven, Norwalk, Shelton, South Norwalk, Torrington, Wallingford, Waterbury, and Yale University. The Bridgeport team also played two teams from New York City, plus the Rochester club of the Eastern League, the Springfield club in Massachusetts, and the Hackensacks of New Jersey. They even played the New York Giants on October 1, 1895, losing 16–7, inspiring a sportswriter to quip "The Victors Played Like Victims."[31]

But baseball is not just about winning and losing games; it's also very much about making and losing money. For this goal, Jim had all the right experience. He had managed two National League clubs. In Buffalo he built a new ballpark. He was ready to graduate to the next level in the baseball industry: team owner.

Fortunately, there were three parks in Bridgeport vying for his business: the Pleasure Beach amusement park; Athletic Park on the East Side of Bridgeport, "not a long walk"[32] from the Barnum Avenue trolley line; and Avon Park in Stratford, just over the Bridgeport line, where the Osceolas of 1868 played. All three venues had a lot to offer and were willing to make improvements.[33]

The owners of the Pleasure Beach amusement park promised to haul in 25,000 square yards of dirt, enough to create a smooth and level ballfield. The venue, located on an island, already boasted a covered grandstand and bleachers. The park also sported a roller coaster, midway, and other attractions. Two boats ran from a dock in downtown Bridgeport every half hour to the island. Plus a trolley line ran down a peninsula to a point less than a baseball throw from the island. A launch taxied patrons the last leg of the trip. The Bridgeport Victors played their first game at Pleasure Beach, on June 15, beginning a tradition of playing important games at the spacious venue. The inaugural game was against a "consolidated" team from Yale. The Victors lived up to their nickname 21–5.

Apparently, Jim was still designing uniforms for his teams, as a reporter could not resist pointing out:

> The new uniforms of the Victors are more serviceable than handsome. They consist of light blue material, black stockings, dark blue belt and cap.[34]

The Pleasure Beach ballfield, on the other hand, received rave reviews for its design aesthetics:

> The grounds were in an excellent condition. Like all "skinned" [grassless] diamonds, they are very fast. Hard hit balls come at the infielders with terrific speed; let the rolling spheres once get by the outfield and it is a home run or a three bagger every time. Wild throws to first or third will also prove costly as there are no "bleachers" [angled in] to stop them. The going and coming from the ground was made in good time. The game was over quickly and in time to catch the 5:30 boat.[35]

In late June, four Connecticut clubs that had taken wing during the 1895 season decided to establish a nonsignatory league, that is, outside the purview of the National Agreement and the strictures of organized baseball.[36] The game plan for the 1895 league was outlined in the *Bridgeport Post* of June 25:

> The managers of the base ball teams in Hartford, Meriden, Waterbury and this city have decided to from a league and the first games will be played July 2. By the arrangements which have been made between them each club will play four games a week, two at home and two abroad. A schedule has been made out for two weeks and if it works satisfactory another one will follow to the first of

September. There is no reason why these four cities should not have a nice little contest.

But after a few games, even this plan fell through when it was discovered the Waterbury team "could not get its grounds."[37] Since the four contesting teams failed to play each other the requisite number of games, there was no champion; at least not one unanimously recognized. Typically, in these ad hoc scenarios, bravado and self-promotion play a large role in establishing a pecking order. The Hartfords attempted to arrange a five-game series with Bridgeport "to decide the championship of the state."[38] In the best tradition of Connecticut baseball in 1895, this, too, failed to take place.

A century later, the SABR Minor League Committee and the Encyclopedia of Minor League Baseball recognized O'Rourke's team as the 1895 Connecticut State League champions based on research supplied by historian Frank Williams, who also determined from an analysis of box scores that Jim had amassed a .429 average, racking up 15 hits in 35 at bats.

The 1895 season wound down, fittingly, amid new rumors of a Connecticut State League. On October 17, the *Meriden Journal* reported that the traction company owners planned to establish teams in Bridgeport, New Haven, Meriden, Hartford, Waterbury, New Britain, Middletown, Derby and Danbury. But as with all the previous schemes this one, too, failed to see fruition.

On October 29, the *Bridgeport Post* reported that O'Rourke had been approached by D. A. Long, an organizer of a new Atlantic League, but Jim said he was not interested when he learned that former major league player Sam Crane was behind the scheme. According to a *Bridgeport Post* reporter:

> Manager O'Rourke does not have a very high opinion of Mr. Crane and from his experience with that gentleman while [O'Rourke was] in the New York team it may be said that he has good grounds for it.... O'Rourke then informed Long that he would have nothing to do with anything that Crane was in any way connected and that ended the matter.[39]

I do not know what "good grounds" Jim had for not trusting Sam Crane, who later became a sportswriter and wrote a glowing biography of O'Rourke as part of a newspaper series entitled "The Fifty Greatest Ball Players."

Crane played second base for the Buffalo Bisons in 1880, the year before Jim took over the team. His next major league team was the New York Mets, where he would have been a teammate of John O'Rourke. (Is the distrust Jim has of Crane based on reports from his brother?) In 1884, Crane played for the Cincinnati team of the one-season-wonder Union Association, a league John contemplated joining in Boston. In 1885, 1886 and 1887 Sam Crane played in Detroit, St. Louis and Washington, all National League clubs that Jim competed against. During the 1890 Baseball War, Crane crossed the picket line to play for the Pittsburgh and New York National League team. (Did Crane undermine Brotherhood solidarity?) In an interview with *The Sporting News*, Jim was diplomatic and circumspect:

O'Rourke's Plans for 1896

Special to *Sporting News*. BRIDGEPORT, Conn., October 21.— James H. O'Rourke, the well-known ex-ball player, says he will not enter a team in the new Atlantic Association.

There is talk of a new league being formed by Connecticut and New Jersey clubs. J. Dennis, Secretary of the Arlington Athletic Club is interested in the project and O'Rourke believes that a good circuit could be formed.[40]

But when the United Press issued a story on November 2 that quoted Crane, as saying Bridgeport was to be a member of his new Atlantic Association, Jim took off the gloves. A follow-up interview with O'Rourke, appearing in *The Sporting News* of November 9, 1895, ran under the headline:

O'Rourke Is Outspoken

Jim Will Boycott Any Association Sam Crane
Is Connected With

In the interview, Jim had this to say about Crane:

Now, I know Crane of old and would not willingly cooperate with him in anything. He was connected with the Wilkes-Barre and Metropolitan Base Ball Clubs and with other lesser organizations at different times. I am afraid that he has borne the reputation of being a sower of discord wherever he was connected with ball players. After leaving baseball ... he embarked in the newspaper profession. He worked first on the New York *Press*, and afterward on the New York *Advertiser*.

After making it crystal clear that he would have nothing to do with Sam Crane Jim offered his recipe for an "ideal league": Patterson and Newark in New Jersey, and from Connecticut, Bridgeport, Derby, Hartford, and Meriden.[41]

A league did come together, but without representation from New Jersey. A group of Connecticut clubs— that were already organized with players and ballparks—coalesced into a new professional circuit. Compared to the shuttle diplomacy of 1895, it was all rather anticlimactic. At an organizing meeting on November 22, Jim met with representatives from other Connecticut cities to formalize the organization. All eight member clubs were from small industrial towns located principally along the Naugatuck River valley: Ansonia, Bridgeport, Derby, Meriden, New Haven, Torrington, Wallingford, and Winsted. They called themselves the Naugatuck League.

The new organization was professional in every sense of the word, with a regular schedule of championship games, a constitution, and board of directors. D. W. Porter, owner of the Derby-Shelton club and the president of the Derby Traction Company, was elected president.[42] T. M. Burns of Torrington was elected secretary. Two committees were formed: one to recruit additional cities to the league and a committee to draft bylaws. Attorney O'Rourke served on both.[43]

Most of the backers of the new circuit were owners of the electric trolley lines in their respective towns. The transportation companies looked upon ownership of ball clubs as vertical integration. They were giving townsfolk places to go. The *Bridgeport Post* reported that President Andrew Radel of the Bridgeport Traction Company had announced plans to erect "a fine grand stand" and to finance other improvements to the ball grounds at Stratford's Avon Park. With only slight exaggeration of the importance of this news to the Greater Bridgeport community, the *Post* editor appended the following commentary:

> This will be good news to the lovers of the game in this city. They have been anxiously waiting for just such an announcement. And when the season has opened and the cranks having journeyed over to Stratford to see the new grounds find that they are all anyone could wish for we can guarantee that President Radel may safely think of running for mayor.[44]

Comparing the relative ease with which the Naugatuck League came together in 1896 versus Jim's fruitless ordeal the year before, the *Bridgeport Post* printed the following analysis:

> It is recognized that there is business in the organization this time, and that there will be no disappointing fizzle as there was in the state league attempt last season. This of course is due in a measure to the different kind of men back of it. In the venture last spring Manager O'Rourke soon found out that there was nobody of any standing behind the representatives of the other cities and the result was failure. It is entirely different this time. Manager O'Rourke is satisfied that everybody means business.[45]

With the organizing complete, Jim turned his attention to arranging pre-season exhibition games. The first outing of the 1896 season was a benefit on April 13.[46] Harry Wright had passed away six months earlier and a number of his friends organized games to raise money for a monument in his honor.

Three days after "Harry Wright's Day" the Bridgeport Victors again welcomed the Cuban Giants to the Park City. Bridgeport won this contest 12–9.[47] In a return match the following month, the Cubes downed the Victors 9–8.[48] An odd feature of the second game was that each of the Cuban Giants scored one run and no more.

While many other owners extended invitations to black ball clubs, O'Rourke was the only magnate with a black player on his roster. When the Victors turned pro in 1896, Harry Herbert became the only black player in professional baseball.

Although only an average batter in 1896, hitting .264, Herbert had the good habit of getting his hits when men were on base and he had hands that balls stuck to. Even the *New York Herald* took note of the Park City leftfielder:

> In left field Harry Herbert lifts the boys on the bleachers from their seats by wonderful running catches.[49]

Herbert was also reliable, playing in all 40 games of the season; he had a good eye at the bat, drawing a team-leading 20 walks, and he came through in the clutches, as on June 6, 1896. Bridgeport was down two runs against league-leading Torrington. In the ninth inning, with two outs and two strikes against him, Herbert walloped a three-run homer to win the game 7–6. The Victors won the 1896 pennant by one game.[50]

Jim did his share, too, leading his team by example as catcher and manager. He hit a whopping .437 and drew 17 free passes to first base. In one game he was six for six with three home runs.[51]

But professionals do not play baseball just for the love of the game. The business side is critical, too. By this measurement, Jim did very well, earning $4,000 (about $80,000 today) from his club in the Naugatuck Valley

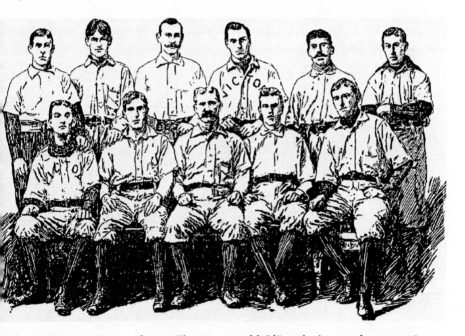

The Bridgeport Victors of 1896. The 46-year-old O'Rourke is seated center; 18-year-old "Pop" Foster is standing third from right. Foster would play four years in the majors. Second from right is Harry Herbert (engraving: *Bridgeport Herald*, October 4, 1896).

League.

Knowing he had a good thing going, Jim called his buddy Roger Connor, who was still living in Waterbury, and encouraged him to enter a club in the league. He did.

On March 15, 1897, the league was again reorganized and renamed the Connecticut State League. Senator Sturgis Whitlock was elected president, and Jim secretary and treasurer.[52] Bristol and Waterbury replaced Ansonia, New Haven, Wallingford, and Winsted. Except for New Haven, the cities that dropped out were just too small to support a professional ball club, and have not had a paid nine since. New Haven returned the following year. The league, like the waters of the Naugatuck River, was seeking its proper level.

For the 1897 season, Harry Herbert was back as the starting left fielder. He hit a career-high .327 and coaxed 20 walks out of opposing pitchers.[53]

The Bridgeport entry in the Connecticut State League did not have a nickname, so the sportswriters conferred upon the team the soubriquet Soubrettes, "coquettish maids in French comic opera."

In 1897, in spite of the stigma of an uninspiring nickname, the Soubrettes finished third. Jim's personal stats were historic. He won his second straight batting title in the Connecticut State League with a .405 average and led the circuit in hits (130), doubles (28) and triples (9).[54] In recognition of his pace-setting performance, the sportswriters elevated the team's moniker to the Orators for 1898.

Jim celebrated by building a new ballpark.

26

New Home for the Bridgeports (1898–1900)

Each year the Bridgeport team played a majority of its games at the Pleasure Beach ballpark, attracted by its billiard-table field and large covered grandstand. However, there was one significant drawback to the venue. Because the grounds were located on an island, fans had to take at least two trolleys to reach the shore of Long Island Sound, then take a ferry to the island. Once they arrived at the dock they still had to walk a half mile to the ballpark, while negotiating barkers, cotton candy and other manners of distractions along the midway.

By a fortunate coincidence, the final leg of the trolley route passed right by the old O'Rourke farmland now owned by Jim and John.[1] For the 1898 season, Jim built a ball diamond and covered grandstand on his half of the inheritance. He called it Newfield Park.

The Bridgeport fans and media were appreciative of the time and money that Jim had invested to bring professional sports entertainment to Bridgeport. A local newspaper printed the following editorial:

> The *Telegram* does not know whether Jim O'Rourke has or has not made any money in the game this season, but it hopes he has. It does know though that he has furnished wholesome recreation for hundreds of Bridgeport people who admire him for the courage he has displayed in persevering where his unfair critics would have made a most miserable failure, even if they had the means at his command. He has never been troubled with "swelled head" and has gone right ahead in spite of curs that have been yelping at his heels, not even turning to notice them, when their actions have been exasperating in the highest degree.[2]

For the 1898 season, Jim ushered the Connecticut State League into organized baseball by signing the National Agreement.

The 1898 season also marked the end of Harry Herbert's playing career, cut short after only 10 games, not by prejudice, but by the bane of all athletes:

injury. In an account of one game, Herbert was identified as "one of Mr. O'Rourke's reconcentradoes."[3] Herbert is listed on page 4 of *Minor League Baseball Stars,* Vol. 3, a publication of the Minor League Committee of the Society

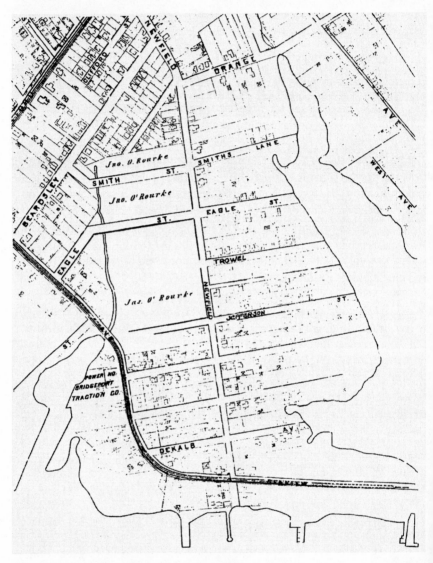

Field of Dreams: O'Rourke property in the East End of Bridgeport. Note that brother John owned the northern half of the property, which was developed for housing and a neighborhood school. The lower portion became Newfield Park in 1898. The heavy lines were trolley routes. Newfield would remain the home of Bridgeport professional teams through 1941 (Atlas of the City of Bridgeport, 1896. Historical Records Department, Bridgeport Public Library).

for American Baseball Research (SABR). Historian Frank Williams[4] concludes that Herbert was given an opportunity to compete in the national sport because "O'Rourke believed in integrated baseball." Indeed, I do not know of any black player in the nineteenth century who played on the same team in organized baseball four years running. Most were hooted off the field by fans, rival managers, or even their own teammates.

O'Rourke had not forgotten the attempt by the New York Giants in 1887 to hire black pitching ace George Stovey. It was eight years before Jim was in a position to overturn the order of Spalding and Anson against blacks in baseball, but once he had the power to do so, he wasted no time in overturning the precedent.

Herbert may also have been the first black umpire. At Newfield Park, on September 10, 1898, for the final game of the season:

> No official umpire put in an appearance, and Harry Herbert, an ex–Bridgeport player, was pressed into service. He did fairly good work. There was much kicking at him from the spectators and the visiting players, but on the whole his work was well done.[5]

It would be another half century before another owner would have the courage to hire a black player. That player was Jackie Robinson.

At the end of the 1898 season, the Orators were again in third place. By this time the league had matured into a tight-knit circuit of eight clubs, all contained within the borders of Connecticut. This helped to keep down travel costs, and made overnight hotel stays unnecessary. Of the two sides of baseball management — winning pennants and making money — the latter is just as elusive as the former.

Jim realized early that the long-term route to profitability was to recruit, groom, and then sell the most talented players to the major leagues. Moving players along as quickly as their skill allowed hurt a club's chances to win pennants, but it brought in revenue for owners and benefitted the players.

Jim had a real gift for spotting potential in a player. With 22 years of major league experience under his belt — five of them as a manager — he was also adept at coaching rookies to improve their performance.

By 1898, Jim was ready to begin harvesting talent. Some of the players he sent up were from his club and some were members of other teams in the Connecticut State League; but it was usually Jim's recommendation that earned the minor leaguer a tryout, as these sample newspaper accounts attest:

> February 23, 1898 — Twirler Donovan, the strapping pitcher recommended to Earl Wagner by Jim O'Rourke, is exercising in a Philadelphia gymnasium, and will report in Washington on March 31.[6]
> June 4, 1898 — Phil Corcoran ... will be sampled by [Cincinnati Manager Buck] Ewing ... with the endorsement of Jim O'Rourke.[7]

THOMAS E. DOWNEY

Thomas E. Downey, Cincinnati's active young infielder, was first given a trial on the professional diamond in 1903 by James H. O'Rourke, Bridgeport's veteran manager. After three years with Bridgeport he played in the then outlaw Tri-State League and eventually landed with Birmingham, of the Southern Association. He played at second, third and short for that team in 1908, and in 1910 for Cincinnati filled in at both third and short.

	G.	B.	F.
1908	142	.280	.928
1909	119	.231	.909
1910	109	.270	.895

BASE BALL SERIES 400 DESIGNS
SWEET CAPORAL CIGARETTES
The Standard for Years
FACTORY Nº 42 4½ DIST. N.C.

Two stars sent up by O'Rourke: Patsy Dougherty (left), and Tom Downey. Dougherty played 10 seasons in the majors, Downey six (1911 T205 Gold Border cards).

Within 10 years the majors included 11 graduates of Jim O'Rourke's baseball university:

> The Connecticut League, the snug little circuit which Orator Jim O'Rourke, the 55-year-old ex–Giant, acts as guardian of, is mighty proud of its products. Fred Parent and Hobe Ferris, of the Boston Americans; Wild Bill Donovan, of Detroit; Pat Dougherty [of the Chicago White Sox]; Dan Murphy, of the Philadelphia Athletics; Danny Hoffman, of the Yankees; Charlie Armbruster, of the Boston Americans; Harry Howell, of the St. Louis Browns; Heine Batch, of Brooklyn; Eddie Phelps [of Pittsburgh; and] Dave Altizer, of the Washington team ... are all Connecticut League grads.[8]

To be sure, some were cups of coffee, like Waller, who pitched one inning for the Giants, striking out one and giving up three hits; and a catcher named John Robinson. Jim arranged a tryout for Robinson with the Giants. After catching his third — and last — game, the New York Times wrote the epitaph for his brief baseball career: "The new man was not able to catch Mathewson's delivery, and four passed balls were marked to his account.[9]"

Jim also discovered some future stars, like Patsy Dougherty, who posted a .342 batting average in 1902, his rookie year with the Boston club of the American League. Dougherty went on to lead the new league in runs in 1903 and 1904, and in stolen bases (47) in 1908.

Although many sportswriters thought of the league as O'Rourke's, no one can really *own* a league or even control it absolutely. Because of Jim's success, others began to covet what he had created. Before the start of the 1899 season, his old friend Tim Murnane began angling to annex the Connecticut State League. Tim headed the New England League, an aggregation of small towns in the Boston area. Many of the burgs were too small to adequately support a team. As a result, an average of two clubs turned over each year. Recently, Murnane's circuit had shrunk to six teams. Tim reasoned that if he could siphon off four of Jim's cities and combine them with his four strongest teams, he would have a more stable league.

Only one problem: Jim was not about to let Tim dismantle his prized Connecticut State League. Even though Murnane was planning to retain Bridgeport (along with Waterbury, New Haven and Meriden), four of Jim's cities would be left high and dry without a league. O'Rourke and his buddy Roger Connor of Waterbury blocked the merger bid:

> The New England League officials were anxious to bring the deal to a focus, but could not do so on account of the opposition of those well-known baseball veterans—Roger Connor, formerly of the New Yorks, who owns the Waterbury franchise, and Jim O'Rourke, also once a "Giant," who owns the Bridgeport franchise, and is Secretary of the League. Roger said he would drop out of the league before he would give his consent. The objection was based on the increased expense in traveling. President Murnane was on the scene Monday and Tuesday but could not induce his brothers of days gone by to accede to his views. Both sections will go on their own lines.[10]

Tim had appealed to Jim's business instincts, claiming that a combined league of the largest cities would be the most profitable. In pursuing this strategy, Murnane had not factored in Jim's love for the game and his paternal instincts toward the other owners in "his" league. It might have made sound business sense, but it wasn't right.

Nor did Jim need to strengthen his league. The Connecticut State League was stable and would remain unchanged through the next two years.

Murnane did not give up on his design to strip Jim's league of its strongest clubs. But he would have to wait for a moment when Jim was vulnerable.

In 1900, the Orators placed third in the eight-team Connecticut State League, behind the batting of its 50-year-old founder, who hit .358. The Orators also boasted the league's top three base stealers, with a combined 173 thefts.[11] Inside baseball was alive and well in Bridgeport.

27

Defending the Minor Leagues (1900–1903)

Peace had come to baseball. In hindsight, it was because Spalding had won. All opponents had been vanquished from the field and the National League was the only major league left standing.

As the century turned, the status quo of organized baseball was solidified by a new National Agreement, signed by the National League and minor league representatives, including James H. O'Rourke on behalf of the Connecticut State League. The *Chicago Tribune* heralded the signing of the baseball treaty:

> Washington, D.C., April 13–[Special.]— Eleven minor leagues, embracing 76 clubs, will start the season of 1900 under protection of the national agreement. The organizations, together with their officers, as registered at National league headquarters are as follows:
>
> American league, B. B. Johnson, President — Chicago, Ill.; Cleveland, O.; Kansas City, Mo; Indianapolis, Ind.; Milwaukee, Wis.; Detroit, Mich.; Minneapolis, Minn.; Buffalo, N.Y.
>
> Eastern league. P. T. Powers, President — Montreal, Que.; Toronto, Ont.; Rochester, N.Y.; Syracuse, N.Y.; Providence, R.I.; Worcester, Mass.; Springfield, Mass.; Hartford, Conn.
>
> Atlantic league. Horace S. Fogel, President — Elmira, N. Y.; Scranton, Pa.; Wilkesbarre, Pa.; Allentown, Pa.; Reading, Pa.; Athletics of Philadelphia, Pa.; Newark, N.J.; and one other yet to be selected.
>
> Interstate league ... New Western League ... New York State league ... Virginia league ... Canadian league ... Central league ... Indiana league....
>
> Connecticut State league, James H. O'Rourke, secretary — Waterbury, Derby, New Haven, Meriden, New London, Norwich, Bridgeport, Bristol.[1]

By signing the National Agreement, leagues and clubs recognize the sanctity of one another's territory and reserve lists. No league in organized baseball could place a team within five miles of a team in another league; let alone place teams in a city belonging to another league or bribe a club to switch leagues.

Jim was protected from the politics and intrigue of baseball — and from jealous league presidents. Or so he thought. There was a time bomb ticking in the above announcement. Note the name of the first league in the above list and the size of the cities that would make up its intended circuit. Although the new American League failed to launch in 1900, "owing to a lack of financial support in Philadelphia,"[2] its bully organizer, Ban Johnson, returned to the field in 1901, but not as the head of a "minor" league. He challenged the National League's monopoly on "major" league status. You can almost see the bats waving in the air as Johnson challenged the status quo:

> Nothing could be more mistaken than the impression that our league is asking favors of the parent body [Johnson is referring to the National League]. We did not ask permission to go into Chicago, but we are well established there. If we decide to take in Baltimore and Washington we will not ask the National's consent. Of course we fully realize that in order to take in the two last named cities our league must henceforth be conducted on a national basis. There can be no drafting of players [by the National League] or any other restriction placed upon the American by the National league. We will come in here on an equality with the National league or go it alone as an Independent organization.[3]

This was the equivalent of a declaration of war, and Jim's Connecticut State League would be caught in the coming crossfire.

Reminiscent of the Players' League War a decade before, the press reported on the jockeying among the leagues for the best players:

> The Players' Protective association is in accord with the new league [the American League], and most of its members will be induced to jump if they can see good financial backing for the clubs. The Brooklyn [National League] club promises to be the principal loser in the matter of players, no fewer than nine of its men having promised to jump to the latter organization. If it loses such men as Pitchers McGinnity, Kitson and Kennedy, Catcher McGuire, First Baseman Jennings, Shortstop Dahlen, Third Baseman Lave Cross, and Outfielders Keller, Keeler, and Jones, it will be a death-blow to the club, and the chances are that these stars will secede.
>
> Other clubs will suffer, but not so badly. Nearly all the Cincinnati players are dissatisfied with their treatment by President John T. Brush and have expressed their willingness to take a jump. Chicago will lose several of its best players, including two pitchers. Pittsburg will be minus two of its star twirlers, who did so much to land the team in second place. Three of Philadelphia's players are said to have promised their services and men from other clubs have also given their words to join the [American] league.[4]

Sporting Life editor Frank Richter summed up the situation at the end of the 1901 season, showing the inevitability of another baseball war:

> Being unable to come to terms with the National League for franchises for Washington, Baltimore and Philadelphia, the American League withdrew from the National Agreement, occupied Washington, Baltimore, Boston and

Philadelphia, and made a successful raid on National League players, the
Boston, Brooklyn and Chicago teams being hard hit.[5]

The National League board knew its member clubs would have to hire
away a good number of players from the minor leagues to replenish the players they were losing to the upstart American League. So in the fall of 1901,
President N. E. Young of the National League "decided to abrogate the
National agreement" with the minor leagues. This would leave the National
League clubs free to "draft" players without compensating the lower clubs.
This move to grab player resources took the minor leagues by surprise. In
fact, they had already forwarded $6,200 in "protection" money to the league
for the 1902 season.[6]

At that moment there was no National Agreement. There was no association — guided by law or tradition — that could be considered organized
baseball. It was every league for itself.

In response, Jim and nine other minor league officials, including Tim
Murnane of the New England League, banded together for "mutual protec-
tion" by creating the National Association of Professional Base Ball Leagues.
They drafted their own National Agreement on October 24, 1901, at the Fifth
Avenue Hotel in New York.

The *Washington Post* was direct and to the point regarding the motivation for forming the NAPBL:

New Organization Formed to Frustrate National and American [League]
Attempts to Strengthen Their Teams by Raiding the Minors— Board of Arbitra-
tion Vested with Supreme Authority— Heavy Fines Provided for Players Who
Jump Contracts.[7]

O'Rourke and Murnane were two of the five members elected to the
National Board of Arbitration, the governing body of the organization.[8] The
published role of the NAPBL would be to settle player disputes, territory
conflicts, and other issues among the member leagues.

The delegates drafted a new National Agreement that set rules as well
as fines for their infraction. Even "before anything was decided, all the delegates present pledged themselves to uphold and recognize in every detail
the new agreement for the next ten years."[9]

Salary limits were set for the monthly payrolls: for clubs in class "A"
leagues, $2,000; class "B," $1,200; class "C," $1,000; and class "D," $900.[10]
The Connecticut State League was designated class "C."[11]

Henry Chadwick, "the father of baseball," was elected an honorary
member of the association; he, O'Rourke, Murnane, and four other league
presidents were named to a Rules and Contract Committee.[12] A standard
player contract was adopted, "almost identical to the old form used by the
National League."[13]

The Fifth Avenue Hotel in New York, where the generals of the baseball wars planned their grand strategies (engraving: Van Wyck, *Recollections of an Old New Yorker*).

Another purpose of the NAPBL board was to represent the minor leagues in negotiations— or war — with the major leagues. By this time, the American League had begun to assert itself as a major league. As such, it did not join the NAPBL. The American, like the National League was the enemy.

The NAPBL took the bold initiative of bypassing the heads of the major league and sending letters directly to the American and National League *club* owners asking for cooperation. Jim and his fellow board members soon realized that National League president Nick Young had not bothered to consult with *his* board members when he announced the disavowal of the National Agreement with the minor leagues. Some clubs wrote back to the

NAPBL to promise their support. Others said that they would reply after they had a chance to meet with their fellow club presidents at the upcoming league meeting in November 1901. A letter from Pittsburgh club president Barney Dreyfuss disclosed that "Several of the magnates ... are very angry over the matter, and trouble is promised when the National League meets."[14]

In this case, the pen actually was mightier than the sword. The strategy of the minor leagues of "banding together" worked, partly because the other side was anything but organized, thanks to Spalding. As *Sporting Life* editor Frank Richter explained:

> At the annual winter meeting of the League in New York the organization became deadlocked in a battle over the presidency, Messrs. N. E. Young and A. G. Spalding having received four votes each. After the 25th ballot the Young delegates left the room, and then Col. John I. Rogers, acting as chairman, ordered the 26th ballot, and declared A. G. Spalding elected. The latter assumed charge of the National League records, but the Young delegates refused to acknowledge his election and secured an injunction. To this the Spalding faction filed a demurrer. The case dragged along all Winter until March 29, when Judge Truax overruled the Spalding demurrer. The National League met on April 1 [1902], when Mr. Spalding resigned the presidency he had claimed, and Mr. Young also withdrew his candidacy, thus ending the factional fight and the legal proceedings. Messrs. Temple, Ward, Soden, Talcott, Elliott and Pulliam all refusing to accept the nomination for the presidency, it was decided, on April 3, to leave the presidential office vacant. Mr. Young was elected secretary-treasurer and a Board, consisting of Messrs. Brush, Soden and Hart, was appointed to conduct the affairs of the League during the 1902 season. Mr. Brush was appointed chairman of this committee, with power to act.[15]

To deter players from signing with a "non-cooperating" major league or nonsignatory minor league, the minor leagues passed a resolution to levee fines for this infraction, ranging from $300 for a class "C" player to $1,000 for class "A." In 1901, these were hefty fines indeed, representing a third to a half of a one-year salary.[16]

Granted, it would be difficult to collect the fine after a player jumped to a major league. However, if the player ever wanted to rejoin a signatory league to the new National Agreement, he would have to make good the fine to "get back into the club or maintain his original standing."[17]

By the third and final day of the inaugural NAPBL convention, the delegates were "confident that their new organization will be able to live against the greater baseball organizations— the American and National Leagues."[18] With their new confidence, "The new association has decided to discountenance the practice of farming players. A resolution was adopted making it a punishable offense for any one club to employ a player under the farming system."[19] Farming, the practice of a higher league loaning a player to a lower league for an indefinite period, had benefits for both clubs involved. The lower club received surplus major-league caliber players, and was reimbursed for the player's salary. The higher club was able to skirt the limits on rosters by farming out surplus players. Yet many financially secure minor league owners resented the system, because it deprived them of control over their players. The higher club could recall a farmed-out player on a moment's notice. Seasoned owners also understood that stars developed a following among local fans and this built attendance. But when the fans know the star is just visiting, they do not form the same strong attachment.

While engaged in the business of reorganizing organized baseball, Jim also resumed his participation in local Bridgeport politics. He received an appointment to the fire commission on June 1, 1901, and served until January 1, 1904, including one year as president of the four-person commission.[20]

During his term, a new mayor was elected: hard-drinking Dennis Mulvihill. The two could not have been more at odds and as a consequence, O'Rourke's tenure was stormy. The *New York Times* did not ordinarily cover rhubarbs within suburban administrations, but the Orator made pronouncements that were just too colorful to pass up. To wit:

> James H. O'Rourke called Mulvihill a political hyena, and said he had demoralized the Fire Department.[21]

And this was mild. O'Rourke once introduced a state bill to "curtail the mayor's powers," arguing that Mulvihill was "unfit for office by reason of his viciousness, perniciousness and mischievousness."[22] At city hall some of Jim's arguments with hizzoner were so heated they had to be broken up by the police.

Although Jim devoted many hours to his volunteer positions with the City of Bridgeport, there *were* compensations. One day when Jim was catching, New London manager and centerfielder Mickey Finn swaggered up to the plate spitting tobacco juice and boasting that the game would be over with the next pitch. He was awaiting the throw when all of a sudden he whirled and began swearing at O'Rourke. Perhaps it was wrong of Jim to comment on the derivation of Finn's family name just at that moment, but whatever the cause, Counselor O'Rourke was not going to tolerate foul language in any ballpark he owned. He demanded Finn be arrested for "using obscene language." The Bridgeport officer seemed almost eager to oblige.[23]

For the 1901 season the Orators finished second with a 61–44–2 record. The Orators dropped to third in 1902 with a 53–58 performance.

In 1902, Springfield, MA, joined the Connecticut State League. It was therefore no longer a state league, so its name was changed to the Connecticut Valley League.[24] All the cities in the circuit, except Bridgeport, were located along the Connecticut River Valley. In 1903, the League name was shortened simply to Connecticut league.

On the national scene, Jim was reelected to the board of the NAPBL at its second annual convention in October 1902.[25] Attesting to the effectiveness of the new organization in carrying out its mission, J. H. Farrell, secretary of the minor league association, announced:

That so far as he knew, neither the National nor American League had taken any minor league players at the close of the season, in violation of the National agreement.[26]

The NAPBL board still had to devote significant time and energy to avoid being hit in the crossfire of the latest baseball war. The American League was trying to climb up the baseball ladder to attain a level equal to the National League; and the latter was fighting just as hard to maintain its monopoly on the highest plateau of baseball. Thanks to the NAPBL, the minor leagues were, so far, unscathed and still prosperous.

When National League officials suggested an affiliation with the NAPBL, the later responded that it "would remain independent of any other organization."[27] This episode shows how weakened the once-omnipotent National League had become as a result of its continuing war with the American League. The NAPBL demurred because to align with one of the behemoths would invite raiding by the other. But the minors could hold *both* major leagues at bay, since each was afraid the other might negotiate a unilateral treaty with the minors, thus cutting off its best source of new quality talent. However, after some reflection and debate, the NAPBL passed a conciliatory resolution that left the door open and delineated terms under which it would consider an affiliation:

O'Rourke in 1902. This year, Jim celebrated 31 years of continuous service in the professional ranks of the national game, more years than any other player.

In the event of a joint invitation being received from the National and American Leagues by the National Association [of Professional Baseball Leagues] in the interest of tripartite agreement, the National Board of the new organization [the NAPBL] would preserve its present from of government and individuality intact. In other words, the National Association will decline to act with the two older leagues until their differences have been settled, and then only on a basis of equality of representation in baseball councils.[28]

The National League eventually accepted that the American League was here to stay, and recognized it as an equal major league. A peace treaty between the two mega-leagues was signed on January 10, 1903.[29] To confirm the new status of the American League, its 1903 pennant winner was invited to face the National League champions in a post-season World's Series.

The NAPBL immediately seized the initiative to propose a framework for organized baseball under the postwar landscape with two separate but equal major leagues. On February 18, 1903, Jim and fellow NAPBL board members met in New York to draft a new National Agreement that would encompass all leagues. The *Washington Post* reported out the NAPBL's vision for the proper working relationship between the major and minor leagues:

> There is said to be no doubt but the National Association [of Professional Baseball Leagues] will demand an equal representation upon the proposed new national board with the American and National Leagues. Under the old regime the old national board of the National League settled all disputes between clubs and players of the minor leagues, and the latter had no representatives on the board.[30]

But Ban Johnson of the American League was reluctant to sign any agreement between the leagues until he "could be certain there would be no friction in the workings of the peace agreement."[31] This was magnate-speak for unresolved player-ownership disputes.

When all cases were eventually resolved, leaders of the National and American Leagues met in Buffalo in August 1903, and adopted a new National Agreement. Ominously, the new constitution of organized baseball was created without representation from the NAPBL, even though, as the *New York Times* pointed out, it was the "organization which embraces all the professional baseball associations in this country, with the exception of the two big leagues."[32]

The minor leagues could no longer play the two strongest leagues against one another. They were united. Order had also been restored to the National League, the magnates having finally agreed on a new president, Harry Pulliam, who would serve for six years.

In the fall of 1903, NAPBL president P. T. Powers called a meeting of the board to discuss and respond to the new National Agreement drafted by the major leagues.

One of the sticking points was an article that created a National Commission for the purpose of enforcing the terms and provisions of the agreement. That in itself would not have been objectionable, except that the three-member commission was to be composed of the owner of the National

League Cincinnati club, August Herrmann; the president of the American League, Ban Johnson; and National League president Harry Pulliam.[33] The NAPBL wanted representation on the National Commission.

Although the agreement excluded representation from the NAPBL, it appeared to be a genuine attempt to protect the rights of all leagues. The majors had at least been listening. The *New York Times* detailed the major provisions of the new National Agreement:

> Should the measures be adopted by the National Association of Minor Leagues, these minor organizations will have absolute control of their own affairs. Under the terms of the agreement, the major leagues shall adopt all rules governing the game of baseball.[34]

Those first two articles might have been a bit condescending, but the next provision can only be scored a win for the NAPBL:

> The practice of "farming" is prohibited. All right or claim of a major league club to a player shall cease when such player becomes a member of a minor league club, and no arrangement between the clubs for the loan or return of a player shall be binding between the parties to it or recognized by other clubs.
>
> The right of a minor league club to its players shall be absolute, except that from Aug. 15 to Oct. 15 of each year major leagues shall have the privilege of selecting players from National Association clubs for the following season upon payment of $750 for each player so selected from clubs in Class A leagues; $500 for each player so selected from clubs in Class B leagues; $300 for each player so selected from clubs in Class C leagues; and $200 for each player so selected from clubs of a lower class.
>
> A major league club may at any time purchase the release of a player from a minor league club, to take effect forthwith or at a specified date, provided such purchase is recorded with the Secretary of the commission for promulgation within five days of the date of the transaction.[35]

The draft differs from farming in that a farmed player may be recalled at any time from a minor league club, while a club is at risk of losing a drafted player only during a two-month period. Still, the minor league representatives objected to a two-month window (it had been only one month under the prior National Agreement). They also felt the purchase prices were too low under the draft scheme.[36] As a result, the NAPBL board voted to reject the proposed National Agreement.[37]

On September 10, 1903, a delegation from the NAPBL met in Cincinnati with the National Commission to hammer out the few differences, and on September 12 a new National Agreement was signed by representatives of the National League, American League and NAPBL.[38] Jim and his colleagues won some points, and lost others. The major leagues refused to accept minor league representation on the National Commission. (The minors would continue to pursue this goal.)

However, a request to reduce the drafting period was agreed to.[39] Then, on October 26, 1903, the National Commission (without consulting with the NAPBL) asserted "the absolute right of the major leagues to draft players from the minor leagues" and passed two amendments to the National Agreement that refined the rules applying to the draft:

> Rule 24 provides that each club must send to the Secretary of the National Commission before August 26 in each year, a list of its purchased players, and that none not on such lists, can ever be claimed after that date.
>
> Rule 25 provides that there shall be no purchases of releases of players made during the drafting period; that such purchases would not be allowed as against the draft of any such players. A definite interpretation was made so that the drafting period would be from Sept. 1 to Oct. 15, with no sales permitted during that time.[40]

A requested increase in the draft price paid to class "A" clubs, from $750 to $1,000 was refused, but a request to pay half the draft price at the time of the draft, and the balance on June 1, was agreed to by the big leagues. The "half payment idea" was a safeguard to prevent a major league team from drafting a player, giving him a tryout at the start of the season, then telling the minor league club they changed their mind if the player did not pan out. A number of the major league teams were abusing the privilege by drafting more players than they needed, and then culling the roster during spring training. The splitting of the payment protected both sides. It guaranteed a minimum benefit to the lower club even if the player was returned; and it gave the higher club an out prior to June 1, by which it would save half the draft price.[41] As it turned out, the postseason draft of 1903 was "very heavy." The Southern League alone received $4,750 cash on the barrelhead "for the men drafted, and that much more if they make good in fast company."[42]

A request to reduce the number of players a major league could draft from a class "A" club to one (instead of two), and from clubs in other classes to four, was denied.[43] (This would cause no end of dissension in the NAPBL.) An article in the *Washington Post* tried to soothe the worried minor league magnates and managers over the gutting of their starting line-ups by the just-ended 1903 draft:

> Heretofore, only about five per cent of the minor leaguers have remained in fast company, and unless there is an unusually large number of good players in the crops which have just been harvested the minor league clubs need not be worried much, for most of their men will be returned to them. All they need is enough players to open the season, for many of the drafted men will last a month or so in fast company before their inability is detected.[44]

Although the NAPBL delegation obtained only half the concessions they sought, the *Chicago Tribune* reported that "President Powers, speaking for the National Association, indorsed [sic] every article and said the amended agreement meets the full approval of the minor leagues."[45]

Powers, it turned out, was overstating the unanimity within his ranks. The class "A" American Association and Eastern League "strongly objected to indorsing [sic] the National Agreement on the grounds that the draft conditions and purchase prices were not satisfactory."[46] The class "A" delegates felt betrayed and staged an attempted coup on October 23 at the opening session of the 1903 NAPBL annual convention in Cincinnati. When this was thwarted, they walked out, leaving President Powers "dumbfounded."[47] An all-day session of the board on the following day "failed to effect a harmonious settlement" of the class "A" league grievances.[48] The class "A" leagues would continue to press for special considerations at future NAPBL meetings, creating strife and distraction in an organization that

Spalding Glove at turn of the century. Note the beginning of a web and the crescent-shaped pad running along the thumb and the base of the palm (engraving: Spalding Catalog).

should have been challenging the National and American League domination of the National Commission and National Agreement, not each other.

Taking a respite from the turmoil within America's idyllic pastime, Jim and the other delegates to the 1903 NAPBL convention found a few free hours to visit the World's Fair in St. Louis. The *Spalding Guide* of the following spring carries a group photo of the 58 conventioneers arrayed on the steps of what is now the St. Louis art museum. Board members Powers, Sexton, Murnane and O'Rourke are in the front row.

28

The Bridgeport Orators
(1903–1907)

On the home front, 1903 was a special year for Jim, as it was the year his son, Jim Jr., joined the Orators. To distinguish between the two Jim O'Rourkes, the fans began to refer to senior as "Uncle Jeems."

Jimmy also followed in his father's footsteps academically, studying law at Yale for three years (1900–01 through the 1902–03 academic year). In his freshman year he made the varsity baseball team as shortstop.[1]

Jim Senior must have taken particular pride when the Yale nine of 1901 whipped the New York Giants 5–4 at the Polo Grounds in a pre-season exhibition game.[2] But perhaps not so joyful when the Yale youngsters beat the Bridgeport Orators 7–5 the following month.[3] Senior's chest swelled again when, on June 1, 1901, Yale beat Princeton in the final inning, the winning run brought in by Jimmy O'Rourke.[4]

Jimmy was ineligible in 1902, but for the 1903 season he again made the team, covering third base well enough to garner notice by the press:

> O'Rourke, at third, son of Tom O'Rourke, of the famous old Metropolitans, covered an acre of territory around his position and managed to pull in three bad ones.[5]

As sure as you can count on the Yankees wearing pinstripes next season, you can be sure that when Uncle Jeems read this, he sent a congratulatory letter to his son immediately after firing off a telegram to the *Washington Post* suggesting they fine the sportswriter who made errors on both his name and his team name.

Playing for Yale, 22-year-old Jimmy was seeing a good portion of the Northeast. Besides the usual foes at Harvard, Georgetown, and Princeton, Yale beat Navy at Annapolis in the spring of 1903. In another scrapbook-worthy account, the *New York Times* noted the winning run "was scored by O'Rourke."[6]

After the close of the college baseball season in late June 1903, "against his father's advice, young Jim decided to become a professional" ball player.[7] The sports editor of the *Chicago Tribune* commented:

> Bridgeport, Conn., is not the only place where a father and son have played on the same ball nine. A. C. [Cap] Anson used to play the game with his father on the nine at Marshalltown, Ia., and between them they made it interesting for all comers. Jim O'Rourke and his son are now playing at Bridgeport. If O'Rourke junior is as good an orator as his father used to be the umpires in the Connecticut league must have a hard time.[8]

The Anson duo, although earlier, was on an amateur nine. The O'Rourke pairing was the first instance of a father and son playing on the same professional team at the same time.[9] The *Washington Post* remarked on the intergenerational teammates:

> It was a unique spectacle ... when Father Jim made a quick line throw from behind the bat to second base to head off a base stealer and his son caught the ball for a swift put-out.[10]

Jimmy helped his dad bring the Orators back up to third place in 1903, with a 59–47 record for the year.

Following the baseball season, Jimmy, practiced law in his father's office.[11]

In 1904, Jim Senior had the opportunity to play one last game in the majors. It was on September 22 for the New York Giants against St. Louis. If the Giants won the game, they would win the pennant. Manager John McGraw figured it couldn't hurt to have a catcher in the lineup from the last winning season. (Superstition is no stranger to a baseball clubhouse.)

On this day O'Rourke became the first major leaguer to play in four decades. Jim was 1 for 4 at bat; and at age 54, he became the oldest player to hit safely in the National League. Jim caught all nine innings, which also earned him the distinction of being the oldest player to complete a major league game.[12]

The Giants' pitcher was Joe McGinnity, the eighth Hall of Fame pitcher that O'Rourke caught during his career. (The others were Al Spalding, Johnny Ward, Jim Galvin, Buck Ewing, Tim Keefe, Mickey Welch, and Amos Rusie.[13]) No other Hall of Famer has caught as many Hall of Fame pitchers. The next highest is five, a distinction shared by King Kelly, Buck Ewing, and Bill Dickey.

The Giants won the game and the pennant on that day in 1904. *The Sporting News* recounted Jim's final game as a Giant:

> Jim O'Rourke, the grand old man of baseball, beside whose records those of Pop Anson and other veterans fade into insignificance, yesterday made his first appearance in many years at the Polo Grounds and handled the delivery of Iron

Man McGinnity without a flaw.... Those who expected to see a spavined "has been" behind the bat saw a man who has the activity of a youngster combined with the practical experience of a Warner, a McGuire or a Robinson. Not one of the Iron Man's shots got away from "Jeems" nor did he make a wild throw. His one error was the muff of a throw from McGinnity to the plate to force a runner, and this was due to over-anxiety to complete a double play at first base. At the bat O'Rourke made a hit and got to third on a bad throw by Steinfeldt. He blazed his way around the bases like a minor league colt.[14]

The following month a contest was arranged between the 1889 champion Giants and the 1904 pennant winners. The game was a benefit to raise money for the employees of the Polo Grounds. Dan Brouthers, who was the Giants groundskeeper at the time, covered left field for the veterans.[15] Others old rebels were there, too. Jim O'Rourke caught and Roger Connor played first base.

There were also players from the 1889 championship team who had opted to play for the National League in 1890 instead of joining the Players' League.

The former Baseball War combatants were amiable, as Civil War veterans were in reunions of northern and southern soldiers at a famous or forgotten battle site, for they understood what their former enemies had endured. When Buck Ewing passed away two years later, Jim O'Rourke called him "The greatest baseball player who ever lived ... and one of the greatest leaders any nine ever had."[16] Within a decade, Spalding would write his memoirs, and while it is easier for victors to be magnanimous, his recounting of the war was noticeably without rancor.

Relations between Jim and his fellow owners were not so convivial. It may have been unavoidable that some of his peers would be resentful of the Bridgeport owner's influence over the Connecticut League. Although the president in 1904 was Sturgis Whitlock, Jim was secretary and treasurer and performed all of the work of the league, without pay. His years of volunteer service gave him a moral authority.

O'Rourke spoke out against syndication (owning more than one team in the same league). He was concerned about the owner of the New Haven club, attorney Cornelius Danaher, who also had an interest in the Meriden club. The arrangement enabled Danaher to switch pitchers between teams for a tactical advantage.[17] Jim's efforts to maintain a level playing field infuriated Danaher, who became increasingly belligerent, challenging Jim's decisions and undermining his authority. Finally, in September 1904 Danaher organized a coup to wrest control of the Connecticut League from its founder. As the neutral *Hartford Times* reported:

Cornelius J. Danaher of New Haven aspires to Jim O'Rourke's place as leader in the league. To this end he opposes every move by the veteran. Danaher has created trouble ever since he broke into the league. The league has survived under O'Rourke who is not so bad as he is painted, while more paint is needed in the case of Danaher.[18]

When it was announced that the Connecticut League had scheduled its annual meeting for November 15, 1904, the *Bridgeport Post* added ominously:

> The election of offices is also on the program and it is then no doubt that Manager Danaher will start his great attempt to "throw Manager O'Rourke out of organized baseball."[19]

Jim survived the Danaher onslaught and within two years the New Haven owner sold out and retired from the league.

Since Jim was the owner of the Bridgeport club as well as the catcher, a local sportswriter imagined what the annual contract negotiations were like:

> OWNER: Have you decided to affix your signature to a contract?
> JAMES: No, not for the dough you paid me last year.
> OWNER: But the environment ... is nowhere finer than in the Bridgeport club, for here you will have all the benefit of my long experience in the National League.
> JAMES: See here, I don't play baseball for the environment. What I want to know is this: Am I going to get more salary this season ... or not?[20]

I presume counselor O'Rourke helped the owner and catcher reach an amicable compromise.

In 1905, the Orators finished third in the Connecticut League, winning 64 games and losing 49. In five years, the club had won 55 percent of its games.

In 1906, Jim was reelected secretary of the Connecticut League; W. J. Tracy of Bristol was elected president, replacing Sturgis Whitlock of New Haven; and T. P. Prindeville of Holyoke, treasurer.[21] All three gentlemen served without pay. Jim could afford to be generous with his time. By now his personal fortune was estimated at $75,000[22] ($1.5 million in current dollars).

One day his conflicting responsibilities collided. Jim had a run-in with rookie umpire Bill Klem, who got his start in the Connecticut League in 1902. When Klem ejected one of the Orator's players, the Bridgeport manager (and league secretary) fumed: "You'll never umpire another game in this league." To which the unflappable Klem retorted: "Maybe so, but I'll umpire this one."[23]

Because of his spunk, Klem advanced to the majors where he served for 37 years and umpired in 18 World's Series.[24] After retiring, Klem was inducted into the Hall of Fame.[25]

Years later, Jim had another altercation with an umpire; this one involving a called ball on a pitch that clearly nicked the outside corner of the plate. The Orator let loose a tirade on the man in blue, who was under-

Left: Lawyer O'Rourke. According to a fellow attorney, Jim's work as a lawyer was mainly as a counselor. O'Rourke sought to avoid litigation when, in his opinion, the interests of his clients would be advanced (*Bridgeport Herald*, September 11, 1904). *Right: Uncle Jeems Points Out an Umpire's Error* (engraving: *Bridgeport Herald*, August 20, 1905; illustration by Barber).

standably indignant. Jim could see that the umpire wasn't sure if it would be a good idea to fine his boss for using abusive language. (At the time, O'Rourke hired and fired the umpires.) So Jim removed his catcher's mask and addressed the crowd: "As President of the Connecticut League I hereby fine player James O'Rourke ten dollars for swearing at the umpire."[26] Crisis averted.

On the field in 1906, "Uncle Jeems" O'Rourke played his last full season, batting .244. He realized his days in uniform were numbered. To prepare his son to take over the leadership of the team, O'Rourke made Jimmy the team captain in 1906.[27] "But," added a sportswriter, "as Orator Jim is seldom out of the game, the duties are not heavy."[28] Still, 25-year-old Jimmy took his new role seriously, even providing encouragement to the most experienced player on the team: "Hit it out, dad, make him pitch to you; that's the boy."[29] Boy?

By 1907 Jim was spending more time on national baseball politics, and less time actually playing the game. O'Rourke Senior appeared in only 24 games that year. But 27-year-old son Jimmy was hitting his stride. In 1908, he hit .303, scored 98 runs— second highest in the league — and led the Orators with 48 stolen bases.[30] As a batter and base runner, he had learned his lessons well.

During the 1908 season, O'Rourke felt his son was ready to move up to the big leagues, and so advised his contacts at the New York Highlanders (later the Yankees) of the American League. A terse announcement appeared in the press toward the end of the season:

BRIDGEPORT, Conn., Aug. 15.— Second Baseman James O'Rourke of the Bridgeport Connecticut league baseball team, was notified yesterday that he had been sold to the New York Americans, and ordered to report in New York immediately.[31]

Jimmy O'Rourke (*Bridgeport Herald*, April 14, 1901).

When he joined the Highlanders, Jim Junior became only the second son of a major leaguer to play in The Show.[32] Jimmy's inaugural game was on August 15, 1908, against Cleveland. He was 1 for 5 at the bat.[33] Jimmy's primary position was at second base, but he was also tried at short, third, and the outfield. Unfortunately, he enjoyed only "fair success"[34] in his 34 games with the Highlanders, and was sold to the Columbus Senators of the American Association.[35] Jimmy remained in the high minor league for six more years before retiring to pursue a career in the law.

29

The NAPBL (1907)

As his on-field playing declined, O'Rourke's duties in the national minor league organization demanded an increasing amount of attention. Each year dozens of cases had to be adjudicated by the Board of Arbitration of the NAPBL. Most were small disputes among clubs or between clubs and players. But there was also at least one major case each year that would require a great deal of deliberation, the hearing of testimony, and often a visit to the seat of the conflict.

Although time-consuming, his work on the NAPBL board provided Jim the opportunity to see many old friends in the baseball community on a regular basis.

On January 8, 1907, at the NAPBL annual meeting at the Fifth Avenue Hotel, Johnny Ward was on hand to represent the six-week-old Atlantic League. He was also present to represent a club in the Pennsylvania, Ohio and Maryland League in a dispute over the pennant. The *New York Times* outlined the particulars of the case:

> John M. Ward was a conspicuous figure in a case in which the club at Uniontown, Penn., appealed from the decision of President Richard Guy of the Pennsylvania, Ohio, and Maryland League, declaring that Uniontown and Braddock had tied for the championship. Mr. Ward was the counsel for the Uniontown Club. The evidence showed that the championship race was close between Uniontown, Waynesburg, and Braddock, with the former having a slight advantage. That club at first was declared the winner, but at a subsequent meeting of the league, games were taken away from both Uniontown and Braddock, which left them a tie in the final record. While the board decided that President Guy had acted in good faith, his proceeding was against the law, and therefore the championship goes to Uniontown.[1]

Chalk up a win for attorney Ward. This case is an example of the numerous but relatively routine disputes that O'Rourke and his fellow board members were required to settle.

On the other hand, the Atlantic League issue was one of the more serious cases that O'Rourke would hear in 1907. The Atlantic League, comprised of clubs in Trenton, Wilmington, Chester, Reading, Allentown, and Pottsville (the last four in Pennsylvania), had applied to join the NAPBL and thereby receive protection for its players and territory under the National Agreement. Ward was present to give reason why protection should be accorded to the Atlantic League. In the meantime, the Tri-State League, which had also applied for protection under the National Agreement, announced plans to place teams in Trenton and Wilmington in order to reach the minimum population of 400,000 in order to be admitted as a class "B" circuit. In retaliation, the Atlantic League threatened to invade Newark and Patterson.[2] Ward lost this contest.

The Tri-State League was admitted into the NAPBL and that league was awarded Trenton and Wilmington. The Atlantic League's application was tabled because the board felt its "chances for playing organized baseball were slim."[3]

These cases give a good idea of the type of issues that Jim had to deal with on an almost-constant basis to orderly and properly sort out which players belonged to which clubs and which clubs belonged to which leagues. Baseball lawyer O'Rourke must have performed these duties to the satisfaction of his fellow league magnates, for he was again elected to the board of the NAPBL in 1907. The full lineup of the seven-member body included:

> Eugene T. Bert of San Francisco, president of the Pacific Coast League; J. D. O'Brien of Milwaukee, president of the American Association; Judge W. H. Kavanaugh of Little Rock, president of the Southern League; T. H. Murnane of Boston, president of the New England League; D. M. Shively of Kansas City, president of the Western League; M. H. Sexton of Rock Island, ex-president of the Three I League, and James H. O'Rourke, secretary of the Connecticut League. (The board, with the exception of Mr. O'Brien, who takes the place of Ed Grillo of Toledo, is the same that existed last year.)[4]

J. H. Farrell also served on the board in his capacity as NAPBL secretary. President Powers was also reelected, unanimously, in spite of efforts by "one or two malcontents" to engineer his defeat. To forestall similar shenanigans, Powers was given a four-year term."[5]

The NAPBL also voted to change the date of the annual meeting back to October, so the eighth convention was also held in 1907, October 29–31. The attendance at these events had grown steadily. At this meeting, held at the venerable Fifth Avenue Hotel in New York, 150 delegates were on hand, representing 23 of the association's 36 member leagues.[6]

As the confab opened, the class "A" leagues swaggered up to the podium to demand more than equal treatment. The request by the American Association and Eastern League for a new "AA" status with drafting privileges on a par with major leagues was unanimously ignored.

A more serious issue was looming: a case that would test the power of the National Association against the major league-controlled National Commission. Remember the territory dispute between the Atlantic and Tri-State Leagues that was settled without bloodshed? Well, a week later it all unraveled. As sometimes happens, financiers do not come through with promised capital. When this happens, league organizers need to scramble for replacement cities. Sometimes, "illegally," they look for these new clubs in territory owned by another league. This is what the Tri-State League did, and as punishment the league was thrown out of the NAPBL, making it an "outlaw" league.

The risk of being outlawed was the only clout organized baseball had for keeping leagues in line. A banished league found it more difficult to recruit players, because a player that signed with an outlaw club would never be able to transfer to a league associated with organized baseball. Advancing to a higher league would not be a career option.

Jim was incensed by the action of the Tri-State, particularly after he and his fellow board members took two plum cities from the Atlantic League, represented by his friend Johnny Ward, and handed them to the duplicitous Tri-State gang. This was a betrayal of the trust upon which all businesses rely. Jim had lived through too many eras of baseball chaos. The law had to be respected and upheld, even baseball law.

In retaliation (retribution?), Jim introduced a measure at the October 1907, NAPBL meeting to induce the players who had broken valid contracts to jump to the Tri-State League to return to their former clubs. The news story in the *Washington Post*, carried under the headline: "Jumpers Must Return to the Clubs They Jumped," read in part:

> NEW YORK, Oct. 31.— At the final session of the National Association of Professional Baseball Clubs this afternoon, a resolution of J. H. O'Rourke, of Bridgeport, Conn., was adopted, by which all players adjudged guilty of contract jumping and placed upon the ineligible list by the national association shall be forever debarred from playing with any clubs of the association, excepting those of the Tri-Sate League. The Tri-State League was excepted from the provisions of the measure on account of the agreement by which it came into the association. Twenty-two players are affected by the decision.[7]

One of the players, infielder Al Odell, jumped from Jim's Bridgeport Orators to the Lancaster Club of the Tri-State League. All the players covered by the measure jumped to the Tri-State League while it was outside the NAPBL and not covered by the National Agreement.[8]

The O'Rourke resolution was not about the players or the Tri-State League. (The wayward league had mended its ways and had been reaccepted into the NAPBL within weeks of turning outlaw.[9]) Instead, Jim had created a test case about one of his favorite issues: who shall rule baseball? More specifically, what rights shall the minor leagues have over their affairs? The Tri-State League was forgiven its transgressions and readmitted by NAPBL only by agreeing to certain terms and conditions. According to the *Chicago Tribune*,

> When the Tri-State league was taken into the ranks of organized ball it was agreed by all the parties to the national agreement that players who had jumped contracts and gone to the Tri-State should not be allowed to play elsewhere than in the Tri-State. Recently, the national commission reinstated several players in this category. The National Association [of Professional Baseball Leagues] objects to such reinstatements.[10]

In the words of a *Chicago Tribune* writer, O'Rourke was telling the National Commission, that in matters pertaining to the minor leagues, the commission should "keep its hands off"[11] that it did not have the authority to reverse or alter rulings by the NAPBL. An article appearing four months later in the *Chicago Tribune* gives an idea of how vexing the resolution was:

> Garry Herrmann of Cincinnati and Pulliam of the National league, straightened out their differences today on the matter of the widely discussed O'Rourke "blacklist" resolution adopted by the minor leagues last fall. A meeting of the national commission, which was held in Pulliam's office, brought them together. Ban Johnson, the third member of the commission, also was on hand as well as John E. Bruce, secretary of the commission.
>
> These baseball men were behind locked doors for three hours, and when they adjourned Secretary Bruce announced the clouds had cleared away.[12]

O'Rourke had stared down the National Baseball Commission, and the commissioners blinked. National League president Harry Pulliam, when asked to comment on the National Commission's reversal of position because of the O'Rourke resolution, said only: "All's well that ends well."[13]

Although the 22 errant players who broke their contracts were unreinstated by the National Commission, all were then reinstated in good standing by the NAPBL.[14]

This battle ended peacefully, with the major leagues backing down, but the war for power within baseball would continue between the National Commission and the trust-busters at the NAPBL.

30

Hanging Up the Glove (1908–1910)

"A man's never old till he'll admit it."[1]

— James Henry O'Rourke

In an exhibition game between present and past Boston players, O'Rourke resented being teamed with the "old-timers."[2] Although Jim was spending an increasing amount of time on administrative duties, he was not ready to retire from the game altogether. In 1908, he played in 18 regular season games.

There is some debate over Jim's age. O'Rourke's birth year has variously been reported as anywhere from 1849 to 1854. The source of the conflicting information may have been the Orator himself, who could not resist tampering with our perception of his age.

Reunion of Boston Old-Timers, September 24, 1908. During homecoming week in Boston, the former major leaguers contested a nine of former college stars. The battery was Spalding and O'Rourke. Murnane guarded the first sack. The vintage baseball game was conducted under 1879 rules before a crowd of 5,000. The professionals won 7–2.

Jim O'Rourke (#3) is 58 years old in this photograph, Tim Murnane (#7) is 56 and Al Spalding (#12) is 58 (1909 Spalding Guide).

241

From 1885, when Jim was interviewed for a number of publications after winning the 1884 batting title, until 1996 when the official records were changed, based on new research, it was universally accepted that James Henry O'Rourke was born on August 24, 1852. However, recently unearthed evidence points to an 1850 birth year. Herewith the authoritative (and precise) references to Jim's age.[3] You be the judge.

- Lifelong acquaintance Tim Murnane, writing in the *Washington Post* in 1906 and 1910 supports the 1852 birth year. O'Rourke and Murnane were teammates in 1870, when Tim was 18. Murnane admits to being born June 4, 1852.[4]
- *Graduates of the Yale Law School 1824–1899*, published by Roger W. Tuttle (Tuttle, Morehouse & Taylor) in 1911, lists August 24, 1852, as Jim's birth date.
- An obituary written in 1919 (the *New York Times?*) states that Jim was born in 1852.[5]
- On Jim's original Hall of Fame bio sheet, August 24, 1852, was typed on the document, probably in 1845, when Jim was inducted. The sheet was sent to Jim's youngest daughter, Edith, for confirmation, either in 1945 or perhaps in 1968, when she was interviewed by Hall of Fame historian Lee Allen. The date has since been written over in black marker: "Sept. 1, 1850."
- *The Baseball Encyclopedia,* Published by Macmillan in 1969, "the official record of Major League Baseball" listed a birth date of August 24, 1852. However, the most recent edition of the "Big Mac," published in 1996, shows September 1, 1850, as O'Rourke's date of birth.
- The seventh (2001) edition of *Total Baseball* also gives September 1, 1850.

Why the change from August 24, 1852, to September 1, 1850? During the 1990s, Rich Bozzone, a member of SABR, researched vital records of the State of Connecticut to establish the birthdates of Jim O'Rourke and his brother, John. He found two definitive documents, which he described in a letter to Frank Williams on October 2, 1999:

1. "A record of guardianship paper dated September 7, 1869, showing that the mother, Catherine, was named as guardian for the children: John age 20 (making birth year probably 1849), James age 18 (making birth year 1851 or 1850) and Sarah age 14."

2. "The Bridgeport, CT birth-tape, which is #1428299. On page 65, I found a record of birth for James O'Rourke of September 1, 1850, with the parents showing as Hugh and Catherine O'Rourke. Also, there was the earlier listing for John O'Rourke with a record of birth as August 23, 1849, with Hugh and Catherine O'Rourke showing as parents."

Frankly, I was somewhat dubious that information published during Jim's lifetime — presumably provided by him or a relative — was wrong. Also, there were two problems with the new evidence. First, the guardianship paper indicates Jim was only 18. Regardless of whether he was born on August 24 or a week later on September 1, his birth year would be 1851, not 1850. If we are to allow that the admittedly illiterate Catherine miscalculated by one year, the correct birth year could just as likely be 1852 as 1850. The math does support an 1849 birth year for John, but as evidence to resolve Jim's true birth year, I find the guardianship paper inconclusive.

That leaves the record of birth. This certainly seems like a smoking gun. There was not another couple living in Bridgeport, that we know of, named Hugh and Catherine O'Rourke. But why, if this is "our" Jim, did he and his family give as his birthday, throughout his lifetime, August 24 instead of September 1? In light of these doubts, I set out to prove one of the dates wrong by consulting the census records.

Earlier attempts to find Jim in census data had failed to turn up his name. He was there, but poor indexing of the records kept him hidden. I went back and searched on variations and misspellings like "Rourke" and "Orourke" and began to have better luck. I also learned to look for known neighbors, assuming the O'Rourkes would be on the same census page, or near it. More successes. At this point, I still was missing some census years, but by scrolling through census reports page by page, I was able to find almost every record.

I wanted as many census years as possible to doublecheck Jim's age, because I was convinced any one given year might be wrong. I was right. Like most other documentation of Jim's birth year, the census data was self-contradictory. I suspect Jim was having fun with the census takers, too. Here's what I found. The first number is the ages of Jim given to the census taker (presumably by his mother, Catherine). The second number is Jim's computed birth year, based on the assumption he was born in August or September (the only months ever offered) and the month in which the census was taken, which appears in parentheses:

- 1860 Census (June) 10 — 1849.
- 1870 Census (August) 19 — 1850.
- 1880 Census (June). James and John are not listed in the Bridgeport census, both residing in Boston, where they are teammates on the Red Caps.
- 1890 Census. No O'Rourkes found.
- 1900 Census (June) 46 — the census asked for the month and year of birth, which were given as August 1853 for Jim.
- 1910 Census (April) 62 — 1847.

So here we have the answers to the same question asked over a span of half a century, and no two are the same. You can see why I am skeptical of government documents. Clerks make mistakes. People interviewed by census takers make mistakes when answering questions about the age of family members. However, the above information, when taken as a whole, does seem to support an 1850 birth year for Jim, but not a September birth month. I suspect that by the time of the 1900 census, Jim had prepped everyone to add three years to his real birth year. (But why would you lie about your birth month?) And in 1910, I think his wife, Annie, just got tangled up in the complicated math of computing Jim's "media" age and blew it completely. She probably had enough trouble deriving her own public age from her real age. She had only been aging nine years every decennial census.

By the 1900s Jim's birth year had clearly moved four years forward to 1854.

Authorities reporting this later birthdate include Alfred H. Spink in his 1910 baseball history, *The National Game*.[6] The 1854 birth year also appears in a 1906 *Washington Post* article.[7] A collection of articles in the Hall of Fame's O'Rourke file, written between 1909 and 1919, also give Jim's birthdate as August 24, 1854. The authors seem to have copied from each other, thereby perpetuating another myth: that Jim played for the 1871 Hartford Oriels, a team that did not even exist.

Jim was in his '50s and still playing when the post–1900 pieces were written. The gradual shift of his birth year from 1850 to 1852 and finally to 1854 is most easily explained by an athlete wishing to appear younger in a profession that prized youth.

In 1907, a *New York World* sportswriter admitted:

> Nobody seems to know just how old O'Rourke really is and he won't tell. When asked point blank he is likely to change the subject.[8]

Two years later, a *Chicago Tribune* interviewer fared no better:

> O'Rourke does not answer questions about his age.[9]

A decade later, even a hometown editor did not feel secure in giving O'Rourke's age, and merely stated what by then was the only thing a journalist could reliably report:

> Jim O'Rourke was a native of Bridgeport, the exact date of his birth being rather obscure.[10]

For the purposes of this book, the birthdate of Jim O'Rourke is assumed to be September 1, 1850, and brother John's as August 23, 1849.

Regardless of whether Jim was born in 1850 or 1852, his stamina and longevity as a professional player is deservedly legendary.

When Jack O'Connor of the St. Louis Browns was scouting the Connecticut League in 1909, he reported that its "most promising catcher was a youngster named Jim O'Rourke."[11]

In 1910, when asked the secret to a long and healthy life, Uncle Jeems responded:

> I lived a clean life. I never touched liquor in any form, nor did I ever use tobacco. I always took care of myself.[12]

Jim's favorite drink was milk.[13] It's not that he was a teetotaler, he simply did not care for liquor.

Regarding happiness, a woman reporter a century ago elicited these nuggets from the Orator:

1909 Studio Portrait.

- The man is happiest who has some honorable work. That work should take a great deal of his time so that he does not have time to worry about debts, death and like "mortal inconveniences."
- Everyone also ought to have an interest outside of work. Learn to play golf or tennis, take long walks or even tango.
- Keep a close touch with nature. Enjoy the woods and appreciate all the good things that are here for our pleasure.
- And don't travel by boat, "whatever the attraction might be."[14]

Jim also believed in serving one's community. In addition to the fire commission already mentioned, he was appointed to the Bridgeport Sewer and Paving Commission when it was formed on July 1, 1909.[15] He was reappointed to six-year terms for life.[16]

Tracking a Pop-up. In 1909, Jim played in only one game, on August 21, late in the season. His career as a starting player was over, but the annual game with Uncle Jeems would become a tradition (*New York Herald,* January 16, 1910).

Jim played in only one ballgame in 1909, on August 21, late in the season. It was the first game of a double-header against Holyoke. Jim had retired from regular duty as a baseballist. He realized, however, that if he played in at least one game a year under a professional contract, he would continue to extend his record as the player with the longest professional career.

As a manager and owner he was still very much engaged in the day-to-day events of the Bridgeport club. In a heads-up play by an owner, he was able to squeeze a few more quarters into the turnstile one day in 1909. He noticed that Comiskey's Chicago White Sox would have to lay over in New York on Sunday, June 13. He wrote to Commie to suggest the Sox play an exhibition game against the Orators at the ball grounds on Pleasure Beach. Commie replied that he would accept the invitation if Jim would guarantee the club $500 against a share of the gate. Jim agreed and the game was on.[17]

For the first two innings, the only run scored was the result of a home run by Frank Hilt over the center field fence into Long Island Sound. (I'm sure this wasn't the only reason, but Jim granted Frank permission to marry daughter Ida at the close of the season.) The Sox won the game, 12–4.[18]

Jim also arranged exhibition games with the New York Giants and Detroit Tigers in 1909. Although Bridgeport lost all three games against the major league teams, it gave the local fans a chance to see national stars up close and personal right in their own back yard.

O'Rourke continued to work just as hard as a league officer. In 1909, the other owners in the Connecticut League finally began to appreciate his significant efforts on their behalf. In October 1909, the board elected O'Rourke to a two-year team as secretary and treasurer and for the first time authorized a $500 annual salary. League president W. J. Tracy was still serving a two-year term that would end after the 1910 season. [19]

For Jim, playing was fun; managing was work. He therefore put the word out among his contacts in the industry that the Orators were for sale. On February 2, 1910, Jim found a buyer, New York Yankees scout Gene McCann. John H. Freeman, a good friend of Yankees owner Frank Farrell, financed the $7,500 purchase.[20] The Bridgeport club was, for all intents and purposes, a farm club for the Yankees.

With the stroke of a pen, Jim signed away his roles as manager and owner. Life was now considerably simpler for O'Rourke, but within four months, tragedy would again visit the family. The *New York Times* reported on June 15, 1910, a month after Jim's 38th wedding anniversary:

Mrs. James H. O'Rourke Dead

BRIDGEPORT, Conn., June 14 — Mrs. James H. O'Rourke, wife of Secretary O'Rourke of the Connecticut Baseball League and former owner of the Bridgeport team, died to-day. Death was due to the effects of a fall suffered several months ago. She leaves, besides her husband, [seven] children.

Fortunately, all of their children were grown. The youngest, Edith, was 20. His girls had their own families. Jimmy was nearly 30 and away from home, playing in the American Association.

Then a month after he lost his wife, Jim received shocking news from Columbus: his son was hit in the head by a pitch and severely injured. According to a contemporary newspaper account, Jimmy required hospitalization:

O'Rourke is no Better
Columbus Player Hit in Head by Pitched
Ball Still Speechless

COLUMBUS, Ohio, July 21.—"Jimmie" O'Rourke, third baseman of the Columbus American Association nine, who was hit in the head yesterday by a pitched
ball by "Vinegar" Bill Essick, of the Kansas City nine, is still speechless at Grant
Hospital. O'Rourke dropped like a log when he was hit, and the blow paralyzed
his vocal cords.[21]

Fortunately, Jimmy made a full recovery and returned to the Columbus lineup. Indeed, the following season, veteran sportswriter Jacob said:

Columbus has some very good ball tossers, including the former Yale star,
young Jimmy O'Rourke.[22]

Tragedies come in threes. The following year, on June 23, 1911, John
O'Rourke died of a heart attack. Gone now was Jim's only brother in blood.
They had played together on the same fields in the East End of Bridgeport
and in the National League. As the fast train from Boston stopped in Bridgeport on its way to New York, Jim would often be waiting on the platform to
shake his brother's hand and relay family news. "John in turn was ever on
the watch to greet him and perhaps throw out a bundle of papers for future
reading on topics in which they were both interested."[23]

With his wife and brother deceased, his children grown, and his team
sold, the Connecticut League and the NAPBL became increasingly important to Jim, filling the voids of his life.

31

Baseball's Elder Statesman
(1911–1913)

In 1911, when the November conference of the NAPBL was scheduled in San Antonio,[1] Jim thought it a perfect opportunity for his family to see some of America, so he bundled off all six daughters onto the train for a cross-country adventure.

The NAPBL had grown considerably in the decade since its founding. "Forty-seven organizations, embracing 132 cities and towns of America and Canada, qualified for membership in 1911." Over 10,000 ballplayers were employed in the minor leagues.

In the 10 years of the existence of the National Association, $2,090,150 had been paid out to its member clubs for players. Baseball had become a big business, even in the minor leagues.[2]

Each year, Jim was reelected to the board of the NAPBL; and each year several of the highest minor leagues threatened to secede from association unless they were given special status and drafting rights equal to that enjoyed by the major leagues. In 1911, it was the American Association, Eastern Association, and Pacific Coast League that were arguing the loudest. To appease these organizations, the convention created a new league classification of "AA" between major league and Class "A."[3]

The convention drafted a number of additional proposals that were also recommended to the National and American League conventions. Attesting to the clout of the NAPBL, all the measures were adopted by the major leagues as well. These included a rule that minor leaguers receive a raise during major league tryouts, and a fixed payment schedule to minor league clubs when players were drafted. The draft season was again shortened from 15 days to a five-day window beginning September 1 of each year.[4]

The NAPBL meeting was capped, fittingly, by a ballgame: The East defeated the West 6–2. O'Rourke and Murnane played for the winning East side.[5]

Board member O'Rourke was instrumental in formulating and pushing resolutions through the mire of the NAPBL's democratic process. According to historian Daniel Pearson, the Orator "earned notoriety in minor league gatherings which rivaled his reputation as a player" because of a forceful manner of speaking and assertive demeanor.[6] *Sporting News* said of advocate O'Rourke:

> When he arose to speak, tossed his great mane of gray hair, stamped his foot, and grasped the back of his chair, ... brave indeed was the man who would combat his ideas in a league meeting or on a convention floor.[7]

In proceedings closer to home, Jim was elected president, secretary and treasurer of the Connecticut League for the 1912 season. His salary, now $2,000, indicated his responsibilities occupied a great deal of time. Jim had served as president of the league since 1907, and as secretary and treasurer since 1896, the year he helped to establish the circuit.[8]

In 1912, bookmakers must have continued to infect the national sport, for O'Rourke found it necessary to take "drastic" measures to counter their influence:

TO OUST BASEBALL GAMBLERS
Special to the New York Times

NEW HAVEN, Conn., May 10 — President James H. O'Rourke of the Connecticut Baseball League announced to-night that drastic steps have been ordered by the Directors looking toward the suppression of gambling on any of the league grounds by either players or spectators in any form of pool selling, betting, or wagers. Any spectators detected in betting will be ejected from the grounds. O'Rourke, who is a former New York Giant, is an official of the National Association of Minor League Clubs. He says that this organization will push every movement inaugurated by the National and American Leagues to check baseball gambling, and will inaugurate some moves of its own besides.[9]

To strengthen the Connecticut League financially, O'Rourke required each club to deposit a performance guarantee of $2,000 "in real money"[10] (as opposed to a bond, which would have been harder to collect). These funds would be forfeited if the team failed to complete the season. According to a *Sporting News* correspondent:

> This action will prevent such fizzles as have happened in the past and will especially tend to check and prevent irresponsible parties from holding franchises on prospects.
> Heretofore the financial affairs of the league have been run in a sort of hit and miss fashion and the unwisdom of that policy struck the magnates with force the past season when the Holyoke and Northampton teams disbanded early in the race, with resulting loss to the players and magnates, not to mention the undesirable notoriety the league itself received in the base ball world.
> But during the past winter the affairs of the league have been put upon a firm business basis, and under the guidance of that old war horse James O'Rourke, will be in a position to weather severe storms.[11]

Storms would not be long in coming.

On September 14, 1912, league president O'Rourke caught for the New Haven Wings in a game against the Waterbury Spuds. It was his 41st season as a professional ballplayer.[12] The *New Haven Union* reported on the performance of the 62-year-old baseballist:

> President James H. O'Rourke of the Connecticut League ... skipped about the diamond like a yearling.... The applause that greeted him as he donned the mask, mit[t] and windpad, will be remembered by the great old veteran for years to come.[13]

Soon afterward, the Connecticut League owners changed the name of the organization to the Eastern Association, in deference to its three Massachusetts clubs (Springfield, Pittsfield, and Holyoke). The cosmopolitan circuit still included five clubs from Connecticut (Bridgeport, Hartford, New Haven, New London, and Waterbury). Jim was elected president of the Eastern Association for the 1913 season in spite of an attempt by rival owners to knock the Orator out of the box. As *The Sporting News* reported:

> The opposition to the election of President James O'Rourke to head the new Eastern Association failed in its purpose, as the veteran commanded enough votes to set at naught the scheme of [James H.] Clarkin of Hartford and Dan O'Neil of Holyoke to depose him from his position. The retention of Mr. O'Rourke was in keeping with some of the wise policies the league has adopted in the last year or so and I look to see the affairs of the new organization handled in fully as capable a manner as was exhibited during the past year by the genial O'Rourke.[14]

The political infighting and conniving to wrest control of the league from Jim may have begun to take a toll on his health, as *The Sporting News* noted:

> Dan O'Neil of Holyoke and Eugene McCann of Bridgeport were selected by the league to represent the Eastern Association at Milwaukee during the meeting of the National Association [of Professional Baseball Leagues]. President James O'Rourke generally is selected, but on account of ill-health will forego the pleasure for the first time since the founding of the national body.[15]

A year later, poor health again interfered with an important event: the annual game with Uncle Jeems. "He was anxious to keep up the 'playing' and take part in the closing game of the year in 1913, but illness prevented."[16]

We can only imagine how disappointed Jim must have been at reaching the end of his career season streak. The *New York Times* marked the closing of O'Rourke's professional career:

> When Jim O'Rourke failed to step to the bat before the Eastern Association closed its season last week, he closed a continuous record extending over thirty-six years. The veteran has played at least one game every season since he joined the national League in 1876, and thereby established a record for continuous playing.

O'Rourke was anxious to keep up his
record this season, but, acting on the
advice of his physician, he decided to
quite baseball and athletics, owing to a
severe illness last winter.[17]

However, by November of the following year, Jim had regained his health and
so attended the 1913 meeting of the
National Association of Professional Baseball Leagues. Each year for the NAPBL, Jim
was required to address a growing caseload
from the association's 43 leagues and 302
teams. In the fall of 1913 alone, 700 cases
came to the attention of the Board of Arbitration.[18]

In 1913, O'Rourke was also appointed
to two important NAPBL committees: one
on contracts[19] and a special committee to
consider revisions to the NAPBL constitution,[20] and by extension the relationship of
the organization to the major leagues.

At the 1913 annual meeting, the constitution committee presented a number of
resolutions. The most substantive provision was to tighten up a loophole in the
draft:

H. Eugene McCann. Prior to the
start of the 1911 season McCann
sold his interest in the Bridgeport club to his backer, John
Freeman, but stayed on to manage through mid–June of the 1913
season (engraving: *Bridgeport
Herald*, June 15, 1913).

President Tearney of the Three-I [League]
started the movement for a reform in the system of drafting players and was
supported in a fight against the practice of major league clubs in claiming a
large number of players and then making cancellation of the draft. During the
discussion President Dreyfuss of the Pittsburgh Club charged that violations of
the rules by the National Commissioners themselves were responsible for the
trouble that had occurred. It was plainly the sense of the convention that such
procedure should be checked.

Base ball as a business has been treated by several well meaning magazine
writers whose horizon was limited to the major leagues and the height of whose
knowledge was the salary Mathewson is supposed to get. The National Association of Professional Base Ball Leagues forms the backbone of the national pastime. The majors with the star players and the World's Series each autumn grab
the lion's share of press notices. The minors with a deficit in the treasury about
July 4 and a stock assessment to get the clubs up to Labor Day, develop the players, serve as feeders for the major leagues and get a lot of fun out of it. Civic
pride is responsible for most of the minor leagues. The leading business men of
the cities, as a rule, believe the towns should have base ball, so they get it.[21]

The Sporting News described the fireworks in its report on the NAPBL annual meeting with the headline:

MINOR LEAGUERS HAND A REBUFF TO THE COMMISSION.
Reject Suggestion for Uniform Contracts— Rules That No
Drafts Shall Be Canceled and Move to Further Restrict Farming.[22]

While O'Rourke's work with the NAPBL was no doubt rewarding and important to the national game, it must also have been fatiguing, and Jim faced continuing problems within his own league.

In 1913, the New York-New Jersey League changed its name to the Eastern League. Jim protested, pointing out "the liability of players and patrons to confuse the two organizations, to the possible disadvantage of the Eastern Association."[23] Jim was correct in his prediction, as several newspaper articles confused the two leagues. The Eastern League backed off. But Jim could savor victory only briefly, for a much more serious threat was looming.[24]

32

The New England
Baseball War (1913–1919)

Jim ruled the Eastern Association with a fair but firm authority. In the summer of 1913, a new cabal of conspirators, led by Hartford owner James Clarkin, began scheming to vote themselves into control of the league. The *Bridgeport Herald* reported on the brewing discord:

> James H. Clarkin, owner of the Hartford Baseball team, seems to have a special grudge against James H. O'Rourke, main office holder in the league, the brains of the organization. At every opportunity, Mr. Clarkin jumps into print with something to say about President O'Rourke.[1]

At the October 1913 annual meeting to elect officers, the Massachusetts owners sided with Clarkin in an attempt to oust O'Rourke as president. When the vote was taken, Jim barely held onto the league he had founded two decades earlier. According to the *New York Times*:

> At a stormy meeting of the Eastern Baseball Association, late this afternoon, James H. O'Rourke of Bridgeport was re-elected President, Secretary, and Treasurer, defeating Daniel O'Neil of Springfield [Massachusetts] 5 to 3. President Clarkin of Hartford and [William E.] Carey of Springfield then left the meeting. The constitution was then amended, and Mr. O'Rourke's term as President was made five years.[2]

An unidentified sportswriter celebrated Jim's election:

> The Eastern Association has re-elected James O'Rourke as its president, thus admitting, though splendid talent as his successor was advanced, that his administration of league affairs is not to be improved upon. Even were only sentiment involved, the base ball world generally would have regretted the retirement of the veteran O'Rourke from a part in the game, and now hopes that he will live to head his league as long as has Tim Murnane, the perpetual president of the New England League. For Jim O'Rourke is the real old-timer of the game, making some other so-called veterans appear like new-comers.[3]

Although the line about serving as long as Murnane would prove to be bitterly ironic, Jim had, for now, had outmaneuvered the conspirators. But O'Rourke had to remain vigilant to maintain the peace and keep the circuit intact.

Jim often used humor and friendly cajoling rather than stern authoritarianism to enforce discipline. Just prior to the start of the 1914 season, Bridgeport sportswriter T. F. Magner, in a column appropriately titled "Circuit Gossip," reported:

> President O'Rourke of the Eastern Association has issued an order that at the next meeting of the directors, Clarkin of Hartford and Carey of Springfield must salute the flag [buy a round for the board of directors]. They were found guilty of some foolish criticism of the president and now they must pay the penalty. If the salute is not made at the time specified, Admiral [Sid] Challenger [a Bridgeport sportswriter] has been ordered to bring his heavier guns to bear upon the greasers. The admiral's flagship, the Piffle, has steam up and is ready to fire a broadside of 12-point type against the two....
> If the cabinet of the president orders that Jim Clarkin is compelled to buy a round, it will be a terrible blow for him, and he would prefer to take back all he said about the president rather than loosen up. But the flag of the league must be saluted.[4]

This inning, Jim won. In fact, prior to the start of the 1914 season, the Eastern Association owners, in an uncharacteristic spirit of brotherhood, voted 7 to 1 to set aside 10 percent of all gate receipts to create a fund for the support of franchises that encountered financial emergencies, such as a lack of sufficient cash to meet payroll.[5] This action showed that most of the board members were on speaking terms with one another, and had the professional discipline to cooperate and keep on-field feuds out of the boardroom.

The 1914 season passed without incident, but gate receipts declined. The waning fan support was blamed on competition from the Federal League, a new major league that was siphoning off stars from the minors to fill its ranks. In November 1914, Jim and his fellow NAPBL board members issued a strong denunciation of the Federal League for not respecting the reserve lists of the minor leagues:

> The Federals have nothing to offer to the minor leagues which will be of benefit to the latter. Therefore the Federal League cannot expect the minor league body to take any interest in outlaw baseball.[6]

Ironically, the reserve clause shoe was now on the other foot, and club owner Jim O'Rourke resented the Federal League stealing his bought-and-paid-for talent. The most notable loss was star player Bennie Kauff, "The Ty Cobb of the Federal League," who played for Bridgeport and Hartford in the Eastern Association before jumping to the Feds, where he led the new league in batting two years on a row.

The Fed's response to the NAPBL denunciation was to organize its own minor league farm system, the Colonial League. President Gilmore of the Federal League unabashedly announced in January 1915, "We are going to invade Eastern [Association] and New England [League] territory."[7] The infighting in Jim's Eastern Association had made the national news, and the Federal League backers assumed it would be easier to make inroads in Jim's territory. Murnane's league was also vulnerable. These were difficult times economically for the minor leagues.

According to Jim's adversaries, the Eastern Association owners lost approximately $60,000 during the 1914 season.[8] The discouraging business results were confirmed even by pro–O'Rourke magnates. John H. Freeman, owner of the Bridgeport club, reported in an interview with the *Bridgeport Herald*:

> This has been the poorest season for baseball financially speaking, that I have had to contend with since I purchased the Bridgeport team a few years ago. [Freeman purchased the club from Gene McCann, who had purchased it from O'Rourke prior to the 1910 season.] Up to the present time I have dropped over $5000. My team has been playing good enough baseball for the most ardent fan and up to late this week we have been no lower than third place for the past two months....
>
> With a team fighting in third place and only drawing 250 and 300 on week days there must something wrong. I imagine if my club was in last place the players would have to sit in the grand stand between innings to make a good crowd.[9]

The difficult financial times even made it possible for the Clarkin-Carey faction to recruit an additional ally, George M. Cameron, owner of the New Haven club. The press dubbed the anti–Orator faction the "Three C's."

To keep from losing any more money, Clarkin, Carey and Cameron suggested the Eastern Association lay fallow during the 1915 season. They argued that the loss suffered by the magnates was "ample reason for an investor to decline to continue, when conditions were hardly favorable."[10] And this is what they did: the Three C's took their balls and bats and went home.

I suspect this was a power play to embarrass O'Rourke and weaken the Eastern Association. If they could destroy Jim's league from within, the Three C's then would be in a position to organize a new league (or join another league) with a more tolerant standard of business and baseball ethics.

Jim reminded the secessionists that less than two years ago they had signed five-year agreements to stick together. But to no avail. The Three C's refused to muster their players for the 1915 season.

Jim's counterstrategy was to try to remove the Three C's as Eastern League franchise holders and to replace the Hartford, New Haven, and Springfield clubs with new franchisees in those cities or other cities within the Eastern Association territory. If he could pull this off on short notice, he would be rid of the pesky conspirators for good.

Since the Three C's had no intention of playing the 1915 season, at least not in the Eastern Association, they did not bother to submit the hefty $2,000 annual bond to the league headquarters as demanded by stickler O'Rourke. (The bond was to insure a city would play out the season, and not fold if times became difficult financially.) Jim then called a meeting of the Eastern Association board of directors (the club owners) for March 16, 1915. The outcome was recorded in the *New York Times*:

> HARTFORD, Conn., March 16, — The storm clouds which have been hovering over the Eastern Baseball Association broke today when three of the Directors met here and declared forfeited the franchises of the New Haven, Hartford, and Springfield Clubs. This leaves as a nucleus of the league — Bridgeport, New London, and Pittsfield.
>
> Directors J. H. Clarkin of Hartford, William Care[y] of Springfield, and George Cameron of New Haven — the latter through proxy — declined to attend the meeting on advice of counsel. These three Directors claim that the meeting of the Directors of the other three clubs was not legal, as no quorum was present.
>
> Directors Hugh Reddy of Bridgeport, Eugene McCann of New London, and John Zeller of Pittsfield met with President James H. O'Rourke behind closed doors for two hours. After the meeting O'Rourke announced that the New Haven, Hartford, and Springfield Clubs had failed to post the necessary bond of $2,000 to finish the season, and therefore the franchises had been declared forfeited under the constitution of the association.
>
> O'Rourke said that an adjourned meeting would be held in New Haven next Friday [March 19], when the matter will be discussed further. He declared that at this time the league would receive applications for franchises from Waterbury, Danbury, and possibly from Hartford.
>
> C. J. Danaher of Meriden, who is counsel for the three clubs refusing to attend the meeting, said tonight that in his opinion today's action was invalid and that an appeal would be made to the National commission.[11]

Reporting on this follow-up meeting, the *New York Times* added:

> Milton H. Baker, of New York, made application for a team at Danbury, and Thomas F. Fogarty, President of the Jersey City club of the International League, applied for a franchise at Waterbury. [12]

In spite of the fact that replacement clubs appeared to be available, the Three C's were given a second chance to post the required bonds at the March 19 meeting. They refused. The Three C's also appealed to the NAPBL to overturn their disenfranchisement by O'Rourke.

This was a sound tactic by Jim's opponents, for even if the NAPBL sided with Jim, confirming that the Hartford, Springfield and New Haven franchises were forfeited back to the league, the review process would delay Jim's efforts to organize replacement clubs for the 1915 season.[13] Whether or not this was the intention of the tactic, a week later, the *Times* reported that making a federal case of the dispute was indeed hindering Jim's efforts to sign up replacement clubs:

EASTERN IN DISTRESS
**Legal Entanglements May Keep It Out of
Competition This Year.**

NEW HAVEN, Conn., March 25, — No action was taken by the Directors of the Eastern Baseball Association here today in filling the vacancies caused by the forfeiture of the New Haven, Hartford, and Springfield franchises. In making this announcement after two hours' deliberation behind closed doors, President O'Rourke added that no steps would be taken until word had been received from Secretary Farrell of the National Association, to whom the matter has been referred.

There are applicants for franchises in three or more cities, O'Rourke said, but the applicants are desirous of having the legal entanglements unraveled before attempting to take hold.

O'Rourke reiterated his former statements that the league would surely start the season, but admitted that the opening would be delayed for ten days or more. It was learned from other sources, however, that O'Rourke's feeling of optimism is not shared by at least two of the Directors. It is said that there is a growing sentiment in favor of discontinuing the league for the present season.[14]

The Three C's did submit a formal appeal to Secretary Farrell of the NAPBL, who refused to hear the evidence supporting the expulsion of the three clubs, thus supporting and letting stand O'Rourke's actions to expel them from the Eastern Association. [15]

But that was not the end of it. The Three C's then went over the head of the NAPBL and appealed the findings to the National Commission.

O'Rourke received word of the appeal from August Hermann, chairman of the National Commission, on April 8, just prior to a planned meeting of the loyal directors of the Eastern Association to award franchises to fill the vacancies left by the Three C's. However, in light of this new appeal, action was again tabled. It was decided to reconvene "when the National Commission's decision is received, a matter of a few days at the most." The "few days" part required an inordinate faith in bureaucracy. The clock was ticking.[16]

In a letter sent to *Sporting Life* on April 5, which the editor titled "President O'Rourke's Temperate Statement," Jim made a public case against the Three C's by putting the following words in their mouths:

While we are violators of the Constitution and intend to wreck the Eastern Association, the conclusive evidence of which we have already given by dismantling our clubs, by sale and release of players, the malignant attacks upon the Eastern Association, plus our publicly-expressed intention in the press never to play in a six-club league, or with New London or Pittsfield [two small-gate towns] in the league, and that we will not allow the protests of the other club members to complete the circuit, to interfere with the consummation of our objects, to destroy the Eastern Association, because we can then merge with the New England League, or perhaps get a berth in the International League.[17]

To keep up the pressure, Jim initiated measures to blacklist the Three C's for their nefarious conduct and violation of written contracts. On April 15, 1915, the National Board of Arbitration of the NAPBL, by unanimous vote, banished Clarkin, Carey and Cameron from organized baseball.[18]

Shortly thereafter, O'Rourke received a letter from the president of the National Commission, informing him of the reply the commission had made to the counsel for the expelled magnates. It read, in part:

> Relative to the appeal filed by you from the National Association Board's decision in the matter pertaining to the Eastern Association, I beg to say that the appeal is not sustained.[19]

The commission added that it would never again accept an appeal of a decision of the NAPBL, confirming the precedent set by the 1907 "O'Rourke Resolution" as to sovereignty of the minor leagues association relative to the National Commission. This was one of Jim's better days.

An elated O'Rourke immediately called a meeting for Saturday, April 24, to award Eastern Association "franchises to those who present the best propositions." According to O'Rourke, he had interest from Hartford, Springfield, New Haven, Waterbury and Danbury.[20] However, in the statement to the press, an ominous note was appended:

> To safeguard the interests of the successful bidders guarantees will probably be given that the new owners will not suffer through any legal action which might be taken by the deposed owners, Clarkin, Carey, and Cameron.[21]

After the April 24 meeting, Jim issued a follow-up release stating confidently "that the league would open its season on May 12, with a six-club circuit."[22] However, reading between the lines, it appears this may have been a media curve. The reporter was unable to extract any details from the usually talkative Orator, and advised readers that:

> Mr. O'Rourke declined to give out the make-up of the circuit, as he said one of the franchises had not yet been awarded. Another meeting will be held next week.
> Those at the meeting today included, besides Mr. O'Rourke, H. Eugene McCann of New London; Hugh Reddy, Secretary of the Bridgeport Club, and Harry Cornen and August Knorr of Norwalk, the two latter being present in the interest of Danbury, which is said to be seeking a franchise.[23]

With opening day only two and a half weeks away, there should have been more organizers present at the meeting. In spite of Jim's positive predictions, I suspect the potential replacement magnates were concerned about "legal action" or else they were having difficulty coming to scratch.

Soon thereafter Jim came to the conclusion that he would not be able to muster out even a six-club league in time for the 1915 season. Ironically, he had won his case both at the NAPBL and the National Baseball Commission levels, but too late to restart the league prior to the opening of the season.

He contacted Secretary Farrell of the NAPBL to request permission for the Eastern Association to suspend operations for a year, but to retain its territory (including Springfield, Hartford and New Haven). Jim planned to use the time to "try to settle the league's troubles" in order to reopen for the following season.[24] Farrell granted the request.

But the Three C's were the bigger winners. They got exactly what they wanted: a suspended Eastern Association. For the 1915 season, Clarkin, Carey and Cameron transferred their clubs to the Feds' new Colonial League. Their teams would be stocked with players farmed out from Federal League clubs.[25]

But the new league was a fiasco. Reports of the Colonial League's lack of success during the 1915 season must have warmed the cockles of O'Rourke's heart. A July 9 article in the *New York Times* carried the headline: "Colonial League on Rocks" and reported that the organization had

decided today to drop Fall River and Taunton from their circuit and to play the Pawtucket team on the road all the time. Poor patronage accounts for these changes.

And on September 7, the *Times* added:

The [Colonial] league is under the auspices of the Federal League. Attendance has been poor for the greater part of the season, and it is said the Federal League suffered a considerable financial loss.

O'Rourke's hometown weekly, the *Bridgeport Herald*, was jubilant:

EASTERN ASSOCIATION WILL COME BACK
WITH BELLS ON NEXT YEAR
Fans Sick of Colonial Junk

Only the apparently unlimited means of the Wards [owners of the Brooklyn Federal League club; no relation to Johnny and Helen] keeps the Colonial league, known as the Siberia of the Federal league, from complete collapse all of which falls upon the ears of President O'Rourke, of the eastern association (temporarily defunct), like water on a famished flower.... And there is every indication now that the Eastern association will come back stronger than ever next year. That is it will if baseball in general recovers from the slump which undermined many minor leagues this summer.

The Eastern association should be especially strong next year in New Haven, Hartford, and Springfield, where the fans have become entirely disgusted with the syndicate stuff furnished by the Colonial league. The recent death of George Malcolm Cameron, the owner of the New Haven club, ... is likely to have its effect on the future of the league of which he was a member.

While Cameron was openly a member of the revolting three C's— the other two being Clarkin of Hartford, and Carey of Springfield — he was not with them in all of their schemes. He was only lukewarm for a merger of the Eastern association and the New England league.[26]

Tim Murnane's New England League had fared no better and began to covet anew the sizable — albeit disloyal — baseball cities of O'Rourke's Eastern Association: Hartford, New Haven, and Springfield.

To further complicate matters, the International League also began to eye Hartford and Springfield as replacements for franchises in Newark and Baltimore that it lost in 1915 to Federal League claim jumpers. On October 19, the *New York Times* reported on the mission of one E. W. Wicks of the International League to parley with the Three C's:

> After a long conference with W. E. Car[e]y, President of the Springfield Athletic Association, which operated the Springfield club in the Eastern Association before that league suspended operations, Mr. Wicks said he would report favorably on Springfield to President E. G. Barrow of the International League. He said he had come to this section as the personal representative of Mr. Barrow and would go over the situation in Hartford tomorrow with James H. Clarkin, who was the owner of the Eastern Association franchise in that city.
>
> Mr. Wicks stated that it was the intention of his league to go to the meeting of the National Association [of Professional Baseball Leagues] in San Francisco next month with a proposition that the International League receive permission to place clubs both in Springfield and Hartford. Neither Springfield nor Hartford had clubs in organized baseball this year, but James H. O'Rourke of Bridgeport, Conn., who was President of the Eastern Association, says the territory is held by that organization and cannot be encroached on by any clubs in organized baseball.[27]

So, at the end of the 1915 baseball season, two usurpers were vying to place teams in the heart of the Eastern Association just as Jim was struggling desperately to resurrect it.

It was just such muddled matters that the Board of the NAPBL existed to arbitrate and the intrigue boiled up at its November 1915 meeting in San Francisco.

Friend Tim Murnane would play it coyly. Feigning disinterest, he claimed he had traveled to San Francisco mainly for a vacation, explaining that there was "nothing doing in Boston" (the headquarters of his New England League, his home, and his job as baseball editor for the *Boston Globe*). Tim was well known to other sports editors and therefore had no difficulty planting the following red herring in *The Sporting News* that appeared during the week of the NAPBL annual convention:

> I am on my way to attend the annual meeting of the National Association at San Francisco, probably the last that I will attend as the president of a minor league and a member of the National Board, though I expect to meet with these

jovial baseball men a good many times at other meetings in some capacity or other. The San Francisco meeting will not be a big convention in point of numbers, judging from the indications, but it will be an important one nevertheless to the minors. There are a number of important matters to be discussed and one bit of news I hear is that an attempt will be made to redistrict minor league territory pretty generally, some seeming to fancy that it will be for the best in the minors to line cities up in new leagues with reduced mileage and more intercity rivalry. In this connection doubtless the proposed merger of my own league, the New England, with certain cities that have been in the Eastern Association will be discussed.[28]

As part of a not-so-subtle public relations campaign to influence the NAPBL, additional self-serving notices appeared just prior to the national convention, like this one in the *New York Times* of October 29:

BOSTON, Oct. 28.—The New England Baseball League tonight appointed a committee to consider a merger by which the New England would absorb the clubs of the Eastern Association which were formerly placed at Springfield, Hartford, and New Haven. Discussion among the members of the league, according to President Timothy H. Murnane, favored retaining five of the clubs of the New England League as at present constituted.

Note how Tim deftly refers to the Eastern Association in the past tense. The strategy of feigning indifference may have led Jim to believe it was unnecessary for him to make the arduous cross-country trek to San Francisco to protect his territory claims. He did not attend the convention, but instead gave his proxy to vote — and, he hoped, defend his Eastern Association — to Secretary Farrell of the NAPBL.

I suspect that the baseball battles had exacerbated his health concerns and this was the reason he chose to remain in Bridgeport. He must have been under a great deal of stress from the incessant battles with the Three-C's. And now, *et tu*, Timothy?

I believe it is noteworthy that Jim held so tenaciously to his league and to his tenets as to how baseball magnates should conduct themselves. He certainly did not need the money, or the aggravation. He fought on for love of the game, and the example it could provide, when players and owners were at their best, on and off the field.

But O'Rourke's influence within the NAPBL was eroding. In light of his missing a second annual convention in four years, and his league lying fallow, Jim, for the first time since he helped to found the minor league body 15 years earlier, was not reelected to its board. The 10 directors who were elected would serve five-year terms, from 1916 through 1920.[29]

The Sporting News marked his passing from the head of the baseball parade:

Orator Jim O'Rourke was notable for his absence. He had put his proxy as president of the alleged Eastern Association in the hands of Secretary Farrell and made his plea to have the claims to his territory recognized in writing, letting it go at that, depending upon Farrell's influence, and it also was up to Farrell anyway to defend his own action in granting O'Rourke the protection he had claimed. The gap in the proceedings made by the absence of Orator Jim's usual speech was silent evidence of the passing of the old guard, or at least some of it.[30]

The Sporting News provides an idea of what O'Rourke's annual orations must have been like:

> At minor league gatherings for many years his speeches were the outstanding feature. He had strong views on any and all subjects and insisted on giving those views an airing. Always he did not talk to the point, but what he lacked in direct argument, he made up in flights of rhetoric and resounding phrases and was listened to with interest by those who knew him and with amazement by those who were hearing him for the first time.[31]

Jim would no more stir the baseball leadership to action.

Murnane, on the other hand, who had renounced any interest in a future role in the minor league organization, ran for and was elected vice president of the NAPBL.

Tim had laid the groundwork well for raiding the Eastern Association. Murnane's strategy was to create a new league out of the strongest towns of the Eastern and New England Leagues. It was the same strategy he attempted to employ in the spring of 1899. The two leagues were intertwined within a crowded geography between Bridgeport, Connecticut, and Portland, Maine.

To sort out the conflicting claims to the Hartford, Springfield, and New Haven franchises, a special committee was appointed at the November 1915 annual meeting of the NAPBL. Secretary Farrell, Ed Barrow of the International League, and Tim Murnane. Even "Curry" (no relation to Foley), the Hartford reporter for *The Sporting News*, was taken aback by the composition of the committee:

> HARTFORD, Conn., November 19.— The theory of an Arbitration Committee is that it is supposed to be made up of disinterested parties, but the minor leagues or the National Board, which named the committee that is to settle the International-New England-Eastern Association dispute over territory must have forgotten the theory. The committee named is made up of three men who are directly concerned in the issues involved, the three being Barrow of the International, Murnane of the New England and Secretary Farrell, who as chairman of the Board, gave the Eastern Association the rights that now are contested.
>
> Therefore, the investigation will be conducted by three men seeking as many different outcomes. President Barrow of the International League has made no secret of the desire of his circuit to annex Springfield and Hartford, a move inimical to Mr. O'Rourke's long-cherished hope to revive the Eastern Association. If the dope is right, Mr. Murnane has his own New England League to consider and there is a majority of his club owners who would like to see a merger with the best cities in the Eastern Association. As Secretary Farrell, the

other member of the committee, held O'Rourke's proxy at the San Francisco meeting, it is assumed that he will continue to exercise his influence to secure what the Bridgeport man wants.[32]

It was almost a month before the press heard of any new developments. Most of the players in this drama were lingering (conspiring?) on the West Coast, inaccessible to the eastern press. As one sportswriter speculated after a month of silence: "Something's brewing, that's for sure. Of course, I may be wrong, but all this secrecy means something."[33]

I believe a deal was being cooked up between Barrow of the International League and Murnane of the New England League (two of the three members of the special committee). Curry, the Hartford-based sportswriter, pieced together the following theory that appeared in *The Sporting News*:

HARTFORD, Conn., Nov. 27 — There is reason to believe that President Ed Barrow has been assured by those high in authority in baseball that he can have what he needs for rebuilding his International League circuit and that his privilege of choice extends to cities that have made up the New England League as well as the old Eastern Association. A hint of this is given in the fact that Ed Wicks, representing Barrow, has been lately looking over the field at Worcester one of the New England League cities....

The conclusion, of course, is that the New England would not yield any claim to a city unless it had an understanding that it would be given something in return, which makes it appear that the New England and the International have reached an agreement on the merger proposition by which, after the International has chosen the one city or perhaps the two it needs for its circuit, the New England will be given claim to what remains.

O'Rourke Has Lost Out.

Logically, this means that James O'Rourke's claims to privileges in this section of the baseball world will not be recognized as valid. The report is he was told he would have to give a guarantee that he would operate the territory he claimed and that failing to do this the rights he alleged to have to dictate as to what the future of baseball in New England should be were cast aside.[34]

I think this is exactly what happened. Consider this December 9 article in *The Sporting News*:

Announcement that Tim Murnane is in favor of the so-called New England-Eastern Association merger, which should really be termed a New England League expansion, is hailed as indication that the plans for a Greater New England League will go through. Timothy has heretofore been rather lukewarm toward the proposition. What has caused his change of heart is not stated, but it may be guessed that in spite of his announced determination to retire from the presidency of the New England, he still is willing to head the expanded organization. The only fault to be found with Murnane is that he seems obsessed with a notion that because a man has been in baseball for a time — long or short — that man has vested rights that take precedence over the desires of the public. Where Timothy got his notions of divine right are not clear, certainly they do not coincide with American ideas.

Intrigue was definitely afoot, but little notice was taken outside the cities directly involved, for as the baseball fates would have it, the war between organized baseball and the outlaw Federal League was approaching its climax. The Eastern Association-International League-New England League war would be resolved in smoke-filled rooms, out of the national spotlight that was focused squarely on the Federal League War.

The Feds were attacking the seat of organized baseball's power — the National Agreement — by bringing an antitrust suit to dissolve the National Baseball Commission. The suit was being tried by none other than Judge Kenesaw Mountain Landis of the United States District Court of Chicago. The Feds claimed, rightly, that the national sport was being operated by the National Commission as a trust and that

> many of their methods violated the Sherman anti-trust law in restraining trade. After a lengthy hearing Judge Landis reserved decision and has not handed down his finding. The Federal League now agrees to withdraw this suit.[35]

Landis did not want to break up the baseball trust, feeling that the National Agreement among the leagues— with its reserve clause — was a necessary accommodation to preserve order in the national sport. So that he would not have to rule on the question, he coerced the parties to settle out of court. In the settlement, the Federal League, weakened by two years of warring with organized baseball, was dissolved. Its principal backers were given the opportunity to buy into National and American League clubs. The Federal League players, on the other hand, would have to fend for themselves. For his wisdom on the bench, Kenesaw Mountain Landis was offered the job as national baseball commissioner, a new position, with supreme authority over the national sport.

On December 15, the peace announcement concerning the latest national baseball war was carried under headlines spread across the sports pages of newspapers coast to coast. A much smaller article that day, appearing in the *New York Times*, told of a meeting between Tim Murnane, Ed Barrow, Carey, Clarkin, and New England League club owners.[36]

The decision of the NAPBL special committee of Murnane, Barrow, and Farrell was formally announced in the press on December 17:

> It was decided to give the Eastern Association thirty days in which to reorganize, and if at the end of that time the organization is not on a business basis, the principle cites of both leagues will be merged into one league. It is proposed to have Lynn, Portland, and Lawrence, of the New England League, and New Haven, Hartford, Bridgeport, and Springfield, of the Eastern Association, in the new organization.[37]

The most galling aspect of the ruling was that it required O'Rourke to rescind the earlier blacklisting of the Three C's and "accept them with full rights restored."[38] This was an important win for Murnane. Although Clarkin, Carey and Cameron had agreed to merge with Tim's league, he could not accept them if they were banned from owning clubs in organized baseball.

As *The Sporting News* observed, regarding the restoration of the Three C's:

> That in itself was a bitter enough pill for O'Rourke to swallow, for he long since read them out of Organized Ball, never to return.[39]

Nevertheless, the official ruling of the NAPBL committee at least had an appearance of fairness, in that it gave Jim an opportunity to save his league, and a more balanced merger, with four clubs from each league, if he did not. The additional team from the Eastern Association in the merger plan was Bridgeport. This was an obvious concession to Jim, because, although he no longer owned the team, he did still own the Bridgeport ballpark.

It was a week before Christmas. Jim had until January 17 to organize six clubs, line up playing fields in each city, and put the league on a sound "business basis." An almost impossible task, which Murnane was no doubt assuming. It took Jim and the Brotherhood a year to perform the same feat a generation earlier. And he could not count on any cooperation from the established magnates in three of the strongest cities in his territory, the ever-difficult Three C's.

Curry obviously thought it was the bottom of the ninth with two out:

> That O'Rourke can organize his personally conducted league by the 17th of January or by any other date is just as likely as that Henry Ford will have the soldiers out of the trenches by Christmas.[40]

The last jibe was a reference to the automaker's personal peace mission to end The Great War, a not unrelated simile, for the war in Europe had altered the economics of baseball and made it more difficult to operate ball clubs profitably. In 1915 the *Lusitania* was sunk, and so was minor league baseball. The red-brick munitions factories of New England were smoking to meet the urgent demand for war materiel. Factory owners were offering far more in wages than the baseball industry could afford to pay. Jim's hometown of Bridgeport was supplying machine guns, artillery shells, trucks, even submarines to combatants on both sides of the conflict. The reserve clause was little protection against a booming war economy.

Confident of the eventual dissolution of Jim's league, the magnates of the New England League were already squabbling over who would be admitted into and who would be shut out of the new "Connectichusettes" league.[41]

On the other hand, the *New York Sun* and Jim's hometown *Bridgeport Herald* were more optimistic. A December 26 *Herald* article sported the headline: "UNCLE 'JEEMS' O'ROURKE JOYOUS AT SUCCESS IN HOLDING E. A. TOGETHER."[42]

At the same time Jim was organizing replacement clubs to restart his Eastern Association, Murnane and company were attempting to win over its three remaining loyal members. The object was to obtain the unanimous consent for the merger by the current board of directors of the Eastern Association. He already had the votes of Hartford, New Haven and Springfield (the Three C's). If only he could convince New London, Bridgeport, and Pittsfield to change sides, he would pull a fast one on O'Rourke. It would be legal, and if effected before Jim reorganized the Eastern, the merger would be a *fait accompli*.

Murnane approached Morton Plant, the wealthy owner of the New Haven Planters. He willingly went over to the conspirators. That left Bridgeport and tiny Pittsfield, headed by Jack Zeller. Bridgeport would be difficult, but since O'Rourke was no longer the owner of the club, not impossible.[43]

They were convinced that if they could bag Zeller, they would bring in Freeman — the Bridgeport businessman who had lost money recently on his franchise — "in on a stretcher."[44]

But the conspirators hadn't much time. The NAPBL special committee was scheduled to deliver its final ruling on January 17, 1916. Tim Murnane's "mergerites" needed to buy out the holdouts, and soon.

Clarkin and Carey met Jack Zeller of Pittsfield and Hugh Reddy, secretary of the Bridgeport club on January 11, 1916, at the Allyn Hotel in Hartford.[45] New London manager (and former Bridgeport owner) Gene McCann shuttled between the factions, huddled in private rooms.

First, Pittsfield. Jack Zeller offered to sell his franchise (and vote) for $8,000 plus $1,600 to cover O'Rourke's salary for the year.[46] The conspirators did not believe the asking price reasonable and "couldn't have paid it if they had."[47] The Three C's responded that "If Mr. Zeller would make a fair offer, in proportion to the amount invested in Pittsfield, the mergerites would meet him half way and the deal closed at once." But Zeller held firm. The high price acted like a modern poison pill to prevent a hostile takeover. Pittsfield remained loyal to O'Rourke.[48]

Hugh Reddy, the secretary of the Bridgeport club, answered that the Bridgeport franchise would also stick by Jim's efforts to reconstitute the Eastern Association for 1916.[49]

The outcome of the New England War, then, would hinge on Jim's ability to organize a critical mass of credible clubs by the January 17 deadline.

On January 12, 1916, Jim received heartening news. Promoters Harry Cornen and Gus Knorr accepted the Waterbury franchise in the new Eastern Association.[50]

And on January 13, more good news. O'Rourke received assurances from backers in New Haven that they would underwrite a franchise in the Elm City. That made six clubs—the minimum Jim needed to retain his league. The clubs would be located in Hartford, Springfield and New Haven (under new owners), Bridgeport, Pittsfield, and Waterbury. He called a meeting of the directors for the afternoon of January 14 to reestablish the circuit. Confidently, Jim announced to the press:

> There does not now appear to be anything in the way of the Eastern's starting the 1916 season on time, as Messrs. Irwin and [Roger] Connor, who will operate the Hartford and Springfield franchises are quite enthusiastic over prospects. Both have refused to have anything to do with James H. Clarkin and William E. Carey, the former Hartford and Springfield magnates who were ousted from the league last April.[51]

On January 16, after the meeting, Jim O'Rourke announced that the Eastern Association had been successfully reorganized. To give evidence that there was considerable substance behind his assertion, Jim enumerated not only the names of the clubs, but the investors in each city, even the playing sites.[52] Moreover, Jim extracted the following written commitment from each of the Eastern League owners:

> This is to certify that we, as individual owners of franchises in the Eastern Baseball Association agree as men of honor to bind ourselves to stand together as a unit to carry out all the obligations imposed by the constitution and hereby pledge ourselves individually, not to dispose, sell, transfer or assign our interest in the respective franchises, awarded to us as members of the Eastern association, unless such disposal, sale, transfer or assignment receives the unanimous vote of the directors of the said Eastern association.[53]

The *Herald* editor rendered the opinion that:

> As the action [of violating the covenant] would mean loss of franchise in addition to loss of esteem, it looks as though the Eastern was on a firm footing again.
>
> It looks as though the merger crowd had been decisively set back. When the Eastern association goes before the National commission's specially appointed committee one week from tomorrow at New York [the final meeting of the special committee of the NAPBL had been postponed from January 17 to the 24th], it will be able to show a circuit composed of six clubs, with backers on hand in all of the cities.[54]

The editor summarized the situation as: "At present Clarkin, Carey and company appear to be gasping for wind, while O'Rourke and his crowd are breasting the tape."[55]

On Monday, January 24, President O'Rourke and "directors of the six Eastern Association clubs" went to New York to give assurances to the NAPBL committee that they had complied with its order to perfect an organization of six clubs. According to *Bridgeport Post* sports editor Earl C. Donegan, "They were

handed one of the worst frosts that was ever dealt out by professed representatives of fairness and honesty." Instead of ruling on whether the Eastern Association had met the test, the committee (Farrell, Barrow, and Murnane), after
hearing O'Rourke's arguments, also entertained a proposal by Clarkin, Carey,
and other merger advocates for a 10-team combination of the strongest clubs
from each league.[56]

The committee deferred ruling on the Eastern Association matter to allow
time to investigate the claims of each faction, and to evaluate their respective
abilities to conduct a baseball league. Farrell planned to tour the northeastern
cities to examine, among other indictors, leases for ball grounds.[57]

Jim declared the new merger plan insane and vowed to fight it in the
courts should the NAPBL accept it in opposition to recognizing the legitimacy of his Eastern Association. It was commonly recognized that Jim had
baseball law on his side.

But this was war.

On January 31, 1916, in a desperate all-or-nothing maneuver, Murnane
expelled from his New England League all of his franchisees opposed to the
merger plan.[58] His directors now spoke with one unanimous voice.

On the evening of Wednesday, February 9, the National League celebrated its 40th anniversary at a banquet at the Waldorf Astoria. The player
who made the league's first hit was one of its honored guests.[59]

Five days later, Secretary Farrell handed down the decision of the special committee: the Eastern Association must merge with the New England
League.

Jim's reaction was to exclaim, "It is the most unfair decision I have ever
heard of since I have been in baseball."[60]

On February 15, 1916, the plans for the merger of the Eastern Association and New England Leagues were approved by the special committee of
the NAPBL. According to the *New York Times:*

> The committee, consisting of Mr. Farrell, E. G. Barrow, President of the Inter-
> national League, and T. H. Murnane, President of the New England League,
> finds that the best interest of baseball will be conserved by allowing the merger.
>
> Upon the conclusion of certain formalities, for which 15 days are allowed, the
> order for a 10-club circuit becomes effective. The circuit comprises the Towns
> of Lowell, Lawrence, Worcester, Portland, and Lynn of the New England
> League, and Bridgeport, New Haven, Hartford, New London, and Springfield of
> the Eastern Association.
>
> J. A. Zeller of Pittsfield is allowed $3,500 for the dissolution of his franchise,
> and President James H. O'Rourke of the Eastern Association is allowed $1,000
> for expenses....
>
> Chief opposition to the merger, the report recites, came from President J. H.
> O'Rourke of the Eastern Association, but satisfactory proofs that the association
> had a local organization in each city of its circuit were not presented to the
> committee.[61]

The following day, O'Rourke dashed off a rebuttal to the *Times:*

BRIDGEPORT, Conn., Feb. 16, — That the proposed merger of the Eastern Base-ball Association with the New England League will be opposed by those inter-ests in the former body which are not recognized by the decision [the cities left out of the proposed merger] of the National Board of Arbitration was indi-cated today, when President James H. O'Rourke of the Eastern Association notified Secretary John H. Farrell of the board that he would file an appeal from the merger decision at once.

Mr. O'Rourke, who has fifteen days in which to make the appeal, says that he may bring equity proceedings [a lawsuit].[62]

Tim Murnane (1909 T204 Ramly card).

This regional baseball war was being fought in the theater of public opinion. The letters to the sports editors were like the volleys of artillery then being heard on European battlefronts.

On February 20, Jim issued a written appeal against the merger.[63] The original letter is not available, but a letter sent to a fellow minor league pres-ident — "leaked" to the press — reveals Jim's position and attitude:

The decision will go down into baseball history unparalleled for disregard of the rules and laws not only of organized baseball but of the laws of the land....

Just think of Murnane being a member of the committee disregarding the ethics, ... and the National constitution which reads: "Article 5, Section 3 — No member shall sit or vote in the trial of any clause in which his league is inter-ested."

Let me quote his letter of September 24, 1915:

"Dear Jim: Take of your own knitting and you can always count on me, but not as the president or officer of any baseball league in the United States of America. Will be in a stronger position to make a lot of bad actors wince under the lash of criticism. Don't ever bother your head about what you may see in the papers. The needle ever points to the pole, and 'old sport' has never been known to change colors and quit a friend."

Oh, what slush and gush. Could or would any judge of honor accept a place on a committee disqualified of the constitution, render judgment, and then accept an office at the hands of one or the other of the parties to the contro-versy?[64]

But Jim's cause was lost.[65] Murnane had won.

The new combine took the name Eastern League. Of the five teams from

Murnane's New England League, only three survived the 1916 season. Within two years, only one remained afloat; while all of Jim's clubs were still active.

Clearly the stronger circuit prior to the forced merger was the Eastern Association. Yet Murnane, who brokered the deal, had the votes in his pocket to guarantee his election as president of the new league and force Jim out.

It never was a game.

33

The Baseball Wars: A Look Back

A sportswriter, in surveying the baseball wars, observed: "It is becoming more and more apparent that friendship and honor in baseball go little further than dollars and cents."[1] Although professional baseball was less than a half century young in 1916, it had already suffered numerous civil wars:

- 1876 National Association coup that created the National League,
- 1884 destruction of the Union Association by the National League,
- 1890 war between the owners and players,
- 1891 National League conquest and absorption of the original American Association,
- 1901–1903 unsuccessful National League attempt to quash the new American League,
- 1914–1916 Federal League War.

And this is only a list of the national campaigns.

At first I thought the Great War to End All Baseball Wars, the Brotherhood uprising of 1890, was a class conflict between labor and capital, but it has more in common with the other baseball wars between leagues; that is, between opposing armies of owners. The Brotherhood War had in fact brought in capitalists as partners to provide financial backing. And the players chose not to ally themselves with the burgeoning union movement of the late nineteenth century. It wasn't class warfare; it was just warfare.

Clearly, ever since the founding of the National League, the magnates did everything they could to keep the players in their place, through perpetually renewable contracts, the blacklist, and control of the job market. However, they were just as ruthless toward one another.

Consider, for example, the 1882 case of the National League throwing out the Troy and Worcester clubs. The victims here were the capitalists as well as the players. According to the *Clipper*:

271

The directors of the Troy Club have been at great expense this year in laying out new grounds, and according to the constitution of the League no club can be expelled unless it has violated the League rules.[2]

The league admitted the franchises had not violated the rules, but they were out anyway. In a display of unity and support for their capitalists,

The Troy players express[ed] indignation at the way the Troy Club has been used, and say that they will remain there next season in preference of going to any other city.[3]

But this sentiment, too, was soon overwhelmed by the basic economic urges driving all capitalists and workers. The Troy players drifted down the Hudson River to Manhattan and changed their name to the New York Giants.

These were all economic wars: wars of greed, between one group of men that held a monopoly, of valuable territory (franchises), the better players (the reserve), or indeed over the entire baseball industry (the National Agreement).

War inevitably broke out whenever an upstart group of capitalists—or players—organized to carve out a piece of this bounty for themselves. Murnane coveted the strong clubs in O'Rourke's Eastern Association and took them.

The stars of O'Rourke and Murnane had traveled in parallel for more than half a century, as teammates in three leagues and as leaders within the National Association of Professional Baseball Leagues.

Each winter as they journeyed together by train to the annual NAPBL convention, the two old friends would catch each other up on their lives, their families, and their careers; and relive moments shared on ball fields long ago. However, at the end of their careers, and lives, these veteran baseballists were not on speaking terms.

Murnane passed away within a year of their regional war; and Jim not long thereafter.

On January 1, 1919, Jim O'Rourke was to meet with a woman being evicted from her home. He waited for a trolley that never came, then walked to his office to keep the appointment, contracting pneumonia. He died one week later at the age 68.[4]

At the time of his death, he still owned Newfield Park, the family farm that he had converted into his own field of dreams. In his will, he asked that "the park be used for baseball as long as possible."[5]

It still is.

34

Epilogue

Adrian C. "Cap" Anson. Although the least politically correct of any baseball manager, he was the best player of his era. His final major league season was in 1897, when he was 45 years old. His lifetime batting average is .333. He managed the Chicago White Stockings for 19 years, corralling five pennants. Anson is in the Hall of Fame.[1]

Hugh "One-Arm" Daily won 73 games in his major league career,[2] including a no-hitter. He once struck out 20 batters in a single game, setting a record that lasted a hundred years.[3] Daily ranks third among all pitchers for the most strikeouts in a season: 483. Daily was never heard from again after leaving the major leagues. He is not in the Hall of Fame.

Helen Dauvray. Johnny and Helen separated at the start of the 1890 season, from the strain of the Baseball War and irreconcilable differences. Helen opened her 1890 season on September 29, at the Standard Theatre in New York, with *The Whirlwind*, a light comedy. It received cool reviews and closed a month later. After several attempts at reconciliation, Johnny and Helen divorced in 1903.

James Stephen O'Rourke Jr. After playing for his father on the Bridgeport Orators for six years (1903–1908), Jimmy played 34 games for the Highlanders during the second half of the 1908 season. In 1909 he was purchased by the Columbus Senators of the "AA" American Association.

James Jr., at age 28, married his first wife, Emma, on March 11, 1909, in New York City.[4] In 1911 they had a child, James John O'Rourke III.[5]

In 1913, Jimmy was sold to the St. Paul Saints, also of the American Association. He was in St. Paul through the 1914 season. In 1915 he played for Syracuse of the New York State League.[6]

In 1916, Jimmy divorced Emma. He was 36 years old, a stage when ballplayers must take stock and face the reality of a future that may not accept them as a player. Emma, too, may have been reassessing her life as the wife of a minor league ballplayer, with its uncertainties, low wages, and absentee husband. At an auto meet in 1914, a "Mrs. James O'Rourke, Jr., in a small

Saxon" raced "Mrs. Rosella Cippola in a Ford car, the prize being a silver cup." Emma won the cup.[7]

Soon after his divorce, Jimmy married a woman from Baltimore. He moved to the area and settled down for what would become a lifelong career at Bethlehem Steel in Sparrows Point, Maryland. Bethlehem was serious about its baseball club and had organized its own league in 1917. Each of its six plants around the country had a team.[8] In the middle of the 1918 season, the minor leagues were shut down because ballplayers were required to fight or work in a defense plant, allowing Bethlehem to pick up 36 former major leaguers. Jimmy had found his home. He was still at Sparrows Point when he passed away on December 22, 1955, four days before his 75th birthday.[9]

In 13 years in the minor leagues (1903–1915), Jimmy had racked up 277

James John O'Rourke III, baseballist (Bridgeport *Herald*, March 16, 1913).

stolen bases and a lifetime batting average of .253, very respectable for an infielder during the deadball era.[10]

Albert Goodwill Spalding moved to California and joined the Theosophians, a religious denomination. Spalding is in the Hall of Fame for putting baseball and its players under the control of the magnates and for his superb pitching. He won 80 percent of his games during a six-year career as a starting pitcher.

John Montgomery Ward. After the Baseball War, Johnny went on to manage the consolidated Brooklyn club and later the New York Giants. He retired as a player after the 1894 season to practice law and golf. Ward has the all-time lowest on-base percentage for pitchers (.254).[11] In December 1911, along with James E. Gaffney, he purchased 945 of the 1,000 shares of the Boston Braves for $177,000.[12] Ward was elected President of the club, but the following year sold his interest to Gaffney.[13] Ward died in 1925 in Augusta, Georgia, where he was entered in the Masters Gold Tournament.[14] Ward is a member of the Hall of Fame

Jim "Deacon" White. Jim's first year as a major league player was in 1871, the inaugural season of the National Association (the first league run by and for the players). His last season was with the Players' League Buffalo team, in which he was a major investor. In his 20-

year career he amassed a lifetime batting average over .300 and led the majors in hitting two years and in RBI three years. He died on June 8, 1939, of a broken heart. It was four days prior to baseball's grand centennial celebration at Cooperstown, and the player who made the real first major league hit was not invited. The Deacon is not in the Hall of Fame.

Appendix A

Jim O'Rourke's Professional Statistics

The Majors

	LG	TEAM	G	AB	RUNS	HITS	AVE	RANK	OBP	SB	POS	FA
1872	NA	Middletown	23	101	25	31	.307		.320	1	ss, c, 3b	.727
1873	NA	Boston	57	280	79	98	.350	9	.381	4	1b, of, c	.916
1874	NA	Boston	70	331	82	104	.314		.322	11	1b	.943
1875	NA	Boston	75	358	97	106	.296		.313	17	cf, 3b,1b	.800
1876	NL	Boston	70	327	61	102	.312	10	.358	na	of, 1b, c	.856
1877	NL	Boston	61	265	68	96	.362	4	.407	na	of, 1b	.846
1878	NL	Boston	60	255	44	71	.278		.292	na	of, 1b, c	.860
1879	NL	Providence	81	362	69	126	.348	2	.371	na	of, 1b, c, 3b	.785
1880	NL	Boston	86	363	71	100	.275		.315	na	of, 1b, ss, 3b, c	.907
1881	NL	Buffalo	83	348	71	105	.302		.352	na	3b, of, c, ss, 1b	.821
1882	NL	Buffalo	84	370	62	104	.281		.305	na	of, ss, c, 3b	.866
1883	NL	Buffalo	94	436	102	143	.328	5	.350	na	of, c, 3b, ss, p	.866
1884	NL	Buffalo	108	467	119	162	.347	1	.392	na	of, 1b, c, p, 3b	.894
1885	NL	New York	112	477	119	143	.300		.354	na	of, c	.940
1886	NL	New York	105	440	106	136	.309	9	.365	14	of, c, 1b	.926
1887	NL	New York	103	433	73	149	.344		.352	46	c, 3b, of, 2b	.890
1888	NL	New York	107	409	50	112	.274		.319	25	of, c, 1b, 3b	.960
1889	NL	New York	128	502	89	161	.321		.372	33	of, c	.893
1890	PL	New York	111	478	112	172	.360	3	.410	23	of	.930
1891	NL	New York	136	555	92	164	.295	6	.334	19	of, c	.906
1892	NL	New York	115	448	62	136	.304	10	.354	16	of, c, 1b	.913
1893	NL	Washington	129	547	75	157	.287		.354	15	of, 1b, c	.927
1904	NL	New York	1	4	1	1	.250		.250	0	c	.800
23 years		·	1995	8556	1729	2679	.313		.353	224		

The Minors

	LG	TEAM	G	AB	RUNS	HITS	AVE	RANK	SB	POS	FA
1895	Conn	Bridgeport	8	35	8	15	.429		3	c, of	na
1896	Naug	Bridgeport	33	135	47	59	.437	1	14	c, of	na
1897	Conn	Bridgeport	73	321	75	130	.405	1	20	c	na
1898	Conn	Bridgeport	79	316	36	96	.304		11	c	.964
1899	Conn	Bridgeport	93	356	50	102	.287		14	c, of	na
1900	Conn	Bridgeport	93	352	61	126	.358		12	c, of	.951
1901	Conn	Bridgeport	80	318	47	105	.330		6	c	na

	LG	TEAM	G	AB	RUNS	HITS	AVE	RANK	SB	POS	FA
1902	Conn	Bridgeport	83	310	27	76	.245		5	c	.973
1903	Conn	Bridgeport	101	400	42	110	.275		9	c	.968
1904	Conn	Bridgeport	66	245	28	70	.286		4	c	.977
1905	Conn	Bridgeport	68	238	15	60	.252		3	c, of	.950
1906	Conn	Bridgeport	93	348	26	85	.244		5	1b	.980
1907	Conn	Bridgeport	24	83	3	16	.193		4	of, c	.963
1908	Conn	Bridgeport	18	57	2	9	.158		1	1b, c, of	na
1909	Conn	Bridgeport	1	3	0	1	.333		0	c	na
1912	Conn	New Haven	1	4	0	0	.000		0	c	na
16 years			914	3521	467	1060	.301		111		

Major league stats are taken from O'Rourke Player Card at the Hall of Fame Library; *Daguerreotypes*, Sporting News, 1990; *Total Baseball*, 7th Ed., 2001. Minor league stats are based on research by Frank Williams, *Spalding* and *Reach* Guides, and *Daguerreotypes*. RANK=Batting Average rank in league (only recorded if placed among top 10 in majors or led league in minors), OPB=On-Base Percentage, SB=Stolen Bases, FA=Fielding Average.

Appendix B

Evolution of the Rules of Baseball

The following are the significant developments, first as reflected in the New York rules attributed to Alexander Joy Cartwright, that were then embellished by the National Association of Base Ball Players founded in the 1850s. In 1871, the National Association of Professional Base Ball Players assumed custody of the rules of baseball. Finally, as of 1876, the rules herein outlined are those of the National League, the dominant force in the national pastime during the last quarter of the nineteenth century.

The minor leagues tended to follow the major leagues, taking the best ideas from the various senior circuits, and sometimes lagging behind in the implementation of new rules, taking a wait-and-see attitude.

Most rules were written to maintain a balance between offense and defense. Over the years, as pitching became swifter and "trickier," the rule makers adjusted the restrictions placed on the delivery, the number of balls needed for a walk, and the distance from the pitcher's box to the plate. To gauge how they were doing, the rule makers monitored batting averages and ERAs. If one began to shift up or down — because the pitcher or batter found a loophole in the old rules or perfected a new technique — then a rule change was invoked to relevel the playing field.[1]

Originally, the job of the pitcher was to deliver the ball to the batter so he could hit it. Section 3 of the original rules of baseball required that: "The ball must be pitched and not thrown for the bat."[2]

The duel was not between pitcher and batter, but between the striker and the fielders. The pitcher was not a factor in the game.

There were no called balls or strikes. The pitcher tossed up balls until the batter hit one, and the batter could and would wait until one came by he liked. So pitchers had no incentive to try to throw anything by the batter. No batter would swing at a fast or curving pitch or one that just grazed the corner.

A New York Mutual player once took 50 pitches before swinging.[3] This lack of pressure on the batter, coupled with a very lively rubber-core ball, produced triple-digit scores in the 1840s and 1850s.

However, from the very beginning, three pitches *struck at and missed*, was an out. That is, unless the third strike was dropped by the catcher. Then, well, it depends.

THE DROPPED THIRD STRIKE (or, why it's never easy to write a perfect rule). One of the original rules of baseball, adopted September 23, 1845, states:

> Three balls being struck at and missed, and the last one caught is a hand out; *not caught*, is considered fair, and the striker bound to run.

It should be pointed out that in 1845, and even through the 1879 season, a catcher could reel in the ball on the fly or after one bounce to count as being caught (and thereby not a *dropped* third strike).

If the third strike is dropped by the catcher, it was the same as a hit and the batter was obliged to run to first. This happened to O'Rourke early in his career. It was on June 2, 1873, in a game between the Brooklyn Atlantics and Boston Red Stockings:

> The Bostonians had three men on the bases when O'Rourke came to the bat. After having two strikes called on him he struck out, but Barlow failed — purposely — to catch the ball. O'Rourke now had to run to first base, and thus force all the other men off. Barlow instantly picked up the ball, touched the home-plate, putting out [Deacon] White, who was forced off third, and then threw to first base in time to capture O'Rourke.[4]

Many players were naturally reluctant to run to first on a DTS for fear of looking foolish trying to beat out the throw. To give runners a sporting chance (when no bases were occupied and therefore no opportunity for a force-out), catchers began throwing the ball around the horn (to third, to second, to first) after a dropped third strike.

Today, throwing around the horn is done only if the third strike is *caught*, as ritual for reasons long forgotten. If the third strike is dropped, a modern catcher will throw directly to first.

The arcane DTS rule would give fits to rule makers and umpires for at least half a century, until all possible situations were thought through and accounted for in the ever-thickening rulebook.

But why do we even have this rule? So what if the catcher drops the third strike?

It is not a rule of rounders, a game that many believe to be an antecedent to American baseball. The DTS rule does appear on an 1860 list of rules for the Massachusetts Game, a branch of baseball's evolutionary tree that eventually withered and died.[5] A description of baseball from 1834 makes no mention of the DTS.[6] It therefore appears to be a purely American invention of the 1840 perhaps it was a gentlemanly granting of a chance to run to first if unable to hit the ball. The job of the battery, originally, was merely to put the ball into play.

Or the DTS rule may merely have been for consistency. Besides three strikes, the only way to get a batter out was to catch a batted ball; and failing that, to throw the ball to first base before the batter could run there. The DTS says pretty much the same thing: catch the third strike to legitimize the out, or throw to first base before the runner reaches the bag.

In the 1840s and through the 1860s, first basemen were gloveless and the catcher stood well back of the plate. It is therefore conceivable that during this preprofessional era, the runner might beat the throw after a DTS — or the first baseman might muff the catch — often enough to make it worth his while to run.

However, the game evolved in a way to make the DTS rule anachronistic. Players began wearing gloves in the mid–1870s. The skill of the players, and fielding averages, also improved.

1864. But the change in the game that most ran counter to the DTS was a rule adopted in 1864 to make the game more manly by eliminating the "boyish practice" by fielders of catching the ball on the bounce. From then on, a fair ball had to caught on the fly for an out. Still, there was no mention of catching a *third strike* on the fly. That would have created too much danger for the catcher, requiring him to play up close behind the plate. (In 1864, there was no protection for the catcher.)

1880. But beginning with this season, the catcher *was* required to nab a third strike on the fly to complete the out.[7] (Although the rule is not specific on this point, a dropped *foul tip* was treated as a foul ball.) As a result, catchers began playing closer to the plate, and therefore closer to *second base*. Now it gets interesting.

On a dropped third strike, with a runner on first, a batter attempting to beat the catcher's throw could offer the opponents an opportunity to turn a double play, for the catcher could throw to *second* instead of first. (This is what happened to Jim in the 1873 game against the Brooklyn Atlantics.) The tactic was still being employed in 1879. In an account of a June 26 game between Boston and Providence, O'Rourke's team was again the victim of the ploy, when Boston catcher Charlie Snyder, "purposely missing Hague on Strikes" was able to turn a triple play.[8]

So batters were coached never to run on a dropped third strike with a man on first.

1881. The rule was then updated to cover the practice of not running by stating that a batter was out if he failed to run to first.[9]

Of course, one solution always leads to a new problem. Johnny Ward found a loophole in the new rule. In a game with a man on first and one out, he hit a grounder right at the shortstop for an easy double play. Ward stood his ground. The shortstop tossed the ball to second, beating the runner, and the second baseman then threw to first. Double play, right? Not so fast. Ward was called out by the umpire for failing to run, so there were not too many runners on the base paths and therefore no force at second. Ward was out, to be sure, but the runner now standing on second was safe. The next batter drove him in.[10]

1884. Prior to the start of the season, the rules were again modified. On November 21, 1883, at the eighth annual meeting of the National League in Washington, DC, "The rule requiring batsmen to be declared out for failure to run to a base after three strikes was abolished."[11] As *Sporting Life* explained:

> One of the principal reasons why the rule by which a batsman could, after three strikes, prevent the making of a double or triple play by merely standing still was rescinded, was because it was found that under the operation of this rule a double or triple play could be prevented in the same way even after a fair hit had been made; that is, by failing to run the batsman was out, and in consequence, no base runner was forced.[12]

Harry Wright was not happy with the new rule again requiring a batter to run to first base after the third strike. Wright reasoned:

> This gives the fielders a chance to make double or triple plays. The batsman, especially if young and inexperienced, with two or three men on base, is much more nervous in this case, where an entire side is liable to be put out, than in a case where only he himself is concerned, and if he makes a strike or has one called on him, the chances are that he will be struck out and his side disposed of. Of course a double or triple play is made, but there is nothing brilliant about a play of this kind as there would be in a case where a hard hit, and a good catch or fine stop is made.[13]

This unfair situation was then remedied by the following rule amendment:

> The Batsman is out ... if, while the First Base be occupied by a base runner, three strikes be called on him by the Umpire, except when two men are already out.

This was still the rule in 2003. The precise modern language of rule 6.05(c) is:

> "A batter is out when a third strike is not caught by the catcher when first base is occupied before two are out."

In other words, the batter is automatically out on a DTS in situations when a double play would be possible were he forced to run. There was then just one last loophole to close up.

1888. On November 14, 1887, a joint rules committee met in Pittsburgh and refined the DTS rule to cover the situation where the third strike might be deflected or interfered with, thus by chance aiding or hampering the batter's opportunity to reach first base before the catcher could send the ball to the base:

> The batter shall be called out on a third strike when the ball hits his person or his clothing.[14]

This rule was still in effect in 2003.

Well, that should wrap up the infuriating DTS rule, right? Not quite. What if the third strike is a *foul tip*?

1890. THE FOUL TIP. According to the 1890 rules, the consequences of a foul tip differ from that of a foul hit (foul ball), in that a foul ball caught on the fly is an out, whereas a foul tip caught on the fly is not an out. In 1890, it was not even a strike.

And just what is a foul tip? According to the 1890 *Spalding Guide*, Rule 38 stipulates a Foul Ball

> not rising above the Batsman's head and caught by the Catcher playing within ten feet of the Home Base, shall be termed a Foul Tip.

If an umpire declared a foul tip, the runners would have to return to their bases (without danger of being put out in the process). The purpose of this is obvious. A tipped pitch can easily result in a ball getting away from the catcher, allowing runners to advance. This is inherently unfair, as this is almost impossible to do intentionally so that the offense should not be rewarded for a fluke, nor should a catcher be penalized with a passed ball. For this purpose, a foul tip is treated no different than a foul ball.

Today, a foul tip that is caught is a strike and the ball is in play. The precise definition (in 2003) of a "foul tip" is:

> A batted ball that goes sharp and direct from the bat to the catcher's hands and is legally caught. It is not a foul tip unless caught and any foul tip that is caught is a strike, and the ball is in play.

Today, catching a foul tip on the third strike puts the batsman out, as would catching a foul ball. (If it is *not caught*, it is treated as a foul ball; that is, it is a strike only if the batter has no strikes or only one strike. A foul tip cannot count as the third strike unless caught.) If it is not caught, it is a foul ball.

CRYING FOUL

1875. THE FAIR FOUL. Home plate was placed outside the foul line, with the front tip of the square plate just touching the juncture of the first and third base foul lines. This move was made to make it more difficult to hit a *fair-foul* (a ball that would strike the ground in fair territory and then angle foul). At the time, a fair-foul was a legal hit.[15]

In 1877, home plate was placed inside the foul lines.[16]

1881. A base runner could not be put out while returning to his base after a foul ball had been hit.[17]

1883. FOUL BOUND ELIMINATED. Beginning in 1883, a foul ball had to be caught on the fly for an out.[18] Previously, a foul ball caught on one bounce (a foul bound) was an out. The rule was amended at the seventh annual meeting of the National League, in Providence, on December 6, 1882. (From the beginning of time through the 1882 season a foul ball caught on one bound was an out.) The *Clipper* noted the passing of this ancient convention:

In section 3, Rule 51— Class 5 — a very important amendment was made, the words "or after touching the ground but once" being struck out. This does away with the foul-bound catch, and establishes the complete fly-game for the first time in the history of baseball.

1894. A foul bunt was a strike.[19]

1895. A foul tip was a strike for the first time.[20] ("But only if caught by the catcher within the 10-foot lines of the catcher's box.")[21]

1901. (National League; 1903 American League) a foul ball was a strike, unless the batter already had two strikes.[22]

This rule was enacted to discourage the practice of intentionally "fouling off" pitches in an effort to tire the pitcher. The tactic was slowing down the game. According to Frank Richter, "Intentional fouling had been penalized with a called strike, but the question of intention raised such incessant argument that umpires permitted the rule to fall into desuetude."[23]

PITCHING DISTANCE and PITCHER'S POSITION

1845. The forward line of the pitchers' box was 45 feet from home plate. The pitcher's line was 12 feet long and bisected by an imaginary line running from home to second base.

1858. The pitcher was permitted to make a short run-up to the line before delivering the ball.[24]

1864. A pitcher's box, 12 feet wide by 3 feet deep, was added to the field, to shorten the run-up the pitcher could take.[25]

1866. The pitcher's box was made 4 feet deep. It was still 12 feet wide.

1867. The pitcher's box was redrawn as a 6-foot square.

1868. The pitcher's box was narrowed to 4 feet. It was still 6 feet deep.

1869. The pitcher's box was again widened to 6 feet and remained 6 feet deep.

1879. The pitcher's box was narrowed to 4 feet, from 6 feet wide,[26] so the pitcher couldn't dance around so much before delivering the ball. Previously, some pitchers would start at the rear of the 6-foot-deep box, in one corner, and by a very distracting hop, skip and dance wind up in the opposite corner and then throw across his body in the opposite direction.

1881. To give the beleaguered batters a break, the pitcher's box was moved back 5' to 50' from home plate. (It is currently 60' 6".) The difference then and now is not as great as it may appear. Today, the pitcher must start his delivery with his back foot on the rubber, and he can take one giant step with his front foot, and roll his body over the lead foot and release the ball well in front of the 60' 6" mark. In 1881, the pitcher had to begin his delivery with his back foot at the *rear* of the pitcher's 6' foot deep box, or 56' from home plate.

1886. The pitcher's box is changed to 4 feet wide by 7 feet deep.[27] (This had the effect of lengthening the pitching distance to 57 feet.)

1887. The pitcher's box was again reduced: from 4 feet wide by 7 feet deep, to 4 feet wide by 5.5 feet deep. This brought the pitcher to 55.5 feet from home plate, but he was permitted to take only one step before delivering the ball.[28]

The pitcher was also required to hold the ball up in front of him before beginning his delivery, so that it was visible to the batter and umpire. This was to counter the practice of some pitchers of concealing the ball behind their body, then whirling and throwing. This made it difficult for the batter to pick up the ball in its half-second flight to home plate.

1893. The last major changes to the pitching rules were in 1893, when the pitcher was moved back to the modern distance of 60 feet 6 inches from the plate; and the pitcher's box was replaced with a marble slab 12 inches wide and 4 inches deep.[29] "The pitcher was obliged to place his rear foot against the slab "from which he could take but one step, his movement in all other ways being unrestricted."[30]

1895. The pitcher's "rubber" was lengthened to 24 inches by 6 inches deep.[31]

1903. The height of the pitcher's mound was limited to 15 inches.[32]

1968. The pitcher's mound was lowered to 10 inches.[33]

BALLS AND STRIKES

1860. CALLED STRIKES. Batters brought a called strike upon themselves when they adopted the habit of letting even good pitches go by with runners on base, hoping a ball would get past the catcher, thus allowing the runners to advance; or at least to give the runners plenty of opportunities to steal.[34]

In the first attempt to speed up the game, a new section was added to the rules at the annual baseball convention of March 17, 1860:

Should the striker stand at the bat without striking at good balls repeatedly pitched to him, for the apparent purpose of delaying the game, or of giving advantage to a player, the umpire, after warning him, shall call one strike, and if he persists in such action, two and three strikes.[35]

Officially, it was three strikes and yer out, but umpires gave a warning of "good ball!" if the batter looked at what today would be a called third strike. If a batter let another such ball go by, he would be called out.[36] A batter would be called out if he *swung at* and missed a pitch after having two strikes being called on him.

1881. The "good ball" warning was dropped, making three strikes an out in all cases.

1887. For this one year only, the batter was again allowed four strikes.

1888. Again, three strikes meant an out. Johnny Ward did not like the return to three strikes, but Spalding did "because under the four strike rule some clubs had ordered their weak batters not to hit at the first two good balls, taking chances of reaching first on called balls."[37]

1909. A bunt on a third strike was a strikeout.[38]

STRIKE ZONE.[39]

The width of the zone has always been the width of home plate, or 17". The height of a "legal" pitch, however, has changed often.

1845. There were no called strikes, so there was no strike *zone*.

1860. A new section, number 37, was added to the official rules to penalize a batter for delaying the game by refusing to strike at good balls. A batter could now be put out on "called strikes" (fair pitches that he does not swing at). The concept of a strike zone began to develop. Section 5 of the set of rules adopted by the National Association of Base-Ball Players, at their annual convention in New York on March 14, 1860, read in part:

The pitcher must deliver the ball as near as possible over the center of the home base and for the striker.[40]

Henry Chadwick, who edited *Beadle's Dime Base-Ball Player*, explains that "and for the striker" was intended to prohibit pitchouts.[41]

1867. The 1860 rule was slightly modified to read: "and *fairly* for the striker"[42] meaning a ball he could hit. Although the rules did not define a specific "strike zone," Chadwick, in notes accompanying the rules as printed in *Beadle's Dime Base-Ball Player*, offered the following guidelines to umpires:

All balls delivered by the pitcher, striking the ground in front of the home base, or pitched over the head of the batsman, or pitched to the side opposite to that which the batsman strikes from, shall be considered unfair balls.[43]

Although the strike zone was still poorly defined in 1867, the batter, beginning with this season, was entitled to his base after four unfair balls had been called by the umpire. (See "Called Balls.")

1870. Beginning this year, a batter could call for a high or low pitch.[44] There were therefore two strike zones: (1) from the bottom of the knee to the belt; (2) from the belt to the top of the shoulder.

O'Rourke would always call "low." His favorite pitch was down around the knees.

1887. The privilege of the batter to call for a high or low pitch was eliminated. The new 1887 strike zone included the combined area of the previous "high" and "low" zones: that is, "not lower than the knee of the batsman nor higher than his shoulder."[45]

1950. The strike zone was reduced to the area from the armpit to the top of the knees.

1963. The 1887 strike zone was reinstated (top of the shoulder to the bottom of the knees).

1969. The strike zone again reverted to the smaller 1950 standard: armpit to top of knees.

1988. The upper limit was changed to the midpoint between the top of the uniform pants and the top of the shoulders.

1996. The lower limit of the zone was lowered to "the hollow beneath the kneecaps."

It was after strikes began to be called on fussy strikers that pitchers began to throw deceptively and faster. Pitchers began to nibble at the corners of the plate, hoping to lure the striker into going after a bad pitch.

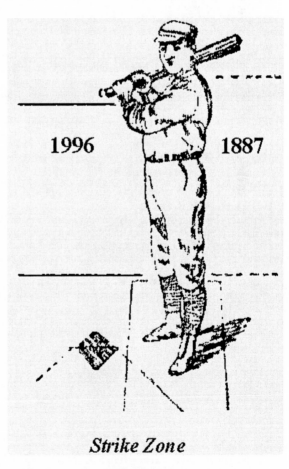

Strike Zone

Strike Zone; 1996 zone added by author (engraving: *Sporting News*, January 29, 1887).

CALLED BALLS. Just as the batters brought about the necessity for called strikes by their poor sportsmanship, so too did the pitchers call down upon their tribe the wrath of the rule makers for throwing junk. In 1867, the following rule first appeared:

> Sec. 6. Should the pitcher repeatedly fail to deliver to the striker fair balls, for the apparent purpose of delaying the game, or for any cause, the umpire, after warning him, shall call one ball, and if the pitcher persists is such action, two and three balls; when three balls have been called, the striker shall take the first base.[46]

The guidelines for called balls were quite muddled, and as a result, inconsistently applied by the umpires. For example, the umpire was not permitted to make a call on the first pitch until 1875. There were also different kinds of called balls. There were *wides* that were not over the plate, as well as *unfair balls* that were not in the player's requested strike zone. To really get your head swimming, read William Ryczek, *Blackguards and Red Stockings* (1992), page 75.

Umps originally called out "unfair ball," since shortened to "ball."

The number of balls required for a walk fluctuated over the initial years as the rule makers groped for the right balance:

- In 1876 a batter did not walk until he received 9 balls;
- in 1880 it was 8;
- in 1881 it was 7;
- in 1884 it was 6 in the National League (7 in the AA and UA);
- in 1886 it was 7 again in the National League (6 in the AA);
- in 1887 it was 5;
- in 1889, it was 4 balls.

After 1889, balls and strikes would never again be tampered with.[47]

THE DEVELOPMENT OF NEW TECHNIQUES BY PITCHERS and THE RULE MAKERS' EFFORTS TO BOX THEM IN.

1845. New Rule: PITCHING RESTRICTION: Section 3 of the first set of baseball rules read:

> The ball must be pitched and not thrown for the bat.[48]

The pitching rule was modified only slightly during baseball's first two decades. In 1867 it read:

> Sec. 7. The ball must be pitched, not jerked or thrown, to the bat.[49]

In notes accompanying the 1867 rules as published in *Beadle's Dime Base-Ball Player*, editor Henry Chadwick provided the following descriptions of illegal deliveries:

The ball shall be considered jerked, in the meaning of the rule, if the pitcher's arm touches his person when the arm is swung forward to deliver the ball; and it shall be regarded as a throw if the arm be bent at the elbow, at an angle from the body, or horizontally from the shoulder, when it is swung forward to deliver the ball. A pitched ball is one delivered with the arm straight, and swinging perpendicularly and free from the body.[50]

1858. Innovation: FASTBALL. Jim Creighton introduced "heat" in 1858. Creighton ignored the requirement to keep the arm stiff and straight and toss the ball underhand. He instead employed an underhand throw, which he got by the umpires and opposing batters. Swift pitching was perfected by the start of the Civil War, although the rules still tried to thwart its use.[51] By the end of the Civil War, pitchers were throwing as fast as they could, as in modern fast-pitch softball. There were no radar guns in the nineteenth century, so the best I can offer is my estimate that between 1845 and 1895, the swiftest balls pitched equaled the year (i.e., 70 mph in 1870).

1861. Innovation: THE BEANBALL. With faster pitching came the opportunity for intimidation. Henry Chadwick wrote in 1864 of

the unfair style of pitching that was in vogue in 1861, '62 and '63 [of] trying to intimidate the batsmen by pitching the ball at them instead of for them as the rules require.[52]

1863. New Rule: PITCHING RESTRICTION. The pitcher must keep both feet on the ground when delivering the ball. This ruling was a reaction to stretching the rule permitting the pitcher to take a few steps in delivering the ball. Over time this had led to a "hop, skip and jump" and other antics.

This would be the cycle of ever-changing rules for decades. A rule was enacted to permit a reasonable action; the rule was abused; the rule was tightened or rescinded or a new rule was enacted to relevel the playing field.

1864–68. Innovation: A rudimentary CURVEBALL was invented probably in the late 1850s and perfected by Candy Cummings (or one of the other claimants to its invention) by the mid–1860s. As early as 1860, baseball commentator Henry Chadwick was advising would-be aces to add a curveball to their arsenals:

The pitcher, who can combine a high degree of speed with an even delivery, and at the same time, can, at pleasure, *impart a bias or twist* to the ball is the most effective player in that position.[53]

By 1868, the curve began to torment batters on a regular basis.

1868. New Rule: PITCHING RESTRICTION. Pitchers could move around as much as they liked, as long as they remained within their box.[54]

1872. New Rule: THE FASTBALL AND CURVE were legalized. Pitchers were allowed to "snap" the ball on delivery, but they had to release the

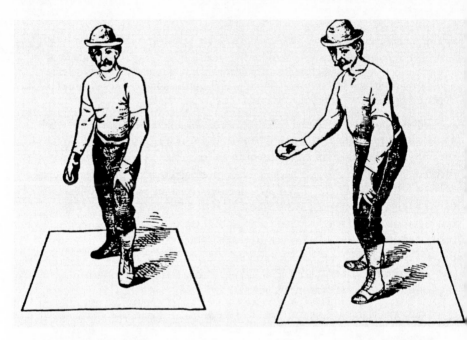

Pitching in the 1870s. Left: A legal pitch, with the arm straight, parallel to the body. Right: An illegal — although commonly used — underhand throw (engraving: *DeWitt's Base-Ball Guide*).

ball below the waist.[55] Still, the pitcher could bend over and thereby throw the ball with considerable force. Prior to 1872, the pitcher was required to toss or pitch the ball — as in horseshoes.

Some historians have misinterpreted the 1872 rule that allowed "throwing," assuming this to mean overhand, when in fact the rule makers were referring to the practice of throwing underhand, the motion used to skip rocks. Tim Keefe used this technique as do some modern-day pitchers. The throw from a five o'clock position allows the pitcher to curve the ball without having to twist his hand and arm, a motion that shortened the career of many a hurler.

For a time, two pitching styles co-existed. Slow-pitch adherents like Harry Wright practiced something closer to the original and authentic underhand lobbing. The advantages were that a pitcher could last easily through nine innings and decades of pitching without the arm giving out. It was also easy on the catcher, who could play closer to the plate to keep runners on, there were fewer passed balls, and the catcher of slow pitching suffered fewer injuries than the backstop who had to take heat.

The slow pitcher could curve the ball by spinning it counterclockwise as it was released below the waist. Such a ball would curve to the left.

A swift-pitch adherent threw with more of a sidearm motion. This pitching was faster and curved the ball naturally, because the fingers were on the side of the ball when it was released, giving it a rotation around a vertical axis. The spin would be clockwise if looking down on the ball, causing it to curve to the right.

1874. New Innovation: THE CHANGE OF PACE was well established by this time. Both fast and slow styles had a changeup version, which eliminated the wrist and finger snap at the end of the delivery. This modern-sounding term was applied to Spalding in a July 25 article in the *New York Clipper*:

> His forte in delivery is the success with which he disguises a change of pace from swift to medium, a great essential in successful pitching.

1876. New Rule: PITCHING RESTRICTION. To shore up batting averages and enliven the game, the arm movement of the pitcher was rigidly proscribed. Rule IV, Sec. 2, of the original rules of the National League read in part:

> The ball must be delivered to the bat with the arm swinging nearly perpendicular at the side of the body, and the hand swinging forward must pass below the *hip* [emphasis added].[56]

Section 3 elaborated on the intent of this rule:

> Any outward swing of the arm, or any other swing save that of the perpendicular movement referred to in section 2 of this rule, shall be considered an overhand throw.

1878. New Rule: PITCHING RESTRICTION. Rule III, Sec. 2, of 1876 was modified to read:

> The ball must be delivered to the bat with the arm swinging nearly perpendicular at the side of the body, and the hand swinging forward must pass below the *waist* [emphasis added].

The arm was creeping higher.

1879. New Rule: PITCHING RESTRICTION. To reduce distracting moves, the pitcher had to face the batter as he began his motion.[57]

1881. Innovation: SIDEARM. In the early 1880s, the pitcher's arm began to inch still higher.[58] Baseball historian Preston Orem cites an account of "Grasshopper" Jim Whitney's style:

> Whitney makes no attempt to pitch as per the rules. With all the strength he can bring to bear, he draws his arm and hand back on a level with the shoulder and then, with a mighty effort, slugs the ball towards the catcher, unmindful of the striker's whereabouts; and was not in the least disconcerted by knocking the wind out of five Providence players last week. The league rules are just a farce if not enforced.[59]

New Rule: HITTING THE BATTER. Umpires were empowered to fine pitchers for *deliberately* hitting a batter. However, the unpopular and difficult-to-enforce rule (how does the umpire *know* it is an intentional beaning?) was scrapped at the end of the 1881 season.[60] Besides, as *Sporting Life* correctly pointed out:

> This penalty alone will not stop the pitcher from striking the batsman with the ball.[61]

1883. New Rule: SIDEARM SANCTIONED. To again bring the rules up to date with what was by then common practice, sidearm was sanctioned. A pitcher could release the ball shoulder high. Rule 27 for 1883 stated:

> A Fair Ball is a ball delivered by the pitcher while wholly within the line of his position and facing the batsman with his hand passing below his shoulder, and the ball passing over the home base at the height called for by the batsman.[62]

The great underhand pitchers like Jim Galvin stuck to the tried and true tossing. They were too old to learn new tricks and the smooth horseshoe pitching motion of underhand was easier on the arm.

1884. OVERHAND SANCTIONED. Since pitchers always fudge on the restrictions on delivery, in 1883 many were releasing the ball above the shoulder (since shoulder-high was then legal). At the National League convention in November 1883, the rule makers threw up their hands and removed all restrictions on the pitching motion. This was a practical decision, as it was too difficult to enforce the delivery rules. The "foul balk," rule 30, was also rescinded, since this was the penalty for an illegal pitch.[63]

The pitcher was still required to face the batter when he started his windup, and he was restricted to taking only one step before delivering the ball.[64]

Overhand pitching resulted in a number of broken arms, not to the batsmen, but to the thrower, as in this dramatic eyewitness account:

> Quinn, the celebrated left-handed pitcher of the Stillwater, met with a peculiar accident a few days ago. As he went to pitch a ball his arm suddenly broke above the elbow with a loud snap, which was heard over the entire field and among the people in the grand stand. The pain was so great that Quinn uttered a loud cry and fell in the box. His misfortune was somewhat allayed by a purse of $75 raised in the grand stand in a few minutes.[65]

My guess is that this type of injury occurred when the arm was subjected to the duel stress of an overhand whip throw with simultaneous twisting to induce a curve. *Sporting Life*, in August 1884 observed:

> All pitchers are now showing the effects of the hard, muscular strain of the arm required of them. It is a wonder that the arm can stand the severe wrenching it receives.[66]

It couldn't. The same issue of *Sporting Life* also contained the notice:

At the Milwaukee-Minneapolis game Thursday [August 7, 1884] Pearson, the pitcher for the Minneapolis Club, while delivering the ball, broke his arm above the elbow. It broke with a snapping sound that could be heard all over the diamond.

On September 3, 1884, page 7, *Sporting Life* reported:

Elmer Foster, the pitcher of the St. Paul Club, broke his arm in pitching the first ball in the game at St. Paul with Milwaukee, August 26. Friends of the ground immediately made up a handsome purse [of $172] for him. He was one of the best pitchers in the Northwestern League, and a number of clubs had their eyes on him. It seems singular how a man can break his arm in this manner, and yet if one will try to pitch a ball with great speed, he will readily perceive how the twist and jerk can snap a slender bone.

The following week, the publication told of yet another victim:

In Savannah last week a lad named Roberts, about 14 years old, while attempting to throw a curve ball, fractured his right arm between the elbow and shoulder. A doctor was called and attributed the accident to the fact that Roberts, in attempting to give the ball the curve line, brought into play the two muscles of the arm at the same instant.[67]

All told, in 1884, there were at least a half dozen pitchers who broke their arms throwing. The situation had not improved by 1889. As *Sporting Life* summarized at season's end:

Seven pitchers have fractured bones in their arms this year while delivering the ball.[68]

1885. New Rule: PITCHING RESTRICTION. A National League rule amendment required

the pitcher to have both feet touching the ground while making any of the series of motions made by him in pitching. This stops the running throw, and in a measure will check the speed of pitching.[69]

Sporting Life added:

There is among many players a singular misconception of the definition of the new League rule governing the pitcher's position. The idea prevailing that the rule requires both of the pitcher's feet to be on the ground when the ball leaves his hand. The fact is that the rule only requires him to keep the forward foot on the ground; the lifting of the backward foot being of no account, as the pitcher cannot lift that foot until the throw of the ball is made and the ball has left his hand.... Were the pitching rule such as to oblige the pitcher to keep the back foot on the ground after delivery, he would be so restricted in his delivery as to destroy his aim; besides which he would be liable to strain himself.[70]

National League president Nick Young added a further clarification that the forward foot cannot be slid forward either. The forward foot must be "perfectly stationary while the ball is being delivered."[71]

New Rule: BALK. Also for 1885, National League rule 20 defined the modern use of the term:

> A balk: If the pitcher when about to deliver the ball to the bat, while standing within the lines of this position, makes any one of the series of motions he habitually makes when delivering the ball, and then fails to deliver the ball to the bat.

New Rule: BATTER'S BOX. The National League, for 1885, gave the batter a way to reach further out for curves by amending rule number 10, widening the batter's box from 3 feet to 4 feet (6 inches on either side), bringing it 6 inches closer to home plate. In the opinion of *Sporting Life*:

> This is a most important change to batsmen, as it gives them more freedom of movement with which to combat the pitcher and also enables them to rap wide-pitched balls.[72]

1887. New Rules: PITCHING RESTRICTIONS. The new 1887 rules said the pitcher could take only one step in delivering the ball. The pitcher was required to

> stand squarely facing the batsman, take one step forward with the ball in plain sight, and let it go as he pleases.[73]

Formerly, the pitcher could hide the ball behind his back. The pitcher was now required to keep his [rear] foot on the back edge of his box, and he was "not allowed to lift [this foot] until the ball leaves his hand." The pitcher could take a step with his lead foot in delivering the ball, but it could not cross over the centerline of his position. (This was intended to stop the pitcher from moving to his right and then throwing the ball back across his body to the left.) The rules, in effect, were intended to keep the pitcher flat-footed thus "reducing the power to send in very swift balls."[74] The rules restricting his gyrations, coupled with the reduction in speed were designed to make the pitcher or thrower more accurate and cut down on beanballs and wear and tear on catchers. *The Sporting News* said the rules were necessary because overhand pitching was

> placing the batsman in the position of being obliged to devote nearly all his attention to avoid being severely hurt by being hit by the pitched ball.[75]

A significant number of pitchers must still have been using the "old style" underhand throw, as *The Sporting News* discussed how the new rules would affect both classes of pitchers.

1888. New Rule: HIT BY PITCH. The National League rules committee belatedly gave the batter first base if he was hit by a pitch, whether intentionally or accidentally.[76]

New Rule: BALK RULE. If a pitcher makes a motion in the direction of a base, he must throw to that base.[77]

Appendix C

The Bat

1845. In the beginning, there were no restrictions on bat size and shape.[1]

1863. New rules required the bat to be round, not more than 2.5 inches in diameter, and made of wood.[2]

1868. Bat length was restricted to 42 inches.[3] Hitters had been bringing dangerously long bats to the plate to reach curves trailing away.

1885. In light of the record low batting averages of 1884 (when overhand pitching was legalized), the National League passed two new rules in regard to bats:

1. "The bat handle may be wound with twine a distance of eighteen inches from the end."[4]

2. The rules also permitted a slight flattening of the bat on one side. According to *Sporting Life*,

> It is a fact that players have frequently used such bats for a long time without detection. The flattening should not exceed a quarter to a half inch in depth and for a foot in length from the end of the bat.[5]

It was expected that the flat bat would aid place hitters, but not power hitters. It aided neither and was eventually abandoned.[6]

1895. The maximum allowable bat diameter was increased to 2.75 inches.[7]

Appendix D

The Ball

WEIGHTS AND MEASURES.

1845. The ball weighed only three ounces.

1854. The rules required the ball to weigh from 5.5 to 6.5 ounces and to have a diameter between 2.75 and 3.5 inches.[1]

1872. The rules stipulated a ball weigh from 5 to 5.25 ounces, and to have a circumference of 9 to 9.25 inches.[2]

PRODUCTION VOLUME AND TECHNIQUE. It was estimated that by 1883, five million baseballs were produced annually. In an interview appearing in the January 20, 1883, issue of the *New York Clipper*, manufacturer Al Reach described the laborious process of making one:

> In the centre is a round piece of the best Para gum. Then there is the best stocking-yarn. This is stretched first by machinery to its utmost tension. Then it is wound by hand so tight that it resembles one solid piece of material. The winding is done by single strands at a time. This makes it more compact. A round of white yarn is now put in, and the whole covered with a rubber cement. When this becomes hard it preserves the spherical shape of the ball, and prevents the inside from shifting when the ball is struck. Then comes more yarn, and finally the cover. The covering for all the good balls is made of horsehide. Long experience has shown this to be the best. Cow or goat skin will become wrinkled and wear loose. The sewing on of the covers is done by hand, and the thread used is catgut. No one man makes a ball complete. One person becomes proficient in the first winding, then someone else takes it; another man will fit the cover, but there are very few of the workmen who become proficient in the art of sewing the cover. A dozen men in the course of a day will turn out about twenty-five dozen first-class balls, and as a rule they make good wages. Some manufacturers put carpet-list in the balls; but this can easily be detected when the batting begins, because the ball soon loses its shape. Of course, for the cheap balls, such as the boys begin with, not so much care is exercised in the manufacture. They are made in cups, which revolve by fast-moving machinery. The insides are made up of scraps of leather and rubber, and then carpet-listing is wound around the ball. It takes a man about ten minutes to turn one of these out complete.

EVOLUTION OF THE DESIGN OF THE BASEBALL. The following comprehensive history of the baseball appeared in the *Spalding Guide* of 1890. It was most likely authored by Henry Chadwick. I have added explanatory comments in brackets.

In the early days of the national game, when the public interest in the sport was centered in New York and its vicinity [1840s and 1850s], the balls used by the clubs were made by John Van Horn of New York and Harvey Ross of Brooklyn. The demand was comparatively limited and those two original makers of base balls, could supply it very readily without entrenching upon the time required for their ordinary avocations; inasmuch as at that period the leading clubs did not play over a dozen matches a season. The old balls of the period were of simple manufacture, and no two were made exactly alike; Van Horn used to cut up old rubber shoes into strips from which he wound a ball of about from two to two and a half ounces of rubber, and then covering this with yarn and the yarn with a sheepskin cover, the ball of the period was ready for use. It was years after this that anything was done looking to a regular manufacture of base balls. Here is the rule adopted by the National Association in 1857:

"Rule 1st. The ball must weight not less than six nor more than six and a quarter ounces avoirdupois. It must measure not less than ten, nor more than ten and a quarter inches in diameter. It must be composed of India rubber and yarn, and covered with leather. [Note that there was no stipulation as to the amount of rubber.]"

When the ball clubs began to multiply by the hundred throughout the country [after the Civil War], the necessity for a regularly manufactured ball became manifest; and thus it was that a series of experiments, in producing the very best ball for use, culminated in the manufacture of the perfect regulation balls of the period, which are now made by the million each season. In the working out of the several experiments, covering a period of over fifteen years, the fraternity had to play with a variety of balls, and it was found that it was absolutely necessary in reaching out for a perfect condition of play in the rules, that the regulation ball in use should be one to be relied on for equality in its elasticity, for endurance of the hard hitting process, it was subjected to, and for its keeping its form during the test of a prolonged game. [A ball was generally used for an entire game, retiring from service as the prize of the victors.] These requirements were finally reached in the now perfect Spalding League Ball, which the experience of the past four or five years has shown, cannot be further improved upon.

In testing the old time balls by each season's experience on the field it was found that the cotton yarn covering the rubber center was not sufficiently elastic for the purpose. Then too the sheepskin outer covering proved to be too frail to withstand the usage of actual play. Besides which, the rubber strip composing the center of the ball was too uncertain in its elasticity to suit a perfect ball. Then came the small one ounce ball of vulcanized rubber for the center [about one inch in diameter and, unlike the bundled strips of rubber, molded with uniform density and roundness] and the strong horsehide leather replaced the sheepskin outer covers, and the woolen yarn was substituted for cotton for the covering of the rubber center. These improvements, however, failed to yield the perfect ball, for experience proved the improved ball to be uneven in its elasticity, and apt to get out of form before half the game was over. In the seventies, the double cover improvement was introduced, but this failed to give the satisfaction expected, and further experiments were tried. Lastly the Spalding League ball was improved to its present point of excellence by the introduction of a plastic cement in its composition, which was patented, and the effect of this was such as to do away with the unreliable double cover." [The plastic cement was a coating on the yarn.]

The thin plastic cement now used in the Spalding League ball holds the inner ball in place and prevents the yarn from shifting. Unlike the discarded double cover, the plastic cement is pliable, and when hit by the bat yields with the rubber and yarn, makes it more elastic and pliable and soft to the hands, and at the same time it retains its perfect shape. Another point in its favor is the absolute certainty of one ball acting just like another, which is a very important feature in closely contested games."

The National League and American Association adopted the plastic cement ball in 1886 (or at the time of the first Joint Rules committee meeting) and since that time there has been no complaint from players as to elasticity or evenness of the ball."[3]

1910. The CORK CENTER ball, experimented with during 1909, was adopted universally by the National League for the 1910 season. Overhand pitching and a 1901 rule charging a strike to the hitter for a foul ball had reduced batting averages and game action, so the league leaders called upon the ball designers to enliven the ball and thereby the game. Frank Richter explained:

> Means had to be taken to check, or at least minimize, the effects of pitcher dominance, and this was found in 1909, when President Benjamin F. Shibe, of the Philadelphia American League Club — a member of the A. J. Reach Company, of Philadelphia, which manufactures an overwhelming majority of the base balls used in organized ball — invented the cork center for the ball instead of the rubber center heretofore in universal use. The cork center increased the resilience of the ball without in the least changing its specifications, and thereby appreciably increased the batting without affecting the fielding in the slightest degree.[4]

1920. The LIVELY BALL came into existence during World War I. Because of the German blockade, English yarn was difficult to obtain, so Australian yarn was substituted. It seems the hardy Aussie sheep produce a stronger yarn that can be wound tighter without breaking, thereby producing a firmer, more resilient baseball.

SELECTING THE BALL FOR THE GAME. Prior to 1876, the visitors had the privilege of selecting and supplying the ball, since their opponents had the home-field advantage. With the inauguration of the National League in the centennial year, the ball was standardized. All teams would use a Mahn ball made to league specifications. (Gone was the tactic of selecting a lively or dead ball.) In 1887 and from then on, the home team was required to supply two balls. To prevent tampering, the balls were to be packaged in individual sealed boxes. The umpire would then break the seals in the presence of the two captains.[5]

DETERMINING WHICH TEAM GETS FIRST LICKS AT THE BALL. Between 1878 and 1886, the umpire flipped a coin to determine who batted first. Beginning in 1887, the home team had the privilege of batting first or last. Initially, teams preferred to bat first because the balls would often soften up after a few good licks. Later, when the quality of the balls improved and more were made available per game, batting last became the preferred choice. In 1950, the ritual was eliminated and the home team automatically was in first.[6]

LOST BALLS. The original 1876 National League rules stated: "Should the ball be lost during a game, the umpire shall, at the expiration of five minutes, call for a new ball."[7] This rule requiring a five-minute wait before substituting a new ball was not rescinded until 1886.[8] An unidentified newspaper clipping from the Spalding Scrapbooks informed readers that eliminating the mandatory waiting period should "prevent vexations and sometimes intended delays."

A ball hit out of the park was usually returned by a boy hoping to gain free admission for his heroism. If not, it was considered a theft. If fans did not voluntarily return balls hit into the stands, players or ushers would retrieve them with force. This practice did not end until well into the twentieth century. It was only after several fans had been injured in scuffles with ushers that the owners finally decided to let the fans keep the souvenirs.

Notes

Preface

1. Mark Twain.
2. English historian Thomas Babington Macaulay (1800–1859).
3. An exception to this rule is a series of interviews in the Deacon White file in the Hall of Fame library.

Chapter 1

1. Albert G. Spalding, "Our national Game," *The Cosmopolitan* magazine, October, 1888, p. 448.
2. Concept: Michael S. Kimmel, "Baseball and the Reconstitution of American Masculinity, 1820–1920," *Baseball History 3*, 1990, p. 98.
3. Harold Seymour, *Baseball: The Early Years*, 1960, 1989, p. 24.
4. Warren Goldstein, *A History of Early Baseball*, 1889, 2000, p. 12.
5. *Total Baseball*, 7th ed., 2001; *Baseball Encyclopedia*, Macmillan, 10th ed., 1996, p. 1439.
6. Catherine's maiden name was O'Donnell and she was born in County Mayo, according to research by Bernard Crowley.
7. Jim's mother was illiterate and may not have been able to spell her name. According to research by the author, her name is spelled in various ways in public documents, including Catherine, Catharine, and Katherine.
8. On family owning farm: *Chicago Daily Tribune*, August 26, 1906 (page A2), based on interview with O'Rourke.
9. Jim attended the Waterville Grammar School. (*Graduates of the Yale Law School 1824–1899*, Roger W. Tuttle, Tuttle, Morehouse & Taylor, 1911.)
10. Reference to "iron plate" is from Darryl Brock's *If I Never Get Back*, 1990, p. 39.

Chapter 2

1. From *Keystone Kids* (1943); as cited by Philip Bergen in "Roy Tucker, Not Roy Hobbs:

The Baseball Novels of John R. Tunis," *SABR Review of Books*, 1986, p. 91.
2. M. V. Rourke, interview, December 1938, as part of the Federal Writers' Project, Item 11 of 443, W14803, Irish in Bridgeport; Library of Congress.
3. *Bridgeport Herald*, April 26, 1914.
4. A write-up of O'Rourke appearing in the *Reach Guide* of 1885 (which I suspect was based on an interview of O'Rourke) says that he played for the Unions during 1868 and 1869; a *Harper's Weekly* profile appearing in the May 16 issue of 1885, says that Jim played for the Unions during 1871. However, both are probably wrong. Box scores and game accounts definitely place Jim with the Stratford Osceolas in 1868. He was back with the Unions in 1869, then again on the Osceolas in 1871 and 1872. The only years he could have played with the Unions would have been 1867 or earlier.
5. *Washington Post*, January 28, 1906 (page S4).
6. Jules Tygiel, *Past Time*, Oxford University Press, 2000, p. 13.
7. *Ibid.*
8. Cannemeyer charged a 10-cent "tariff." Robert Smith, *Baseball*, 1947, p. 44–45
9. Jules Tygiel, *Past Time*, Oxford University Press, 2000, p. 13.
10. Tim Murnane mentions that Jim attended high school. *Washington Post*, April 29, 1906 (page S2). It is recorded in *Graduates of the Yale Law School 1824–1899*, Roger W. Tuttle, Tuttle, Morehouse & Taylor, 1911, that "O'Rourke gained early education at Waterville School and at Strong's Military Academy, both at Bridgeport."
11. *Beadle's Dime Base-Ball Player*, 1860, p. 16 (section 37 of the rules) and p. 21.
12. Hy Turkin and S. C. Thompson, *The Official Encyclopedia of Baseball*, 1951, 1st Ed., p. 594. (Turkin and Thompson indicate the first stolen base was purloined by Eddie Cuthbert of

the Philadelphia Keystones in 1865 at the Capitoline Grounds in Brooklyn.)

13. George Will, *Bunts*.

14. As reprinted by Irving Leitner, *Baseball: Diamond in the Rough*, 1972, p. 219.

15. *Sporting Life*, April 29, 1885.

16. There was also a "boys" club in Bridgeport in 1866 named the Osceolas.

17. *Norwalk Gazette*, August 11, 1868.

18. *Ibid.*, September 29 ,1868.

19. *Ibid.*, July 28, 1868.

20. *Bridgeport Standard*, Monday October 5, 1868.

21. *Ibid.*, Friday, August 20, 1869.

22. *Ibid.*, September 16, 1869.

23. On March 15, 1859, at the annual meeting of the National Association of Base Ball Players, a new rule was adopted that prohibited anyone playing in a match who received compensation for doing so.

24. John H. Gruber, "Rules of the Game and Their History," *The Sporting News*, December 16, 1915.

25. Richter, *History and Records of Base Ball*, 1914, p. 38. Richter adds that in 1868 four of the Red Stockings were paid "small salaries."

26. John M. Rosenburg, *The Story of Baseball*, 1962, 1972 ed., p.13–14; David Voigt, *American Baseball*, Vol. 1, 1966, 1983, p. 23; Frank Richter, *History and Records of Base Ball*, 1914, p. 40. Warren Goldstein, in *Playing for Keeps*, devotes an entire chapter to "Revolving and Professionalism," pp. 84–100.

27. Marshall D. Wright, *The National Association of Base Ball Players 1857–1870*, 2000, p. 241, gives George's stats as a .629 batting average and 47 home runs. Rosenburg, p. 14, gives George Wright's 1869 average as .518. Burt Solomon, in *Baseball Timeline*, 1997, qualifies the stats by stating that: "George Wright *presumably* hits 59 home runs and bats above .500." Solomon reminds us that Wright's records rely primarily on scorecards maintained by the Red Stockings, and record-keepers were more concerned with runs scored than the cumulative ratio of hits to times at bat. As a result, the .500+ average is mostly conjecture.

28. Tuohey, *History of the Boston Baseball Club*, 1897.

29. A. G. Spalding, "Base-Ball," *Cosmopolitan* magazine, May 8, 1889, p. 605.

30. Harold Seymour, *Baseball: The Early Years*, 1960, 1989, p. 59.

31. Frank Richter, *History and Records of Base Ball*, 1914, p. 39.

32. Darryl Brock, *If I Never Get Back*, p. 118.

33. Jack Selzer, *Baseball in the Nineteenth Century: An Overview*, 1986, p. 7.

34. "The Osceola Club of Stratford, have organized with a first-class nine." *Derby Transcript*, May 13, 1870.

35. *Norwalk Gazette*, Tuesday, June 23, 1868.

36. *Ibid.*, Tuesday, September 21, 1869.

37. *Ibid.*, Tuesday, July 26, 1870.

38. *Bridgeport Standard*, July 27, 1868; *Derby Transcript*, October 14, 1870.

39. *Derby Transcript*, July 22, 1870. The Osceolas had also imported the Bacon boys for its 1868 roster. (See *Bridgeport Standard*, July 27, 1868.)

40. Harold Seymour, *Baseball: The Early Years*, 1960, 1989, p. 176.

41. "Baseball—the Batteries of 1880," *New York Clipper*, December 4, 1880.

42. The first 1870 game account in which Jim appeared was printed in the *Bridgeport Standard* of August 6. He may have played in an earlier game, but contests were infrequent and box scores scarce, and this is the earliest game in 1870 for which there is evidence of Jim appearing in the lineup.

43. *Bridgeport Standard*, August 6, 1870.

44. Tim Murnane, "Gossip on the Game," *Washington Post*, April 29, 1906, p. S2.

45. John Montgomery Ward, "Notes of a Base-Ballist," *Lippincott's Monthly Magazine* 38, August 1886, p. 212–213. Ward and O'Rourke were teammates in 1879 and 1885–1889.

46. John Montgomery Ward, "Our National Game," *The Cosmopolitan* magazine, October, 1888, pp. 450–451.

47. Tim Murnane, "Gossip on the Game," *Washington Post*, April 29, 1906, p. S2.

48. As an example of how even contemporary accounts can be misleading, the *Bridgeport Standard* of Thursday, July 20, says this game "took place yesterday," so one would assume the game was played on Wednesday, July 19. Not so. The game was played on Tuesday, the 18th. The account was written on Wednesday, assuming it would be printed the same day, but the report did not appear until Thursday. Also, the *Standard* gives the score as 29 to 16, in favor of the TBs, but the record of the score by innings clearly shows that the Osceolas amassed only 15 runs. On the other hand, the *Derby Transcript* of July 22 had the date and score correct, but said the Osceola's opponent was the Alphabet Club of Bridgeport. There was no Alphabet Club. (The TBs were sometimes referred to jokingly as the Alphabet Club because of the club's long name: T.B.F.U.S.B.B.C.). Beware casual research.

49. *Derby Transcript*, July 22, 1870; *Norwalk Gazette*, Tuesday, July 26, 1870. The game was played on neutral territory in Bridgeport.

50. *Derby Transcript*, August 12, 1870; *Bridgeport Standard*, August 8, 1870.

51. *Ibid.*, August 12, 1870.

52. *Ibid.*, August 26, 1870.

53. *Ibid.*, September 2, 1870.

54. *Ibid.*

55. *Bridgeport Standard*, September 7, 1870.
56. *Derby Transcript*, Friday, October 7, 1870. According to Tim Murnane, this was the first game for which Jim was paid. Murnane, who was catching, was also eager to inform us that the Osceolas lost because outfielder O'Rourke dropped a fly ball in the ninth inning (*Washington Post*, April 29, 1906, p. S2).
57. *Derby Transcript*, September 23, 1870.
58. *Ibid.*, Friday, October 7, 1870.
59. *Ibid.*
60. *Ibid.*, Friday, October 14, 1870.
61. Robert Gelzheiser, *The Great Baseball Rebellion*, 1991, p. 16.
62. William Ryczek, *Blackguards and Red Stockings*, 1992, p. 12–14.
63. Her father was James Kehoe. A Kehoe (Michael) first appears in the Bridgeport Directories in 1873, at 310 Pembroke Street. The Kehoes lived at 310 Pembroke, the O'Rourkes at number 258.

My guess is Jim and Annie met in 1870, but it might have been 1871 or 1872. She arrived in the U.S. that year, and they were married in May 1872.

According to the 1900 census, County of Fairfield, Town of Bridgeport, Bridgeport City, Ward 11-L (Sheet #5, Supervisor's District 26, Enumeration District 44) Anna O'Rourke, age 45, was born in June, 1854, in Ireland and immigrated to the United States in 1870. The O'Rourkes were interviewed for the census on June 6, 1900, so Anna's birthday must have been on June 7 or later in the month. On the 1880 Census, page 665 (enumerated on June 12), she appears as "Annie" age 27. This would indicate a birth year of 1852 or 1853. My guess is the 1880 census was correct, for according to an analysis of census data from 1880 to 1910, Anna aged only nine years each decade. Therefore, she was probably 17 or 18 in 1870.
64. David Arcidiacono, *Middletown's Season in the Sun*, 1999, p. 48.
65. *New Haven Palladium*, September 11, 1871.
66. *Ibid.*
67. *Bridgeport Standard*, September 11, 1871.
68. *Ibid.*
69. David Arcidiacono, *Middletown's Season in the Sun*, 1999, p. 48; Palmer, *Athletic Sports*, 1889, p. 579; *Hartford Post*, September 18, 1871.
70. *New Haven Register*, September 18, 1871.
71. *Bridgeport Standard*, September 18, 1871.
72. *New Haven Palladium*, September 18, 1871.
73. *New Haven Register*, September 18, 1871.
74. *New Haven Palladium*, September 18, 1871.
75. David Arcidiacono, *Middletown's Season in the Sun*, 1999, p. 50.
76. *Bridgeport Standard*, September 18, 1871.

77. *Middletown Press*, April 26, 1910.
78. *New York Clipper*, April 20, 1872.
79. Preston Orem, *Baseball (1845–1881) From the Newspaper Accounts*, 1961, p. 145.
80. John Thorn, *Treasure's of the Baseball Hall of Fame*, 1998, p.22; William Ryczek, *Blackguards and Red Stockings*, 1992, p. 35.

Chapter 3

1. F. C. Lane, *Batting*, 1925, 2001, p. 18. Lobert's career was similar to Jim's in that both played in the big leagues for many years, including multiple seasons with the New York Giants; both managed major league teams, and both managed the Bridgeport minor league club.
2. *Ibid.*
3. CNN/SI Web site www.cnn.com.
4. Bernard J. Crowley, "James Henry O'Rourke," *Baseball's First Stars*, SABR, 1996, p. 124.
5. *Middletown Penny Press*, February 8, 1917, as cited by David Arcidiacono, *Middletown's Season in the Sun*, 1999, p. 92.
6. William Ryczek, *Blackguards and Red Stockings*, 1992, p. 152, who cites Daniel Sutherland, *The Expansion of Everyday Life 1860–1876*. New York: Harper and Row, 1989, p. 178. The parlor car was introduced in 1875.
7. Chadwick Scrapbooks, cited by David Arcidiacono, *Middletown's Season in the Sun*, 1999, p. 81.
8. David Arcidiacono, *Middletown's Season in the Sun*, 1999, pp. 133–134.
9. *New Haven Palladium*, Saturday, July 6, 1872.
10. The *New Haven Palladium* carried the following notice on Thursday, August 15, 1872: "The Mansfield base ball club, which has earned an enviable reputation, has disbanded."
11. The Osceolas were no more, having themselves been decimated by the Mansfield piracy.
12. July 3, 1878, telegram from M. Barron; *April 22, 1878 letter from J. F. Antisder; Letter from W. Davis of Cincinnati Omnibus, May 1, 1878*, Harry Wright Correspondence, Spalding collection, New York Public Library.
13. The $82 transportation amount is for a trip from Milwaukee to St. Louis.
14. N. T. Appolonio to Harry Wright, July 17, 1878; Harry Wright Correspondence, Spalding collection, New York Public Library.
15. Harry Wright Correspondence, Spalding collection, New York Public Library
16. *Brooklyn Eagle*, Monday, August 12, 1872.
17. *Ibid.*
18. *Ibid.*, Wednesday, August 14, 1872.
19. David Nemec, *The Great Encyclopedia of 19th Century Major League Baseball*, 1997, p. 39.

20. Harry Wright Correspondence, Spalding collection, New York Public Library (Letter from Jim O'Rourke to HW dated December 24, 1872).

21. *Ibid.*

22. Harry Wright Correspondence, Spalding collection, New York Public Library.

23. *Boston Herald,* April 2, 1873, p. 1.

24. Bridgeport *Standard,* Thursday, April 10, 1873.

Chapter 4

1. "We must make the game worth witnessing and there will be no fault found with the price of admission. A good game is worth 50 cts, a poor one is dear at 25 cts." Letter from Harry Wright to Nick Young, March 28, 1873; Harry Wright Correspondence, Spalding Collection, New York Public Library.

2. Lee Allen, the HOF historian, in the February 10, 1968, issue of *The Sporting News,* p. 28.

3. *Bridgeport Post,* January 9, 1919, and other sources for this oft-repeated tale, with more than one variation.

4. O'Rourke actually received his offer from Wright in December 1872. Murnane did not receive his offer until January 1873. (Letter from Harry Wright to Murnan, January 7, 1873, Letter # 458, Harry Wright Correspondence, Spalding Collection, New York Public Library.)

5. *Washington Post,* April 29, 1906 (page S2).

6. Robert Gelzheiser, *The Great Baseball Rebellion,* 1991, p. 134.

7. Robert Smith, *Baseball,* 1947, p. 41–44.

8. Wife's name: Darryl Brock, *If I Never Get Back,* p. 175. Location of home: "A Compliment to the Champions" *New York Clipper,* November 14, 1874.

9. *Middletown Press,* April 26, 1910, as cited by David Arcidiacono, *Middletown's Season in the Sun,* 1999, p. 108.

10. O'Rourke was the lowest-paid starter on the Boston roster. The highest salary was $1,800. Two substitutes, Beals and Hall, at $500 per year, earned less than Jim. Arthur Bartlett, *Baseball and Mr. Spalding,* 1951, p. 42.

11. Notebook #2, Harry Wright Note and Account Books, Spalding Collection, New York Public Library.

12. Gould file, National Baseball Library, Cooperstown.

13. Letter to Hicks Hayhurst, December 26, 1871, Harry Wright Correspondence, Spalding Collection, New York Public Library.

14. *Boston Herald,* March 17, 1874. Reporting date was March 15.

15. In 1875, the team "limbered up" at the Tremont gymnasium (*Boston Herald,* March 14, 1875). A *Boston Globe* article of April 7, 1878, reported the players conditioned at the YMCA on Eliot Street.

16. March 11, 1878, letter to H. B. Philips, manager of the Hornellsville, New York, club, Harry Wright Correspondence, Spalding Collection, New York Public Library.

17. I am guessing this is from the *Herald.* The quote is from an article, c. August 13, 1874, in a scrapbook in the Spalding Collection at the New York Public Library.

18. Sam Crane in No. 3 of a series of articles about the "Fifty Greatest Ball Players," [first name of publication missing] *Journal,* a New York publication, O'Rourke folder, National Baseball Hall of Fame Library, Cooperstown. The date was probably late in 1911. (The George Wright bio, No. 2 in the Crane series, appeared November 23, 1911.)

19. Robert Smith, *Baseball,* 1947, p. 44.

20. Robert Smith, *Heroes of Baseball,* 1952, p. 75.

21. *New York Clipper,* December 19, 1874.

22. James White a preacher: Byron E. Clarke, "Jim White Was Fast Behind Bat," article from unidentified newspaper, White file, National Baseball Library, Cooperstown.

23. David Voigt, *American Baseball,* 1966, 1983, Vol. 1, p. 88. Voigt cites *DeWitt's Base Ball Guide,* 1876, pp. 18–37. Also typed notes of circa 1930 interview of Deacon White by Dale Lancaster of the *Aurora Beacon Journal,* James White file, National Baseball Library, Cooperstown.)

24. From typed notes of circa 1930 interview of Deacon White by Dale Lancaster of the *Aurora Beacon Journal,* James White file, National Baseball Library, Cooperstown.)

25. Arthur Bartlett, *Baseball and Mr. Spalding,* 1951, p. 45.

26. *New York Clipper,* July 25, 1874.

27. Typed notes of circa 1930 interview of Deacon White by Dale Lancaster of the *Aurora Beacon Journal,* James White file, National Baseball Library, Cooperstown.

28. *Bill James Historical Baseball Abstract,* 1988, 2001, p. 8; David Voigt, *American Baseball,* Vol. 1, 1966, 1983, p. 88; *Beadle's Dime Base-Ball Player,* 1860, p. 23.

29. *St. Louis Post Dispatch,* June 4, 1874.

30. "The Baseball Tourists," *New York Clipper,* July 25, 1874

31. *Bridgeport Herald,* September 28,1913; *London Standard,* August 4, 1874.

32. *Bridgeport Herald,* April 26, 1914.

33. *Atlanta Constitution,* February 26, 1894.

34. Quip about drinking is by Bob Carroll and appeared in David Nemec's *The Great Encyclopedia of 19th Century Major League Baseball,* 1997, p. 41.

35. "The Baseball Tourists," *New York Clipper*, July 25, 1874.

36. Dan Gutman, *It Ain't Cheatin' If You Don't Get Caught*," 1990, p. 11.

37. *Ibid.*

Chapter 5

1. "The American Base Ball Players and Cricketers," Dublin *Mail*, August 25, 1874.

2. Boston *Herald*, c. August 12, 1874.

3. William Ryczek, *Blackguards and Red Stockings*, 1992, p. 162, who cites the New York *Clipper*, August 29, 1874.

4. Peter Levine, *A. G. Spalding and the Rise of Baseball*, 1985, p. 18. Originally it was thought the baseball games would be regular championship contests, "but wiser heads later prevailed. They would be exhibitions." (William Ryczek, *Blackguards and Red Stockings*, 1992, p. 140.)

5. Harry Wright Correspondence, Spalding Collection, New York Public Library, letter # 392 to Ferguson March 13, 1874.

6. *Players' National League Guide*, 1890, p. 27. Boston beat the Athletics, 12 to 7 (Chadwick diaries, 1874, Spalding Collection, New York Public Library.)

7. This wonderful story of American brashness meeting English reserve is told by Al Spalding in his autobiography *America's National Game*, 1911, 1992, p. 181.

8. Boston *Herald*, September 3, 1874.

9. Mark Alvarez, "William Henry Wright," First Stars, SABR, 1996, p. 177–178.

10. Boston *Herald*, August 30, 1874.

11. Quoted by H. J. Kempton ("Kemp") in his August 17, 1874 dispatch to the Boston *Herald* (published August 30)

12. Bridgeport *Standard*, August 15, 1874. The New York *Times* of August 16, 1874, says it was 122 yards.

13. Kempton, Boston *Herald*, August 30, 1874 [written August 17].

14. New York *Times*, May 15, 1900, page 8.

15. Tuohey, *The History of the Boston Base Ball Club*, 1897, p. 36.

16. The *Abbotsford* sank off the coast of Ireland the following year. (New York *Tribune*, July 24, 1875, p. 1.)

17. Soden's age: Marty Appel; *Slide, Kelly, Slide*, 1999, p. 110. Soden remained a principal partner in the club until 1906.

18. Francis Richter, *History and Records of Base Ball*, 1914, p. 109; Arthur Bartlett, *Baseball and Mr. Spalding*, 1951, p. 70–71.

19. From a series of letters between Harry Wright and O'Rourke: Harry Wright Correspondence — Volume 1, 1874–75, Spalding Collection, New York Public Library. The Wright letters are dated December 8 and 31, 1874; January 29, February 8, and March 4, 1875. O'Rourke's letters no longer exist, but the diplomatic and meticulous Wright recounts Jim's arguments in his replies.

20. *Ibid.*

21. *Ibid.*

Chapter 6

1. As cited by Lawrence S. Ritter, *The Glory of Their Times*, 1966, p. 20.

2. Burt Solomon, *Baseball Timeline*, 1997; Mike Egner, "The Evolution of the Baseball Glove," *The Vintage & Classic Baseball Collector* #16, July-August, 1998, p. 40.

3. *New York Clipper*, January 2, 1875.

4. Alvarez, Mark. "William Henry Wright." *First Stars*, Society for American Baseball Research, 1996, p. 178; John H. Gruber, "Rules of the Game and Their History," *The Sporting News*, December 23, 1915.

5. The *Globe* article appeared in 1887 per David McDonald, "Some Milestones in the Evolution of the Tools of Ignorance," *The National Pastime, no. 16*, SABR, 1996, p. 22.

6. *Sporting Life*, August 27, 1883. Holbert enjoyed a 12-year major league career as a catcher, beginning in 1876 with Louisville.

7. Albert G. Spalding, *America's National Game*, 1911, 1992, p. 479.

8. Burt Solomon, *Baseball Timeline*, 1977; Solomon gives the date as April 11. Bob Richardson, "James Alexander Tyng," *Nineteenth Century Stars*, SABR, 1989, p. 128.

9. Albert G. Spalding, *America's National Game*, 1911, 1992, p. 479.

10. Harry Wright Correspondence, Spalding Collection, New York Public Library.

11. *Boston Globe*, Friday, April 13, 1877.

12. *Ibid.*, Monday, April 16, 1877.

13. *New York Sun*, July 30, 1896, reprinted by Alfred H. Spink, *The National Game*, 1910, 1911, 2000, pp. 384–385.

14. The *New York World* article was reprinted in Al Spalding's *America's National Game*, 1911, 1992, pp. 477–78.

15. *New York Sun*, July 7, 1896; reprinted by Alfred H. Spink, *The National Game*, 1910, 1911, 2000, pp. 384–385.

16. Albert G. Spalding, *America's National Game*, 1911, 1992, pp. 476–77.

17. From typed notes of circa 1930 interview of Deacon White by Dale Lancaster of the *Aurora Beacon Journal*, James White file, National Baseball Library, Cooperstown.)

18. Richard E. Noble, "Saving Face: The Genesis of the Catcher's Mask," Baseball History, Fall 1987, pp. 45–49.

19. *Sporting Life*, August 20, 1883.

20. *Boston Herald*, April 9, 1875.

21. *Boston Globe*, April 7, 1878.

22. *New York Clipper*, September 20, 1879.

23. *Ibid.*, June 19, 1880.

24. *Ibid.*

25. Preston Orem, *Baseball (1845–1881) From the Newspaper Accounts*, 1961, p. 328.

26. *New York Clipper*, April 25, 1881. The store was at 408 Fulton St.

27. *Boston Herald*, March 21, 1875.

28. *Ibid.*, April 4, 1875.

29. *Boston Times*, May 15, 1875.

30. Tuohey, *History of the Boston Baseball Club*, 1897.

31. S. W. C., *Bridgeport Evening Post* April 1, 1902).

32. Troy Soos, *Before the Curse*, 1997. p. 33.

33. *Total Baseball*, Seventh Edition, 2001.

Chapter 7

1. Harold Seymour, *Baseball: The Early Years*, 1960, 1989, p. 172.

2. *New York Clipper*, November 7, 1874.

3. William Ryczek, *Blackguards and Red Stockings*, 1992, p. 145.

4. Donald Honig, *The National League*, 1983, 1987, p. 1.

5. David Voigt, *American Baseball*, Vol. 1, 1966, 1983, p. 41.

6. Albert G. Spalding, *America's National Game*, 1911, 1992, p. 194.

7. John Montgomery Ward, "Notes of A Base-Ballist," *Lippincott's Monthly Magazine*, August 1866, p. 215–216.

8. David Voigt, *American Baseball*, Vol. 1, 1966, 1983, p. 41.

9. William Ryczek, *Blackguards and Red Stockings*, 1992, p. 217, citing the *New Haven Register*, July 30, 1875.

10. Arthur Bartlett, *Baseball and Mr. Spalding*, 1951, p. 102.

11. Peter Levine, *A. G. Spalding and the Rise of Baseball*, 1985, p. 73; Arthur Bartlett, *Baseball and Mr. Spalding*, 1951, p. 99, 101; James D. Hardy, Jr., *The New York Giants Base Ball Club*, 1996, p. 104.

12. The Boston nine has been known over the years by various pseudonyms:

The Bostons (from 1871),
Boston Nationals (from 1876),
Red Stockings (1871 through 1875),
Reds (from 1871),
Red Caps (1876 to 1882),
Beaneaters (1883–1906),
Doves (1907–1910),
Rustlers (1911),
Braves (1912 to 1935),
Bees (1936 to 1940), and finally
Braves (1941 to date, though they left Boston

in 1953, first for Milwaukee, and then Atlanta in 1966).

Then who are the Red Sox? When the American League was organized at the turn of the century, the Boston franchise took on the name of the original Hub nine for brand recognition.

13. As reprinted in the *Bridgeport Daily Standard* of Friday, April 21, 1876.

14. *Ibid.*

15. *Ibid.*

16. *Bridgeport Herald*, April 22, 1876.

17. The *Brooklyn Argus*, July 10, 1876, said the salary was between $1,500 and $1,800.

18. Anecdote corroborated by the *New York Clipper*, July 5, 1879.

19. Most sources place the ballpark at 25th and Jefferson, but Joel Spivak ("Where was the Jefferson Street Grounds?" *The National Pastime*, SABR, 1992, p. 5) suspects it was at 52nd Street, which would place it just two blocks from the Centennial Exposition.

20. Burt Solomon, *Baseball Timeline*, April 22, 1876.

21. This was only the latest indignity. The East-West rivalry dated back to 1870 when the Chicagos organized the second professional ball club with the express purpose of crushing the Red Stockings and asserting their superiority in the national sport. According to the editor of *Sporting Life*, the 1870 White Stockings "defeated the Red Stockings twice in succession, which killed the Cincinnati Club, as that club was disbanded at the end of the season of 1870, the Wright brothers, Gould, and McVey going to the Boston Club." (Frank Richter, *History and Records of Base Ball*, 1914, p. 39.)

22. Arthur Bartlett, *Baseball and Mr. Spalding*, 1951, p. 96.

23. Sam Crane in No. 3 of a series of articles about the "Fifty Greatest Ball Players," [first name of publication missing] *Journal*, NY publication, O'Rourke folder, National Baseball Hall of Library, Cooperstown. The date was probably late in 1911. (The George Wright bio, No. 2 in the Crane series, appeared November 23, 1911.)

24. Arthur Bartlett, *Baseball and Mr. Spalding*, 1951, p. 96–97. The National League played a 70-game schedule in its inaugural year: each of the eight teams were to play the other teams 10 times. (Donald Honig, *The National League*, 1983, 1987, p. 2.)

25. *Total Baseball*, Seventh Edition, 2001.

26. Robert F. Burk, *Never Just a Game*, 1994, p. 60; Donald Dewey and Nicholas Acocella, *The Biographical History of Baseball*, 1995, p. 346; and David Voigt, *American Baseball*, Vol. 1, 1966, 1983, p. 70.

27. Jacob Morse, *Sphere and Ash*, 1888, p. 42. The 50-cent-per day charge to players to cover board on the road was increased to 59 cents in

1881, then eventually repealed in 1887. (Howard Rosenberg, *Cap Anson 1*, 2003, p. 149.)

28. Arthur Bartlett, *Baseball and Mr. Spalding*, 1951, p. 110–111.

29. *Ibid.*, p. 102.

30. *Boston Globe*, May 12, 1877.

31. *Ibid.*, May 17, 1877.

32. *Ibid.*

33. *New York Clipper*, January 10, 1880.

34. Albert G. Spalding, *America's National Game*, 1911, pp. 224–225.

35. James D. Hardy, Jr., *The New York Giants Base Ball Club*, 1996, p. 104; David Voigt, *American Baseball, Vol. 1*, 1983, p. 69.

36. *New York Clipper*, January 20, 1883.

37. Arthur Bartlett, *Baseball and Mr. Spalding*, 1951, p. 103.

38. Xroads.virginia.edu/~HYPER/INCORP/baseball/spalding, 2002.

39. It would be 37 years before the $30 uniform assessment was repealed, at the end of the 1913 season. (Francis Richter, *History and Records of Base Ball*, 1914, p. 276.)

40. *New York Times*, August 9, 1877, page 8.

41. *Washington Post*, July 13, 1890.

42. For example, see *Boston Globe*, May 12, 1877.

43. David Voigt, *American Baseball*, Vol. 1, 1983, p. 76.

44. David Voigt, *Baseball Research Journal*, SABR, 1983, p. 35.

45. Joseph Overfield, "James 'Deacon' White," *Baseball Research Journal 4*, 1975, pp. 1–11.

46. Actually, Soden was only one member of a triumvirate that owned and managed the Boston Red Caps, but he was the largest and most prominent stockholder, and the other owners usually deferred to his judgment. Troy Soos, *Before The Curse (The Glory Days of New England Baseball: 1858–1918)*, 1997, p. 69.

47. *Ibid.*, p. 70.

48. *Boston Globe*, Sunday, February 9, 1878.

49. Preston Orem, *Baseball 1845–1881*, 1961, p. 295. This was John's first full-time professional team. (*Bridgeport Post*, June 24, 1911.)

50. Ted Vincent, *Mudville's Revenge*, 1981, p. 133.

51. The TBs played National Association clubs in Brooklyn, Washington, Hartford, New Haven, and Boston.

52. Preston Orem, "The National League Season of 1879 from the Newspaper Accounts," *Vintage & Classic Baseball Collector* no. 27, May-June, 2001, p. 48.

53. *New York Clipper*, April 12, 1879, page 19.

54. *Ibid.*, July 12, 1879. (Rankings based on stats through July 1.)

55. At Cincinnati on July 11, *New York Clipper*, July 19, 1879; at Cincinnati on July 14, *New York Clipper*, July 26, 1879; at Troy on July 31,

New York Clipper, August 9, 1879. (Which fence was not mentioned in regard to the July 26 homer.)

56. For example, four singles and a double in 10 times at bat would equal a slugging average of .500. A double counts as two hits, a triple three, and a home run four.

57. *New York Clipper*, September 27, 1879.

58. *Ibid.*, October 18, 1879.

Chapter 8

1. *Sporting Life*, January 4, 1884.

2. David Stevens, *Baseball's Radical for All Seasons*, 1998, p. 11.

3. *New York Clipper*, March 20, 1880. The *Clipper* editor indicated that this account first appeared in a "Western exchange."

4. *Ibid.*, July 5, 1879.

5. *Ibid.*, October 25, 1879.

6. *Ibid.*, October 11, 1879.

7. *Ibid.*, October 4, 1879.

8. *Ibid.*, October 18, 1879.

9. *Ibid.*, October 11, 1879.

10. *Ibid.*

11. Lee Lowenfish, *The Imperfect Diamond*, 1980, rev. 1991, p. 41.

12. Noel Hynd, *The Giants of the Polo Grounds*, 1988, p. 17.

13. From SABR files.

14. Harry Wright Correspondence, Spalding Collection, New York Public Library.

15. Soden opinion recorded by part-owner N. T. Appolonio in a letter to Harry Wright dated July 17, 1878, Harry Wright Correspondence, Spalding Collection, New York Public Library.

16. Harry Wright Correspondence, Spalding Collection, New York Public Library.

17. Mark Alvarez, *The Old Ball Game*, 1990, p. 104.

18. *New York Clipper*, December 27, 1879.

19. Location of Boston clubhouse was at 786 Washington Street, above George Wright's store (Preston Orem, "The National League Season of 1878 from the Newspaper Accounts," Vintage & Classic Baseball Collector no. 26, March 2001, p. 55.

20. *Boston Herald*, March 21, 1880, p. 8.

21. *New York Clipper*, October 11, 1879.

22. The *New York Clipper* published details on October 18 and 25, 1879.

23. David Voigt, *American Baseball*, Vol. 1, 1983, p. 57, 77.

24. Boston netted $150 after paying down $2,700 in debt and investing $1,400 into improvements to the grandstand (*New York Clipper*, December 31, 1881). Gate receipts were $19,686, season tickets sales equaled $620, donations from directors were $758, and player

fines $177, making the total receipts $21,647. Expenses included $11,673 for salaries and $3,569 for traveling expenses.

25. "The Boston Club is supposed to have made at least $30,000 profit last year." (*Sporting Life*, January 9, 1884). But according to historian Harold Seymour, the figure was really $48,000. (Harold Seymour, *Baseball: The Early Years*, 1960, 1989, p. 119.) Much secrecy surrounded the true profit figures of baseball clubs, lest more competitors be tempted to enter the industry.

26. David Stevens, *Baseball's Radical for All Seasons*, 1998, p. 16.

27. *Boston Herald*, April 4, 1880.

28. *New York Clipper*, October 25, 1879. The British cricketers were called Daft's noted professionals.

29. *Ibid.*, January 3, 1880.

30. *Ibid.*, November 15, 1879.

31. *Ibid.*, October 9, 1880. Johnny Ward also opened a "baseball emporium" in Providence, at 75 Weybosset Street, in the spring of 1881. (*Ibid.*, March 26, April 25, 1881.)

32. *Ibid.*, December 27, 1879.

33. *Ibid.*, February 14, 1880.

34. *Ibid.*, February 28, 1880.

35. *Ibid.*, April 24, 1880.

36. *Ibid.*

37. *Ibid.*, December 31, 1881.

38. Troy Soos, *Before the Curse*, 1997, p. 69.

Chapter 9

1. *Boston Herald*, "Baseball Jottings," January 18, 1880, p. 2. The contracts indicated that Jim and John would be "released from reservation."

2. *New York Clipper*, September 20, 1879.

3. *Ibid.*, November 27, 1880.

4. *Ibid.*, May 8, 1880.

5. *Ibid.*

6. *New York Times*, May 25, 1880 (page 1).

7. *Washington Post*, May 30, 1880 (page 3).

8. *New York Clipper*, June 26, 1880.

9. *Bridgeport Standard*, July 31, 1880.

10. *New York Clipper*, September 18, 1880.

11. *Ibid.*, September 25, 1880.

12. *Boston Herald*, Sunday, March 28, 1880; Preston Orem, "The National League Season of 1880 From the Newspaper Accounts," *The Vintage & Classic Baseball Collector*, no. 28, July, 2001.

13. *New York Clipper*, October 9, 1880.

14. Preston Orem, "The National League Season of 1880 From the Newspaper Accounts," *The Vintage & Classic Baseball Collector* magazine no. 28, July 2001, pp. 46–47.

15. *Cincinnati Enquirer*, October 5, 1880, as reported by the *Boston Globe*, October 10, 1880;

Preston D. Orem, *Baseball (1845–1881) From the Newspaper Accounts*, 1961, p. 337: National League "Secretary Young reported the release by Boston of the two O'Rourkes, Powers, Sutton, and John H. Richardson."

16. *New York Clipper*, October 23, 1880.

17. *Bridgeport Standard*, October 6, 1880.

18. *Boston Globe*, October 17, 1880.

19. *Bridgeport Post*, June 24, 1911.

20. *New York Clipper*, August 27, 1881.

21. *Ibid.*, October 29, 1881; January 14, 1882; February 18, 1882.

22. *Ibid.*, March 25, 1882.

23. *Ibid.*, April 15, 1882.

24. *Ibid.*, April 29, 1882.

25. *Ibid.*, April 22, 1882.

26. *Ibid.*, May 6, 1882.

27. *Ibid.*, December 2, 1882.

28. *Ibid.*, October 23, 1880.

Chapter 10

1. *New York Clipper*, November 19, 1881.

2. *Chicago Post and Mail*, June 12, 1875, cited by Howard Rosenberg, *Cap Anson 1*, 2003, p. 21.

3. *New York Clipper*, January 1, 1881.

4. *Ibid.*, October 16, 1880.

5. *Ibid.*

6. *Ibid.*, January 1, 1881.

7. *Ibid.*, October 23, 1880.

8. *Ibid.*, April 23, 1881.

9. Cited by Howard Rosenberg, *Cap Anson 1*, 2003, p. 24.

10. *Buffalo Commercial Advertiser*, August 17, 1881, cited by Howard Rosenberg, *Cap Anson 1*, 2003, p. 228.

11. *New York Clipper*, June 18, 1881.

12. Preston D. Orem, *Baseball (1845–1881) From the Newspaper Accounts*, 1961, p. 348–351; *New York Clipper*, August 27, 1881.

13. Sam Crane in No. 3 of a series of articles about the "Fifty Greatest Ball Players," [first name of publication missing] *Journal*, NY publication, O'Rourke folder, National Baseball Hall of Library, Cooperstown. The date was probably late in 1911. (The George Wright bio, No. 2 in the Crane series, appeared November 23, 1911.)

14. *Ibid*

15. *New York Clipper*, April 2, 1881.

16. *Ibid.*, December 10, 1881.

17. As cited by Howard Rosenberg, *Cap Anson 1*, 2003, p. 166–167.

18. Howard Rosenberg, *Cap Anson 1*, 2003, p. 155–172.

19. *New York Clipper*, August 28, 1880; January 1, 1881.

20. *Ibid.*

21. *Ibid.*, August 21, 1880

22. "New York City Club," *Ibid.*, April 30, 1881.

23. *Washington Post*, August 6, 1916.

24. Harvey Frommer, *Primitive Baseball*, 1988, p. 70.

25. Robert Smith, *Baseball*, 1947, p. 115.

26. William H. Dunbar, "Baseball Salaries Thirty Years Ago," *Baseball Magazine*, July 1918, No. 3, p. 291–292.

27. *New York Clipper*, September 16, 1882.

28. *Ibid.*, July 17, 1880.

29. Frank Vaccaro, "One-Arm Daily," *The National Pastime*, no. 19, SABR, 1999, p. 16.

30. *Sporting Life*, June 17, 1883, p. 4.

31. *New York Times*, June 24 and September 23, 1881.

32. *New York Clipper*, January 14, 1882.

33. Irving A. Leitner, *Baseball: Diamond in the Rough*, 1972, p. 156.

34. Hy Turkin and S. C. Thompson, *The Official Encyclopedia of Baseball*, 1st Ed., 1951, p. 583.

35. *Ibid.*

36. Frank Vaccaro, "One-Arm Daily," *National Pastime*, no. 19, SABR, 1999.

37. "Orator O'Rourke–Effective Hitter," unidentified newspaper, January 12, 1919, in the O'Rourke file, National Baseball Hall of Fame Library. (Not *New York Times*, *Tribune*, *Herald*, *World*, *Bridgeport Post*, *Bridgeport Herald*, or *Sporting News*.)

38. Joseph M. Overfield, *100 Season of Buffalo Baseball*, 1985, p. 22.

39. John H. Gruber, "Rules of the Game and Their History," *The Sporting News*, December 23, 1915. These rules took effect in 1879.

40. Quoted in the *New York Clipper*, May 8, 1880.

41. *Ibid.*, September 4, 1880.

42. *Ibid.*, April 29, 1882. The *Clipper* said the ball had to be released below the line of the hip, but the line had been moved up to the waist by 1878. See 1878 *Spalding Guide*.

43. *Ibid.*, February 3, 1883.

44. Arthur Bartlett, *Baseball and Mr. Spalding*, 1951, p. 140.

45. *New York Clipper*, December 18, 1880.

46. *Bridgeport Herald*, September 23, 1913.

47. *New York Clipper*, January 20, 1883.

48. *Ibid.*, April 2, 1881.

49. Howard Rosenberg, *Cap Anson 1*, 2003, p. 36.

50. *Reach Guide*, 1882, p. 80.

51. Geoffrey C. Ward and Ken Burns, *Baseball*, 1994, p.28.

52. *New York Clipper*, April 29, 1882.

53. *Ibid.*, February 11, 1882.

54. This episode is surmised. An account of an actual incidence of mistaken identity on the basepaths, in which the victims were Providence pitcher Hoss Radbourn and first base-man Joe Start, was recalled by Wm. D. Perrin, in number 9 in a series of articles: "Line Drives Then and Now" that appeared in June and July of 1928 in the *Providence Journal* and were reprinted in the SABR publication *Days of Greatness — Providence Baseball 1875–1885*, 1984, p.15.

55. *New York Clipper*, June 24, 1882.

56. Howard Rosenberg, *Cap Anson 1*, 2003, p. 38. The *Cleveland Herald* issue cited was November 28, 1883.

57. This is the uniform worn for the first 1884 game at home, as described by Joseph Overfield, "When Baseball Came to Richmond Avenue," *Niagara Frontier* 2, no. 2 (Summer 1955). I am therefore assuming that, since this was the home uniform in 1881, it was also the home uniform for the balance of 1882 and 1883.

58. *Cleveland Herald*, May 25, 1882.

59. Francis Richter, *History and Records of Base Ball*, 1914, p. 276.

60. *New York Clipper*, September 18, 1880.

61. *Ibid.*, September 30, 1882.

62. Harry Wright Correspondence, Spalding Collection, New York Public Library.

63. *New York Clipper*, September 30, 1882.

64. David Stevens, *Baseball's Radical for All Seasons*, 1998, p. 41.

65. David Voigt, *American Baseball Vol. 1*, 1966, 1983, p. 106.

66. Harry Wright Correspondence, Spalding Collection, New York Public Library.

67. *New York Clipper*, April 15 and 22, 1882.

68. *Ibid.*, May 6, 1882.

69. *Ibid.*, September 30, 1882.

70. *Ibid.*, March 17, 1883; Francis Richter, *History and Records of Base Ball*, 1914, p. 208–209.

71. *Boston Globe*, October 12, 1883, p. 2. According to Mills, clubs were not even "obliged to regularly sign players put on the list, as their reservation is equivalent to having a contract with them."

72. *New York Clipper*, March 17, 1883.

73. Tom Ruane, "Major League Career Hitting Records," *Baseball Research Journal* no. 27, SABR, 1998, p. 28; *New York Times*, September 12, 1985.

74. As reprinted in *Sporting Life*, July 15, 1883.

75. Reprinted May 14, 1884, by *Sporting Life*, whose editor said it fit "Sir James" like the paper fits the wall

76. *Sporting Life*, July 1, 1883.

Chapter 11

1. Reported by Cincinnati president Kramer on November 7 at the *New York Clipper* office, and published November 11, 1882.

2. *New York Clipper*, November 18, 1881.
3. John J. O'Malley, "John Lynch," *Baseball's First Stars*, SABR, 1996, p. 98.
4. *Sporting Life*, April 29, 1883.
5. *New York Times*, April 30, 1883.
6. *New York Clipper*, January 14, 1882.
7. *Sporting Life*, May 6, 1883, p. 3.
8. *Ibid.*, July 15, 1883.
9. *Ibid.*, August 27, 1883.
10. *Ibid.*, September 24, 1883
11. *Bridgeport Post*, June 24, 1911.

Chapter 12

1. *Sporting Life*, May 20, 1883.
2. At the corner of Richmond Avenue and Summer Street. Joseph M. Overfield, *100 Seasons of Buffalo Baseball*, 1985, p. 24.
3. *Sporting Life*, October 15, 1883, p. 3; Joseph Overfield, "When Baseball Came to Richmond Avenue," *Niagara Frontier* 2, no. 2 (Summer 1955).
4. Harold Seymour, *Baseball: The Early Years*, 1960, 1989, p. 193.
5. Joseph Overfield, "When Baseball Came to Richmond Avenue," *Niagara Frontier* 2, no. 2 (Summer 1955).
6. Joseph Overfield, "When Baseball Came to Richmond Avenue," *Niagara Frontier* 2, no. 2 (Summer 1955). The lease was for five years. The rent during the final year of the agreement was $1,800.
7. On June 16, 1884: Joseph G. Donner, "Hitting for the Cycle," *Baseball Research Journal* #10, 1981.
8. *Ibid.*, July 8, 1883, p. 4.
9. *Ibid.*, September 10, 1883.
10. *Sporting Life*, September 17, 1883.
11. *Ibid.*
12. In February of 1887 he was living at 20 Winchester Street in Boston.
13. *Sporting Life*, September 17, 1883.
14. *Ibid.*, October 29, 1883
15. *Ibid.*, January 4, 1884.
16. *Ibid.*, July 2, 1884, p. 6.
17. *New York Clipper*, October 15, 1881.
18. February, 1887, clipping in the Foley file, National Baseball Library, Cooperstown.
19. *Sporting Life*, May 27, 1883, p. 4.
20. *Ibid.*, July 15, 1883.
21. *Ibid.*, October 15, 1883, p. 3.
22. As reprinted in *Sporting Life*, February 20, 1884.
23. *Sporting Life*, April 2, 1884, p. 3.
24. Harold Seymour, *Baseball: The Early Years*, 1960, 1989, p. 119, 193.
25. *Sporting Life*, July 2, 1884, p. 6.
26. O'Rourke interview, *Bridgeport Herald*, September 23, 1913.
27. Mark Alvarez, *The Old Ball Game*, 1990, p. 141.

28. Lee Allen, *The Hot Stove League*, 1955, p. 97; also Burt Solomon, *Baseball Timeline*, 1997, p. 40.
29. Reprinted in *Sporting Life*, May 28, 1884, p. 6.
30. *Sporting Life*, June 4, 1884, p. 6.
31. *Bridgeport Morning News*, April 20, 1886. The charmed bat was used by captain Stewart, Amos Alonzo Stagg and Brenner
32. *Spalding Guide,*1885, p. 20.
33. Marty Apple, *Slide, Kelly, Slide*, 1990, p. 70; Norman Macht, "Michael Joseph Kelly," *First Stars*, SABR, 1996, p. 90.
34. *Total Baseball*, Seventh Edition, 2001, pp 528–531; Frank Williams notes.
35. *Sporting Life*, April 2, 1884, p. 3.
36. *Ibid.*, May 7, 1884, p. 5; also New York *Clipper*, May 11, 1884: "If Manager Hollingshead [of Washington] can succeed in securing John O'Rourke for center field, his nine will be complete."
37. *Washington Post*, May 25, 1884 (page 2).
38. *Sporting Life*, July 2, 1884, p. 6.
39. *Bridgeport Morning News*, September 30, 1885.

Chapter 13

1. Rob Edelman, "On the Silver Screen," *The National Pastime*, no. 17, 1997, p. 107.
2. There is some debate over the exact amount of O'Rourke's 1885 record salary. The 1890 *Spalding Guide* gives it as $4,500.
However, the 1919 *Spalding Guide* says the salary was $6,000. Robert Smith (*Heroes of Baseball*, 1952, p. 77) also says O'Rourke received a $6,000 salary from the Giants. *Sporting News*, in 1884, announced, "Jim O'Rourke has finally made up his mind and signed with the New York League Club" at a salary of $6,000. (*Sporting News*, November 12, 1884, p. 5.)
But then, two months later, *Sporting Life* reported the salary as only $4,200. (*Sporting Life*, January 14, 1885, p. 5). The $4,200 would still have been the record to that date, and seems more believable, in light of the fact that as reported in the same notice, Ward and Ewing were each to earn only $3,000 for 1885. The $6,000 figure may have included a one-time signing bonus or payment of O'Rourke's first-year tuition to Yale Law School or both. *Sporting Life* noted the conflicting reports over the amount:
There is still considerable speculation as to O'Rourke's salary. Those who know say that it is exactly $4200, which is not likely to be lessened by fines, as O'Rourke never needs disciplining in any way. (*Sporting Life*, "Notes and Comments," June 24, 1885.)

If you prefer a figure somewhere in the middle, the *New Haven Union* reported in December 1885, after interviewing O'Rourke, that his salary was $5,000.

Whatever the exact amount ($4,200, $4,500, $5,000 or $6,000), it was many times the average annual wage of a factory worker of the 1880s, and more than Jim's professors earned at Yale. (Daniel M. Pearson, *Baseball in 1889*, p. 67.) In the 1880s, an industrial worker earned approximately $650. (John Rossi, *The National Game*, 2000, p. 33.)

Two decades later, in 1906, the highest baseball salary was paid to "Mr. Shortstop," Bobby Wallace, who earned $6,000. (Donald Honig, *The National League*, 1983, 1987, p. 3.)

3. *Sporting Life,* October 22, 1884, p. 5; "More Reserves," *Ibid.*, October 8, 1883.

4. *Spalding Guide*, 1890, p. 21, Note 2.

5. *Sporting Life*, November 7, 1883.

6. *Ibid.*, November 28, 1883.

7. As to moving closer to home: *Ibid.*, October 29, 1884, p. 5.

8. *Ibid.*, May 27, 1885, p 7.

9. *New York Clipper*, November 15, 1883.

10. Frank Richter, *History and Records of Base Ball*, 1914, p. 57.

11. *Sporting Life*, July 2, 1884.

12. *Ibid.*, July 16, 1884, p. 6, column 5.

13. *Ibid.*, April 22, 1885, p. 6, column 4.

14. *New York Clipper*, June 12, 1880.

15. *Sporting Life*, October 29, 1884, p. 3.

16. *Ibid.*, December 17, 1884, p. 5.

17. *Ibid.*, May 20, 1885, p 7.

18. David Stevens, *Baseball's Radical for All Seasons*, p. 29.

19. *New York Times*, April 2, 1885 (page 2).

20. *Ibid.*, April 10, 1885 (page 2).

21. *Ibid.*, June 1, 1885 (page 2).

22. *Ibid.*

23. *Ibid.*, July 8, 1888 (page 2). Information based on "statistics furnished by the *Sporting Times*."

24. *Ibid.*, June 1, 1885 (page 2).

25. *Ibid.*, July 23, 1885 (page 2).

26. "Veteran Player, Magnate, and Oldest Man in Baseball, O'Rourke," *Cincinnati* (?) *Enquirer*, March 7(?), 1916; O'Rourke File, National Baseball Hall of Fame Library.

27. *Sporting Life*, May 6, 1885.

28. *Washington Post*, April 28, 1885 (page 4).

29. *Ibid.*

30. *New York Clipper*, July 28, 1882.

31. *Sporting Life*, November 26, 1884, p. 3.

32. *Ibid.*, July 8, 1885, "Notes and Comments."

33. Ron McCulloch, *From Cartwright to Shoeless Joe*, Warwick Publishing, 1998, p. 53, 181.

34. David Montgomery, *The Fall of the House*

of Labor, 1989, p. 27; as cited by Gelzheiser, p. 119.

35. *Boston Herald*, October 18, 1885; David Stevens, *Baseball's Radical for All Seasons*, 1998, p. 41.

36. John Montgomery Ward, *Players' National League Guide*, 1890, pp. 3, 7.

37. David Stevens, *Baseball's Radical for All Seasons*, 1998, p. 42–43.

38. *New York Clipper*, February 10, 1883.

39. *Bridgeport Morning News*, November 19, 1885.

40. As reprinted in the *Bridgeport Daily Standard* of Friday, April 21, 1876.

41. *New Haven Union* interview with O'Rourke, reprinted in the *Bridgeport Herald*, December 26, 1885.

Chapter 14

1. *New Haven Register*, October 1, 1885, page 1.

2. *Yale Daily News*, November 17, 1885.

3. *Ibid.*, May 5, 1886.

4. *Ibid.*, December 17, 1885.

5. *Boston Herald*, October 18, 1885.

6. As reprinted in the *Bridgeport Herald*, December 26, 1885.

7. *Yale Daily News*, June 14, June 22, 1886.

8. Lowell Reidenbaugh, *Baseball's Hall of Fame: Cooperstown*, 1997, p. 170. A story in the *Chicago Daily Tribune* of March 6, 1890, reports that he was served with a writ during the Baseball War "when about to leave New York for Princeton."

9. David Stevens, *Baseball's Radical for All Seasons*, 1998, p. 28.

10. *New York Clipper*, February 24, 1882.

11. *Yale Daily News*, March 29, 1886.

12. *Ibid.*, April 29, 1886.

13. *New Haven Union*, as reprinted in the *Bridgeport Herald*, December 26, 1885.

14. As regards O'Rourke's support of youth organizations, Volume 65, p. 777 of the records in the town clerk's office of the City of Bridgeport, attests that James H. O'Rourke signed a surety bond of $300 on March 29, 1886, for the treasurer, Peter Rowen, of the Bridgeport TL&B Association, which sponsored a boys baseball team. TL&B members were required to eschew spirits. The Rowens were friends of the O'Rourkes. Eddie Rowen played for Bridgeport and with Jim on the Boston Red Caps.

15. David Stevens, *Baseball's Radical for All Seasons*, 1998, p. 43, 47.

Chapter 15

1. David Stevens, *Baseball's Radical for All Seasons*, 1998, p. 46.

2. *Ibid.*

3. *Washington Post*, June 27, 1886 (page 1).

4. Grantland Rice, *New York Tribune*, c. March 1, 1925 (Ward File, National Baseball Hall of Fame Library, Cooperstown, New York). Ward was referring to his years with Providence.

5. *New York Times*, November 25, 1886 (page 5).

6. *Ibid.*, January 12, 1886 (page 8). This was the first such contract Jim signed.

7. *Ibid.*, October 12, 1886 (page 2); *New Haven Register*, April 1, 1887: "O'Rourke has been one of the reserve[d] players [of the Giants], notwithstanding erroneous reports to the contrary"; *New Haven Register* of April 6: "James H. O'Rourke, the Yale law school senior, who was reserved by the managers on the New York Giants, went to New York Monday."

8. *Sporting Life*, January 12, 1887.

9. *Sporting News*, December 4, 1886, page 1, column 3.

10. *New York Tribune*, April 17, 1887.

11. *New Haven Register*, March 28, 1887.

12. *New York Times*, April 3, 1887 (page 7).

13. *New Haven Register*, April 2, 1887.

14. *New York Times*, April 3, 1887 (page 7).

15. *New Haven Register*, April 6, 1887.

16. *Ibid.*, April 9, 1887.

17. An August 14, 1887, note in the *New York Times* advised: "In the future Ewing and O'Rourke will alternate behind the bat and at third base." The *New York Times* of June 19 (page 6) reported: "Hereafter both Ewing and O'Rourke will play regularly on the New York team. The man not catching will play the outfield."

18. *Sporting News*, December 4, 1886, page 1, column 3.

19. *Ibid.*, May 31, 1886, page 1, column 3.

20. *New York Times*, November 5, 1887 (p. 10).

21. The name James H. O'Rourke appears in the 1885–86 *Catalog of Yale University* as a junior; and in the 1886–87 *Catalog* as a senior.

22. *Bridgeport Directory*, 1888.

23. *Sporting Life*, December 21, 1887.

24. Robert Smith, *Heroes of Baseball*, 1952, p. 82.

25. *New York Tribune*, July 19, 1887.

26. Larry Bowman, "The Helen Dauvray Cup," *The National Pastime*, 1997, SABR, pp. 73–76; Bryan Di Salvatore, *A Clever Base-Ballist, The Life and Times of John Montgomery Ward*, 1999, p. 206–207.

27. "Helen Dauvray's Choice," article at the top of page in unknown newspaper dated October 12, 1887, Ward File, National Baseball Hall of Fame Library, Cooperstown, New York.

28. Larry Bowman, "Baseball's Intriguing Couple," *The National Pastime*, no. 17, SABR, 1998, pp. 69–72.

29. Helen was born in San Francisco on February 14, 1859. (Larry Bowman, "The Helen Dauvray Cup," *The National Pastime*, pp. 73–76, SABR, 1997.)

30. On August 19, 1889, in Worcester, Massachusetts, when the Giants were in Boston for a three-game series. (New York *Times*, August 23, 1889, page 3.)

31. Lee Allen, "Cooperstown Corner" column, Unidentified newspaper, April 4, 1964, Keefe file, National Baseball Library, Cooperstown. And like their in-laws, would also remain childless (Keefe obituary, *Boston Globe*, c. April 24, 1933, Keefe file, National Baseball Hall of Fame Library, Cooperstown, New York.)

32. *New York Times*, August 13, 1886, p. 2. The game, against New York, was on August 12.

33. *New York Clipper*, April 16, 1881.

34. *Ibid.*, April 23, 1881. Burdock witnessed a Boston-Harvard game on April 15.

35. *Ibid.*, February 3, 1883.

36. The sale was consummated on February 14, 1887. Noel Hynd, *The Giants of the Polo Grounds*, 1988, p. 48; Burt Solomon, *Baseball Timeline*, 1997.

37. John Montgomery Ward, *Lippincott's Monthly Magazine*, August 1887, pp. 318.

38. John Montgomery Ward, "Is the Base-Ball Player a Chattel?" *Lippincott's Monthly Magazine*, August, 1887, p. 314.

39. Harold Seymour, *Baseball: The Early Years*, 1960, p. 109.

40. John Montgomery Ward, "Our National Game," The *Cosmopolitan* magazine, October, 1888, p. 446.

41. Robert Smith, *Baseball*, 1947, p. 87. For a description of Kelly, see also Frank Menke, "Slide, Kelly, Slide," *Fireside Book of Baseball*, 1956, p. 245.

42. For an entertaining account of Mike's larceny on the base paths, see Robert Smith, *Baseball*, 1947, pp. 88–89.

43. Unidentified newspaper (*Sporting Times*?), March 23, 1887, O'Rourke file, National Baseball Hall of Fame Library, Cooperstown, New York.

Chapter 16

1. Lou Hunsinger, Jr., "George W. Stovey," *The National Pastime*, no. 14, 1994, p. 80.

2. *Sporting Life*, "Notes and Comments," September 8, 1886.

3. Noel Hynd, *The Giants of the Polo Grounds*, 1998, p. 46.

4. Jerry Malloy, "The Pittsburgh Keystones and the 1887 Colored League," *Baseball in Pittsburgh*, ed. by Paul Adomites and Dennis DeValeria, 1995, p. 51; Lou Hunsinger, Jr., "George W. Stovey," *The National Pastime*, no. 14, 1994,

p. 80–82. Hunsinger cites the Trenton *True American* of June 21, 1886, regarding Stovey playing in Canada.

5. Jerry Malloy, "The Cubans' Last Stand," *The National Pastime*, no. 11, 1992, p. 11.

6. Lou Hunsinger, Jr., "George W. Stovey," *The National Pastime*, no. 14, 1994, p. 80–82.

7. David Stevens, *Baseball's Radical for All Seasons*, 1998, p. 53; John Bowman and Joel Zoss, *Diamonds in the Rough*, 1989, p. 138.

8. Bryan Di Salvatore, *A Clever Base-Ballist, The Life and Times of John Montgomery Ward*, 1999, p. 330–331.

Chapter 17

1. Sam Crane in No. 3 of a series of articles about the "Fifty Greatest Ball Players," [first name of publication missing] *Journal*, New York publication, O'Rourke folder, National Baseball Hall of Fame Library, Cooperstown, New York. The date was probably late in 1911.

2. *Ibid.*

3. *Bridgeport Morning News*, August 3,1887.

4. Quoted by J. Earl Wagner. *Washington Post*, October 12, 1896, p. 8.

5. Quoted by *Washington Post* sports editor. *Washington Post*, March 5, 1898, p. 8.

6. Quoted by George Davis. *Washington Post*, April 29, 1898, p. 8.

7. Quoted by *Washington Post* sports editor. *Washington Post*, October 10, 1898, p. 8.

8. Quoted by Washington Manager Arthur Irwin. Washington *Post*, May 29, 1899, p. 8.

9. Quoted by Arthur Irwin. *Washington Post*, July 9, 1899, p. 23.

10. Quoted by pitcher Billy Donohue. *Washington Post*, September 25, 1899, p. 8.

11. Quoted by *Washington Post* sports editor. *Washington Post*, October 4, 1899, p. 8.

12. *Chicago Daily Tribune*, August 23, 1923, p. 15.

13. *Bridgeport Morning News*, August 3, 1887.

14. Excerpts from letter printed in *Sporting Times*, November 23, 1890.

15. *Sporting Life*, April 12, 1890, p. 9, "Hub Happenings."

16. John Kiernan, "Sports of the Times," *New York Times*, August 3, 1929, p. 19.

17. David Stevens, *Baseball's Radical for All Seasons*, 1998, p. 63. According to Burt Solomon, *Baseball Timeline*, Hopper read "Casey" for the first time on May 18, 1888, at Wallack's Theatre in New York City.

18. Frederick Van Wyck, *Recollections of an Old New Yorker*, 1932, p. 173.

19. The Giants wore tuxedos to the theater: David Stevens, *Baseball's Radical for All Seasons*, 1998, p. 63.

20. The *New York World*, as cited by Al Ker-

misch, "From a Researcher's Notebook," *Baseball Research Journal*, no. 24, 1995, p. 162.

21. The phrase "glorious uncertainty" appeared in the New York *Clipper* on August 16, 1879. The full citation was: "What would the national game do without that essential element of exciting interest, its 'glorious uncertainty.'" The earliest usage of the phrase in connection with baseball that I have found was in the *New York Times* of August 19, 1865, page 8: "One of the most striking illustrations of the 'glorious uncertainty' of base ball seen this season, was shown yesterday afternoon at Newark, on the occasion of the contest for the championship between the Atlantic Club, of Brooklyn, and the Eureka, of Newark." The Atlantics edged out the Eurekas 21–20.

22. John Bowman and Joel Zoss, *Diamonds in the Rough*, 1989, p. 379.

23. *New York Daily Tribune*, June 9, 1888.

24. Bryan Di Salvatore, *A Clever Base-Ballist, The Life and Times of John Montgomery Ward*, 1999, p. 222.

Chapter 18

1. *Leslies Illustrated*, September 1, 1888.

2. David Nemec, *Great Baseball Facts and Feats*, 1997, p. 270.

3. 1889 Irwin catalog.

4. *New York Times*, May 15, 1887 (page 7).

5. *Bridgeport Herald*, January 28, 1906.

6. Bryan Di Salvatore, *A Clever Base-Ballist*, 1999, p. 244.

7. *New York Tribune*, November 21, 1888. The meeting was held on November 20.

8. Harry Palmer, *Athletic Sports*, 1889, p. 199.

9. *Washington Post*, March 24, 1889, p. 7.

10. Pfeffer file, National Baseball Hall of Fame Library, Cooperstown, New York: probably *Sporting Life*, May 31, 1890.

11. *Washington Post*, March 24, 1889, p. 7.

12. Ted Vincent, *Mudville's Revenge*, 1981, p. 192–93.

13. *Sporting Life*, January 23, 1884.

14. *Ibid.*, February 27, 1884.

15. *Ibid.*, December 3, 1884, p. 5.

16. *Ibid.*

17. *New York Clipper*, June 8, 1889, as cited by Daniel M. Pearson, *Baseball in 1889*, 1993, p. 51.

18. David Stevens, *Baseball's Radical for All Seasons*, 1998, p. 85.

19. Harry Wright Correspondence, Spalding Collection, New York Public Library.

20. Jacob Morse, *Sphere and Ash*, 1888, p. 42.

21. *Spalding Guide*, 1878.

22. Harold Seymour, *Baseball: The Early Years*, 1960, 1989, p. 208–209.

23. On a slip from a book of preprinted tear-out National League receipts, Geo. R. Watson, treasurer of the New York Giants, signed for $258.65 as the visitors' share of the gate from a May 15, 1883, game at Detroit.

24. *Ibid.*

25. *Los Angeles Tribune*, November 23, 1888.

26. *Ibid.*

27. Burt Solomon, *Baseball Timeline*, 1997.

28. Jacob Morse, *Sphere and Ash*, 1888, p. 53.

29. David Stevens, *Baseball's Radical for All Seasons*, 1998, p. 79–80.

30. Daniel M. Pearson, *Baseball in 1889*, 1993, p. 51.

31. Harold Seymour, *Baseball: The Early Years*, 1960, 1989, p. 109.

32. Johnny Ward, as quoted by Ted Vincent, *Mudville's Revenge*, 1981, p. 189. See also page 197 for a discussion of emasculation as player motivation for the war.

Chapter 19

1. Geoffrey C. Ward and Ken Burns, *Baseball*, 1994, p. 40.

2. Daniel M. Pearson, *Baseball in 1889*, 1993, p. 43.

3. David Stevens, *Baseball's Radical for All Seasons*, 1998, p. 85; *New York Times*, June 18, 1889; *New York Clipper*, July 6, 1889, as cited by Daniel M. Pearson, *Baseball in 1889*, 1993, p. 65.

4. *New York Times*, November 5, 1889, p. 8.

5. Daniel M. Pearson, *Baseball in 1889*, 1993, p. 78.

6. *Ibid.*, 1993, p. 66.

7. John Ward, *Players' National League Guide*, 1890, p. 4.

8. Daniel M. Pearson, *Baseball in 1889*, 1993, p. 95.

9. *Spalding Guide*, 1890, p. 26.

10. Richter, *History and Records of Base Ball*, 1914, p. 121.

11. Bryan Di Salvatore, *A Clever Base-Ballist, The Life and Times of John Montgomery Ward*, 1999, p. 292.

12. John Ward, *Players' National League Guide*, 1890, p. 4.

13. *New York Times*, September 6, 1889, p. 6.

14. John Ward, *Players' National League Guide*, 1890, p. 4–5.

15. "The Schemers," *Sporting Life*, October 9, 1889. The St. Louis *Republican* in a front-page story on September 23, 1889, stated each club was to be capitalized through the sale of $20,000 in capital stock, "half of which can be held by the players."

16. David Stevens, *Baseball's Radical for All Seasons*, 1998, p. 134. Voigt, *American Baseball*, Vol. 1, 1966, 1983, p. 165, says the capital of each Players' League club was "at least $50,000."

17. *Chicago Daily Tribune*, February 26, 1890 (page 6).

18. *Sporting Life*, September 18, 1889, 1.

19. Joe Overfield, "'Deacon' White," *BisonGram*, October-November, 1993.

20. Jules Tygiel, *Past Time*, Oxford University Press, 2000, p. 45.

21. William H. Dunbar, "Baseball Salaries Thirty Years Ago," *Baseball Magazine*, no. 3, (July 1918) p. 291–292.

22. Joseph Overfield, "When Baseball Came to Richmond Avenue," *Niagara Frontier* 2, no. 2 (Summer 1955).

23. Robert Gelzheiser, *The Great Baseball Rebellion*, 1991, p. 197.

24. *Ibid.*

25. *Sporting Life*, February 26, 1890, "News, Notes and Comments."

26. *Ibid.*, October 9, 1889, "The Revolt."

27. *New York Clipper*, January 18, 1890, p. 748, column 1.

28. *Sporting Life*, February 12, 1890, p. 5.

29. *New York Clipper*, Saturday, January 18, 1890.

30. *Sporting Life*, February 12, 1890, p. 5.

31. *Chicago Daily Tribune*, February 19, 1890 (page 6).

32. Philip Lowry, *Green Cathedrals*, SABR, 1986, p. 36.

33. *Sporting Life*, February 12, 1890, p. 5.

34. Richard "Dixie" Torangeau, "Remembering the Congress Street Grounds, *The National Pastime*, no. 24, 2004, p. 71–72.

35. *Sporting Life*, February 12, 1890, p. 5.

36. *New York Times*, March 8, 1890.

37. O. P. Caylor, "Opening of the Base-Ball Season of 1890," *Harper's Weekly*, May 3, 1890, p. 354.

38. *Sporting Life*, September 11, 1889; *The Sporting News*, September 14 and 21.

39. Daniel M. Pearson, *Baseball in 1889*, p. 136.

40. The offer was from James Coogan. Daniel M. Pearson, *Baseball in 1889*, p. 137.

41. Dean A. Sullivan *Early Innings*, 1995, p. 187.

42. *New York Times*, September 23, 1889, p. 2.

43. According to Charles C. Alexander, *Our Game: An American Baseball History*, 1991, p. 53, Ren Mulford in Cincinnati and Frank Richter of *Sporting Life* in Philadelphia sided with the players. Steven P. Gietschier, in his forward to the 2000 reprint of Alfred Spink's 1911 *The National Game*, says, "*The Sporting News* took an editorial position supporting the Players' League." Tim Murnane, who at the time was sports editor for the *Boston Globe*, also sided with the players. (Troy Soos, *Before the Curse (The Glory Days of New England Baseball: 1858–1918)*, 1997, p. 27.)

44. David Stevens, *Baseball's Radical for All Seasons*, 1998, p. 106.

45. Ted Vincent, *Mudville's Revenge*, 1981, p. 199.

46. Lee Lowenfish, *The Imperfect Diamond*, 1980, rev. 1991, p. 41.

47. *Sporting Life*, October 9, 1889.

48. *Ibid.*, May 31, 1890 (includes engravings of Keefe and Becannon).

49. "Like the Players' League," *Sporting Life*, March 26, 1890, p. 2.

50. *New York Times*, October 14, 1889 (page 2).

51. *Sporting Life*, October 9, 1889, "The Revolt."

52. *Ibid.*, October 23, 1889, "Club Vs. Player."

53. Howard Rosenberg, *Cap Anson 1*, 2003, p. 6.

54. *Sporting Life*, November 6, 1889, p. 1, "Chicago Gleanings."

55. *New York Times*, November 8, 1889, p. 5. A *Sporting Life* stringer reported that the St. Louis papers revealed on November 1, 1889, that "Comiskey, the Browns' great captain, had signed a Brotherhood contract with the Chicago team." ("Alleged Details of the Players' League," *Sporting Life*, November 6, 1889, p. 1.)

56. *New York Times* interview, January 18, 1890, p. 8.

Chapter 20

1. Daniel M. Pearson, *Baseball in 1889*, 1993, p.175; *New York Times*, October 21, 1889, p. 5.

2. *Spalding Guide*, 1890, pp. 69–70.

3. *New York Times*, October 21, 1889, p. 5.

4. *Ibid.*

5. Alter-ego concept from Daniel M. Pearson, *Baseball in 1889*, 1993, p. 85.

6. Ron McCulloch, *From Cartwright to Shoeless Joe*, Warwick Publishing, 1998, p. 312.

7. *New York Times*, October 19, 1889.

8. Jerry Lansche, *Glory Fades Away*, 1991, pp. 154–182; Daniel M. Pearson, *Baseball in 1889*, 1993, p. 174.

9. *New York Times*, October 24, 1889 (page 3).

10. *Ibid.*

11. *New York Times*, October 24, 1889 (page 3); David Stevens, *Baseball's Radical for All Seasons*, 1998, p. 99.

12. Daniel M. Pearson, *Baseball in 1889*, 1993, p. 107.

13. *Ibid.*, October 26, 1889 (page 2).

14. Game description from Jerry Lansche's, *Glory Fades Away*, 1991, pp. 154–182; Burt Solomon, *Baseball Timeline*, 1997, October 26, 1889; *New York Times*, October 27, 1889; and

Daniel M. Pearson, *Baseball in 1889*, 1993, p. 180.

15. *New York Times*, October 27, 1889 (page 2).

16. *Ibid.*

17. "Notes and Gossip," *Sporting Life*, October 23, 1889.

18. Box score: *New York Times*, October 27, 1889.

19. Daniel M. Pearson, *Baseball in 1889*, p. 182. Pearson cites the *New York Clipper* of November 9,1889. The *Washington Post*, July 7, 1907 (page S4) said the share was $200.

Chapter 21

1. Geoffrey C. Ward and Ken Burns, *Baseball*, 1994, p. 39.

2. *New York Times*, November 5, 1889 (page 8). The *Washington Post* of the same day said the committee to draft the players' manifesto was O'Rourke, Ward, Hanlon and Andrews.

3. *New York Times*, November 5, 1889 (page 8).

4. Frank Richter, *History and Records of Base Ball*, 1914, p. 63.

5. Geoffrey C. Ward and Ken Burns, *Baseball*, 1994, p. 39.

6. Lee Lowenfish, *The Imperfect Diamond*, 1980, rev. 1991, p. 41.

7. Harold Seymour, *Baseball The Early Years*, 1960, 1989, p. 235.

8. Albert Spalding, *America's National Game*, 1911, 1992, pp. 295–297.

9. *Sporting Life*, October 6, 1889, "Notes and Comments."

10. *Ibid.*, February 26, 1890, "A Sharp Rap" and "Injurious Acts." The titles of these articles reflect the press' growing disaffection with the National League's immoral encouragement of contract jumping.

11. *Chicago Daily Tribune*, February 18, 1890 (page 3).

12. *Ibid.*, February 19, 1890 (page 6).

13. Ted Vincent, *Mudville's Revenge*, 1981, p. 203.

14. *Chicago Daily Tribune*, March 24, 1890 (page 6).

15. Harold Seymour, *Baseball: The Early Years*, 1960, 1989, p. 234.

16. David Voigt, *American Baseball, Vol. 1*, 1966, 1983, p. 163.

17. *Sporting Life*, February 5, 1890.

18. *New York Times*, January 10, 1890, p. 8.

19. *Washington Post*, March 27, 1890 (page 6).

20. *New York Times*, December 11, 1889, p. 8.

21. *Chicago Daily Tribune*, March 6, 1890 (page 2).

22. "Law and Ball, "*Sporting Life*, March 12, 1890.

23. Lee Lowenfish, *The Imperfect Diamond*, 1980, rev. 1991, p. 41.

24. Richard McKelvey, *For It's One, Two, Three, Four Strikes You're Out at the Owner's Ball Game*, 2001, p. 10.

25. *Sporting Life*, dated January 29, 1890, and published February 5.

26. Howard Rosenberg, *Cap Anson 1*, 2003, pp. 145, 253.

27. *New York Times*, January 10, 1890, p. 8.

28. *Sporting Life*, February 12, 1890.

29. *Chicago Daily Tribune*, March 16, 1890 (page 3); Tim Murnane, "Training in the South," *Washington Post*, March 18, 1906.

30. *Ibid.*

31. James D. Hardy, Jr., *The New York Giants Base Ball Club*, 1996, p. 107.

32. Harold Seymour, *Baseball: The Early Years*, 1960, p. 232.; James D. Hardy, Jr., *The New York Giants Base Ball Club*, 1996, p. 131.

33. *Sporting Life*, April 12, 1890, p. 9, "In Battle Array." *Sporting Life* published a chart showing the source of players for each of the leagues and teams. It shows that the Players' League and National League recruited 81 versus 37 National League players of the prior season, a two to one ratio. The variance in data among sources can probably be explained by when they took their surveys, as these numbers changed over the course of the season, and by definition. For example, is a "former National League player," one who was reserved by a National League club at the end of 1889 or merely one who played for a National League club at some time during 1889? Might the definition also embrace a forgotten National League veteran called out of retirement?

34. O. P. Caylor, "Opening of the Base-Ball Season of 1890," *Harper's Weekly*, May 3, 1890, p. 354.

35. Harold Seymour, *Baseball: The Early Years*, 1960, 1989, p. 235; *Spalding Guide*, 1890, p. 26.

36. *Spalding Guide*, 1890, pp. 64–65, 148.

37. Players' League. O. P. Caylor, "Opening of the Base-Ball Season of 1890," *Harper's Weekly*, May 3, 1890, p. 355.

38. *Chicago Herald*, May 11, 1890; as quoted by Peter Levine, *A. G. Spalding and the Rise of Baseball*, 1985, p. 61.

39. Noel Hynd, *The Giants of the Polo Grounds*, 1988, p. 34.

40. Michael Gershman, *Diamonds*, 1993, pp. 48–49.

41. *Ibid.*

42. Accounts in quotes from the *New York World*, April 20, 1890.

43. *Ibid.*

44. Dual umpires had been tried earlier, without much success. To a reader suggestion for two umpires (one to call balls and strikes, and one to rule on plays in the field), a *New York Clipper* editor responded February 7, 1880: "Our correspondent does not seem to be aware of the fact that this cumbrous contrivance of two umpires was abolished a quarter of a century ago."

45. Michael Gershman, *Diamonds*, 1993, p. 49; David Stevens, *Baseball's Radical for All Seasons*, 1998, p. 122. Note, the *World* says 12,013 were at Brotherhood Park.

46. Unidentified newspaper (probably *Sporting Life*), April 26, 1890, Ward File, National Baseball Hall of Fame Library, Cooperstown, New York.

47. "A whisper from O'Rourke," *Sporting Life*, August 22 (?), 1890.

48. Geoffrey C. Ward and Ken Burns, *Baseball*, 1994, p. 39.

49. Albert G. Spalding, *America's National Game*, 1911, 1992, pp. 287–8.

50. David Nemec and Saul Wisnia, *Baseball: More Than 150 Years*, 1997, p. 57; David Stevens, *Baseball's Radical for All Seasons*, 1998, p. 107; David Voigt, *American Baseball, Vol. 1*, 1966, 1983, p. 162.

51. *Chicago Daily Tribune*, July 31, 1890 (page 6).

52. Frank Williams research published in the SABR *Baseball Records Committee Newsletter*, December 1997.

53. Arthur Bartlett, *Baseball and Mr. Spalding*, 1951, p. 214–216.

54. Harold Seymour, *Baseball: The Early Years*, 1960, 1989, p. 238.

55. *Spalding Guide*, 1891, p. 15.

56. *Sporting Life*, March 12, 1890.

57. *Spalding Guide*, 1890, pp. 7–19; ostensibly a history of organized baseball, but actually a lengthy tirade against the striking players by Spalding.

58. *Chicago Daily Tribune*, August 9, 1890 (page 6).

59. *Ibid.*

60. Unidentified newspaper, probably the *New York Clipper*, October 4, 1890, Harry Wright file, National Baseball Hall of Fame Library, Cooperstown, New York.

61. David Stevens, *Baseball's Radical for All Seasons*, 1998, p. 133.

62. *Ibid.* Deacon White believed a crucial error on the part of the Players' League was the purchase of the Cincinnati franchise. Even Harry Wright, a National League manager, questioned the wisdom of that decision. When asked by a reporter, he answered candidly: "Why, I don't see what the Players' League can buy there. They can get the grounds and its lease, no doubt, but they cannot be certain about the players. Besides, if the Cincinnati Club is sold to the Players' League there is nothing to prevent the National League from put-

ting a club in there also, and if such was done it might be that almost all of the old players would stick to the National League Club." (Unidentified newspaper, probably the *New York Clipper*, October 4, 1890, Harry Wright file, National Baseball Hall of Fame Library, Cooperstown, New York.)

63. Robert Smith, *Baseball*, 1947, pp. 132–33.

64. Harold Seymour, *Baseball: The Early Years*, 1960, 1989, p. 238; Noel Hynd, *The Giants of the Polo Grounds*, 1988, p. 72.

65. Soden would remain a primary owner of the Boston club until selling out in 1906. This year is approximate. ("History of Owners of the Braves," Boston Braves file, National Baseball Hall of Fame Library, Cooperstown, New York.)

66. David Stevens, *Baseball's Radical for All Seasons*, 1998, p. 134.

67. New York *Times*, November 21, 1890 (page 8).

68. Unidentified newspaper, Ward File, National Baseball Hall of Fame Library, Cooperstown, New York, November 15, 1890.

69. Unidentified newspaper, probably the *New York Clipper*, November 22, 1890, James White file, National Baseball Hall of Fame Library, Cooperstown, New York.

70. David Voigt, *American Baseball Vol. 1*, 1966, 1983, p. 166.

71. This great line summarizing the endgame of the baseball war is from Thomas Gilbert, *Superstars and Monopoly Wars*, 1995, p. 133. In Gilbert's opinion, "Ward's players' League could have—and probably should have—succeeded."

72. Unidentified newspaper, probably the *New York Clipper*, November 22, 1890, James White file, National Baseball Hall of Fame Library, Cooperstown, New York.

73. *Sporting Life*, December 6, 1890.

74. Ron McCulloch, *From Cartwright to Shoeless Joe*, Warwick Publishing, 1998, p. 368–69; The New York *Times*, "Short Stops," January 21, 1891, p. 3, column 2.

75. Alfred H. Spink, *The National Game*, 1910, 1911, 2000, p. 29.

76. Jules Tygiel, *Past Time*, Oxford University Press, 2000, p. 45.

77. Connie Mack, *My 66 Years In the Big Leagues*, 1950, pp. 78–79.

78. *Chicago Daily Tribune*, February 7, 1891 (page 6).

79. *Ibid.*, December 4, 1890 (page 6).

80. *Ibid.*, February 26, 1890 (page 6).

81. *Ibid.*, April 21, 1891 (page 6).

82. *Bridgeport Evening Post*, March 22, 1895. The *New York Times*, September 22, 1904 (page 10), indicated O'Rourke was still a stockholder of the Giants. I found no later references to O'Rourke as a Giants stockholder, nor did I find any notices that he had sold his shares.

83. *New York Times*, March 10, 1894 (page 6).

84. *Bridgeport Evening Post*, March 22, 1895.

85. *New York Times*, April 1, 1891 (page 3).

86. *Chicago Daily Tribune*, February 7, 1891 (page 6).

87. *Ibid.*, February 15, 1891 (page 6).

88. *New York Times*, February 14, 1891 (page 1).

89. *Spalding Guide*, 1891, p. 13.

90. *Chicago Daily Tribune*, March 4, 1891 (page 2).

91. *Los Angeles Times*, October 21, 1890 (page 5). In the March, 1890, issue of the *Railroad Trainman's Journal* a John O'Rourke of 27 Gray Street in Boston is listed as one of the four members of the Board of Grand Trustees. The Boston City Directory lists a John O'Rourke with the occupation of "baggagemaster" at 27 Gray Street in Boston. The Bridgeport City Directory lists a John O'Rourke at 258 Pembroke as a "Ball Player" in 1883, and at the same address as "baggagemaster" from 1884–1905. The residence at 258 Pembroke was also Jim O'Rourke's address from 1875 to 1881. All the dots connect. The grand trustee of the railroad union was John O'Rourke the ballplayer, Jim O'Rourke's brother. I suspect John's Bridgeport address was his permanent legal address, although he was spending more time in Boston when he worked for the railroad.

92. *New York Times*, July 22, 1890.

93. *Los Angeles Times*, October 21, 1890 (page 5).

94. *Ibid.*

95. *Chicago Daily News*, April 7, 1891.

96. *New York Times*, April 18, 1891 (page 1).

97. *Ibid.*

98. *Chicago Tribune*, June 16, 1891.

99. *Ibid.*, September 20, 1891.

100. *Ibid.*, October 6, 1891.

101. *Ibid.*, October 9, 1891 (page 7).

102. *Los Angeles Times*, May 25, 1895.

103. *Bridgeport Post*, June 24, 1911.

Chapter 22

1. *Sporting Life*, Feb. 27, 1892.

2. Quote from unidentified newspaper [*New York Clipper*?] post-season article of 1889–90 entitled "Unhappy O'Rourke," and dealing primarily with Players' League.

3. Bridgeport Land Records, Vol. 92, page 709; researched by Charles Brilvitch.

4. *Total Baseball*, Seventh Edition, 2001.

5. *New York Times*, April 13, 1892 (page 2).

6. Frank Richter, *History and Records of Base Ball*, 1914, p. 66.

7. *Baseball Encyclopedia*, 10th Edition, Macmillan, 1969.

8. Noel Hynd, *The Giants of the Polo Grounds*, 1988, p. 33.

9. Interview with Giants' batboy, Nick Engle's son: *New York Times*, September 28, 1957 (page 187).

10. James D. Hardy, Jr., *The New York Giants Base Ball Club*, 1996, p. 143–144. (An excellent account of this episode.)

11. *New York Times*, September 11, 1892 (page 6).

12. "Washington will get ... O'Rourke from the New York club." *Washington Post*, September 16, 1892 (page 6).

Chapter 23

1. Harold Seymour, *Baseball The Early Years*, 1960, 1989, p. 235.

2. *Total Baseball*, Seventh Edition, 2001.

3. Frank Richter, *History and Records of Base Ball*, 1914, p. 106.

4. Howard Rosenberg, *Cap Anson 1*, 2003, p. 35.

5. *Washington Post*, March 29, 1893 (page 6).

6. *Ibid.*, March 7, 1893 (page 6).

7. *Ibid.*, September 18, 1892 (page 4).

8. *Ibid.*, March 29, 1893 (page 6).

9. *Ibid.*, March 27, 1893 (page 6).

10. *Ibid.*, March 29, 1893 (page 6).

11. *Ibid.*, October 22, 1893 (page 2).

12. *Ibid.*, March 29, 1893 (page 6). Toward the end of the season, Jim amended his assessment of the effect of the new rule: "It is not the five-foot extra that is making the heavy batting, but the fact that the pitcher is confined to the one-foot rubber plate." (*Ibid.*, August 27, 1893 [page 6].)

13. *Total Baseball*, Seventh Edition, 2001.

14. *Washington Post*, December 11, 1916 (page 4).

15. *Ibid.*, May 4, 1905 (page 9).

16. *Ibid.*, May 4, 1905 (page 9).

17. David Nemec, *The Great Encyclopedia of 19thCentury Major League Baseball*, 1997, pp. 829–30.

18. Shirley Povich, *The Washington Senators*, New York, 17–18; *Washington Post*, November 14, 1893 (page 6). A notice appeared in the August 30, 1893, issue of the *Atlanta Constitution*, that "Gus Schmelz goes to Washington and succeeds Jim O'Rourke as manager."

19. *Atlanta Constitution*, February 26, 1894, p. 5.

Chapter 24

1. *Sporting Life*, May 21, 1884, p. 6.

2. *Chicago Tribune*, March 2, 1894.

3. *Washington Post*, April 20, 1894.

4. *New York Times*, April 24, 1894 (page 3).

5. *Washington Post*, April 24, 1894 (page 6).

6. Hall of Fame Umpire Bill Klem said, "The best way to avoid trouble was to favor the home team." Klem saw a lot of trouble. Bill Klem, "I Never Missed One in My Heart," *Collier's* magazine, March 31, 1951, p. 30.

7. *New York Times*, April 25, 1894 (page 3).

8. *Bridgeport Post*, April 30, 1894, quoting the *New York Sun*.

9. *Washington Post*, May 4, 1894 (page 6).

10. *New York Times*, May 19, 1894 (page 6).

11. *Washington Post*, June 22, 1894 (page 6).

12. *Ibid.*, July 1, 1894 (page 15).

13. *Sporting Life*, June 17, 1883, p. 4.

14. *Bridgeport Herald*, April 26, 1914.

15. *Washington Post*, June 24, 1894 (page 15).

16. John Schwartz, "From One Ump to Two," *Baseball Research Journal #30*, SABR, 2001, p. 86.

17. *Washington Post*, September 18, 1894.

18. *Ibid.*, September 21, 1894.

19. *Ibid.*, June 8, 1895.

20. *New York Times*, July 7, 1896 (page 6).

21. *Ibid.*, July 9, 1896 (page 6).

22. *Washington Post*, January 28, 1906 (page S4).

23. *Bridgeport Herald*, September 28, 1913. He set up an office in room 27 of the Fairfield County Court House at 172 Golden Hill Street, in Bridgeport. The courthouse still stands.

24. *Atlanta Constitution*, May 26, 1890; reprinted from the Pittsburgh *Press*.

25. Lee Allen, *The Hot Stove League*, 1955, 2000, p. 95.

26. *Bridgeport Post*, June 3, 1895.

27. *Ibid.*, June 8 (Saturday), 1895.

28. *Ibid.*, June 26, 1895.

29. *New York Times*, April 21, 1896.

30. *Bridgeport Post*, June 1, 1896. (May 30 was a Saturday.)

31. *New York Times*, June 7, 1896 (page 3).

32. *Ibid.*, June 6, 1897 (page 4).

33. Edward Shugrue, "Between Ourselves," *Bridgeport Post*, April 27, 1945. The *Washington Post*, January 28, 1906 (page S4), based on an interview of Jim, also indicates the St. Josephs were semipro.

34. *Bridgeport Post*, March 31, 1929, says the St. Josephs beat the Bostons. Not so. They lost 10 to 1.

35. *Ibid.*, September 17, 1894.

36. *Graduates of the Yale Law School 1824–1899*, Roger W. Tuttle, Tuttle, Morehouse & Taylor, 1911.

37. *Bridgeport Post*, October 19, 1894.

38. *Ibid.*, October 23, 1894 (page 1).

39. *Ibid.*, November 7, 1894.

40. *Ibid.*

41. *Ibid.*

42. *Ibid.*, October 28, 1894.
43. *Ibid.*, October 19, 1894.

Chapter 25

1. During the prior season, a local sports-writer suggested "Bridgeport could make up a pretty good team by picking from the various clubs in the city" and suggested players for each position from among the St. Josephs, East Sides, and the YMCA team (*Bridgeport Post*, August 1, 1894.)
2. *Ibid.*, August 24, 1894.
3. *New York Times*, March 6, 1894 (page 8).
4. *Ibid.*, December 6, 1894.
5. *Ibid.*, December 21, 1894.
6. *Ibid.*, December 28, 1894.
7. *Ibid.*, January 15, 1895.
8. *Ibid.*, January 16, 1895.
9. *Ibid.*, February 21, 1895.
10. *Ibid.*, January 28, 1895.
11. *Ibid.*, February 21, 1895.
12. *Ibid.*
13. *Ibid.*, February 4, 1895.
14. *New York Times*, February 5, 1895 (page 7).
15. *Bridgeport Post*, February 4, 1895.
16. *Ibid.*, February 6, 1895.
17. *Bridgeport Herald*, February 10, 1895.
18. *Bridgeport Post*, February 14, 1895.
19. *Washington Post*, February 24, 1895 (page 5).
20. *Bridgeport Post*, February 19, 1895.
21. *Ibid.*, March 3, 1895.
22. *Ibid.*, March 7, 1895.
23. *Ibid.*, March 8, 1895.
24. *Ibid.*, March 13, 1895.
25. *Ibid.*, March 16, 1895.
26. *Ibid.*, June 19, 1895.
27. *Ibid.*, June 30, 1895.
28. Herbert was listed in the Bridgeport City Directory as a musician, residing at 467 State Street (renumbered 841 State Street in 1910), between Seeley and Iranistan.
29. *Bridgeport Post*, September 13, 1895.
30. *Ibid.*, August 14, 1895.
31. *Ibid.*, October 2, 1895.
32. *Ibid.*, April 11, 1895.
33. Jim convinced the traction company to extend its line to Athletic Park. (*Ibid.*, April 24, 1895.)
34. *Bridgeport Herald*, June 16, 1895.
35. *Bridgeport Post*, June 17, 1895.
36. The Connecticut League of 1895 is considered a continuance of nonsignatory Connecticut State Leagues of 1894, 1891, 1888, 1885, and 1884. (Research by Frank Williams.)
37. *Bridgeport Post*, July 6, 1895.
38. *Ibid.*, September 6, 1895.
39. *Ibid.*, October 29, 1895.

40. *The Sporting News*, November 2, 1895.
41. *Ibid.*, November 9, 1895, p. 5.
42. League president: based on research by Frank Williams.
43. *Bridgeport Post*, November 22, 1895.
44. *Ibid.*, March 6, 1896.
45. *Ibid.*, November 23, 1895.
46. *Ibid.*, April 14, 1896. According to the *Atlanta Constitution* of April 20, 1896, the game raised $10 for the Wright Memorial.
47. *Ibid.*, April 17, 1896.
48. *Ibid.*, May 3, 1896.
49. *New York Herald* August 9, 1896. (The *Herald* does not mention Herbert's ethnicity.)
50. Based on research by Frank Williams.
51. The date was June 24, 1896. (Based on research by Frank Williams.)
52. *Bridgeport Herald*, July 27, 1913. William J. Tracy of Bristol succeeded Whitlock as president on October 15, 1906.
53. Based on research by Frank Williams.
54. Frank Williams research.

Chapter 26

1. "The lot on which the veteran Jim O'Rourke pitched hay when he was a boy." Unidentified newspaper, circa October, 1913, in the O'Rourke file at the National Baseball Hall of Fame Library, Cooperstown, New York.
2. *Bridgeport Morning Telegram*, September 7, 1898.
3. *Bridgeport Herald*, May 22, 1898.
4. Research notes of Frank Williams.
5. *Bridgeport Herald*, September 11, 1918.
6. *Washington Post.*
7. *Ibid..*
8. *Ibid.*, July 2, 1906 (page 8).
9. *New York Times*, September 7, 1902 (page 14).
10. *Washington Post*, March 2, 1899.
11. *Spalding Guide*, 1901, p. 135; *Reach Guide*, 1901, p. 126.

Chapter 27

1. *Chicago Tribune*, April 14, 1900 (page 6).
2. *Ibid.*, October 25, 1900 (page 6).
3. *Ibid.*
4. *Ibid.*
5. Frank Richter, *History and Records of Base Ball*, 1914, p. 70.
6. *New York Times*, October 25, 1901 (page 10).
7. *Washington Post*, October 26, 1901 (page 8).
8. *New York Times*, October 25, 1901 (page 10). The other three members were J. T. Hickey, St. Joseph, Missouri; M. H. Sexton, Rock Island;

and W. H. Lucas, Portland, Oregon. J. H. Farrell of Auburn, New York was elected secretary.

9. *Washington Post*, October 26, 1901 (page 8).

10. *Ibid.*

11. *New York Times*, October 27, 1901 (page 16, column 5).

12. *Ibid.*, October 26, 1901 (page 7).

13. *Ibid.*, October 27, 1901 (page 16, column 5).

14. *Ibid.*, October 25, 1901 (page 10).

15. Francis Richter, *History and Records of Base Ball*, 1914, p. 71.

16. *Washington Post*, October 26, 1901 (page 8).

17. *Ibid.*

18. *New York Times*, October 27, 1901 (page 16).

19. *Ibid.*

20. *Bridgeport Municipal Register*, 1901–1903.

21. *New York Times*, May 21, 1903.

22. *New York Herald*, May 21, 1903.

23. *Bridgeport Herald*, September 14, 1903; *Springfield Republican*, September 13, 1903. The game was on September 12, 1903.

24. The *Spalding Guide* of 1903, p. 150, referred to the circuit as the Connecticut Valley League.

25. At the Fifth Avenue Hotel in New York.

26. *New York Times*, October 26, 1902 (page 17).

27. *Chicago Tribune*, October 24, 1902 (page 6).

28. *New York Times*, October 26, 1902 (page 17).

29. *Ibid.*, August 30, 1903 (page 3, column 4); Frank Richter, *History and Records of Base Ball*, 1914, p. 212.

30. *Washington Post*, February 19, 1903 (page 8).

31. *Ibid.*

32. *New York Times*, August 30, 1903 (page 3, column 4).

33. *Ibid.*

34. *Ibid.*

35. *Ibid.*

36. *Ibid.*

37. *Ibid.*, August 31, 1903 (page 7, column 3).

38. *Chicago Tribune*, September 11, 1903 (page 8).

39. *Ibid.*, September 11, 1903 (page 8); October 25, 1903 (page 13).

40. *New York Times*, October 27, 1903 (page 10).

41. *Chicago Tribune*, September 11, 1903 (page 8).

42. *Washington Post*, October 25, 1903 (page D11).

43. *Chicago Tribune*, September 11, 1903 (page 8).

44. *Washington Post*, October 25, 1903 (page D11).

45. *Chicago Tribune*, September 11, 1903 (page 8).

46. *Ibid.*, October 25, 1903 (page 13).

47. *Los Angeles Times*, October 23, 1903 (page 11).

48. *Chicago Daily Tribune*, October 25, 1903 (page 13).

Chapter 28

1. *New York Herald*, January 9, 1919; *Washington Post*, August 13, 1906 (Page 6).

2. *New York Times*, April 11, 1901 (page 7).

3. *Chicago Tribune*, May 4, 1901 (page 4).

4. *New York Times*, June 2, 1901 (page 8).

5. *Washington Post*, April 10, 1903 (page 9).

6. *New York Times*, April 11, 1903 (page 11).

7. *Washington Post*, January 28, 1906 (page S4).

8. *Chicago Tribune*, July 5, 1903 (page 9).

9. *Ibid.*, August 9, 1903 (page 11).

10. *Washington Post*, February 14, 1904 (page B2).

11. *Chicago Tribune*, August 26, 1906 (page A2); *Washington Post*, August 13, 1906 (Page 6).

12. Bert Randolph Sugar, *Rain Delays*, 1990, p. 23.

13. Jean Pierre Caillault, "Hall of Fame Batteries," *Baseball Research Journal, no. 32*, SABR, 2004, p. 99. Caillault credits Jim with catching only seven Hall of Fame pitchers, as he did not include Spalding from the National Association era. But even with seven, Jim is still two ahead of the runners-up, King Kelly, Buck Ewing, and Bill Dickey, who caught five each.

14. As reprinted by Lee Allen, *The Hot Stove League*, 1955, 2000, p. 67.

15. *Bridgeport Post*, October 1, 1904; *New York Times*, October 8, 1904.

16. *Chicago Tribune*, October 21, 1906 (page A3). William Buckingham Ewing was 47. He died of "diabetes and paralysis" at his home in Cincinnati.

17. *Bridgeport Herald*, September 11, 1904.

18. As reprinted in the *Bridgeport Evening Post*, September 2, 1904.

19. *Ibid.*, October 29, 1904.

20. *Bridgeport Herald*, March 9, 1902.

21. *New York Times*, October 16, 1906 (page 7).

22. *Chicago Tribune*, August 26, 1906, p. A2.

23. Bill Klem, "I Never Missed One in My Heart," *Collier's* magazine, March 31, 1951, p. 30.

24. David Anderson, *Deadball Stars of the National League*, 2004, p. 24.

25. Lowell Reidenbaugh, *Baseball's Hall of Fame: Cooperstown*, 1983, p. 182.

26. Lee Allen, HOF historian, *The Sporting News*, February 10, 1968, p. 28.

27. *Washington Post*, August 26, 1906 (page 6).
28. *Ibid.*
29. *Ibid.*
30. *Bridgeport Post*, September 30, 1907.
31. *Chicago Tribune*, August 16, 1906 (page B1).
32. Larry Ekin, *Baseball Fathers, Baseball Sons*, 1992, pp. 53–180. At the time, the Yankees were known as the Highlanders. The first son of a major leaguer to play in the majors was Jack Doscher.
33. *New York Times*, August 16, 1908 (page S2).
34. *Ibid.*, February 21, 1909 (page S1).
35. *Washington Post*, February 21, 1909. Alfred H. Spink, *The National Game*, 1910, 1911, 2000, p. 252, says he was sold to Omaha, but this is incorrect.

Chapter 29

1. *New York Times*, January 8, 1907 (page 7, column 4).
2. *Ibid.*
3. *Ibid.*, January 9, 1907 (page 6, column 3).
4. *Ibid.*, January 10, 1907 (page 6, column 4).
5. *Ibid.*
6. *Ibid.*, October 30, 1907 (page 7, column 2), October 31, 1907 (page 7, column 5).
7. *Washington Post*, November 1, 1907 (page 9).
8. *Ibid.*
9. A *Washington Post* headline of December 6, 1907, referred to the Tri-State as the "Former Outlaw League."
10. *Chicago Tribune*, November 1, 1907 (page 6).
11. *Ibid.*
12. *Ibid.*, February 26, 1908 (page 6).
13. *Ibid.*, February 26, 1908 (page 6).
14. *New York Times*, January 5, 1909 (page 11), February 4, 1910 (page 8). Some of the more blatant scofflaws were required to pay fines of $50 to $200.

Chapter 30

1. *Chicago Tribune*, August 26, 1906 (page A2).
2. *Boston Globe*, September 20, 1908; as reprinted in Albert G. Spalding, *America's National Game*, 1911, 1992, p. 353.
3. There are other, ambiguous sources, such as the very first biographical sketch of Jim, which appeared in an October 1879, issue of the *New York Clipper*, that said O'Rourke "was born about 26 years ago."

4. *Washington Post*, April 29, 1906 (page S2), and *Washington Post*, July 22, 1910 (page S2).
5. O'Rourke file, National Baseball Hall of Fame Library, Cooperstown, New York.
6. Alfred H. Spink, *The National Game*, 1910, 1911, 2000, p. 252.
7. *Washington Post*, January 28, 1906 (page S4).
8. *New York World*, May 12, 1907 (section 9).
9. *Chicago Tribune*, August 29, 1909 (page C3).
10. *Bridgeport Times*, April 29, 1906, p. 1.
11. From an unidentified newspaper in the O'Rourke files of the National Baseball Hall of Fame Library, Cooperstown, New York, c. February 3, 1910.
12. Unidentified newspaper, February 10, 1910, O'Rourke file, National Baseball Hall of Fame Library, Cooperstown, New York.
13. *Washington Post*, August 13, 1906 (Page 6).
14. *Bridgeport Herald*, April 26, 1914.
15. "Last Honors Paid Today..." *Bridgeport Post*, January 11, 1919.
16. *Bridgeport Herald*, January 12, 1919, p. 10. *Bridgeport Municipal Register*, 1909, 1913, 1916.
17. *Chicago Tribune*, June 9, 1909 (page 12).
18. *Ibid.*, June 14, 1909 (page 10).
19. *New York Times*, October 19, 1909 (page 8).
20. *Hartford Daily Times*, February 5, 1910; *Bridgeport Herald*, March 19, 1911.
21. *Washington Post*, July 22, 1910 (page 8).
22. J. C. Morse, "Changes in the World of Baseball," *Baseball Magazine*, September, 1911, No. 5, p. 39–44.
23. *Bridgeport Post*, June 24, 1911.

Chapter 31

1. Dates of the San Antonio NAPBL conference are based on reports in the *New York Times*, November 16 and 19, 1911. Bernard Crowley has identified a photo of Jim's family, allegedly taken in Texas while Jim "was on a business trip." I presume the "trip" was to the only NAPBL meeting in Texas, as I can think of no other reason why a Bridgeport lawyer or Connecticut League official would have "business" in Texas. However, Crowley indicates that one of the women as "Annie" (Jim's wife, who died in 1910). So one of us is wrong. Either the older woman is not Annie (It could be Jim's sister, Sarah) or else the photo was taken elsewhere.
2. *New York Times*, November 16, 1911 (page 11, column 1).
3. *Ibid.*, November 19, 1911 (page 7, column 7).

4. *Ibid.*, December 15, 1911 (page 14, column 1).
5. *Ibid.*, November 19, 1911 (page 7, column 7).
6. Daniel M. Pearson, *Baseball in 1889*, 1993, p. 194.
7. *Sporting News*, January 16, 1919.
8. *Bridgeport Herald*, July 27, 1913.
9. *New York Times*, May 11, 1912 (page 9).
10. *The Sporting News*, March 21, 1912.
11. *Ibid.*
12. Unidentified newspaper, 1913, O'Rourke file, National Baseball Hall of Fame Library, Cooperstown, New York.
13. Troy Soos, *Before the Curse*, 1997, p. 141.
14. George McGlynn, *The Sporting News*, November 14, 1912.
15. *Ibid.*
16. Unidentified newspaper, c. October 21, 1913, O'Rourke file, National Baseball Hall of Fame Library, Cooperstown, New York.
17. *New York Times*, September 14, 1913 (page S2).
18. *The Sporting News*, November 20, 1913.
19. With Frank Leavitt, Chairman; N. J. O'Neill; James Frank; and C. A. Cline.
20. With A. T. Baum, Pacific Coast League; E. G. Barrow, International League; R. W. Road, Ohio State; Nick Corish, South Atlantic
21. *The Sporting News*, November 20, 1913.
22. *Ibid.*
23. *New York Times*, December 14, 1913 (Part V, page 4, column 6).
24. There is no record of an Eastern League in 1914.

Chapter 32

1. *Bridgeport Herald*, July 27, 1913.
2. *New York Times*, October 24, 1913 (p. 7, column 1).
3. Article entitled "He Makes the So-called Veterans Look Young," from unidentified clipping in the O'Rourke file at the National Baseball Hall of Fame Library, Cooperstown, New York.
4. *Bridgeport Herald*, April 19, 1914.
5. "Eastern Association in Session," *New York Times*, March 5, 1914.
6. *Ibid.*, November 10, 1914 (page 9, column 1).
7. *Washington Post*, January 31, 1915.
8. *The Sporting News*, November 25, 1915.
9. *Bridgeport Herald*, August 9, 1914.
10. *The Sporting News*, November 25, 1915.
11. *New York Times*, March 17, 1915 (page 12).
12. *Ibid.*, March 20, 1915 (page 11).
13. *Ibid.*, March 19, 1915 (page 12).
14. *Ibid.*, March 26, 1915 (page 11).
15. *Sporting Life*, April 17, 1915.
16. *Ibid.*
17. *Ibid.*, April 17, 1915.
18. *Bridgeport Herald*, March 22, 1916.
19. *New York Times*, April 21, 1915 (page 11).
20. *Ibid.*, April 22, 1915 (page 10). Only one applicant was mentioned by name: Mickey Finn of New Haven, who had pennant-winning experience as a manager in the Southern League and the Eastern Association, in which he had managed the Waterbury team.
21. *Ibid.*, April 22, 1915 (page 10).
22. *Ibid.*, April 25, 1915 (page S1).
23. *Ibid.*
24. *Ibid.*, May 15, 1915 (page 14).
25. *Ibid.*
26. *Bridgeport Herald*, August 29, 1915.
27. *New York Times*, October 19, 1915 (page 12).
28. "Tim Finds Time to Take a Vacation," *The Sporting News*, November 11, 1915. (The article was written by Murnane on November 6 while en route to the West Coast.)
29. *Ibid.*, November 18, 1915.
30. "Pickups from the Meeting of the Minor Magnates," November 18, 1915.
31. *Ibid.*, January 16, 1919, p. 5.
32. "Here's a New Idea in Arbitration Board," November 25, 1915.
33. *Ibid.*, December 16, 1915; with a Providence, December 13 dateline.
34. *Ibid.*, December 2, 1915.
35. *New York Times*, December 15, 1915.
36. *Ibid.*
37. *Ibid.*, December 17, 1915 (page 13, column 4).
38. *The Sporting News*, December 23, 1915.
39. *Ibid.*
40. *Ibid.*
41. *New York Times*, December 31, 1915, and January 6, 1916; *The Sporting News*, December 23 and 30, 1915.
42. *Bridgeport Herald*, December 26, 1915 (page 26).
43. *Ibid.*, January 16, 1916.
44. *Ibid.*
45. *Bridgeport Post*, January 11, 1916.
46. *Ibid.*
47. *Bridgeport Herald*, January 16, 1916.
48. *Bridgeport Post*, January 11, 1916.
49. *Ibid.*
50. BaseballLibrary.com. The former owner was Lee Fohl, who was also a playing manager. Cleveland hired him to manage in 1915. He brought the Indians up to second place by 1918. But in a 1919, he was fired when he displayed poor judgment for *not* walking Babe Ruth with the bases loaded. He also managed for the St. Louis Browns and Boston Red Sox.
51. *Bridgeport Post*, January 13, 1896.
52. *Bridgeport Herald*, January 16, 1916;

Bridgeport Post, January 15, 1916. The New Haven franchisee was James E. Canavan, who piloted a team to the Eastern Association pennant in 1902. In 1915 he had thrown in with the ill-fated Federal organization's Colonial League. The directors voted to start the season on April 26 and close on September 10.

53. *Bridgeport Herald*, January 16, 1916.
54. *Ibid.*
55. *Ibid.*
56. *Bridgeport Post*, January 30, 1916.
57. *Ibid.*, January 25, 26, 1916.
58. *Ibid.*, February 1, 1916.
59. *Ibid.*, February 10, 1916.
60. *Bridgeport Herald*, February 20, 1916.
61. *New York Times*, February 15, 1916 (page 13).
62. *Ibid.*, February 17, 1916 (page 12).
63. *Bridgeport Herald*, February 20, 1916.
64. *Ibid.*, March 22, 1916.
65. *New York Times*, February 22, 1916 (page 12).

Chapter 33

1. Sports editor Earl C. Donegan, *Bridgeport Post*, February, 1916.
2. *New York Clipper*, September 30, 1882.
3. *Ibid.*
4. O'Rourke died of pneumonia at 4:00 p.m. on January 8, 1919 (*New York Times*, January 9, 1919, (p. 8, column 2).
5. *Bridgeport Telegram*, April 26, 1945.

Chapter 34

1. *Total Baseball*, Seventh Edition, 2001.
2. *Ibid.*
3. Al Kermisch, "From a Researcher's Notebook," *Baseball Research Journal*, no. 8, 1979, pp. 12–13.
4. *Bridgeport Herald*, March 20. 1910.
5. *Ibid.*, March 16, 1913.
6. *Ibid.*, December 26, 1915.
7. *Bridgeport Post*, August 2, 1914.
8. *Spalding Guide*, 1919, p. 307.
9. I am not certain when Jimmy moved to the Baltimore area. I know he was there in 1919.
10. Including 1915 season in Syracuse. Data compiled by Frank Williams.
11. David Stevens, *Baseball's Radical for All Seasons*, 1998, p. 28.
12. *New York Times*, December 20, 1911 (page 8, column 1).
13. "History of Owners of the Braves," Boston Braves file, National Baseball Hall of Fame Library, Cooperstown, New York.
14. Thomas Gilbert, *Superstars and Monopoly Wars*, 1995, p. 136–137.

Appendix B

1. For an excellent discussion of the evolution of pitching styles and speeds, see William Ryczek, *Blackguards and Red Stockings*, 1992, pp. 16–17, 55.
2. Arthur Bartlett, *Baseball and Mr. Spalding*, 1951, p. 14.
3. John Rossi, *The National Game*, 2000, p.18.
4. *New York Times*, June 3, 1873, p. 8.
5. Preston Orem. *Baseball From the Newspaper Accounts (1845–1881)*, 1961, pp. 6–7.
6. *Ibid.*
7. The rule was adopted at the National League meeting on December 5, 1879. Jacob Morse, *Sphere and Ash*, 1888, p. 7, 44, 46; Burt Solomon, *Baseball Timeline*, 1997. Preston Orem, *Baseball From the Newspaper Accounts (1845–1881)*, 1961, p. 316; David Nemec, *The Rules of Baseball*, 1994, pp. 33, 34, 93, 2.38.
8. *New York Clipper*, July 5, 1879.
9. Jacob Morse, *Sphere and Ash*, 1888, p. 46.
10. *Sporting Life*, January 16, 1884.
11. Jacob Morse, *Sphere and Ash*, 1888, p. 48.
12. *Sporting Life*, January 16, 1884.
13. *Ibid.*, January 30, 1884.
14. Jacob Morse, *Sphere and Ash*, 1888, p. 52.
15. Robert H. Schaefer, "The Lost Art of Fair-Foul Hitting," *The National Pastime*, no. 19, SABR, 1999, p. 5.
16. Harold Seymour, *Baseball, The Early Years*, 1960, p. 178.
17. BaseballLibrary.com, adapted from: Glen Waggoner, Kathleen Maloney, and Hugh Howard, *Spitters, Beanballs and the Incredible Shrinking Strike Zone*, Triumph Books, 2000.
18. Jacob Morse, *Sphere and Ash*, 1888, p. 48; *The Official Encyclopedia of Baseball*, 1951, 1963, 3rd Ed., p. 2331–2336.
19. *The Official Encyclopedia of Baseball*, 1951, 1963, 3rd Ed., p. 2332.
20. *Ibid.*, p. 2331–2336.
21. David Nemec, *The Rules of Baseball*, 1994, p. 34.
22. *The Official Encyclopedia of Baseball*, 1951, 1963, 3rd Ed., p. 2333.
23. Francis Richter, *History and Records of Base Ball*, 1914, p. 257.
24. BaseballLibrary.com, adapted from: Glen Waggoner, Kathleen Maloney, and Hugh Howard, *Spitters, Beanballs and the Incredible Shrinking Strike Zone*, Triumph Books, 2000.
25. According to Section 5 of the official rules as extensively revised at the December 9, 1863, convention of the National Association of Base-Ball Players, as published by Francis Richter, *History and Records of Base Ball*, 1913, p. 231–232.
26. Harold Seymour, *Baseball: The Early Years*, 1960, p. 177.

27. BaseballLibrary.com, adapted from: Glen Waggoner, Kathleen Maloney, and Hugh Howard, *Spitters, Beanballs and the Incredible Shrinking Strike Zone*, Triumph Books, 2000.

28. BaseballLibrary.com, adapted from: Glen Waggoner, Kathleen Maloney, and Hugh Howard, *Spitters, Beanballs and the Incredible Shrinking Strike Zone*, Triumph Books, 2000.

29. *The Official Encyclopedia of Baseball*, 1951, 1963, 3rd Ed., p. 2332.

30. Francis Richter, *History and Records of Base Ball*, 1913, p. 256.

31. *Ibid.*

32. *The Official Encyclopedia of Baseball*, 1951, 1963, 3rd Ed., p. 2331-2336.

33. *Ibid.*, p. 2336.

34. Harold Seymour, *Baseball: The Early Years*, 1960, P. 40. Dan Gutman, *It Ain't Cheatin' If You Don't Get Caught*, 1990, p. xxxiii., says called strikes were initiated in 1858. Ron McCulloch, *From Cartwright to Shoeless Joe*, Warwick Publishing, 1998, says the first called strike was in 1860.

35. Ron McCulloch, *From Cartwright to Shoeless Joe*, Warwick Publishing, 1998, p. 53, 27.

36. Harold Seymour, *Baseball: The Early Years*, 1960, p. 176.

37. *Washington Post*, November 22, 1887, p. 1.

38. *The Official Encyclopedia of Baseball*, 1951, 1963, 3rd Ed., p. 2333.

39. *Official Baseball Rules*, The Sporting News, various years. *Spalding Guide*, various years. *Baseball Encyclopedia*, 10th Edition, Macmillan, 1969; Paul Dickson, *The New Dickson Baseball Dictionary*, 1999, p. 483. [Note: these sources are not in complete agreement.]

40. *Beadle's Dime Base-Ball Player*, 1860, p. 12.

41. *Ibid.*

42. *Beadle's Dime Base-Ball Player*, 1867, p. 15. The rule was adopted at the annual meeting of the National Association of Base-Ball players on December 12, 1866.

43. *Ibid.*

44. BaseballLibrary.com, adapted from: Glen Waggoner, Kathleen Maloney, and Hugh Howard, *Spitters, Beanballs and the Incredible Shrinking Strike Zone*, Triumph Books, 2000.

45. *The Sporting News*, January 29, 1887, p. 6.

46. *Beadle's Dime Base-Ball Player*, 1867, p. 15. The rule was adopted at the annual meeting of the National Association of Base-Ball players on December 12, 1866.

47. Bryan Di Salvatore, *A Clever Base-Ballist, The Life and Times of John Montgomery Ward*, 1999, p. 125.

48. Henry Chadwick, *Beadle's Dime Base-Ball Player*, 1860, p. 7; Arthur Bartlett, *Baseball and Mr. Spalding*, 1951, p. 14.

49. *Beadle's Dime Base-Ball Player*, 1867, p. 15. The rule was adopted at the annual meeting of the National Association of Base-Ball players on December 12, 1866.

50. *Ibid.* The rule was adopted at the annual meeting of the National Association of Base-Ball players on December 12, 1866.

51. Mark Alvarez, *The Old Ball Game*, 1990, p. 136.

52. *Ibid.*

53. *Beadle's Dime Base-Ball Player*, 1860, p. 22; Barry Sloate has also uncovered an article in the August 6, 1860, Brooklyn *Eagle*–probably written by Chadwick–that indicates the game's first superstar hurler, Jim Creighton, was pitching a "deceptive curve" before Cummings. (*Vintage & Classic Baseball Collector*, no. 27, May-June, 2001, p. 36.)

54. David Nemec, *Rules of Baseball*, 1994, p. 151.

55. Hy Turkin and S. C. Thompson, *The Official Encyclopedia of Baseball*, 1951, 1st Ed., p. 493.

56. *Spalding Guide*, 1878, p. 28; Harold Seymour, *Baseball: The Early Years*, 1960, p. 176. Seymour wrote that the pitcher "had to deliver the ball with the throwing arm swinging nearly perpendicular to the side of the body, in order to make certain that the hand passed below the hip." This would be more akin to sidearm. The rule actually said "perpendicular, *at* the side of the body," meaning: perpendicular to the ground, not the body.

57. David Nemec, *Rules of Baseball*, 1994, p. 151; BaseballLibrary.com, adapted from: Glen Waggoner, Kathleen Maloney, and Hugh Howard, *Spitters, Beanballs and the Incredible Shrinking Strike Zone*, Triumph Books, 2000.

58. Arthur Bartlett, *Baseball and Mr. Spalding*, 1951, p. 140.

59. Preston Orem, *Baseball From the Newspaper Accounts, (1845–1881)* 1961, p. 346

60. *Ibid.*

61. *Sporting Life*, March 26, 1884, p. 3.

62. *Sporting Life*, November 28, 1883.

63. *Ibid.*

64. BaseballLibrary.com, adapted from: Glen Waggoner, Kathleen Maloney, and Hugh Howard, *Spitters, Beanballs and the Incredible Shrinking Strike Zone*, Triumph Books, 2000.

65. *Sporting Life*, August 6, 1884, p. 7.

66. *Ibid.*, August 13, 1884, p. 7.

67. *Ibid.*, September 10, 1884, p. 5.

68. *Ibid.*, October 9, 1889, "Notes and Comments."

69. *Ibid.*, November 26, 1884, p. 3.

70. *Ibid.*, February 4, 1885, p. 5.

71. *Ibid.*, April 1, 1885, p. 4, "Important Definition."

72. *Ibid.*, November 26, 1884, p. 3.

73. *The Sporting News*, January 29, 1887, p. 6.

74. *Ibid.*
75. *Ibid.*
76. Arthur Bartlett, *Baseball and Mr. Spalding*, 1951, p.200; Bryan Di Salvatore, *A Clever Base-Ballist, The Life and Times of John Montgomery Ward*, 1999, p. 124.
77. BaseballLibrary.com, adapted from: Glen Waggoner, Kathleen Maloney, and Hugh Howard, *Spitters, Beanballs and the Incredible Shrinking Strike Zone*, Triumph Books, 2000.

Appendix C

1. BaseballLibrary.com, adapted from: Glen Waggoner, Kathleen Maloney, and Hugh Howard, *Spitters, Beanballs and the Incredible Shrinking Strike Zone*, Triumph Books, 2000.
2. *Ibid.*
3. *Ibid.*
4. *Sporting Life*, November 26, 1884, p. 3.
5. *Ibid.*
6. *Ibid.*, February 25, 1885, p. 8.
7. BaseballLibrary.com, adapted from: Glen Waggoner, Kathleen Maloney, and Hugh Howard, *Spitters, Beanballs and the Incredible Shrinking Strike Zone*, Triumph Books, 2000.

Appendix D

1. BaseballLibrary.com, adapted from: Glen Waggoner, Kathleen Maloney, and Hugh Howard, *Spitters, Beanballs and the Incredible Shrinking Strike Zone*, Triumph Books, 2000.
2. *Ibid.*
3. *Spalding Guide*, 1890, pp. 35–36.
4. Francis Richter, *History and Records of Base Ball*, 1913, p. 257.
5. David Nemec, *The Rules of Baseball*, Lyons & Burford, 1994, p. 38.
6. Bryan Di Salvatore, *A Clever Base-Ballist*, 1999, p. 124.
7. Arthur Bartlett, *Baseball and Mr. Spalding*, 1951, p. 100.
8. Harold Seymour, *Baseball The Early Years*, 1960, p.178; David Nemec, *The Rules of Baseball*, Lyons & Burford, 1994, p. 40.

Bibliography

Newspapers and Periodicals

The Atlanta *Constitution* (1875 through 1919)
Baseball Magazine (1909 through 1918)
Baseball Research Journal
Boston *Globe*
Boston *Herald* (March 1–May 7, 1871; February 22–April 30, 1880)
Bridgeport *Daily Standard* (1862–1890)
Bridgeport *Herald* (1892 through 1919)
Bridgeport *Post* (1895 through 1921)
Chicago *Tribune* (1890 through 1919)
Derby (CT) *Transcript* (1868 through 1871)
National Pastime
New Haven Palladium (May 1 through September 30 1868, 1869, 1871, 1872)
New Haven Register (1871; plus academic years 1885–1887)
New York Clipper (April 1, 1879, through March 31, 1883)
New York Times (checked printed index plus digital search 1868 to 1919)
New York Tribune (August 20–October 9, 1880; plus index searched 1894 through 1899)
New York World (checked hand-written index at New York Public Library plus January 1919)
Norwalk (CT) *Gazette* (May 1 through October 31 1868 through 1870)
Railroad Trainman's Journal (1889 through 1896)
Sporting Life (January 1, 1883, through December 31, 1885)
Vintage & Classic Baseball Collector (issues no. 1 through no. 38, except no. 7)
Washington Post (1878 through 1919)
Yale Daily News (academic years: 1885 through 1887)

Articles

Akin, William E. "The Best Fielders 1880–1899." *Baseball Research Journal*, no. 10 (1981).
Bergen, Philip. "Roy Tucker, Not Roy Hobbs: The Baseball Novels of John R. Tunis." *SABR Review of Books* (1986).
Bowman, Larry. "Baseball's Intriguing Couple." *The National Pastime*, no. 17 (1998).
____. "The Helen Dauvray Cup." *The National Pastime* (1997), pp. 73–76.
Caillault, Jean Pierre. "Hall of Fame Batteries." *Baseball Research Journal*, no. 32 (2004).
Casway, Jerrold. "A Monument to Harry Wright." *The National Pastime*, no. 17 (1997).

Caylor, O. P. "Opening of the Base-Ball Season of 1890." *Harper's Weekly*, May 3, 1890.

Crane, Sam. "Fifty Greatest Ball Players." O'Rourke File, National Baseball Hall of Fame Library, unidentified New York publication (ca. fall 1912).

Donner, Joseph G. "Hitting for the Cycle." *Baseball Research Journal*, no. 10 (1981).

Dunbar, William H. "Baseball Salaries Thirty Years Ago." *Baseball Magazine*, July 1918, p. 291–292.

Edelman, Rob. "On the Silver Screen." *The National Pastime*, no. 17 (1997).

Egner, Mike. "The Evolution of the Baseball Glove." *Vintage & Classic Baseball Collector*, no. 16 (July–August 1998) .

Hunsinger, Lou, Jr. "George W. Stovey." *National Pastime*, no. 14 (1994).

Kermisch, Al. "From a Researcher's Notebook." *Baseball Research Journal*, no. 8 (1979), no. 24 (1995).

Kimmel, Michael S. "Baseball and the Reconstitution of American Masculinity, 1820–1920." *Baseball History Three* (1980).

Klem, William J., with William J. Slocum. "I Never Missed One in My Heart." *Collier's* magazine, March 31, 1951. p. 30.

Malloy, Jerry. "The Cubans' Last Stand." *The National Pastime*, no. 11 (1992).

McDonald, David. "Some Milestones in the Evolution of the Tools of Ignorance." *The National Pastime* 16 (1996).

Morse, J. C. "Changes in the World of Baseball." *Baseball Magazine*, September, 1911, p. 39–44.

Noble, Richard E. "Saving Face: The Genesis of the Catcher's Mask." *Baseball History*, Fall 1987.

Orem, Preston. "The National League Season of 1878 from the Newspaper Accounts." *Vintage & Classic Baseball Collector* 26 (March 2001).

_____. "The National League Season of 1879 from the Newspaper Accounts." *Vintage & Classic Baseball Collector* 27 (May–June 2001).

Overfield, Joseph. "James 'Deacon' White." *Baseball Research Journal* 4 (1975).

_____. "When Baseball Came to Richmond Avenue." *Niagara Frontier* 2 (Summer 1955).

_____. "'Deacon' White." *BisonGram*, October–November 1993.

Ruane, Tom. "Major League Career Hitting Records." *Baseball Research Journal* 27 (1998).

Schaefer, Robert H. "The Lost Art of Fair-Foul Hitting." *National Pastime* 19 (1999).

Schwartz, John. "From One Ump to Two." *Baseball Research Journal* 30 (2001).

Spivak, Joel. "Where Was the Jefferson Street Grounds?" *National Pastime* 11 (1992).

Torangeau, Richard "Dixie." "Remembering the Congress Street Grounds." *The National Pastime*, no. 24 (2004).

Vaccaro, Frank. "One-Arm Daily." *The National Pastime* 19 (1999).

Ward, John Montgomery. "Is the Base-Ball Player a Chattel?" *Lippincott's Monthly Magazine* 40 (August 1887), pp. 310–319.

_____. "Our National Game." *The Cosmopolitan* 5 (October 1888), pp. 443–455.

_____. "Notes of a Base-Ballist." *Lippincott's Monthly Magazine* 38 (August 1886), pp. 212–220.

Baseball Annuals

Beadle's Dime Base-Ball Player, 1860

Players' National League Guide, 1890

Reach Guides, 1919, 1920

Spalding Guides, 1877, 1878, 1879, 1880, 1882, 1884, 1885, 1890, 1905, 1909,1919

Books

Alexander, Charles. *Our Game: An American Baseball History*. New York: Henry Holt, 1991.

Allen, Lee. *The Hot Stove League*. New York: Barnes, 1955, 2000.

Alvarez, Mark. *The Old Ball Game*. Alexandria, VA: Redefinition, 1990.

Anson, Adrian C. *A Ball Player's Career*. Chicago: Era, 1900. Reprint: Mattituck, NY: Amereon House, n.d.

Appel, Marty. *Slide, Kelly, Slide*. Lanham, MD: Scarecrow Press, 1999.

Arcidiacono, David. *Middletown's Season in the Sun*. East Hampton, CT: self-published, 1999.

Bartlett, Arthur. *Baseball and Mr. Spalding*. New York: Farrar, Strauss and Young, 1951.

Baseball Encyclopedia. 10th ed. New York: Macmillan, 1996.

Brock, Darryl. *If I Never Get Back*. New York: Crown, 1990.

Burk, Robert F. *Never Just a Game*. Chapel Hill: University of North Carolina, 1994.

Campbell, Frederick Ivor, ed. *Baseball's First Stars*. Cleveland: Society for American Baseball Research, 1996.

Carter, Craig, ed. *Daguerreotypes*. 8th ed. St. Louis: Sporting News Book Publishing, 1990.

Dewey, Donald, and Nicholas Acocella. *The Biographical History of Baseball*. New York: Carroll and Graf, 1995.

Dickson, Paul. *The New Dickson Baseball Dictionary*. New York: Harcourt Brace, 1999.

Di Salvatore, Bryan. *A Clever Base-Ballist: The Life and Times of John Montgomery Ward*. New York: Pantheon, 1999.

Einstein, Charles, ed. *Fireside Book of Baseball*. 1st ed. New York: Simon and Schuster, 1956.

Ekin, Larry. *Baseball Fathers, Baseball Sons*. White Hale, VA: Betterway, 1992.

Frommer, Harvey. *Primitive Baseball*. New York: Atheneum, 1988.

Gershman, Michael. *Diamonds*. New York: Houghton Mifflin, 1993.

Gilbert, Thomas. *Superstars and Monopoly Wars*. New York: Grolier, 1995.

Goldstein, Warren. *A History of Early Baseball*. New York: Barnes & Noble Books, 2000. Originally published as *Playing for Keeps*. Ithaca, NY: Cornell University Press, 1989.

Gutman, Dan. *Banana Bats and Ding-Dong Balls*. New York: Macmillan, 1995.

_____. *It Ain't Cheatin' If You Don't Get Caught*. New York: Penguin, 1990.

Hardy, James, Jr. *The New York Giants Base Ball Club*. Jefferson, NC: McFarland, 1996.

Honig, Donald. *The National League*. New York: Crown, 1983, 1987.

Hynd, Noel. *The Giants of the Polo Grounds*. New York: Doubleday, 1988.

James, Bill. *Bill James Historical Baseball Abstract*. New York: Villard, 1988, 2001.

Lane, F. C. *Batting*. New York: Baseball Magazine Co., 1925. Reprint: Cleveland: Society for American Baseball Research, 2001.

Lansche, Jerry. *Glory Fades Away*. Dallas: Taylor, 1991.

Leitner, Irving A. *Baseball: Diamond in the Rough*. New York: Criterion, 1972.

Levine, Peter. *A. G. Spalding & the Rise of Baseball*. New York: Oxford, 1985.

Lowenfish, Lee. *The Imperfect Diamond*. New York: Stein & Day, 1980. Rev. ed. New York: Da Capo Press, 1991.

Mace, James E. *Collectible Gloves*. San Luis Obispo, CA: Welltek, 1990.

Mack, Connie. *My 66 Years In the Big Leagues*. Philadelphia: John C. Winston, 1950.

McCulloch, Ron. *From Cartwright to Shoeless Joe*. Toronto: Warwick, 1998.

McKelvey, Richard. *For It's One, Two, Three, Four Strikes You're Out at the Owner's Ball Game*. Jefferson, NC: McFarland, 2001.

_____. "The Pittsburgh Keystones and the 1887 Colored League." *Baseball in Pittsburgh*. Paul Adomites and Dennis DeValeria, eds. Cleveland: Society for American Baseball Research, 1995.

Morse, Jacob. *Sphere and Ash.* Boston: J. F. Spofford, 1888. Reprint: Columbia, SC: Camden House, 1984.

Nemec, David. *Great Baseball Feats, Facts & Firsts.* New York: Signet, 1997.

_____. *The Great Encyclopedia of 19th Century Major League Baseball.* New York: Donald L. Fine, 1997.

_____. *The Rules of Baseball.* Lyons & Burford, 1994.

_____, and Saul Wisnia. *Baseball: More Than 150 Years.* Lincolnwood, IL: Publications International, 1997.

Orem, Preston. *Baseball from the Newspaper Accounts (1845–1881).* Altadena, CA: self-published, 1961.

Overfield, Joseph M. *100 Years of Buffalo Baseball.* Kenmore, NY: Partners Press, 1985.

Palmer, Harry. *Athletic Sports.* Philadelphia: Hubbard Brothers, 1889.

Palmer, Pete, and John Thorn, eds. *Total Baseball.* 7th ed. Total Baseball, 2001.

Pearson, Daniel M. *Baseball in 1889.* Bowling Green, OH: Bowling Green State University, 1993.

Perrin, Wm. D. *Days of Greatness — Providence Baseball 1875–1885.* Cleveland: Society for American Baseball Research, 1984.

Povich, Shirley. *The Washington Senators.* New York: Putnam, 1954.

Reidenbaugh, Lowell. *Cooperstown.* St. Louis: Sporting News, 1983.

Richter, Frank C. *History and Records of Base Ball.* Philadelphia: self-published, 1914.

Rosenberg, Howard. *Cap Anson 1.* Tile Books, 2003. www.capanson.com.

Rosenburg, John M. *The Story of Baseball.* New York: Random House, 1972.

Rossi, John. *The National Game.* Chicago: Ivan R. Dee, 2000.

Ryczek, William. *Blackguards and Red Stockings.* Jefferson, NC: McFarland, 1992.

Selzer, Jack. *Baseball in the Nineteenth Century: An Overview.* Manhattan, KS: Ag Press, 1986.

Seymour, Harold. *Baseball: The Early Years.* New York: Oxford, 1960.

Simon, Tom, ed. *Deadball Stars of the National League.* Cleveland: Society for American Baseball Research, 2004.

Smith, Robert. *Baseball.* New York: Simon & Schuster, 1947.

_____. *Heroes of Baseball.* 1952.

Solomon, Burt. *Baseball Timeline.* New York: Avon Books, 1997.

Soos, Troy. *Before the Curse: The Glory Days of New England Baseball: 1858–1918.* Hyannis, MA: Parnassus, 1997.

Spalding, Albert G. *America's National Game.* New York: American Sports, 1911.

Spink, Alfred H. *The National Game.* St. Louis: National Game Company, 1910, 1911, 2000.

Stevens, David. *Baseball's Radical for All Seasons.* Lanham, MD: Scarecrow Press, 1998.

Sugar, Bert Randolph. *Rain Delays.* New York: St. Martin's Press, 1990.

Sullivan, Dean A. *Early Innings.* Lincoln: University of Nebraska Press, 1995.

Thorn, John. *Treasures of the Baseball Hall of Fame.* New York: Villard, 1998.

Tiemann, Robert L. and Mark Rucker. *Nineteenth Century Stars.* Cleveland: Society for American Baseball Research, 1989.

Tuohey, George V. *The History of the Boston Base Ball Club.* Boston: Quinn, 1897.

Turkin, Hy, and S. C. Thompson, eds. *The Official Encyclopedia of Baseball.* 1st ed. New York: A. S. Barnes, 1951.

Tuttle, Roger W. *Graduates of the Yale Law School 1824–1899.* New Haven: Tuttle, Morehouse & Taylor, 1911.

Tygiel, Jules. *Past Time.* New York: Oxford University Press, 2000.

Van Wyck, Frederick. *Recollections of an Old New Yorker.* New York: Liveright, 1932.

Vincent, Ted. *Mudville's Revenge.* New York: Seaview Books, 1981.

Voigt, David. *American Baseball,* Vol. 1. University Park: Pennsylvania State Press, 1983.

Ward, Geoffrey C., and Ken Burns. *Baseball.* New York: Knopf, 1994.

Zang, David W. *Fleet Walker's Divided Heart.* Lincoln: University of Nebraska Press, 1995.
Zoss, Joel, and John Bowman. *Diamonds in the Rough.* New York: Macmillan, 1989.

Dissertations

Gelzheiser, Robert Paul. "The Great Baseball Rebellion." Master's thesis, Trinity College, 1991.

Collections

Harry Wright Correspondence, Spalding Collection, New York Public Library
Harry Wright Note and Account Books, Spalding Collection, New York Public Library
O'Rourke file, National Baseball Library

Websites

baseballlibrary.com
bluecurl.com/ncbbp
cnn.com

geocities.com/Colosseum/Bleachers/5573/pl/htm
totalbaseball.com

Index

331

0218 173